Language Policies
and (Dis)Citizenship

Full details of all our publications can be found on http://www.multilingual-matters.com, or by writing to Multilingual Matters, St Nicholas House, 31–34 High Street, Bristol BS1 2AW, UK.

Language Policies and (Dis)Citizenship

Rights, Access, Pedagogies

Edited by
Vaidehi Ramanathan

MULTILINGUAL MATTERS
Bristol • Buffalo • Toronto

For Sandy and Leona who taught me my first lessons in (dis)citizenship

Library of Congress Cataloging in Publication Data
A catalog record for this book is available from the Library of Congress.
Language Policies and (Dis)citizenship: Rights, Access, Pedagogies/
Edited by Vaidehi Ramanathan.
1. Language and languages—Political aspects. 2. Language policy.
3. Citizenship. 4. Nationalism. 5. Linguistic minorities—Government policy. 6. Linguistic minorities—Civil rights. 7. Linguistic minorities—Education. I. Ramanathan, Vaidehi, 1965- editor of compilation.
II. Title.
P119.3.L358 2013
306.44'9–dc23 2013022824

British Library Cataloguing in Publication Data
A catalogue entry for this book is available from the British Library.

ISBN-13: 978-1-78309-019-8 (hbk)
ISBN-13: 978-1-78309-018-1 (pbk)

Multilingual Matters
UK: St Nicholas House, 31–34 High Street, Bristol BS1 2AW, UK.
USA: UTP, 2250 Military Road, Tonawanda, NY 14150, USA.
Canada: UTP, 5201 Dufferin Street, North York, Ontario M3H 5T8, Canada.

Copyright © 2013 Vaidehi Ramanathan.

All rights reserved. No part of this work may be reproduced in any form or by any means without permission in writing from the publisher.

The policy of Multilingual Matters/Channel View Publications is to use papers that are natural, renewable and recyclable products, made from wood grown in sustainable forests. In the manufacturing process of our books, and to further support our policy, preference is given to printers that have FSC and PEFC Chain of Custody certification. The FSC and/or PEFC logos will appear on those books where full certification has been granted to the printer concerned.

Typeset by Exeter Premedia Services
Printed and bound in Great Britain by TJ International Ltd

Contents

Acknowledgements   vii

1   Language Policies and (Dis)Citizenship: Rights, Access, Pedagogies   1
Vaidehi Ramanathan

Part 1: Citizenship: Reproducing, Challenging, Transforming Discourses and Ideologies

2   Language, Gender and Citizenship: Re-framing Citizenship from a Gender Equality Perspective   19
Busi Makoni

3   Problematizing the Construction of US Americans as Monolingual English Speakers   35
Aya Matsuda and Chatwara Suwannamai Duran

4   Keywords in Refugee Accounts: Implications for Language Policies   52
Emily Feuerherm

5   'The World Doesn't End at the Corner of their Street': Language Ideologies of Chilean English Teachers   73
Julia Menard-Warwick

6   A Perfect Storm for Undocumented Latino Youth?: Multi-level Marketing, Discourses of Advancement and Language Policy   92
Gemma Punti and Kendall A. King

7   Education Policy, Citizenship and Linguistic Sovereignty in Native America   116
Teresa L. McCarty

Part 2: Education and Citizenship: Creating (and Constraining) Spaces for Language, Learning and Belonging

8 Citizenship as Social, Spiritual and Multilingual Practice: Fostering Visions and Practices in the Nishkam Nursery Project — 145
   Gopinder Kaur Sagoo

9 Re-imagining Citizenship: Views from the Classroom — 167
   Jacqueline Widin and Keiko Yasukawa

10 Classroom Meanings and Enactments of US Citizenship: An Ethnographic Study — 188
    Ariel Loring

11 (Dis)Citizenship or Opportunity? The Importance of Language Education Policy for Access and Full Participation of Emergent Bilinguals in the United States — 209
    Kate Menken

12 English Learning without English Teachers? The Rights and Access of Rural Secondary Students in Nicaragua — 231
    Rosemary Henze and Fabio Oliveira Coelho

Afterword — 253
Vaidehi Ramanathan

Appendix — 256

Contributors — 281
Index — 287

Acknowledgements

Each of the sterling authors in this volume has been a delight to work with. They have my sincere gratitude for their provocative contributions and for indulging me in thinking about 'citizenship' differently and in promoting Devlin and Pothier's concept of 'dis-citizenship' as one relevant to applied linguistics.

Two anonymous reviewers and Marilyn Martin-Jones gave me excellent feedback and suggestions on strengthening the volume, and to them I remain very grateful. The team at Multilingual Matters remains as always a pleasure to work with.

Mouton de Gruyter gave me kind permission to reprint my very first serious publication in Applied Linguistics, which is in the Appendix. I am including that early paper in this volume so as to draw a straight line from that early start to my current cognitions.

Vaidehi Ramanathan
September 2012

[(Dis)Citizenship] raises questions of access and participation, exclusion and inclusion, rights and obligations, legitimate governance and democracy, liberty and equality, public and private, marginalization and belonging, social recognition and redistribution of sources, structure and agency, identity and personhood, self and other
Devlin and Pothier, 2006: 2

1 Language Policies and (Dis)Citizenship: Rights, Access, Pedagogies

Vaidehi Ramanathan

This volume brings together some leading female scholars writing in areas relating to language policies, globalization, citizenship and pedagogic practices. While each of these domains is well researched, only recently has scholarship begun to address them in relational terms, where implications of investigations in one domain spill into and have consequences for the others. My primary aim with bringing these scholars together under the covers of one book is to probe the borders of our collective understandings about 'citizenship'. Seeking to go beyond viewing 'citizenship' in terms of the passport one holds or one's immigration or visa status, the volume posits that this concept needs to be understood in terms of 'being able to participate fully'. The fuller implications of this phrase, needless to say, depend on local conditions – policies, pedagogic engagements and borders – that do and do not create equitable conditions. In this sense, then, 'citizenship' needs to be understood in very much more than the usual teleological terms – where it is a goal to be attained (to 'become' a citizen or acquire citizenship) – to where it gets understood in terms of what it allows one to do, and where it is viewed as a process amidst tensions, fluid contexts and diverse meanings. Doing so means turning our gaze to where everyday instances of teaching practices, institutionalized discourses and rights awareness become more salient, and where our conjoined sense of civic citizenship gets attired differently. It also means becoming acutely alert to ongoing contexts of (dis)citizenship (Pothier & Devlin, 2006).

While applied linguistics has produced scholarship in citizenship testing and nations (McNamara & Roever, 2006; Shohamy & Kanza, 2009; Stroud, 2001; Stroud & Heugh, 2004; Wodak, 1998) and language policies

(DeFina & King, 2011; Hornberger, 2008; Lane, 2009; McCarty, 2011; Menken, 2008; Ramanathan, 2005), the concept of '(dis)citizenship' has tended to remain underexplored. The term itself raises a variety of questions: under what local conditions does 'dis-citizenship' happen? What roles do language policies and pedagogic practices play? What kinds of margins and borders keep humans from fully participating? Embedded in such questions are concerns about access and rights. With this in mind, it seems fitting to have this volume consist primarily of women scholars, since women, the world over, know 'dis-citizenship' or have strong historical understandings of what it means to not be able to participate fully. While the volume does not specifically address issues of gender, it draws on what the female gender across our planet collectively knows, and we bring this varied and complex understanding to how (dis)citizenship gets enacted, reproduced, questioned, and changed in our multivalent realms of engagements (see my Afterword in this volume for more details on gender and (dis)citizenship).

Searching for a More Inter-related Understanding of Citizenship

Passages from feudal, colonized subjects to modern, agentive citizens are the world over muddled and untidy passages, tense with unfinished conversations about rights and obligations, personal and public lives, individual autonomy and group identities. Our various cultures – institutional, local, national and international – promulgate these distinctions in very particular narratives, which tend to elicit only a narrow range of interpretations (Gee, 1990). These narratives are, and ought to be, open to contestation and retellings. How do we conceptualize our current transnational belongings in ways that go beyond paying lip service to calls for international treaties and global solidarity? The corporeal realities of extreme poverty, exclusions and repressions still remain. Our thinking seems to still be stuck at countering these distinctions on their terms.

My search for a path ahead, then, begins from this difficult, sometimes unpalatable benchmark, and seeks to move our cognitions to another plane so as to complicate our current understandings about citizenship. The world is full of so-called 'undocumented' people. They are the shadowy masses that we do not want to acknowledge, whose grievances we do not want to hear lest they counter our own narratives, whose existence on the peripheries of fuller participation are threatening to us because we are caught up with our stories of limited resources. If we allow ourselves to think of these 'shadowy figures' differently – where histories and languages are foregrounded – a very different picture of citizenship emerges. However, we would need to take a few early steps to re-cognize ourselves. As a start, first we would need to be open to the possibility of a more historicized understanding of our places in the world. We are, each of us, a point in history, with connections to our pasts and a look towards the future. Second, we would need to be open to what translation theory has to offer us about in-between spaces. We are always between languages and meanings. Third, we would have to take account of how language policies in the various realms of our existences serve to draw borders and exclude. At first glance, these might seem like most flimsy guides with which to address citizenship. Yes, you say, of course, we are products of the tellings and retellings of our national histories. Yes, we sometimes need to translate our speech to others who do not speak our tongues. Of course policies marginalize. What does this have to do with (dis)citizenship, globalization and language policies? Everything, I maintain.

Citizenship and globalization

If there is a metanarrative that thrives in applied linguistics today, it is 'globalization'. Seldom do we attend a conference or turn to an article in an academic journal without encountering some attention to the term, cached as it is in a host of related topics, including 'western imperialism', 'border dissolving' and 'interculturality'. In many respects, 'globalization' seems to have become the discursive support of identity politics, the conceptualization that underwrites discourses of cross-cultural encounters, tensions about outsourcing jobs or insensitivity to local cultures. As an imaginary appealing to intellectuals, 'globalization' is, in many ways, a direct outgrowth of colonialism (especially the English language and Great Britain's former Empire); it is also lodged in 'nations', 'borders', 'migrations' and 'resettlements', key words that are at once sacral and most ordinary.[1]

Latent beneath these concepts is, of course, 'citizenship', a modernist term often used to refer to, among other things, belonging to a certain geographic space (Flemming & Morgan, 2011). The spatial nuances of the term are apparent when we consider phrases such as 'the average citizen' or 'the tax-paying citizen' or 'citizenship test', where connections to a specific territory on our planet become a way by which we both present ourselves and/or get read by others. But 'citizenship' in relation to 'globalization' calls for a deeper sociological, historical and philosophical inquiry into the 'bordered' character of social membership and the most local of concerns that inhibit fuller participation (Blackledge, 2005; Block, 2002; Blommaert, 2010; Chilton, 2004; Delanty et al., 2011; Ricento, 2006; van Dijk, 1997; Wodak, 2009; Wodak et al., 1998). Open to historicities, memories and postcolonial migrations, identities – our own and others' – are always crossing borders (Vandrick, 2009). We only need to consider the travel involved in songs that go through phones from Bollywood to San Jose to Chicago to Tokyo and then on to London, Sydney and Dubai, mutating in each city, picking up splinters of each city's insignia, coming back to us in forms that we instantly misrecognize and recognize. It is in these traversals that we confront the newer syntax of our lives, a syntax consisting of different languages, multiple language policies and the most diverse of learning experiences. These criss-crossings have translation flowing thickly through and between them (more on translations presently). What may be lost in the song as it travels from Mumbai to Sydney either linguistically or in terms of semantic moorings may open up other unanticipated venues. Two-way translations – a language-learning pedagogic practice common in many multilingual parts of our planet – may offer some insight here: there opens up a cultural and temporal space in which all of us are modified and 'translated', where mutations and reconfigurations of travelling songs echo back our strains even as they bring in new notes. Border crossings are all about this. The vulnerable at our borders change us as we change them. Citizenship, then, is *processual* and about becoming.

Citizenship and languages: Issues of translations and histories

Continuing with this point about translations, I turn now to addressing the relevance of translations to histories and thus to citizenship. If we consider the fact that it is through language that we proceed in the world and that we are each bearers of our respective histories in our everyday communications, then the interdependency of history and language becomes clearer. When we are with people whose languages and histories are different from our own, we are called on to 'translate' them. By this I do not just mean 'translate them literally', where we engage in literally translating their speech (although it does not discount this). I mean that we view them (and us) as translated texts, at once rhizomatic, uprooted and in-between (Ramanathan, 2006). As Benjamin (1968) points out, a translated text is forever 'in between'; that is, a translated text resides in the gap between the language, culture and history that is translated and the language, culture and history that does the translating. When I translate written or spoken data from Gujarati or Hindi into English, I am uprooting them from their local moorings – geographic and social – and am bringing them into another language (English, say) and another culture. The processes involved are not seamless by any means (see Ramanathan (2006) for a detailed discussion) and go far beyond searching for linguistic equivalents or the 'right' approximate word. The processes belie the idea that translations may be transparent with languages reflecting each other in shared, transparent semantic mirrors. Indeed, they are uncertain terrains, with tensions that sometimes make crossovers highly anxiety-ridden (Maryns, 2005).

Take for example the following bits of data. Here are two pages from an English language textbook used in a 5th standard vernacular-medium class in Gujarat, India, where I am from (see Figure 1.1). I have been engaged for many years now on a project regarding English and the vernaculars in India and some of this work has entailed addressing issues relating to pedagogies in different mediums of education.

Several things occur to me as I look at this text and think about bringing it into the West, all of which touch on issues of translations, histories and globalization and policies. I did not use this in my book *The English-Vernacular Divide* (2005), and I ask myself why I omitted what seems to be a fairly

Figure 1.1
(Excerpt from Standard 6, Purani et al., 1998; 54–55, used with permission)

innocuous text to select another (the one in the following section). Among other things, the gender implications in the presentation of the bangle stall (in the lines 'That is a bangle stall. Who are those girls?') bothered me. Bangles are not only a distinctive mark of femininity; they are also a mark of wedded life and sexuality in Hinduism (traditionally widows in North India do not generally wear bangles; or at least not those bangles that are typically associated with being married).

My discomfort with this aspect of my culture and my embarrassment at possible elaboration countered my discomfort as a feminist at the omission of the implications. It seemed safe to simply use another text. That is part of the story. The other part was the complexity of the task. If 'effective translations' mean also conveying implicit cultural information from the source landscape, then, do readers need to be filled in on some local associations around the children riding on an elephant's back at the fair? While elephants may be an uncommon sight at a fair in the West, they are not unusual in India where decorated temple elephants occasionally come from house to house to collect donations, or may be used at fairs. Would my use of this text in my writing in the West necessitate my elaborating these pieces of information, and how much of it would be seen as exotica? Further, the use of *iddlis* (the name of a Tamilian item of food at the bottom of the page marked 55) calls for some explanation about the movement of people from state to state, but more from the south to the north than the other way around. I could see at once from the names of the authors of the book (Nityanandanam) that one of them was a Tamilian. Was the inclusion of *iddlis* a point of Tamilian assertion, or was it pointing to the undeniable fact that this food item has become pan-Indian over the last 20 years? Where was one to begin or stop? The net result was that this translated text now floats around in my consciousness, not putting down roots anywhere. Embarrassment and complex details that would thicken the description to the point of weariness played their role in selectivity and omission. I chose instead the text that follows, a choice that seemed better from one point of view, but one that now sets me thinking about domesticizing texts.

The Gujarati sections in the piece below, especially points 2, 3 and 4 (see Figure 1.2; on the page marked 20 at the bottom), direct students to:

- first repeat after the teacher (where the teacher reads out the preceding sentences – *That is a farm, That is a mango tree*);
- say these sentences aloud by themselves, singly or chorally;
- read out vocabulary that the teacher writes on the board, copy this down, and draw animals corresponding to *a dog* and *a cow*.

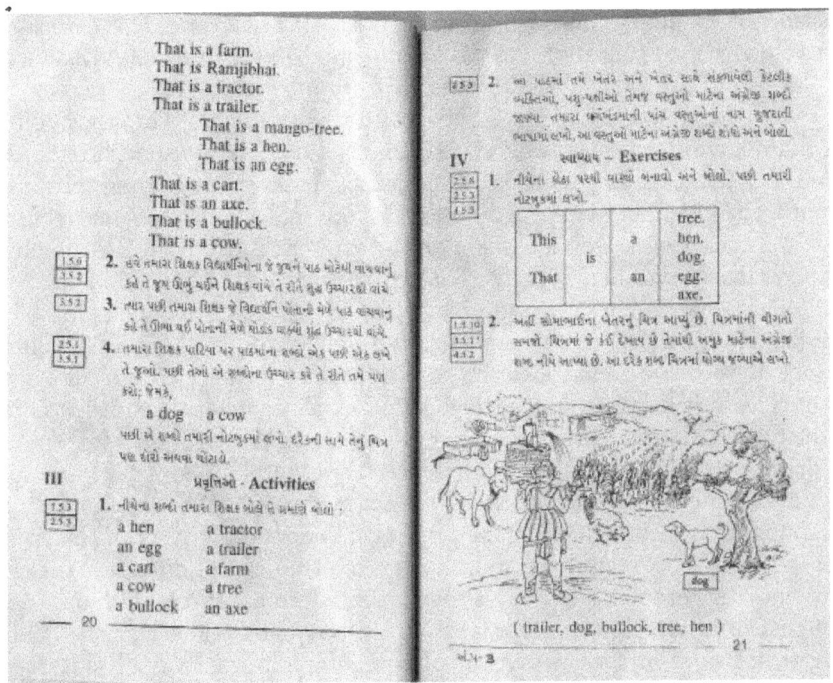

Figure 1.2
(Excerpt from Standard 5, Nataraj and Joshi, 1999; 20, used with permission)

In my previous work, I have drawn on this excerpt (Ramanathan, 2005) to argue against West-based English language teaching practices which have, by and large, critiqued pedagogic practices such as the above (choral recitation, grammar translation) as being generally ineffective because it promotes rote learning. What I did not uncover at the time is that I was making a deliberate choice of a text free(er) of the problems surrounding the other and using a text that could be more easily re-territorialized and domesticated.

These points are directly relevant to the points about histories, translations, globalization and citizenship (Ramanathan, 2011). Moving texts, like moving people (migrants, immigrants and visa-less people) are about de-terriotorializing and re-teritorrializing (and directly impact policies and are indeed impacted by them; more on this presently). What we read of people and what they read of us is partial and selective. Like texts, they are transplanted from their mileu to another, and like texts, written in other languages and emerging from diverse parts of our planet, bringing them into academic arguments in English in the West necessitates some elaboration along with the translation. And as I just pointed out, issues around elaboration are not nearly as straightforward as they may seem.

You are wondering, I'm sure, what all of this points to. What they point to, among other things, are our differences, our perceptions of differences and our language for them. All translations are a way of coming to terms with the foreignness of or differences between languages. Translations – translating ourselves to others and others back to ourselves – involve encounters with 'alien' tongues that in turn affect our language and history. A fuller sense of 'dis-citizenship', of what in our present contexts inhibits fuller participation can only emerge if we unabashedly usher in history into applied linguistics, and view each person speaking an 'alien tongue' as a historicized being, bringing to each encounter their individual connections to their pasts. Crucial here is the need to respect difference and its relevance. Identity, after all, is based on difference: I am who I am because I am not you. Casting it aside and saying it does not matter runs the risk of imposing homogeneity, a 'one-ness,' 'a one size fits all' orientation that can smack of imperialism. On the other hand, though, the language of difference can go too far and become divisive. It is this double-edged nature of difference that we need to now openly address in our debates about globalization. While 'globalization' with its messing up of firm borders is often roundly critiqued (especially by postcolonial scholars) for tending to erase history, it is also a phenomenon that alerts us, now more than ever, to be conscious of history. Translations, histories, and our language of difference, then, are imperative to consider in any and all contexts regarding (dis)citizenship.

(Dis)Citizenship and language policies

I turn now to language policies and their connections to (dis)citizenship. Issues of difference matter here as well. 'The right to participate fully' – the orientation to citizenship that this volume prefers – has at its foundation a key tenet of modern political theory, namely, that all humans are equal in the eyes of the law (have equal access, equal rights and equal claims on public goods). From such an orientation, there seem to be two extensions: (a) that the emphasis is on what citizens have in common; (b) that the policies and laws apply to all in the same way and that rules are blind to individual and group differences (Young, 1998). But such a framework runs risks, especially regarding erasing particularity and difference. Individual and group identities do matter. Different social groups have different histories and world views, and these come into play when they interpret policies and mandates. Creating policies that put pressure on social groups to give up their affiliations to better 'assimilate' disrespects difference and serves to create contexts of dis-citizenship (Kymlicka & Patton, 2003; Ricento, 2006; Turner, 1992; Wiley & Wright, 2004).[2]

It is important, then, that we bring in concerns about difference into our thinking about policies. The orientation of policies happening to people promotes a top-down, structuralist view, where difference can get erased and where homogenizing can be imperialistic. Side-stepping policies and not losing sight of human agency and the transformative potential of humans are important as well (Cooke & Simpson, 2008; Ramanathan & Morgan, 2007). This involves more than denouncing existing structural inequities or voicing concerns about economic deprivation to recognizing the power we each have at hand to make changes, no matter how small they may first appear (Baynham, 2006). To insist against the odds that language policies may be the site of both transit and difference, that it may be a site where we each make a difference is, to suggest another hue in *becoming citizens,* a crucial processual orientation. Policies, while anchored in spaces, also become the routes that transport us to our better selves. Such a view is profoundly transformative, supplementing our cognitions about policies and pedagogies, nation and citizenship and globalization and translations with necessary yet unanticipated complexity.

Winding down

I realize that these above points can be seen as abstract, and thus, marginal to the everyday business of contesting the powers of policies and globalizing surges. However, I do believe that we need to uncover the theoretical back roads of our key concepts (such as 'citizenship') so as to begin to interrogate and eventually displace paradigms of power that maintain status quos. Philosophy, in its language, and orientation is ultimately about awakening us to both representation and then action. To query how we think about citizenship, as this volume strives to do, is to question its current representations; to think about and represent it in the inter-related ways mentioned above is to move us to other domains of engagement. Each of the studies in this volume does this. While not all of them address '(dis) citizenship' as a concept directly (see the Afterword in this volume for more details), they all do address issues around fuller participation, including constraints, rights and pedagogies. As globalizing surges make us aware, while our modernities are heterogeneous, they are translatable; they are also collages of histories, policies, borders and crossings that do not add up to tidy snapshots. To think about citizenship this way is to shift its debates away from being only about visas and passports to more uncertain and contested spaces of interpretation. As the various chapters point out, this is a move that at once broadens edges of our conceptual canvas to where we pay heed to what citizenship allows us to do, namely, participate more fully.

Overview of the chapters

Each of the different chapters in this volume addresses interrelations between policies and (dis)citizenship. Some focus on pedagogies, others on globalizing currents and still others on citizenship testing and refugees. All of the chapters offer situated and ethnographic accounts of very localized contexts of (dis)citizenship. They are grouped into two sections with the first entitled *Citizenship: Reproducing, Challenging, Transforming Discourses and Ideologies*[3] (with Makoni, Matsuda and Duran, Feuerherm, Menard-Warwick, and Punti and King and McCarty) and the second *Education and Citizenship: Creating (and Constraining) Spaces for Language, Learning and Belonging* (with Sagoo, Widin and Yasukawa, Loring, Henze and Coelho and Menken). What follows are brief summaries of the various chapters that have been written primarily by the authors themselves.

Part 1: Citizenship: Reproducing, challenging, transforming, discourses and ideologies

Situating herself in the African context is Busi Makoni who opens the volume with a discussion of how dis-citizenship emerges in the context of having to struggle for rights in the face of traditional norms, often invoked by African patriarchy. Viewing the use of *isihlonipho sabafazi* (women's language of respect) within a courtroom setting through the lens of the distinction between overt/covert or de facto/de jure language policies, her chapter argues that this gendered register of language use puts women in compromising positions. She discusses the importance of the role of language policies not only in defining and regulating the institutional and functional statuses of languages but also in paying attention to register differences, especially along gender lines.

Chapter 2 by Matsuda and Duran addresses how the term 'multilingual' gets used to refer to ESL learners in education-related contexts, and ways in which this term sits dichotomously with non-ESL people who tend get categorized as 'monolingual.' Such a construction, they argue, is not only inaccurate (there are many native-English-speaking US citizens and residents who are multilingual) but also normalizes prevailing ideologies of monolingualism as part of US identity. They maintain that we scholars of language policy, practices, and pedagogy, must collectively and critically examine the ideological construction of mainstream American students with the same sensitivity we bring to the discussion of ELLs and immigrant students, so as to refrain from unintentionally supplying larger monolingual ideologies.

Moving into the realm of community concerns is Feuerherm's chapter (Chapter 4) that situates itself amidst policy concerns around refugee resettlement and the need for agentive voices in applied linguistics research regarding communal transformation. Situated in local ongoing resettlement efforts, some of which she has herself spearheaded, her chapter offers a critical discourse analysis of key works as they emerge in the extended life histories of two Iraqi refugees. Her analysis reveals that the discrimination that Iraqi women face because of wearing a *hijab* or the difficulties in navigating a working world in English emerge in the use of very particular language. This language, key words in particular, occurs in very specific contexts and make us pay attention to what we can change in existing policies to improve conditions for resettlement.

Continuing the focus on language ideologies and ESL is Menard-Warwick's research at a small Chilean university (Chapter 5). Her chapter examines the language ideologies of English teachers in Chile, a nation that is extensively promoting English language learning. Taking a Bakhtinian orientation, she argues that current conceptualizations of globalization can be best understood through dialogue. The questions she explores are: What language ideologies do English teachers in Chile reference in talking about their work? How do they position themselves and their work? What value do they see for English teaching in Chile? Based on interviews with English teachers in Chile, she addresses teachers' ideological struggles as they make sense of their work, to themselves, to their colleagues and in response to local political concerns.

Punti and King (Chapter 6) address concerns around undocumented Latino youth and ways in which multi-level marketing (MLM) schemes such as Herbalife and Amway provide a means – or the discourse of a means – to financial, educational and social advancement. They specifically examine MLM language policies and their discourses of advancement, as well as their uptake and entextualization by undocumented Latino adults. They focus on ways in which two individuals engage with MLM organizations, including how they position themselves and their decisions to invest in an MLM business within their life trajectory. Their analysis reveals how and why MLM discourses get adapted and personalized. This work illustrates how MLM schemes, in conjunction with the dysfunctional US immigration system, create a 'perfect storm' for undocumented Latino youth, thus creating contexts of (dis)citizenship.

In the final chapter of this section, McCarty explores the question: what does it mean to be a 'citizen' in Native America and what are the implications for Native American language and education rights? Her chapter offers first a crucial understanding of the unique legal and political status of Native American people, focusing on concerns about citizenship and sovereignty in the Native American context. Drawing on safety zone theory and tribal critical race theory, she shows how federal education policies have constructed a social, psychological and pedagogical space designed to domesticate Native American cultural difference using language as a mechanism of social control. Her chapter then examines two key policy cases in which safety zone boundaries have been ruptured as Native educators, families and youth have carved out new spaces for indigenous language reclamation. The chapter concludes with a consideration of the broader meaning of the cases, outlining what linguistic sovereignty might look like in practice and arguing for its necessity as a cornerstone of 'full citizenship'.

Part 2: Education and citizenship: Creating (and constraining) spaces for language, learning and belonging

Sagoo's chapter is about the founding of a Sikh-inspired nursery in Handsworth, an inner-city neighbourhood in Birmingham, England. It is part of a series of regeneration projects spearheaded by members of the locally based, transnational Sikh organisation known as Nishkam, driven by a commitment to civic and interfaith engagement, the fostering of shared values and support for lifelong education and holistic wellbeing in ways that combine 'heritage conservation' with 'social innovation' for the 'common good'. Presenting a close analysis of the ways in which English, Punjabi and other linguistic and semiotic resources are drawn upon by nursery practitioners to foster dispositions in the ebb and flow of classroom interaction, she reveals how the nursery's focus on dispositions contributes to broadening notions of – and possibilities for – citizenship, in comparable social contexts.

Also in the area of pedagogy is Widin and Yasukawa's chapter, which explores notions of citizenship and dis-citizenship through the experiences of teachers and learners in four very different classroom settings in Australia: a literacy and numeracy programme for young people disengaged from learning, a vocationally oriented class for speakers of English as an additional language, a numeracy class for adults, and a flexible learning centre for adult basic education students. Taking the classroom as a point of departure, they present citizenship as generative and collectively created in a shared space, and in so doing, offer different possibilities of citizenship. They argue that teachers can work with their learners to create these new spaces of belonging and being.

Loring in Chapter 10 addresses the idea of citizenship in the United States and how particular meanings of language, history and culture are encoded in government policy and practice. Her chapter offers a critical situated account of how four different teachers teaching English language and citizenship classes conceive of 'citizenship'. Classroom enactments around this term can be seen to cluster around: (1) what is believed; (2) what is taught and (3) what is not taught. Her findings reveal that the teachers address this term differently, with some of them fronting legal immigration-related information and others addressing concerns around rights. Her chapter also addresses ways in which English language learning is a Herculean task for many learners who, despite having lived in the United States for many years, have not been able to acquire fluency over the language, and the importance of ESL classes in current times of fiscal crises.

Menken in Chapter 11 addresses (dis)citizenship by examining the loss of bilingual education programmes in New York's city schools in two studies. The first involves qualitative research conducted in city schools that have recently eliminated their bilingual education programmes and replaced them with ESL programmes. School administrators were interviewed to determine the factors that influenced their decision to adopt English-only instruction in their schools. The second study shows how the schooling experiences of these primarily US-educated students can be described as 'subtractive', in that their native languages have not been developed in school and instead have been largely replaced with English. She discusses how these restrictive language policies serve as means of gatekeeping for citizenship, barring many emergent bilinguals from future opportunities and full participation.

Lastly, straddling geographic terrains is Henze and Coelho's chapter (Chapter 12) where they ask: is it possible to develop a viable English language programme in remote rural areas where no English teachers reside? Their chapter documents a partnership whereby a team of English language educators from San Jose State University in California works with a small NGO in Nicaragua to develop English language learning tools for both students and teachers. By critically exploring different perspectives on the role of English and its importance as a means for students to obtain an equal diploma, the paper contributes new insights for educators concerned with linguistic power relations and the meanings of 'global citizenship'.

Notes

(1) In terms of establishing some kind of chronology – after all, the term 'citizenship' does have a history – it is useful to review how early political thinkers such as T.H. Marshall conceived of the term. As the following quote points out, Marshall views citizenship as comprising three elements: the civil, the political and the social:

The civil element is composed of the rights necessary for individual freedom – **liberty of the person; freedom of speech, thought and faith; the right to own property and to conclude valid contracts; and the right of justice.** The last is of a different order from the others, because it is the right to defend and assert all one's rights on terms of equality with others and by due process of law. This shows us that the institutions most directly associated with civil rights are the courts of justice. By the political element I mean **the right to participate in the exercise of political power,** as a member of a body invested with political authority or as an elector of the members of such a body. The corresponding institutions are parliament and councils of local government. By the social element I mean the whole range from **the right to share to the full in the social heritage and to live the life of a civilized being according to the standards prevailing in the society.** The institutions most closely connected with it are the educational system and the social services. (Marshall, in Shafir (1998: 94); my emphasis)

As Turner (1992) notes, this view of citizenship became a cornerstone for ensuing debates, opening up as it did, deliberations regarding what could or could not be included under the terms 'civil', 'political' and 'social.' (And deliberative democracies that view these terms as contested with several interpretations have kept the terms elastic, with current political events – the collapse of the market, the Occupy movements, fiscal conditions in Europe – pointing to the spillage inherent in these terms). It led to, for instance, greater room for working-class struggles for political equality and for a voice in parliamentary processes. In this sense, then, personal and civil rights, embedded as they are in social spheres, become grounds for political articulations.

(2) This domain of how policies influence the unequal distribution of resources is, of course, most contentious, with both scholars and lay people staking out various conceptual domains, some of which run counter to each other (Pogge, 2003).

(3) I thank an anonymous reviewer for suggesting that I change the headings of these sections. He/she suggested that I incorporate the progressive – *ing* ending in keeping with the processual orientation to citizenship that the volume emphasizes. This person recommended alternate headings that I am now using.

References

Baynham, M. (2006) Agency and contingency in the language learning of refugees and asylum seekers. *Linguistics and Education* 17 (1), 2–39.

Benjamin, W. (1968) *Illuminations: Essays and Reflections* (edited by H. Arendt and H. Zohn). New York: Harcourt, Brace and World.

Blackledge, A. (2005) *Discourse and Power in a Multilingual World*. Amsterdam: John Benjamins.

Block, D. (2002) McCommunication: A problem in the frame for SLA. In D. Block and D. Cameron (eds) *Globalization and Language Teaching* (pp. 117–133). London: Routledge.

Blommaert, J. (2010) *The Sociolinguistics of Globalization*. Cambridge: CUP.

Chilton, P. (2004) *Analyzing Political Discourse: Theory and Practice*. London: Routledge.

Cooke, M. and Simpson, J. (2008) *ESOL: A Critical Guide*. Oxford: Oxford University Press.
DeFina, A. and King, K. (2011) Language problems or language conflict: Narratives of immigrant women in the U.S. *Discourse Studies* 13 (2), 163–188.
Delanty, G., Jones, P. and Wodak, R. (2011) *Migration, Identity and Belonging*. Liverpool: Liverpool University Press.
Flemming, D. and Morgan, B. (2011) Discordant anthems: ESL and critical citizenship education. *Citizenship Education Research* 1, 28–40.
Gee, J. (1990) *Social Linguistics and Literacies: Ideologies and Discourses*. Philadelphia: Falmer Press.
Hornberger, N. (2008) *Can Schools Save Indigenous Languages?: Policy and Practice on Four Continents*. London: Palgrave Macmillan.
Kymlicka, W. and Patton, A. (eds) (2003) *Language Rights and Political Theory*. Oxford: Oxford University Press.
Lane, P. (2009) Mediating national language management: The discourse of citizenship categorization in Norwegian media. *Language Policy* 8 (3), 209–225.
Maryns, K. (2005) Monolingual language ideologies and code choice in Belgiam asylum procedure. *Language and Communication* 25, 299–314.
McCarty, T. (ed.) (2011) *Ethnography and Language Policy*. New York: Routledge.
McNamara, T. and Roever, C. (2006) *Language Testing: The Social Dimension*. Malden: Blackwell.
Menken, K. (2008) *English Learners Left Behind: Standardized Testing as Language Policy*. Clevedon: Multilingual Matters.
Nataraj, R. and Joshi, S. (1999) *English Reader, Standard 5*. Ahmedabad: Gujarat State Board of Textbooks.
Pogge, T. (2003) Accomodation rights for hispanics in the United States. In W. Kymlicka and A. Patton (eds) *Language Rights and Political Theory* (pp. 105–122). Oxford: Oxford University Press.
Pothier, D. and Devlin, R. (eds) (2006) *Critical Disability Theory: Essays in Philosophy, Politics, Policy and Law*. Vancouver: UBC Press.
Purani, T., Nityanandanam, S. and Patel, J. (1998) *English Reader, Standard 6*. Ahmedabad: Gujarat: Gujarat State Board of Textbooks.
Ramanathan, V. (2005) *The English-Vernacular Divide: Postcolonial Language Policies and Practice*. Clevedon: Multilingual Matters.
Ramanathan, V. (2006) Of texts AND translations AND rhizomes: Postcolonial anxieties AND deracinations AND knowledge constructions. *Critical Inquiry in Language Studies* 3 (4), 223–244.
Ramanathan, V. (2011) Researching-texting tensions in qualitative research: Ethics in and around textual fidelity, selectivity, and translations. In T. McCarty (ed.) *Ethnography and Language Policy* (pp. 255–270). New York: Routledge.
Ramanathan, V. and Morgan, B. (eds) (2007) *TESOL Quarterly Special Issue: Focus on Language Policy*. New York: TESOL.
Ricento, T. (ed.) (2006) *Ideology, Politics and Language Policies*. Amsterdam/Philadelphia: John Benjamins.
Shafir, G. (1998) *The citizenship Debates: A Reader*. Minneapolis: University of Minnesota Press.

Shohamy, E. and Kanza, T. (2009) Language and citizenship in Israel. *Language Assessment Quarterly* 6 (1), 83–88.
Stroud, C. (2001) African mother-tongue programmes and the politics of language: Linguistic citizenship versus linguistic human rights. *Journal of Multilingual and Multicultural Development* 22 (4), 339–355.
Stroud, C. and Heugh, K. (2004) Language rights and linguistic citizenship. In J. Freeland and D. Patrick (eds) *Language Rights and Language Survival* (pp. 191–218). Manchester: St. Jerome Publishing.
Turner, B. (1992) Outline of a theory of citizenship. In C. Mouffe (ed.) *Dimensions of Radical Democracy: Pluralism, Citizenship, Community* (pp. 33–62). New York: Verso.
van Dijk, T. (ed.) (1997) *Discourse Studies*. London: Sage.
Vandrick, S. (2009) *Interrogating Privilege: Reflections of a Second Language Educator*. Michigan: University of Michigan Press.
Wiley, T. and Wright, W. (2004) Against the undertow: Language minority education policy and politics in the 'age of accountability'. *Educational Policy* 18 (1), 142–168.
Wodak, R. (2009) *The Discourse of Politics in Action: Politics as Usual*. Basingstoke: Palgrave
Wodak, R., de Cillia, R., Reisgl and Liebhart, K. (1998) *The Discursive Construction of National Identity*. Edinburgh: Edinburgh University Press.
Young, I.M. (1998) Polity and group difference: A critique of the ideal of universal citizenship. In *The Citizenship Debates* (pp. 263–290). Minneapolis: University of Minnesota Press.

Part 1
Citizenship: Reproducing, Challenging, Transforming Discourses and Ideologies

2 Language, Gender and Citizenship: Re-framing Citizenship from a Gender Equality Perspective

Busi Makoni

> *Injustice against women is probably no more clearly demonstrated than in the laws of a country and in their interpretation and implementation by the justice system.*
> Haysom, 2009: 3

Introduction

The main focus of this chapter is on the use of *isihlonipho sabafazi* (women's language of respect) within a courtroom setting and viewing it as a gendered category of language, which has been reinforced by the expectation of society towards women. The chapter investigates how *isihlonipho sabafazi* and national language policy are related to each other and how this relationship protects the use of a gendered form of language that leads to discriminatory practices. The Zimbabwean language policy implemented by the government does not overtly include *isihlonipho sabafazi* in its policy statements, and thus, leaving it as a *de facto* language practice that is deeply rooted in the culture of Ndebele speakers. In examining *isihlonipho sabafazi* as an issue of language policy, the covert/overt or *de facto/de jure* distinction in language policy (Shohamy, 2006) indicates that unlike overt language policy, covert language policy is not codified, but functions effectively in society. *Isihlonipho sabafazi*, as a covert form of language policy, enables overt language policy to pay lip service to inclusive language and democratic processes because the covert mechanism functions to execute policies with contrary aims. Although the boundaries of the feminine and masculine use of language are erased in language policies, it is clear that *isihlonipho sabafazi*, as an instance of covert language policy, marginalizes and promotes a certain degree of gender discrimination through the use of language, especially in a courtroom setting.

In a courtroom setting, written and spoken languages are integral parts of the legal process. Effective communication with the accused is an essential aspect of a fair trial (Steytler, 1993) because 'law is a profession of words' (Mellinkoff, 1963: vi). For instance, outside the courtroom, language plays a major role in interactions between police and suspects, in discussions between attorneys and their clients and in statements taken by law-enforcement officers from witnesses and suspects alike. Similarly, inside the courtroom, the interrogation of plaintiffs and defendants, the testimony of witnesses and the pleadings by attorneys all depend on the use of language. Surprisingly, applied linguistics research on the intersection of language and the law is relatively sparse and appears to be rather marginal to the discipline, unless if it is viewed as part of forensic science. In an attempt to fill this gap, this chapter explores the nexus between the use of language, language policy, communication, gender and the socio-legal process in a southern African context by examining 'hidden' social inequalities in the use of indigenous African languages in a courtroom setting. The aim of this chapter is to argue that despite the fact that women have their equality neatly enshrined in the Bill of Rights, Ndebele women and possibly other African women who are subject to the *isihlonipho* language variety are denied full citizenship status and are treated as 'partial citizens' (Bulmer & Rees, 1996: 275), exposing them to a 'cheap and shoddy imitation' (Marshall, 1964: 85) of citizenship or 'a regime of dis-citizenship' (Devlin & Pothier, 2006: 144). Linguistic citizenship, therefore, must consider women's differential linguistic needs in order to ensure that they have genuine equality and full access to public institutions. After all, language rights are human rights, and as such, the use of all varieties of languages spoken by all citizens is part of the process of democracy and of the process of social inclusion. In other words, the ability and opportunity to use one's full linguistic repertoire are central to participation in democratic and social processes.

It has long been established in critical language studies that questions of language policy are largely questions about 'politics and power/(lessness), power over and power to' (Devlin & Pothier, 2005: 2) those whose languages are accorded official status. As Lo Bianco (2009: 113) pointed out, 'power, politics and status differentials' are encoded in language policies. As public texts, language policy documents 'often carry agendas they conceal' (Lo Bianco, 2009: 113), and what is concealed is inequality. Tollefson (2006: 42), for instance, acknowledged that 'policies often create and sustain various forms of social inequality' and that 'policy-makers usually promote the interests of dominant groups'. This means that policies on the use of language are not value-neutral commodities insofar as they have become an arena for giving voice to certain groups of people while silencing and excluding others from active citizenship participation. However, such inequality is very rarely, if ever, examined from an intra-language perspective, where the source of inequality and marginalization may be related to the use of a language variety that enjoys official status. When a language is assigned official status, some variety of it is usually selected and promoted by either quasi-legal authorities or other social institutions, such as schools or media. Yet in real-life situations, no one uses the so-called standard or the more prestigious forms, as these are often encountered in writing or in more formal public settings, creating a dichotomy between the public and the private. This is usually the case in African contexts where a large portion of the population has no formal education and, therefore, uses non-standard varieties associated with the private space. In African contexts, a large part of the population that may not even have encountered the standard varieties are mainly women, who, because of systems of patriarchal domination, are still tied to their cultural practices and use culture-specific varieties of language such as *isihlonipho sabafazi*. Again, for such women, their space is the private sphere and not the public.

The focus in this chapter is on the uses of a culture-specific language variety known as *isihlonipho sabafazi* (women's language of respect) and its disempowering role in a legal setting. Its exclusion of women undermines the principle of equality before the law. Not only is the use of *isihlonipho sabafazi* disempowering but it also highlights the contradictions inherent in language policies: in as much as the intention is inclusion, the result may, inadvertently, be exclusion. Using dis-citizenship as a conceptual framework for analyzing *isihlonipho* talk in the courtroom, the questions that the chapter seeks to answer are as follows: (a) To what extent is the *isihlonipho* language variety as a cultural practice recognized and respected in a courtroom setting by the legal profession? (b) Are women able to participate fully in a legal process when using *isihlonipho sabafazi*, especially in rape trials? (c) Does the use of *isihlonipho* lead to inclusion/exclusion of women in legal processes, such as rape cases?

The chapter is divided into four sections. The first section situates the analysis of *isihlonipho* in a courtroom setting in Zimbabwe by providing contextual background of women's status and some of the relevant proclamations made in the constitution. The next section outlines the basic tenets of dis-citizenship, whereas the third section analyzes courtroom interactions in rape cases and highlights some of the difficulties experienced by witnesses that use *isihlonipho* language variety. The last section offers concluding remarks about the association between use of *isihlonipho,* language policy and dis-citizenship and suggests ways that citizenship can be re-framed to include the use of differential language.

Contextual Background: Language Policies and Law

In terms of the use of language, Zimbabwe is a multilingual country with a large number of languages, although three languages (i.e. English, Shona and Ndebele) enjoy significant prominence under the present Education Act as national languages (Makoni et al., 2006; Makoni et al., 2007). Languages such as Tonga, Kalanga and Nambya only attained official status after intense lobbying by grassroots organizations (Makoni, 2011; Makoni et al., 2008). Thus, the right to use one's language, as one of the specifications of human rights, is considered a cultural right, which is protected by the Zimbabwean Constitution. Although the three original official languages supposedly enjoy parity of esteem, English seems to play a much more prominent role in education and the judiciary, as well as in areas such as trade and industry, mass media and parliament, whereas Shona and Ndebele are central in government structures such as the senate, state media and lower primary education (Thondhlana, 2002). Shona and Ndebele are also used in courtroom proceedings, especially for those individuals with limited language skills in English, although the language of court records is English.

The composition of the judiciary reflects the ethnic and linguistic backgrounds of the so-called 'super-tribes' (Werbner, 2003): the Ndebele and Shona. Hence, many legal professionals speak African languages, although they still operate within the English legal discourse based on Roman Dutch law. In addition, the members of the judiciary have knowledge of African languages as they often use these languages in cross-examination of witnesses without the need for interpreters. It is almost inconceivable that members of the judiciary may not have encountered the *isihlonipho sabafazi* language variety. However, lawyers, judges, magistrates and, in certain cases, court interpreters have not been trained in issues of intercultural communication, the effects of culture-specific uses of language in a courtroom and the ways these may create disadvantage (Carol, 1994). Since the courtroom itself is a cultural institution with its own rules of procedures and the use of language (Eades, 1994, 2010), it is plausible that judiciary members may not be aware of the risks of misunderstanding arising from cultural and linguistic differences (Carol, 1994).

Citizenship and dis-citizenship

The concept of citizenship is historically associated with 'membership in a bordered community' (Jenson, 2006: 4), yet borders have become more fluid with movements of people within and across them (Bosniak, 2000). Thus, full participation may be a particularly important issue to examine, especially for those who have been displaced and are in vulnerable positions; however, even within territorial borders, questions still arise regarding the extent to which individuals are able to participate fully. In other words, even within borders, there are also 'internal' boundaries, wherein rules of inclusion and exclusion are set.

Citizenship, as originally defined by Marshall (1964: 71), includes civil, political and social rights: 'the rights necessary for individual freedom – liberty of the person, freedom of speech, thought and faith, the right to own property and to conclude valid contracts and the right to justice'. Political rights are described as 'the right to participate in the exercise of political power as a member of a body invested with political authority or as elector of the members of such a body' (Marshall, 1964: 72). Social rights are wide-ranging but are most closely associated with education and social services institutions.

While it is indisputable that women are not formally excluded from any of these rights, women experience *de facto* exclusion in most aspects of civil rights. In the political sphere, Zimbabwe, like most African countries, has a constitution with a Bill of Rights that has an equality clause that centralizes gender equality for the realization of equity for women and men alike. Yet gender-based inequities still exist, which is not surprising, because the same constitution also centralizes the respect of all different cultural practices, especially that of indigenous cultures, without any prejudice. Customary law is, therefore, part and parcel of the Zimbabwean legal system. In customary law, women cannot be considered equal to men because African cultural norms, based in patriarchy, view women as children. Women use a variety of language that reflects powerlessness.

If citizenship is the basis of democracy and participation in governance, then Zimbabwean women are exposed to 'a cheap and shoddy imitation' (Marshall, 1964: 85) of citizenship that is inherently disempowering. Since citizenship is closely related to full participation in a democratic society, full participation remains 'pie in the sky' for Zimbabwean women. It is also through citizenship that policies that aim to eliminate any potential and perceived impediments to full participation in governance and civil society by all individuals are developed. In such contexts, citizenship entails the ability to participate in social and cultural institutions. From this perspective, 'citizenship is not just an issue of individual status, it is also a practice that locates individuals in the larger community' (Delvin & Pothier, 2005: 1). If citizenship is viewed as a practice, then issues of access and participation become paramount.

However, evident from this concept of citizenship is that gender as a category is 'absent from many discussions of citizenship' (Walby, 1994: 379). In recent years, researchers in feminist studies have examined the issue of citizenship by locating gender as an integral part of any theory of citizenship (Andersen & Siim, 2004; Hobson & Lister, 2002; Lister, 1990; Siim, 1999). In most of these studies, women experience exclusion, although formally they have *all the rights* of citizenship, which makes them 'denizens' (Hammar, 1990: 13).

Research on the use of *isihlonipho* in the courtroom has focused mainly on translation and the use of interpreters in a bilingual courtroom setting (Moeketsi, 1999; Thetela, 2003). Bearing in mind that a trial is, in simple terms, a dispute that involves two verbal accounts of the same reality (Atkinson & Drew, 1979; de Klerk, 2003; Walker, 1987), language is critically important in establishing which reality is credible. The assumption is that the truth of what really took place will emerge from the verbal representations. In a criminal justice system, not only does the verbal constitute the fulcrum of the representation, but non-verbal forms of communication, such as the demeanor of witnesses, also create problems for *isihlonipho* users, because it requires that women do not maintain eye contact with males and always keep their heads bowed as a sign of respect. Given the importance placed on the 'demeanor' of witnesses as an indication of their truthfulness and credibility (Eades, 2010), *isihlonipho* users run the risk of being dismissed as unreliable witnesses. Yet it has long been established in sociolinguistic and communication studies research that non-verbal forms of communication such as eye contact differ significantly between cultural groups. In other words, different cultural aspects of communicative style in court play a significant role to the extent that a decontextualized view of women's talk in a courtroom setting can potentially create inequality, despite formal proclamations to the contrary. More importantly, a decontextualized view of the *isihlonipho* language variety reveals the inadequacies of language policies. It also reveals the shortcomings of linguistic citizenship rights that do not consider differential linguistic needs and circumstances, thus creating 'imminent others' (Isin, 2002: 45), or 'denizens' (Hammar, 1990). In other words, linguistic citizenship is not sensitive to a regime of dis-citizenship.

Data collection

The analysis draws from a large research project that focused on the role of *isihlonipho* in a courtroom setting where all participants use one language without any form of interpretation taking place. The analysis below is drawn from transcripts of 12 recorded criminal proceedings of rape trials that were collected from January to May 2007 in the Bulawayo Magistrate court. The researcher also set through all the rape trial cases in order to observe the demeanor of all witnesses.

A study of this nature always raises questions about the positionality of the researcher. Feminist research has shown that as insiders, women are the best analysts of their own lives. In this particular study, grounding an analysis of *isihlonipho sabafazi* in the everyday lives of ordinary women was, in my view, the beginning of an improved understanding of social forces that reproduce inequities (and privileges) in language policies. In this particular study I viewed my position as one of an 'outsider-within'. I see myself as a Ndebele woman and a feminist linguist who occupies a unique position of understanding the way in which marginality stems from interlocking systems of societal oppression and socialization. I am also committed to raising awareness about anomalies, distortions and invisibilities of women. Thus, my multiple subjectivities allow me to be an insider and outsider simultaneously and to shift back and forth with some degree of agency.

Data analysis

Extract 1

In the case of the rape of a 23-year-old, the time period in which the rape occurred is in dispute. The alleged rapist has an alibi that places him at a different venue during the time period in which the girl claims to have been raped. *Isihlonipho* forms are all in bold and italics.

1.1	**DC:**	Tshela inkundla ukuthi kwenzekani and at what time it happened. (Tell this court what happened and the time it happened.)
1.2	**W:**	Ngizame ukubaleka wa...wase.... (I tried to run away then...then he....)
1.3	**DC:**	Kwasekusenzekani? (And then what happened?)
1.4	**W:**	Wase ngigwenxa...ngawa wasengifuqela phansi ezama ***ukungembula***. Ngazama ukumfuqelakhatshana kodwa ubelamandla futhi ubephethe inqamu. Wa...**wasengipha isondo**. (He then tripped me...I fell down, he then pushed me down trying to ***uncover me***. I tried pushing him away, but he was very powerful, and he had a knife. He...*he then gave me the* **wheel**.)
1.5	**DC:**	Utshela inkundla ukuthi ***ukuphe isondo?*** (Are you telling this court that he ***gave you a wheel?***)

1.6	**W:**	Yebo baba. (Yes, sir.)
1.7	**DC:**	Ulithethe wena lelo **sondo?** (Did you take **the wheel?**)
1.8	**W:**	(Looks down, sobbing, does not answer.)
1.9	**DC:**	Ngiyakuzwa lokho **okwesondo ulithethe na isondo?** (I understand **about the wheel, but did you take the wheel?**)
1.10	**W:**	(Sobbing, does not answer the question.) Ubephethe inqamu efuna ukungigwaza. (He had a knife; he wanted to stab me.)
1.11	**DC:**	Akesiyitshiye leyo **eyesondo** oliphiweyo. Bekuyisikhathi bani? (Let's leave the story of **the wheel which you were given** aside for a moment. What time was it?)
1.12	**W:**	Ngicabanga ukuthi bekusemini. (I think it was in the afternoon.)
1.13	**DC:**	Uyacabanga...uzama ukutshela inkundla ukuthi awukwazi ukuthi bekuyisikhathi bani? (You think...are you trying to tell this court that you do not know what time it was?)
1.14	**W:**	(Looks down, does not answer the question.)
1.15	**DC:**	Utsho ukuthi bekusemini singathi ngo 3 kumbe u 2? (Are you saying it was 3 or 2?)
1.16	**W:**	(Seems confused) Angazi lutho ngo 3 lo 2 okhulumangaye. **Isithunzi sami bengingasiboni phambi kwami.** (I do not know anything about 3 or 2, which you are talking about. **My shadow was not in front of me.**)

The witness, a young unmarried woman who has been raped by an unknown male, uses *isihlonipho sabafazi* when responding to the defense counsel's questions. However, as the issue in dispute is time, the inability of the witness to provide a precise or exact reference to time renders it impossible for the accused to be found guilty because of the high standard required for conviction in a criminal justice system. The female witness, who can only look down and probably does not even have a wristwatch, uses a gendered temporal formulation of time: the position of her shadow (1.16). As the defense counsel presses her for precision in terms of her reference to time (1.15), the temporal formulation becomes vague (see Thetela (2003)). The defense counsel also takes advantage of the use of *isihlonipho sabafazi* language variety in the witness' testimony to create reasonable doubt by 'manufacturing' and constructing consent, thereby rhetorically erasing the criminality of rape.

Starting from 1.5, the defense counsel asks a rhetorical question, insinuating that the witness accepted the gesture of being given the wheel (i.e. having sex), which the witness unwittingly acknowledges in 1.6. The defense counsel's question in 1.7 appears intended to 'seal the deal' for consensual sex. In 1.8, the witness' response does not help the case. Her avoidance of the question and her non-verbal behavior of looking down suggest evasiveness and easily lead to an interpretation that she is not being truthful and, therefore, lacks in credibility as a witness.

The same strategy of using *isihlonipho* language variety, in a manner in which the witness is disempowered or her words are used against her, is also evident in Extract 2 below. In Extract 2, the witness is asked to explicitly describe what took place during the rape incident. Naturally, as a Ndebele female, she resorts to *isihlonipho sabafazi* because sex discourses are not available to her in the Ndebele language. More so, if she were to use male language, she would be viewed, at least from a customary perspective, as a woman of loose morals, so for her the stakes are high; hence, she has to use the 'appropriate' language.

Extract 2
The defendant claims that sex occurred but was consensual.

2.1   W: Ufuqele *into yakhe entombini*. (He **pushed his thing into the girl**.)

2.2   DC: *Yintobani* ayifuqele *entombini* bengithi ubuwedwa? Ibizo *lentombi* belingubani? (What **thing** did he push into **the girl**? I thought you were alone. What was **the girl's** name?)

2.3   W: (Sobbing) Ye bengingedwa ufuqele *induku yakhe entombini* (Yes, I was alone. He pushed **his knobkerrie into the girl**.)

2.4   DC: *Induku?* Kungani amapholisa ekubuza awuzange uyiqambe leyo eye *nduku* lenye *intombi*. (**Knobkerrie?** Why is that in your statement to the police you did not mention the **knobkerrie?** You also never mentioned the other **girl** but a **cake**. Let me read to you what you said: '*Wafuqela* **impompi** *yakhe ekukwini*... he pushed his pipe in the cake'.)

In the above extract, the witness' testimony shows her avoidance of a sexually explicit register that any male would very easily use. The witness resorts to euphemistic references in 2.1, where she refers to the defendant's penis as '*into yakhe*' (his thing) and her own private part in '*entombini*' (in the girl). Because the court proceedings are adversarial and inquisitorial (see de Klerk (2003); Sigsworth *et al.* (2011); Thetela (2003)), the defense counsel requests precision with regard to 'his thing' and chooses to deliberately 'misunderstand/misinterpret' the *isihlonipho* talk by asking for the girl's name in order to raise credibility issues about this witness, something that he effectively does in 2.4 when pointing out the discrepancies in the witness' statements to the police. Yet, in *isihlonipho* lingua, *induku* (knobkerrie) and *impompi* (pipe) are used interchangeably with reference to a penis, while *intombi* (the girl) and *ikuku* (cake) are synonyms for the vagina. These lexical choices are accessible to all speakers of the language, although they are used almost exclusively as part of the *isihlonipho* lexicon by women. As the defense counsel is also a native speaker of this language, he has knowledge of the culture-specific nature of the meanings of these lexical items but chooses to interpret them as if they were devoid of a cultural context. Therefore, he underscores that, in a court of law, 'explicitness and precision' (Thetela, 2003: 85) are emphasized, rather than *isihlonipho*, which can have multiple interpretations. The defense counsel and the witness are clearly using different frames of interpretation. Female witnesses in rape trials use *isihlonipho sabafazi* as a norm for interpretation, which creates crosstalk because legal professionals (i.e. lawyers, judges and magistrates) use the 'legal' norm to interpret court proceedings. Female courtroom participants draw from cultural interpretative practices grounded on culturally specific meanings drawn from *isihlonipho sabafazi*.

This practice is not only evident in female witnesses but also in female law-enforcement officers. In Extract 3, a statement taken by a female law-enforcement officer uses *isihlonipho* expressions to the detriment of the complainant.

Extract 3
Statement written by a policewoman

Kuthiwa indoda le ithanda **ukudlala umdlalo wokungena emacansini inikana isondo** *lamantombazana noma wona engafuni nje. (This man is accused of liking to* **play a game of getting on the mat** *and* **giving each other the wheel** *with the girls when they do not want.)*

When taking statements from victims, female officers compromise female victims by their use of *isihlonipho sabafazi*. Because sex discourses are not available to females, these officers resort to cultural norms that are antithetical to conducting a legal investigation, thus creating misunderstandings during trials. In the above statement, for instance, the policewoman describes the unwanted sexual encounter as *ukudlala umdlalo* (playing a game), effectively reducing the severity of a violent crime to a sex game (Thetela, 2003). In addition, this so-called game is described as reciprocal in *inikana* (giving each other), which discursively constructs consent. The reciprocal marker in the form of the suffix *ana* is an example of what Eades (2010: 112) described as the 'manufacture of consent'. Put differently, the female police officer, by using *isihlonipho sabafazi*, has inadvertently transformed the victim's experience of a violent crime into one of a consensual sex game. The redefinition of rape as a game is, in fact, a reproduction of patriarchal domination where women have no voice and a 'no' is taken as a 'yes' (Drew, 1992). This is not surprising because the *isihlohipho* language variety is founded on the principle of patriarchal domination. *Isihlonipho* is, therefore, 'a system organized around the subordination and sexual control of women' (Matoesian, 1993: 219).

Interestingly, female attorneys who are also speakers of Ndebele assume a different role in the courtroom. As shown in Extract 4, they exploit the use of the *isihlonipho* register to the advantage of their clients by assuming/performing male roles.

Extract 4
A female defense counsel takes on an elderly married woman who has been raped by someone she knows in the community. The defendant has claimed that they were secret lovers and that sex was consensual.

4.1	DC:	Tshela inkundla ukuthi kwenzakalani ngemva kwalokho? (Can you tell this court what happened after that?)
4.2	W:	Uthe kangivule *isibaya sikababa* ufuna *ingubo*. (He said I must open *father's kraal* because he wanted *blankets*.)
4.3	DC:	Utshoni nxa usithi uthe *vula isibaya sikababa*? Angithi uthe belingathandani? (What do you mean when you say he said open *father's kraal*? Didn't you say you were not lovers?)
4.4	W:	Ubephethe iskhali wathi uzangibulala ngaso nxa *singayanga ecansini*. (He had a weapon and said he would kill me if *we did not go to the mat*.)
4.5	DC:	Angikholwa ukuthi umuntu olodlame kangaka ulakho ukucela *ingubo lokuya ecansini*. Tshela inkundla amazwi awasebenzisileyo. (I do not believe that someone with such violence would ask for a *blanket* and for *going to the mat*. Tell the court the exact words he used.)
4.6	W:	⊗ (Silence...)...Ubekhuluma *inhlamba*. (He was saying obscenities.)
4.7	DC:	Tshela inkundla ukuthi leyo *nhlamba* ibisithini. (Tell this court what these *obscenities* were saying.)
4.8	W:	⊗ (Looks down...silence.) Ngingumama ohloniphekayo. Angikhulumi *inhlamba*. (I am a respectable mother. I do not talk *obscenities*.)

In the above extract, the female defense attorney exploits the witness' expression *isibaya sikababa*, used by married women to refer to their vaginas that are now the possession of their husbands (i.e. father). The defense counsel uses the expression *ukufuna ingubo* (desire for blankets), which is the *isihlonipho* expression for an affectionate request for intimacy, which rhetorically erases the criminality of rape as a violent crime and discursively constructs the encounter as affectionate/intimate and not violent. In 4.3, the defense counsel questions the credibility of the witness, and in 4.5, she emphasizes the weakness of her testimony in her attempt to create reasonable doubt. In 4.6, the witness can only provide an opinion on the nature of what the defendant said without repeating his exact words but explains, (4.8), her inability to repeat his words in terms of her own gendered identity.

All the extracts show that women's powerlessness in the courtroom is most visible when *isihlonipho sabafazi* gets dismissed as imprecise or not meeting the standards required by the criminal justice system. African women, within the context of the courts, have constitutional rights to use their first language but have no socio-legal rights to use the *isihlonipho* language varieties, especially in describing matters of a sexual nature. Put differently, Ndebele women have language rights to use *isihlonipho* variety within a courtroom setting, but the courts do not recognize this variety as appropriate in a courtroom setting, possibly due to the dichotomy between the private and public. In this context, language rights create 'the appearance of equality while masking the pervasiveness of ongoing inequality' (Devlin & Pothier, 2006: 163). Women are, in fact, denied substantive citizenship and 'assigned to the status of dis-citizens'. What these Ndebele women have is 'citizenship minus', which is effectively 'a disabling citizenship' (Devlin & Pothier, 2005: 3). Linguistic citizenship in this context has been used for the 'achievement of social inequality' as well as 'an instrument of social stratification' (Marshall, 1964: 106). Zimbabwe needs to re-conceptualize the notion of citizenship that encompasses women's language of respect and create a new legal vision that does not select which variety of a language it will observe.

By introducing Ndebele within a courtroom setting, a formal right to a fair trial is achieved, but this right also ends there. Language policy that allows women to use their native language in a courtroom setting entails the simple bearing of rights, but not the full participation that accompanies active citizenship. What women have in this context is partial or passive citizenship. The lived experiences of these Ndebele women indicate that the language policies in and of themselves are not sensitive to the realities of a regime of dis-citizenship. In other words, viewing women's *isihlonipho* as 'extra', 'special' or 'extraneous' and unsuitable for court proceedings denies women equal citizenship (see Devlin & Pothier, 2006) and disregards the differential linguistic needs of a differentiated citizenry. As a result, women are turned into 'lingua-denizens', which perpetuates their linguistic dis-citizenship. But from a language policy standpoint, what the use of *isihlonipho* shows is that formal language policies are always at variance with actual language practice.

Conclusion: Re-framing Citizenship from a Gender Equality Perspective

Using dis-citizenship as an analytic tool to reveal exclusions and inequalities experienced by female citizens, this chapter has argued that the boundaries that limit women's access to full citizenship rights are linguistic in nature. If, as Jenson (2006: 4) indicated, '[f]ull citizenship is not simply about having some protections and some rights; it is about having equal rights and protections', then, in this context, Ndebele women are not 'full' citizens but rather 'partial' citizens. In a legal setting, *isihlonipho sabafazi* renders women 'domestic foreigners' or 'fellow strangers'.

While, from a language policy standpoint, introducing the use of indigenous African languages in the courtroom by court participants with limited language skills in English is, prima facie, empowering to women with limited linguistic skills in the languages of the courts, *isihlonipho sabafazi* is equally disempowering to the extent that it does not, in any way, lead to equitable justice. By using *isihlonipho*, the equality clause is somewhat subverted through a cultural choice. Yet the problem is not so much a cultural choice, but the limitation of that choice to a specific gendered body. In this regard, Ndebele women are not adequately included in court proceedings and face recurring marginalization and social exclusion by the criminal justice system. The introduction of African languages in the courtroom has not adequately addressed the linguistic needs of Ndebele women; if anything, it has compounded these problems, especially in rape cases. This resultant inequality is partially due to the distinction between 'overt' and covert language policies (Schiffman, 2006), both of which are immersed in a linguistic culture. Given that 'language policy is not only the specific overt, explicit, *de jure* embodiment of rules in laws or constitutions but a broader entity, rooted in covert, implicit, grassroots, unwritten *de facto* practices that go deep into the culture' (Schiffman, 2006: 112), the use of *isihlonipho sabafazi* falls within *de facto* practices. Bearing in mind that language, as Schiffman (2006) pointed out, is the main vehicle for the construction, replication and transmission of culture, it follows that language policy is primarily a social construct that rests on a range of issues that constitute 'linguistic culture'. Language policy, therefore, falls between ideology and practice; hence, it includes both covert and overt mechanisms, which create and maintain both official policies and *de facto* ones.

Perhaps what is required to truly include women in public institutions such as the courts is a re-framing of the concept of citizenship from a gender equality perspective by broadening it to include substantive equality that is not based on the dichotomy between public and private. As Devlin and Pothier (2006) pointed out, the advantage of such an approach is that it places at the core of any citizenship 'differential needs' because 'substantive equality gives effect to the particularized' rights of persons with different types of needs. Substantive equality requires comprehensiveness to be factored in any policy in order to determine the extent to which the prima facie equality or fairness does not meet the needs of some. Because substantive equality is not necessarily based exclusively on Marshall's (1964) triad (i.e. civil, political and social rights), it is a much broader view of human rights; it is inclusionary and encompasses the plurality of language varieties. Factoring in differentiated linguistic rights may entail further marginalization and possible essentialization. However, lived reality indicates that inequality is part of social life, and the notion of equal citizenship may need reframing. After all, 'the accommodation of differences is the essence of true equality' (Young, 1997: 160).

References

Andersen, J. and Siim, B. (eds) (2004) *The Politics of Inclusion and Empowerment: Gender, Class and Citizenship*. Basingstoke: Palgrave Macmillan.
Atkinson, J. and Drew, P. (1979) *Order in Court: The Organization of Verbal Interaction in Judicial Settings*. London: Macmillan.
Bosniak, L. (2000) Citizenship denationalized. *Indiana Journal of Global Legal Studies* 7 (1), 447–509.
Bulmer, M. and Rees, A. (eds) (1996) *Citizenship Today: The Contemporary Relevance of T. H. Marshall*. London: UCL Press.
Carol, J. (1994) Lawyer's response to language and disadvantage before the law. In J. Gibbons (ed.) *Language and the Law* (pp. 306–315). London: Longman.
de Klerk, V. (2003) Language and law: Who has the upper hand? *AILA Review* 16, 89–103.
Devlin, R. and Pothier, D. (2005) Introduction: Toward a critical theory of dis-citizenship. In D. Pothier and R. Devlin (eds) *Critical Disability Theory: Essays in Philosophy, Politics, Policy and Law* (pp. 1–10). Vancouver: UBS Press.
Devlin, R. and Pothier, D. (2006) Dis-citizenship. In Law Commission of Canada (eds) *Law and Citizenship* (pp. 141–175). Vancouver: UBC Press.

Drew, P. (1992) Contested evidence in courtroom cross-examination: The case of a trial rape. In P. Drew and J. Heritage (eds) *Talk at Work: Interaction in Institutional Settings* (pp. 39–64). Cambridge, UK: Cambridge University Press.
Eades, D. (1994) The case of communicative class: Aboriginal english and the legal system. In J. Gibbons (ed.) *Language and the Law* (pp. 234–264). London: Longman.
Eades, D. (2010) *Sociolinguistics and the Legal Process*. Bristol: Multilingual Matters.
Hammar, T. (1990) *Democracy and the Nation State: Aliens, Denizens and Citizens in a World of International Migration*. Aldershot: Avebury.
Haysom, L. (2009) Women and the legal system. *Agenda* 23 (82), 2–3.
Hobson, B. and Lister, R. (2002) Citizenship. In B. Hobson, J. Lewis and B. Siim (eds) Contested Concepts in Gender and Social Politics (pp. 23–54). Cheltenham: Edward Elgar.
Isin, E. (2002) *Being Political: Genealogies of Citizenship*. Minneapolis: University of Minnesota Press.
Jenson, J. (2006) Introduction: Thinking about citizenship and law in an era of change. In Law Commission of Canada (ed.) *Law and Citizenship* (pp. 3–21). Vancouver: UBC Press.
Lister, R. (1990) Women, economic dependency and citizenship. *Journal of Social Policy* 19 (4), 445–468. doi:10.1017/S0047279400018250
Lo Bianco, J. (2009) Critical discourse analysis (CDA) and language policy and planning (LPP): Constraints and applications of the critical in language planning. In T. Le, Q. Le and M. Short (eds) *Critical Discourse Analysis: An Interdisciplinary Perspective* (pp. 101–119). New York, NY: Nova Science.
Makoni, B., Makoni, S. and Mashiri, P. (2007) Naming practices and language planning in Zimbabwe. *Current Issues in Language Planning* 8 (3), 437–467. doi:10.2167/cilp126.0
Makoni, S. (2011) A critical analysis of the historical and contemporary status of minority languages in Zimbabwe. *Current Issues in Language Planning* 12 (4), 437–455. doi:10.1080/14664208.2011.615104
Makoni, S., Dube, B. and Mashiri, P. (2006) Colonial and postcolonial language policy and planning practices in Zimbabwe. *Current Issues in Language Planning* 7 (4), 377–414.
Makoni, S., Makoni, B. and Nyika, N. (2008) Language planning from below: The case of the Tonga. *Current Issues in Language Planning* 9 (4), 413–439. doi:10.1080/14664200802354419
Marshall, T.H. (1964) *Class, Citizenship and Social Development*. New York, NY: Doubleday.
Matoesian, G.M. (1993) *Reproducing Rape: Domination through Talk in the Courtroom*. Cambridge: Polity Press.
Mellinkoff, D. (1963) *The Language of the Law*. Boston, MA: Little, Brown & Co.
Moeketsi, R. (1999) *Discourse in a Multilingual and Multicultural Courtroom: A Court Interpreter's Guide*. Pretoria, South Africa: J. L. van Schaik.
Schiffman, H. (2006) Language policy and linguistic culture. In T. Ricento (ed.) *An Introduction to Language Policy: Theory and Practice*. Oxford: Blackwell Publishing.
Shohamy, E. (2006) *Language Policy: Hidden Agendas and New Approaches*. London & New York: Routledge.
Sigsworth, R., Vetten, L., Jewkes, R. and Christofides, N. (2009) Policing rape in South Africa. *Agenda* 23 (82), 39–50.
Siim, B. (1999) Towards a gender sensitive framework for citizenship—Comparing Denmark, Britain and France. In J. Bussemaker (ed.) *Citizenship and the Transition of European Welfare States* (pp. 85–100). London: Routledge.

Steytler, N.C. (1993) Implementing language rights in court: The role of the court interpreter in South Africa. In K. Prinsloo, Y. Peeters, J. Tuin and C. van Rensburg (eds) *Language, Law and Equality* (pp. 205–222). Pretoria, South Africa: UNISA.

Thetela, P. (2003) Discourse, culture and the law: The analysis of crosstalk in the Southern African bilingual courtroom. *AILA Review* 16 (1), 78–88. doi:10.1075/aila.16.08the

Thondhlana, J. (2002) Using indigenous languages for teaching and learning in Zimbabwe. In B. Burnaby and J. Reyhner (eds) *Indigenous Languages Across the Community* (pp. 30–39). Flagstaff, AZ: Northern Arizona University, College of Education.

Tollefson, J.W. (2006) Critical theory in language policy. In T. Ricento (ed.) *An Introduction to Language Policy: Theory and Method* (pp. 31–39). Oxford: Blackwell.

Walby, S. (1994) Is citizenship gendered? *Sociology* 28 (2), 379–395. doi:10.1177/0038038594028002002

Walker, A.G. (1987) Linguistic manipulation, power and the legal setting. In L. Kedar (ed.) *Power through Discourse* (pp. 57–80). Norwood, NJ: Ablex.

Werbner, R. (2003) Challenging minorities: Difference and tribal citizenship in Botswana. *Journal of Southern African Studies* 28 (4), 671–684. doi:10.1080/ 0305707022000043467

Young, M. (1997) Sameness/difference: A tale of two girls. *Review of Constitutional Studies* 4 (1), 150–166.

3 Problematizing the Construction of US Americans as Monolingual English Speakers

Aya Matsuda and
Chatwara Suwannamai Duran

In both public and scholarly discourse, US Americans[1] are often constructed as monolingual L1 English speakers. It is especially the case when they are compared with immigrants or English language learners in US school settings. In composition studies, education and some applied linguistics research, we have observed a tendency to use the word *multilingual users* (*speakers* or *writers*) as a replacement or interchangeable alternative to such words as *ESL* (English as a second language), *ELLs* (English language learners), *LEP* (limited English proficient) and *NNES* (non-native English speakers), a trend which seems to reflect a belief that we should acknowledge all linguistic (and other) resources that individuals possess rather than focusing on the 'deficiency' in their English proficiency. While we, the authors, agree with the reasoning behind it, we are also concerned that such practice potentially creates a false dichotomy where students who are *non-ESL*[2] are positioned as *non-multilingual* (i.e. monolingual). It is problematic because it is inaccurate; not only there are many US citizens from multilingual or immigrant families who grew up learning multiple languages but there are also those who learned English as their first language and added another language or languages later on. We also fear that such a construction normalizes monolingualism in this country and solidifies the ideology of English monolingualism as part of the US identity, which excludes and possibly alienates multilingual Americans. Furthermore, such ideology has implications for policies and practices, including those that compromise the English monolingual Americans' opportunity to learn foreign languages (FLs) and gain access to the global community.

We begin this chapter by presenting some examples of how the term *multilingual* is used to refer to the population that are traditionally referred to as *ESL*, and consequently, though unintended, could construct the non-ESL population as English monolingual users. We then problematize the construction of Americans as English monolinguals, especially focusing on the L1-English-speaking population and their future as *global citizens*. The chapter concludes by suggesting actions that language researchers and educators can take to respond to this problem.

The chapter focuses specifically and exclusively on the US contexts, where we believe that the term *multilingual users* has acquired nuances different from other parts of the world. For example, in contexts where both individual and societal multilingualism are maintained through policies and actual practices, what the term implies as well as the potential policy and ideological implications of using the term are expected to differ from what we suggest in this chapter. However, some of the overall arguments presented, such as how a well-intended practice to be inclusive may ironically contribute to the further exclusion of multilingual individuals, may apply to contexts beyond the United States as well.

Conflation of *Multilingual* and *ESL*

One usage of the term *multilingual* that seems to have emerged within the field of composition studies and education in the United States (and some related sub-disciplines within applied linguistics), which seems to have developed independently from the emergence of 'new strands' of multilingualism research that are informed by new theoretical and epistemological perspectives in the last two decades (Martin-Jones *et al.*, 2012), is to use it to refer to the population whose first language is not English. One of the underlying forces for this shift in the use of terminologies in composition studies and education seems to be the desire to change the image of language learners, from one that focuses on their limitations and deficiencies to one that recognizes their potential and resourcefulness.

Toohey (1992: 88), for example, problematized the deficit view of L2 learners and perspective of 'remediation of difficulty and not of maintaining and building upon strengths students have already acquired' found in Canadian schools and urged readers to refer to their students as '(at least) bilingual[3] students'. She argued that such practices may encourage ourselves as well as others to recognize their previous academic and linguistic achievement and regard them as 'young people with talents and abilities, which the school will try hard to enhance and support' (1992: 94) rather than students with limitations and deficiencies that schools will attempt to remedy.

García (2009) also urged TESOL (Teaching English to Speakers of Other Languages) professionals to use the term *emergent bilinguals* to refer to K-12 students they serve because terms such as LEPs and ELLs perpetuate educational inequalities by overlooking their valuable linguistic resources. More specifically, calling these children bilinguals leads to (1) the recognition of positive linguistic resources that students as well as their parents and community possess, (2) pedagogy that builds on students' strengths rather than that focuses on remediation and (3) more rigorous curriculum and more challenging instructional materials.

Cook (1991) has made a similar proposal for a more holistic understanding and construction of language learners with the introduction of the notion of *multi-competence*, or 'the knowledge of more than one language in the same mind' (1996: 65). Cook (2010) argued that 'someone who knows two or more languages is a different person from a monolingual and so needs to be looked at in their own right rather than as a deficient monolingual', challenging the common belief and widely-held assumption in L2 acquisition that successful language learning means progression toward the L1 monolingual speakers' linguistic knowledge. This idea that the mind of a multilingual user is fundamentally different from that of a monolingual speaker is supported by both linguistic (e.g. Mennen, 2004; Spivey & Marian, 1999) and cognitive research (e.g. Bialystok, 2001; Coggins *et al.*, 2004) and has been extended to understand aspects beyond the 'mind' of multilingual users, including their self- and social-identification and social practices (e.g. Pavlenko, 2003).

In composition studies, the term *multilingual writers* emerged as early as the 1990s (e.g. Lunsford & Connors, 1995; Spack, 1997) and now seems to have become the 'preferred equivalent for L2 or ESL writers' (Gentil, 2011: 6). A writing center resource page for faculty explains that a *multilingual writer* is the label favored by students as well as scholars and teachers in the field of L2 writing over such other alternatives as *L2 writer*, *NNES*, *LEP*, *ELL* and *ESL* (Ruecker, 2010), although the latter terms continue to be used as well. One well-respected book series dedicated to L2 writing is called 'The Michigan Series on Teaching Multilingual Writers', and various composition handbooks and writing textbooks include a section dedicated to *multilingual writers*, which addresses various language and rhetorical issues that may pose particular challenges to writers whose first language is not English (e.g. Hacker & Sommers, 2011; Lunsford, 2011; Roen *et al.*, 2009).

A preference for *multilingual* over *ESL* is also evident in various institutional practices in US higher education: the sections of first-year composition courses that are specifically tailored for ESL writers are now often referred to as 'Composition for Multilingual Writers' and support programs for international students and/or L2 speakers of English at US colleges and universities also have *multilingual students* as part of their program names.

We understand why the term *multilingual* may be considered more desirable than ESL in many contexts, as described above. In fact, being multilingual ourselves, we do share a view that language learners should be viewed as a person of multilingual resources rather than as a deficient version of a monolingual speaker of the language (e.g. Duran, 2011a, 2011b, 2012; Matsuda, 2000), and we appreciate that the use of an alternative term has encouraged some teachers and researchers to acknowledge the resourcefulness of these individuals.

However, what concerns us is that *multilingual* individuals are often constructed too narrowly. That is, in some applied linguistics and related scholarship focusing on US contexts, multilingual users (students, speakers or writers) are often conflated with persons whose first language is not English and are now learning English as their second/additional language. Many uses, although not all, of the term *multilingual* we introduced above referred exclusively to such a population.

In her article on racialization of ESL teacher identities, Motha (2006) critiqued the use of words *multicultural* and *diverse* to mean *minority* and the consequential juxtaposition of it:

> One characteristic of this ideology was the use of words such as *multicultural* and *diverse* to mean *minority*, a substitution that is troubling because if a multicultural literature class is marked as multicultural, then a literature class that is not marked as multicultural can somehow come to be understood as not multicultural. This tendency sets mainstream and multicultural classes in opposition to each other, thereby potentially excusing literature classes that are not multicultural from including diverse voices. (Motha, 2006: 505)

We argue that, although most likely unintended, the same kind of juxtaposition takes place when the term *multilingual* is used to refer exclusively to ESL persons, suggesting that non-ESL persons are non-multilingual. In the following sections, we critique this discursive construction of Americans as monolingual English speakers in more depth, with a particular focus on its implications for those who have learned English as their first language.

The Problem of Constructing US Americans as English Monolinguals

The construction of Americans as English monolinguals is problematic for several reasons. In this section, we focus on three of them – the inaccurate presentation of the linguistic repertoire of US Americans, the reinforcement of English monolingualism, and consequent policies and practices that restrict individual multilingualism. Our discussion for the most part focuses specifically on their implications for the L1-English-speaking population, whose language privileges and rights tend to be taken for granted and have not been studied as critically as that of their ESL counterparts.

Inaccurate presentation of the linguistic repertoire of US Americans

While there is a 'popular image of the United States as a nation united by one language' (Mackey, 1977), it is probably safe to say that the presence of languages other than English in the US society is already part of the general public's consciousness (whether it is accepted as a legitimate part of the society is another matter). Even if people do not recognize that numerous languages of indigenous peoples and early European settlers made United States a multilingual nation from its inception, recent high-profile media coverage on the controversies around the education of ELL children serves as a constant reminder that the US society today is multilingual.

What receives less media attention – and by consequently, less social recognition – is that multilingualism in the United States exists not only at the societal level but also at the individual level. In other words, US society today is not simply a collection of monolingual speakers of different languages but comprised a sizable number of individuals who know multiple languages.

For instance, new refugees and immigrants who become US citizens each year quickly become multilingual by adding English to their linguistic repertoire, if they have not already done so upon or prior to their arrival. Many of their children also grow up to be multilingual, using English in school and other public spaces and other language(s) at home. While research shows that immigrants typically become English monolinguals by the 3rd generation (Fishman, 1966; Veltman, 1983), there are always new groups of refugees and immigrants who use English and other languages on a daily basis.

While linguistic diversity is typically associated with the L1 speakers of languages other than English, they are not the only Americans who possess the knowledge of multiple languages; there are the L1-English-speaking Americans who speak other languages. For example, there are those who grew up in multilingual households and have acquired multiple languages, although English may be their strongest language throughout their lives (and they may be perceived as an English monolingual by their peers and teachers). There are those who learn FLs in school or through community programs. Some may grow up knowing only English, but may decide later to learn a language that is part of their heritage. There are also those who have lived abroad and have thereby acquired the host country's local languages.

It is hard to say how many L1-English-speaking Americans have taken advantage of opportunities to learn another language, have attained a certain level of proficiency and are able to use it for actual communication. It is probably safe to assume that such individuals are a minority in the United States. However, our point is that there *are* L1-English-speaking Americans who are also fluent in other languages and use such languages in both professional and personal contexts. Thus, constructing Americans – even those who speak English as their L1 – as English monolinguals, which leaves out this particular group of Americans, results in an inaccurate and incomplete portrayal of people in this country.

English monolingualism and marginalization of multilingual Americans

Besides being an inaccurate description, the construction of Americans as English monolinguals is problematic because it perpetuates the ideology of English monolingualism, which 'sees English monolingualism as a normal – if not ideal – condition' (Wiley & Lukes, 1996: 514). And when the multilingual population is positioned as an exception, their voices are less likely to be reflected in public discourse, allowing or creating a social climate and language policies and practices that reinforce English monolingualism and officially deny multilingualism. The English-only movement, policies that restrict the use of non-English languages in public spaces, and restriction of bilingual education are some well-cited examples of the manifestations of an English monolingual ideology (see Crawford, 2000; Lippi-Green, 2011; and Wiley & Lukes, 1996 for in-depth critiques of English monolingualism).

The English-only movement '[grew] directly out of the immigration-restriction movement' (Crawford, 2000: 4), and it views language diversity 'as largely a consequence of immigration' and 'equates the acquisition of English with patriotism and Americanization' (Wiley & Lukes, 1996: 519). Consequently, the recognized targets and victims of the English-only movement are linguistic minorities (e.g. indigenous people, immigrants and heritage language speakers). However, we further argue that it adversely affects the L1 speakers of English as well. It is true that their knowledge of language other than English tends to be perceived more favorably than that of L2 users of English, which works as the reminder of 'otherness' of refugees, immigrants and children of recent immigrants. But, even for L1 users of English, there are situations where not being an English monolingual could draw unwanted attention or marginalize the person. For example, in the most recent Republican primary race, some people used fluency in languages other than English to construct candidates as non-American. John Huntsman, who has spoken in Chinese during a televised debate and other events during his presidential campaigns, was called 'China Jon' and the 'Manchurian candidate', and his American values were questioned (Summers, 2012). Similarly, Newt Gingrich aired an ad titled *The French Connection*, which 'mock[ed] Romney for being able to speak French' (Summers, 2012). We do not suggest that their ability to speak another language alone has hurt their candidacy; however, the connection between English monolingualism and American identity is so strong in some people's mind that being something other than an English monolingual can be used to challenge one's American-ness.

What is even more disheartening is the fact that multilingualism can (and has) become a *'surrogate means'* (Wiley, 1999) to discriminate against people based on other factors such as race, national origins and religious beliefs, practices that are illegal and socially unacceptable (Boas, 1940; Haas, 1992; Lang, 1986; Lippi-Green, 2011; Phillipson, 1988; Wiley, 1999). The accumulated body of sociolinguistic research has shown that the evaluation of a language (and linguistic variety) is based on the social evaluation of its speakers and that minorities and members of less-privileged social groups get further marginalized and discriminated against because of the unfavorable evaluation of the language associated with the group. This is typically critiqued in relation to the speakers of 'non-standard' varieties of a language or a minority language, but when English monolingualism is perceived as the norm, multilingualism could become a similar tool for masked discrimination. For instance, the critiques of the bilingual fluency of Huntsman and Romney presented above may have been an indirect attack on their faith, as they learned these languages while serving as Mormon missionaries (Wayne Wright, personal communication, 31 January 2012).

In short, we criticize the construction of Americans as English monolinguals because it perpetuates the ideology of English monolingualism. Such ideology marginalizes multilingual Americans – both US born and immigrants, and L1 and L2 speakers of English – and harbors biased practices and discrimination. In the next section, we explore how such ideology and consequent policies and practices affect English monolingual speakers, whose opportunities to learn a new language are considerably compromised.

Compromised opportunities for global citizenship

An example of problematic policy and pedagogical implications that is particularly relevant to this volume, which explores the relationship between policy, education and citizenship, relates to the state of FL education in the United States. That is, the ideology of English monolingualism compromises opportunities for Americans – particularly the ones who grow up as English monolinguals and have not had a chance to learn another language – to become multilingual, which is critical for global citizenship.

Although offered in many elementary, middle and high schools, FL classes are required for high school graduation in only 10 of 50 states, and are often positioned in a marginal place within the overall K-12 curriculum (Lacorte, 2006; Reagan, 2002). The teaching and learning of some languages that are considered 'critical' from the perspective of national security may receive government support (Clifford, 2004; Malone et al., 2005), but overall funding for FL education in the K-12 contexts keeps declining (Clifford, 2004; Rhodes & Pufahl, 2011). And in times of budget crisis, or under the pressure to increase test scores, it is courses like FL (along with other specials like PE and Arts) that get reduced or eliminated (Lipton, 1998).

Lack of support for FL curriculum not only reduces the number of FL classes but also negatively affects hiring and professionalization opportunities. K-12 FL teachers often find themselves in working conditions less favorable compared to their colleagues in other subject areas (López Gómez & Albright, 2009), and the salary for FL instructors in higher education tends to be lower than that of their colleagues in other disciplines (Thornton, 2011). This, combined with the marginalized status of the FL curriculum, makes it difficult to hire qualified teachers. Less support for professional development (e.g. attending conferences) as well as decreased preparation time and larger classes (Keatley, 2004) makes it difficult for teachers to continuously and consistently deliver high-quality instruction in existing FL classes (Rhodes & Pufahl, 2011).

In addition, as stated earlier, a strong English monolingual ideology in the country makes it difficult for students to recognize the importance of learning an FL (Crystal, 2003; Nunan, 2003). Furthermore, the ideology of English as an international language is very powerful outside of the United States as well, and thus English speakers do tend to get accommodated much more so than speakers of other languages, making it (seem) unnecessary for

English monolingual speakers to learn other languages. Students who are unmotivated or have no investment in FL learning are not likely to attain much fluency even if they are enrolled in an FL class, and the lack of demand from students may even encourage schools to discontinue or limit their FL offerings (Curtain & Pesola, 1994; Tedick & Walker, 1996).

In short, English monolingualism – the ideology as well as policies and practices that support it – results in fewer opportunities for English-speaking monolingual Americans to receive quality FL education and to become fluent in a language other than English, a problem which we problematize further in the next section.

Individual multilingualism and global citizenship

The knowledge of multiple languages is a prerequisite for a global citizenship. By *citizenship*, we are of course not referring to one's immigration or visa status or the origin of one's passport – at the global level, which cuts across the border of nation states, such formal ways to recognize one's membership do not exist. Instead, we define *citizenship* in terms of one's ability to participate fully in the community, and thus *global citizenship* refers to one's ability to successfully participate in various international endeavors and become a valuable member of the community, which is characterized by 'the intensification of worldwide social relations which link distant localities in such a way that local happenings are shaped by events occurring many miles away and vice versa' (Giddens, 1990: 64). While English is typically considered and promoted as the key that opens the door to the globalized world (Crystal, 2003; Matsuda, 2003), some scholars have questioned the discursive construction of English as the only international lingua franca (e.g. Kubota & McKay, 2009) and pointed out the importance and advantages of knowledge in multiple languages.

Among various benefits that ranges from increased communicative abilities to cognitive advantages to improved curriculum (Baker & Sienkewicz, 2000), the most salient advantages of multilingualism in the context of today's globalized world are its communication advantages, cultural advantages and economic advantages. Communication advantages in a global context refer to the ability to communicate with more people. With the greater mobility of people worldwide and the advancement of technology such as the internet, we are blessed (or cursed, depending on your perspective) with increased opportunities to interact with people from language and cultural backgrounds that differ from our own. Lack of a common language can 'sometimes [be] a barrier to communication and to creating friendly relationships of mutual respect' (Baker & Jones, 1998: 6), but the knowledge of multiple languages can increase the chance of having a common language, possibly lowering or eliminating such a barrier.

Knowledge of multiple languages also often leads to cultural advantages, specifically the ability to experience and understand different cultures. It is possible to travel to foreign countries or interact and learn from friends and neighbors about their culture without speaking their languages, but the knowledge of the language of that culture is required 'to participate and become involved in the core of a culture' (Baker & Jones, 1998: 7). Furthermore, the process of learning and using multiple languages is often accompanied by a cross-cultural awareness and sensitivity and higher tolerance of cultural differences in general (Friedrich, 2012; Friedrich & Matsuda, 2010). Since we cannot always predict the background of people we will come across in international communication, such meta-awareness of diverse cultures and how it affects our communication are as important as – or perhaps more important than – the knowledge and experience of a specific culture that we gain through learning new languages.

The most obvious form of an economic advantage is increased job opportunities. As Heller (2002) pointed out, in today's global market that is highly multilingual and multicultural, bilingualism has become a commodity, and individuals who know multiple languages are attractive to businesses (see also Baker, 2011). Knowledge of FLs may open up new learning opportunities such as study abroad, or allow one to access information that is available only in another language. Such experience and knowledge not only leads to personal growth but they may also be used to distinguish oneself from the rest of the crowd when competing for a position or promotion.

In short, helping US children to become multilingual is one promising way to prepare them for the globalized world – so that they not only survive in global competition but also become global citizens who can contribute to and gain from their involvement in the community. This future generation of Americans can use the knowledge of multiple languages not only for their individual success and economic advancement but also to work as grassroots diplomats who build mutually respectful relationships that go beyond national boundaries. Unfortunately, the ideology of English monolingualism that permeates the US society today, which limits the opportunity to become multilingual and to become aware of the multilingualism that exists outside the United States, is counterproductive in preparing American children for a highly mobile, multilingual and multicultural global community that they are already part of. And our concern, as we have tried to illustrate, is that our well-meaning practices may be indirectly contributing to this unfortunate state of affairs.

What Needs to be Done

In the previous sections, we suggested how the current use of the term *multilingual users* in scholarly and public discourse in the United States may lead to the construction of Americans as English monolinguals and discussed the possible negative consequences of such a discursive construction, which collectively undermine the future opportunities of American citizens who want to be part of the multilingual and multicultural, globalizing world. Given these concerns, we, applied linguists, must critically examine the construction of L1-English-speaking Americans with the same sensitivity we bring to the discussion of ELLs and immigrants, so that we do not unintentionally feed or reinforce the monolingual ideology in public discourse.

One thing we can do is to be mindful of the precise definition of the terms we use to describe particular populations, and encourage others to do the same. In some cases, the term *multilingual* is chosen because the scholar or teacher intends to capture and understand the multilingual repertoires, resources and language (use) of people who are learning English. In other words, the choice of the term implies a shift of perspectives and construction of this population, which not only influences how scholars understand and describe their experiences, but also what about their experiences are studied. In such cases, the use of the term *multilingual* in fact seems appropriate, even if the group that a particular study focuses on happens to be learning English as a second language. Even so, however, it is still important to acknowledge, perhaps as a footnote, that L1-English speakers can also be *multilingual* and to clarify why the term *multilingual* in chosen over *ESL*. Providing a clear definition and clarifying our standpoint is important with any concept, especially in interdisciplinary and multidisciplinary fields like applied linguistics where scholars often bring different reference points to address the same issues. Such practices seem particularly critical when the conflation of terms may lead to some harmful consequences like the ones discussed in this chapter.

In other cases, we will have to question whether *multilingual* is actually the most appropriate term. For example, for a study that uses the term *multilingual users* but yet is based on the deficit view of language learners, other terms such as *L2 learners* or *non-native speakers* may actually better capture the orientation of the study. Another potentially problematic case is when the term *multilingual* is used as a euphemism to avoid the stigmatizing potential of existing labels (Ortmeier-Hooper, 2008). Although there are benefits in avoiding loaded labels, it needs to be kept in mind that substituting a word is only a temporary solution. Unless we address the sources of the problem, the new word would quickly acquire the stigma and the search for a new, 'clean' alternative must continue.

In addition, we suggest that we engage in more research that investigates the language, language use and experience of multilingual Americans whose L1 is English, which can be as complex and illuminating as that of multilingual Americans who are L2 users of English. There are many applied linguistics studies whose participants are multilingual L1-English-speaking Americans, but their focus is typically on their L2 only (e.g. FL classroom research). The majority of such studies operate from the 'deficit' view of L2 learners that compares the language of L2 users (in this case, FL proficiency of L1-English-speaking Americans) against that of L1 users of the target language. Some studies position such participants as L1-English-speaking *multilingual* language users (e.g. Byrnes *et al.*, 2010), but they are few and far between. Studies that investigate the multilingual resourcefulness or negotiation of NES Americans outside FL classrooms (e.g. Jarmel & Schneider, 2010; Kim, 2008; Sicola, 2005; Tung, 2004) tend to construct participants as special kinds of language users in a unique linguistic circumstance rather than a population that contributes to multilingualism among Americans in general. If we expand our understanding of 'multilingual Americans' by including the research on L1-English-speaking multilinguals (by both drawing from the insights of the existing studies and conducting new research), and if we consolidate them with the increasing body of literature on multilingual Americans who are L2 users of English, we will arrive at a much more comprehensive and nuanced understanding of what it means to be 'multilingual' in this country.

In non-scholarly, public discourse, the kinds of usage that are particularly worrisome are those that explicitly exclude L1 speakers of English from the definition of *multilingual users* and reinforce the false dichotomy between *multilingual* users and *L1 English* users. A school service office or course for *multilingual students*, which caters exclusively to L2 English users, is an example of such use. Such usage is highly visible to the general public (much more so than that found in scholarly journals which are generally read only by scholars), many of whom may uncritically internalize the definition of *multilingual* assumed here as well as the possible consequences we have problematized in this chapter.

What exactly needs to be done about this type of use of the term *multilingual* is rather complicated. On one hand, if a particular group (e.g. service clientele and students) is defined only by the fact that English is not their first language and excludes others, we might as well call them *ESL, ELL* or *NNES* – these terms describe the intended population more accurately. On the other hand, we hesitate to suggest returning to those terms because they promote the deficit view of L2 users, and they are already stigmatized in many contexts in the United States. Given this complex landscape where there are no easy solutions, and that sometimes the change in language use leads to a social change (Holmes, 2006; Lippi-Green, 2011), one approach that may be most realistic and promising is to encourage the use of the term *multilingual,* while working to increase people's awareness of the inclusiveness implied in this term. We may also encourage administrators to re-examine the appropriateness of labels vis-à-vis the needs the program or course is attempt to address. For instance, in a writing program, a different course number and a systematic advising may allow students to be placed in appropriate sections without explicitly labeling it as *ESL* or *multilingual.*

Finally, we would like to propose that we eventually turn around the discourse and move away from presenting English monolingualism as the norm among Americans, a proposal similar to what Ofelia García has made. García (2009: 4) has argued that 'by focusing on the children's emergent bilingualism and making bilingualism the norm, the field of language education would be able to move to the center of all educational endeavors for all children' and urged the language education profession to embrace not just those who speak languages other than English at home, but also L1-English speakers who are becoming bilingual. English-speaking monolingual individuals may be the majority in this society, but that does not necessarily mean that it needs to be the norm. Individual bilingualism and multilingualism, though less common, are in fact a realistic state for which we can all aim. Such a shift in discourse may help us recognize the resourcefulness of children who have had an access to languages other than English early on in their lives (through family language use or other opportunities) as well as the disadvantages of those who have not had such multilingual exposures and require extra support in order to overcome their disadvantage. Furthermore, such a shift in thinking may encourage language policies and practices that would promote multilingualism through the maintenance of languages other than English, high-quality FL education in public schools and increased opportunities for study abroad.

Regardless of the path we take, one thing that seems clear is that we need to become more thoughtful – and perhaps careful and responsible – in the way we use the term *multilingual* in our work, and encourage others to do the same through our scholarship, teaching and professional collaborations. Failing to do so not only leads to confusion and misunderstanding but also to the stereotypical and uncritical construction of a group of people – in this case, Americans as English monolinguals, the kind of practice we often critique and fight against in our work.

Final Remarks

The goal of this chapter was not to criticize the overall use of word *multilingual* or to suggest that it is the only or most powerful force behind English monolingualism in the US society today. Rather, it attempted to point out the ironic and unproductive practices we may be unintentionally taking part in. That is, our use of the term *multilingual,* which has emerged from our desire to support (and even promote) multilingualism and respect the language rights of linguistic minorities, may feed into the ideology, policies and practices of English monolingualism that we fight against. While we may be successful in promoting the appreciation of multilingualism in relation to linguistic minorities, we could potentially create the opposite effects concerning L1-English-speaking Americans by reinforcing the discursive construction of them as English monolinguals and limiting their opportunities to become 'citizens' of the globalizing world. It is our hope that this chapter serves as the reminder of the importance of critical reflection on language use in our scholarship as well as our role in illuminating the language resources of the US citizens, need for quality language education in the US schools and the need to cultivate global citizenship among Americans.

Acknowledgments

We would like to thank Vaidehi Ramanathan, Yasuko Kanno, Matthew Prior, Doris Warriner and Wayne Wright for their helpful comments and Lizabeth Collier for her assistance with the preparation of the manuscript.

Notes

(1) For the rest of the chapter, we use the term *Americans* to refer specifically to *US Americans* in order to avoid wordiness.
(2) *ESL* is being used to represent not only *ESL* but also other similar terms such as *ELL, LEP* and *NNES* in order to avoid wordiness.
(3) In the field of education, the term *bilingual* is more often used to describe an individual student who speaks two languages (e.g. a *bilingual* student) and a group in which only two languages are represented (e.g. a *bilingual* classroom). For the interest of space, this chapter focuses on the use of *multilingual* only, but much of our critique of the term *multilingual* in this chapter also applies to the use of the term *bilingual* that refers exclusively to ELLs.

References

Baker, C. (2011) *Foundations of Bilingual Education and Bilingualism* (5th edn). Bristol: Multilingual Matters.

Baker, C. and Jones, S.P. (1998) *Encyclopedia of Bilingualism and Bilingual Education*. Clevedon: Multilingual Matters.
Baker, C. and Sienkewicz, A. (2000) *The Care and Education of Young Bilinguals: An Introduction for Professionals*. Clevedon: Multilingual Matters.
Bialystok, E. (2001) *Bilingualism in Development*. Cambridge: Cambridge University Press.
Boas, F. (1940) *Race, Language, and Culture*. Chicago, London: The University of Chicago Press.
Byrnes, H., Maxim, H.H. and Norris, J.M. (2010) Realizing advanced foreign language writing development in collegiate education: Curricular design, pedagogy, assessment. *Modern Language Journal* 94 (S-1), i–ii.
Clifford, R. (2004) Remarks at *National Briefing on Language and National Security*, 16 January 2004, National Press Club, Washington, DC.
Coggins, P.E., Kennedy, T.J. and Armstrong, T.A. (2004) Bilingual corpus callosum variability. *Brain and Language* 8 (10), 69–75.
Cook, V.J. (1991) Wholistic multi-competence – jeu d'esprit or paradigm shift? Talk given at first EUROSLA Conference, Salzburg.
Cook, V.J. (1996) Competence and multi-competence. In G. Brown, K. Malkjaer and J. Williams (eds) *Performance and Competence in Second Language Acquisition* (pp. 54–69). Cambridge: Cambridge University Press.
Cook, V.J. (2010) Multi-competence. *Uncut version of a shorter encyclopedia entry*, accessed 13 January 2012. http://homepage.ntlworld.com/vivian.c/Writings/Papers/MCentry.htm
Crawford, J. (2000) *At War with Diversity: US Language Policy in an Age of Anxiety*. Clevedon: Multilingual Matters.
Crystal, D. (2003) *English as a Global Language* (2nd edn). Cambridge: Cambridge University Press.
Curtain, H. and Pesola, C. (1994) *Languages and Children: Making the Match*. White Plains, NY: Longman.
Duran, C.S. (2011a) 'Imagined Communities and Learning Thai as a Foreign Language'. Poster Presentation, Annual Convention of American Association of Applied Linguistics, 26 March 2011.
Duran, C.S. (2011b) 'A Study of Multimodal Literacies and Multilingual Repertoires among Karenni Youth in Arizona'. Paper Presentation at 22nd Penn State Conference on Rhetoric and Composition, 10–12 July 2011.
Duran, C.S. (2012) A study of multilingual repertoires and accumulated literacies: Three Karenni families living in Arizona (28, Chapter 3, pp. 24). Doctoral Dissertation, Arizona State University, Tempe, Arizona.
Fishman, J.A. (1966) *Language Loyalty in the United States: The Maintenance and Perpetuation of Non-English Mother Tongues by American Ethnic and Religious Groups*. The Netherlands: Mouton & Co.
Friedrich, P. (2012) ELF, intercultural communication and the strategic aspect of communicative competence. In A. Matsuda (ed.) *Principles and Practices of Teaching English as an International Language*. Bristol: Multilingual Matters.
Friedrich, P. and Matsuda, A. (2010) When five words are not enough: A conceptual and terminological discussion of English as a Lingua Franca. *International Multilingual Research Journal* 4, 20–30.
García, O. (2009) Emergent bilinguals and TESOL: What's in a name? *TESOL Quarterly* 43 (2), 322–326.

Gentil, G. (2011) A biliteracy agenda for genre research. *Journal of Second Language Writing* 20, 6–23.
Giddens, A. (1990) *The Consequences of Modernity*. Stanford: Stanford University Press.
Haas, M. (1992) *Institutional Racism: The case of Hawai'i*. Westport, CT: Praeger.
Hacker, D. and Sommers, N. (2011) *A Writer's Reference* (7th edn). Boston, MA: Bedford/St. Martin's.
Heller, M. (2002) Globalization and the commodification of bilingualism in Canada. In D. Block and D. Cameron (eds) *Globalization and Language Teaching* (pp. 47–63). London/New York: Routledge.
Holmes, J. (2006) *Gendered Talk at Work: Constructing Gender Identity through Workplace Discourse*. Oxford: Blackwell.
Jarmel, M. and Schneider, K. (2010) *Speaking in Tongues*. California: PatchWork Films. http://speakingintonguesfilm.info/
Keatley, C. (2004) Who is paying the bills? The federal budget and foreign language education in U.S. schools and universities. *The Language Resource Newsletter* (March).
Kim, Y.S. (2008) Communication experiences of american expatriates in South Korea: A study of cross-cultural adaptation. *Human Communication* 11 (4), 505–522.
Kubota, R. and McKay, S. (2009) Globalization and language learning in rural Japan: The role of English in the local linguistic ecology. *TESOL Quarterly* 43, 593–619.
Lacorte, M. (2006) But what am I doing here...?: A qualitative study of perceptions about sociopolitical issues among teachers of Spanish in the United States. *Hispania* 89 (2), 347–357.
Lang, K. (1986) The language theory of discrimination. *The Quarterly Journal of Economics* 101 (2), 363–382.
Lippi-Green, R. (2011) *English with Accent: Language, Ideology, and Discrimination in the United States* (2nd edn). New York: Routledge.
Lipton, G.C. (1998) A century of progress: A retrospective on FLES programs: 1889–1998. *Hispania* 81 (1), 75–87.
López Gómez, C. and Albright, J.J. (2009) Working conditions of foreign language teachers: Results from a pilot survey. *Hispania* 92 (4), 778–790.
Lunsford, A. (2011) *The St. Martin's Handbook* (7th edn). Boston/New York: Bedford/St. Martin's Press.
Lunsford, A. and Connors, R. (1995) *The St. Martin's Handbook* (3rd edn). New York: St. Martin's Press.
Mackey, W. (1977) Foreword. In H. Kloss (ed.) *The American Bilingual Tradition* (pp. vii–ix). Rowley, MA: Newbury House.
Malone, M.E., Rifkin, B., Christian, D. and Johnson, D.E. (2005) Attaining high levels of proficiency: Challenges for foreign language education in the United States. *CALdigest*.
Martin-Jones, M., Blackledge, A. and Creese, A. (eds) (2012) *The Routledge Handbook of Multilingualism*. Abingdon/New York: Routledge.
Matsuda, A. (2000) The use of English among Japanese returnees: A communicative strategy. *English Today* 16 (4), 49–55.
Mennen, I. (2004) Bi-directional interference in the intonation of Dutch speakers of Greek. *Journal of Phonetics* 32, 543–563.
Motha, S. (2006) Racializing ESOL teacher identities in the U.S. K-12 public schools. *TESOL Quarterly* 40 (3), 495–517.

Nunan, D. (2003) The impact of English as a global language on education policies on Asia-Pacific region. *TESOL Quarterly* 37 (4), 589–613.
Ortmeier-Hooper, C. (2008) English may be my second language, but I'm not 'ESL'. *College Composition and Communication* 59 (3), 389–419.
Pavlenko, A. (2003) 'I never knew I was a bilingual': Reimagining teacher identities in TESOL. *Journal of Language, Identity, and Education* 2 (4), 251–268.
Phillipson, R. (1988) Linguicism: structures and ideologies in linguistic imperialism. In T. Skutnabb-Kangas and J. Cummins (eds) *Minority Education: From Shame to Struggle* (pp. 339–358). Clevedon: Multilingual Matters.
Reagan, T.G. (2002) *Language, Education, and Ideology: Mapping the Linguistic Landscape of U.S. Schools*. Westport, CT: Greenwood Publishing.
Rhodes, N.C. and Pufahl, I. (2011) Foreign Language Instruction in U.S. schools: Results of a National Survey of Elementary and Secondary Schools. *Foreign Language Annals* 44 (2), 258–288.
Roen, D., Glau, G.R. and Maid, B.M. (2009) *Handbook for the McGraw-Hill Guide*. New York: McGraw-Hill.
Ruecker, T. (2010) *Multilingual Writers*. University Writing Center, University of Texas-El Paso, accessed 13 January 2012. http://academics.utep.edu/Default.aspx-?tabid=65801
Sicola, L. (2005) 'Communicative lingerings': Exploring awareness of L2 influence on L1 in American expatriates after re-entry. *Language Awareness* 14 (2/3), 153–169.
Spack, R. (1997) The rhetorical construction of multilingual students. *TESOL Quarterly* 31 (4), 765–774.
Spivey, M.J. and Marian, V. (1999) Cross talk between native and second languages: Partial activation of an irrelevant lexicon. *Psychological Science* 10, 181–184.
Summers, J. (2012) John Huntsman's Mandarin moments. *Politico*, accessed 14 January http://www.politico.com/news/stories/0112/71442.html
Tedick, D.J. and Walker, C.L. (1996) *Foreign Languages for All: Challenges and Choices*. Lincolnwood, IL: National Textbook.
Thornton, S. (2011) 2010–11 Report on the Economic Status of the Profession, accessed 16 February 2012. http://www.aaup.org/AAUP/comm/rep/Z/ecstatreport10-11/
Toohey, K. (1992) We teach English as a second language to bilingual students. In B. Burnaby and A. Cummings (eds) *Socio-political Aspect of ESL* (pp. 87–98). Toronto: OISE Press.
Tung, R.L. (2004) Female expatriates: The model global manager? *Organizational Dynamics* 33 (3), 243–253.
Veltman, C. (1983) *Language Shift in the United States*. Berlin: Mouton de Gruyter.
Wiley, T.G. (1999) Comparative historical analysis of U.S. language policy and language planning: Extending the foundations. In T. Huebner, K.A. Davis and J. Lo Bianco (eds) *Sociopolitical Perspectives on Language Policy and Planning in the USA* (pp. 17–37). Philadelphia: John Benjamin Publishing.
Wiley, T.G. and Lukes, M. (1996) English-only and standard English ideologies in the US. *TESOL Quarterly* 30 (3), 511–535.

4 Keywords in Refugee Accounts: Implications for Language Policies

Emily Feuerherm

Introduction

Policies and politics of refugee resettlement in the United States have been debated by the agencies responsible for the resettlement of diverse populations for decades (for a collection of recent debates, see Haerens, 2010). However, these debates have remained under investigated from an applied linguistics perspective and many of those applied linguistic studies have focused only on documenting inequalities, without addressing local, agentive responses. In the special edition of *TESOL Quarterly* on policy enactments, Ramanathan and Morgan (2007) stated that the aim of the collection is to highlight the local and agentive aspects of TESOL's engagement with language policies and planning: 'It seems time that we go beyond documenting and describing how our current language policies often sustain or create inequalities – we accept this as a truism now – to spaces where we become cognizant of our agentive roles in their enactments' (2007: 450). This chapter builds upon this orientation to show how international and local policies of resettlement are locally and individually interpreted by Iraqi refugees. Although the policies investigated here are not language policies, they have implications for language, and language plays a key role in the agentive interaction the Iraqi refugees have with the policies.

Some previously applied linguistic studies on refugee resettlement have focused on inequalities related to the application for refugee status (Blommaert, 2009; Eades, 2009); others on the discrimination and effect of the new environment on refugees (Leudar *et al.*, 2008; Delgado-Gaitan, 1994); and some have highlighted inequalities in educational programs directed toward refugees (Tollefson, 1989). The current chapter builds upon these studies to highlight not only the inequalities that arise through resettlement policies but also the agencies with which Iraqi refugees react to these inequalities.

Through interviews and field notes taken during English as a second language (ESL) class designed for refugees, the effects of international, national and local policies are addressed in relation to Iraqi refugees' abilities and inclinations to adapt to and remain in the United States after being resettled there. To accomplish this, a critical interpretive approach to interview data is used because, as Fairclough (2009: 163) points out, 'critical social research aims to contribute to addressing the social *"wrongs"* of the day (in a broad sense – injustice, inequality, lack of freedom, *etc*) by analyzing their sources and cause, resistance to them and possibilities of overcoming them'. Thus, through critical analysis, resistance, agency and possibilities of overcoming the social wrongs are highlighted over a more simplistic documentation of what the wrongs are.

The questions I will focus on in this chapter are: (1) at what point and under what circumstances do refugees feel as though they belong to their new country of residence? and (2) what effect do policies of resettlement have on refugees' translation of themselves[1] to a new country? Before these questions can be returned to, it is imperative to understand what a refugee is, and what processes they undergo to become a refugee in the United States.

Refugees

According to the 1951 Convention of the United Nations High Commissioner for Refugees (UNHCR), a refugee is defined as anyone who

owing to a well-founded fear of being persecuted for reasons of race, religion, nationality, membership of a particular social group or political opinion, is outside the country of his nationality and is unable or, owing to such fear, is unwilling to avail himself of the protection of that country.

Over the past 10 years, the number of refugees admitted to the United States has fluctuated between 130,000 and 30,000, with the lowest allowance following the attacks on September 11 2001 (Martin & Hoeffer, 2009). In 2010, 73,311 refugees were admitted to the United States, the largest group, at 18,134, had Iraqi nationality (FY 2010 Refugee Arrivals, nd).

Because of the Iraq war in 2003, followed by Iraq's sectarian violence (culminating in the attack of the Al-Askari Mosque in 2006), the United States has been pressured to accept a large quota of Iraqi refugees (Christoff, 2010). Although Iraqis were able to apply for refugee status, they were subjected to enhanced security-screening procedures established by the Department of Homeland Security (Margesson *et al.*, 2010). The full effects of these additional procedures on Iraqi's applications have yet to be documented. Nevertheless, the Immigration and Nationality Act bars asylum and resettlement to any member of a terrorist organization *and* to anyone who has provided what the law terms as 'material support' to 'terrorist organizations' (Acer *et al.*, 2006). 'Material support' can be the provision of money, goods, personnel and/or training to terrorist organizations. This includes support attained under duress or before the individual was 18 years old (Sridharan, 2008). Additionally, the definition of 'terrorist organizations' has broadened since the attacks of 11 September 2001 to include any 'group of two or more individuals, whether organized or not, which engages in, or has a subgroup which engages in, terrorist activity' (Sridharan, 2008: np). This definition includes groups that have assisted in prodemocracy/anti-authoritarian organizations and do not present a threat to the security of the United States (Acer *et al.*, 2006).

What this means for Iraqis who may be admitted to the refugee program in the United States is that they may not have been in the most dire of circumstances (persecution wise), but qualified because there was a quota to be filled and they had avoided providing anything that could be qualified as 'material support' to 'terrorist organizations'; qualities which under the sectarian violence that has been occurring, is quite remarkable.[2] After arrival to the United States, each refugee gets eight months of federal welfare before they are expected to become self-sufficient.[3]

Background for this study

This study is based on work that I have been doing in collaboration with the Sacramento Immigrant Resource Center (SIRC),[4] a private non-profit organization that works with refugees, human-trafficking victims and immigrants in the Sacramento area. In 2009, the volunteer coordinator at the SIRC and I set the groundwork for a program which would focus on helping Iraqi refugees find employment by providing the linguistic skills necessary for applying for and acquiring employment. The program, Refugee Employment Acquisition Program (REAP), began in June 2010 and has met once a week since then. The course itself consists of the following:

- 5–6:30 pm   Vocational ESL courses divided into three levels.
- 6:30–7 pm   Potluck meal.
- 7–8 pm   Individual tutoring and conversation with community volunteers.

From the beginning of REAP in June 2010 until November 2011, the students were mostly men, with only a few women and children. Attendance fluctuated between 2 and 15 students, with an average of 8 students per class, and 1–2 children (childcare was also provided for the duration of the course).

As the co-developer, coordinator and, at different times, teacher and tutor of the program, my investment in the project has motivated the trajectory of this research. More specifically, because of my connection to the program, one of the goals for this research is to understand the needs and experiences of the refugees served by REAP in order to make the program as beneficial as possible to those whom it serves.

Methods

This chapter will be a critical interpretive approach to two semi-structured interviews which elicited refugees' life histories of immigration from Iraq to the United States. This approach is used to highlight societal inequalities as they are observable through semiotic modalities. The social wrong that was identified by SIRC at the outset of the study was that the Iraqi refugees they were working with were struggling to find employment and were often unhappy with aspects of their resettlement, resulting in a secondary relocation soon after being resettled. This situation was approached through the establishment of REAP, thus creating a dynamic source for semiotic research.

The point of entry to this space is two semi-structured interviews and relevant field notes regarding three Iraqi refugees (in two interviews), focusing on their life stories of migration. Life stories were chosen because 'they touch on the widest of social constructions, since they make presuppositions about what can be taken as expected, what the norms are and what common or special belief systems can be used to establish coherence' (Linde, 1993: 3) and because storytelling can be used to make sense of our actions (Weick, 1995). The interview questions were constructed to elicit life stories of the resettlement process and effects of REAP:

- *Tell me about why you decided to come to the* United States?
- *What was the process of coming to the* United States *like?*
- *Tell me about your experiences in the* United States.
- *What did you think of the REAP class?*

These interviews were recorded and transcribed, preserving the content and phrasing, but omitting many of the false starts and back channeling to make the transcript easier to read.

Data were organized by *keywords* (Williams, 1976) identified first by calculating the high-frequency words, then by connecting those terms to their collocations, connotations and synonyms. *Keywords,* as Williams (1976: 74) explains, 'are significant, binding words in certain activities and their interpretation; they are significant, indicative words in certain forms of thought'. Not all high-frequency words were chosen as keywords; the ones chosen for analysis were those which signified larger issues in the resettlement process and signified the shaping and reshaping of the individual throughout this process. In other words, *keywords* are a means for addressing the relationship between discourse and social structures.

The participants[5]

The basis of the data for this chapter are two interviews, as well as 117 hours of observation field notes from the REAP classes and social events associated with the program. While I recognize that my positioning as a teacher/tutor and director of REAP, as well as my identity as a white non-Muslim American woman, may influence the data I collected in the interviews, triangulation through different data sources and recognition of my own positionality is considered. Those I interviewed for this chapter had spent time with me in purely social occasions, and we had developed rapport with each other (Langness & Frank, 1981), which is one reason why I chose to focus on the individuals discussed here.

Participants were chosen from those who had attended REAP. Students have been mostly male Iraqi refugees, who had worked with the US military in Iraq, though a few human-trafficking victims and refugees from other countries attended several classes. Participants were chosen based on the following criteria: (1) that they were Iraqi refugees having lived in the United States approximately one year; (2) I had developed rapport with them (Langeness & Frank, 1981); (3) they had attended all sessions of REAP for at least one six-week term; and (4) that they were able to communicate in English.

Rushdi and Nadia

Rushdi came to the United States with his wife and four daughters (the eldest being Nadia) almost a year before I interviewed them on 19 August 2011. The interview was conducted in their home. Rushdi was in his 50s and had been drafted into the Iraqi military at 19, then spent 30 years working for the Iraqi army. In 2003, he worked with the US army and the emerging Iraqi government as the organizer for foreign dignitaries' visits to Iraq.

His english skills were not as advanced as Nadia's, which is one reason why she joined him for the interview. Nadia had spent a year in college in Iraq, studying civil engineering when they immigrated to the United States. At the time of the interview, she, her sisters, and her mother were planning to move back to Iraq at the end of the month, while Rushdi remained in the United States.

Bashir
I interviewed Bashir on 2 October 2011, in my home office. He is in his 30s and had been an interpreter for the US army in Iraq prior to getting refugee status and immigrating to the United States. At the time of the interview, he was employed in a factory south of Sacramento, and was applying to technical colleges. He had been a student for two terms of REAP before he found a job and was no longer able to attend.

Keywords from the interviews

As I noted above, my approach to the analysis of these interviews will be focusing on the keywords that were repeated (or avoided) during the interviews. The analysis is divided into two sections: (1) refugee status and gender and (2) geographical space, nation and language. While the division of these two sections is in many ways arbitrary – in that they both deal with identity (or more specifically, identities) as Iraqi refugee in the United States – the division is a means for highlighting relevant factors in the narratives of the participants as they explain their motives for coming to the United States and their experiences upon arrival. In each of these sections, the keywords are highlighted, relevant quotations from the interviews are presented and a discussion of their context and meaning in the larger sense of an immigrant/refugee interacting with a new culture and language are explored.

Refugee status and gender

This section addresses issues relating to attaining refugee status from Iraq and the role of gender as it affects the entrance into a new, non-Muslim majority. The keywords focused on in this section are *safety* and *hijab*. As refugees, *safety* is an important word because to attain refugee status, the applicant must prove that their *safety* has been significantly threatened and that they are unable ('or unwilling', according to the UNHCR) to continue living in their home country. However, in these interviews, discourses of *safety* are intertwined with issues of gender, particularly concerning the *hijab* worn by some Muslim women. This section will begin by analyzing *safety* first, then tying that to gender through *hijab*.

In the interviews, *safety* was something sought, yet what *safety* meant was based in the context of war; both international and internal. Bashir's stories of persecution and the threats to his physical safety are contextualized by his association to the US army and his identity as an Iraqi.

B: It's like, kind of ... It was a little bit challenging and, uh, because sometimes you have to work under pressure and different kinds of circumstances. You know it's Iraq, it's not safe country, so, and working with the US army wasn't fun

E: How come?

B: It's fun, but it wasn't fun. You know, I will tell you, it was fun because when you are inside the base it's very safe, you know, you can go to the gym, but when we go outside the people target us, you know, we're a moving target, a live target, some people try to hunt us down

E: Did you have that happen?

B: It happened, like my, the camp where I was, I used to ride twice we get hit with roadside bomb, you know? So, it wasn't that fun, you know. After we stop, I drink like two bottles of water. You know, it's dangerous, it's dangerous ... but it was hard, you know it was hard and sometimes they call us names, you know, like traitors or something like that, but yeah, I mean I did my part. I was thinking like when stuff was start getting bad in Iraq I thought to do something to help the people, I was seeing innocent people was getting killed it was not easy. I was thinking why, why the people die?

This quote from Bashir's interview contains his only two instances of the word *safe*: Iraq is *not safe* and the base is *safe*. However, there are other words and phrases within this section of the interview which implicate the idea of *safety* (or its converse: *danger*). The use of *fun* is equated with *safety* on the base. Here, *fun* undergoes a semantic shift in meaning from something *entertaining* to *safe*. Being a *target* is a metaphor supported by examples of being hit by roadside bombs upon leaving the base. *Dangerous* is repeated twice, alluding to physical danger, but Bashir switches at this point to the more emotional effects of his situation with two instances of *hard* meaning 'difficult'– indicating the emotional hurt caused by being called *traitor* when he was motivated to join the US army *to help the people ... innocent people was getting killed.* The rhetorical question at the end of this section (*I was thinking why, why the people die?*) has a dramatic quality – posed to the self – that indicates an internal dilemma.

Throughout this segment, Bashir sets up a clear dichotomy between *safety* and *danger* and extends that dichotomy beyond geographical space by including emotional injuries (being insulted by *traitor*) which may abide in physically safe spaces. His initial claim that Iraq is *not safe* and the US army base is *safe* avoids the history of the United States as an invader of Iraq, and the creation of a war zone in 2003 with an occupation lasting until 2011. This intentional avoidance may be an effect of being interviewed by an American; or he may believe that the invasion helped Iraqis. In fact, both may be true in certain contexts. In any case, his narrative highlights his intentions to help Iraq by joining the US army, while avoiding the reasons why the US army was there to be joined in the first place. The messiness of this situation, while rationalized in the narrative, becomes bound to the historical context of war and occupation inasmuch as it is bound to the context of the interview (Linde, 1993; Weick, 1995).

Bashir's narrative of persecution above uses the keyword *safe* only twice, but references the notion through other forms such as with semantic shift (*fun, wasn't fun*), its opposite (*dangerous*), metaphor (*target, hunt*), example (*roadside bombs*) and rhetorical question (*why the people die?*). On the other hand, Rushdi's sense of *safety* is one in which he uses the word, but his decision to become a refugee in the United States was not guided solely by the traditional notion of escaping persecution and seeking *safety*.

E: So my first question for you is why did you decide to leave Iraq? And come here, to the United States
R: The first one, uh, the first one, was because of the situation. I thought it was safety for me and for my family
E: Yeah
R: And I need PEACE. And I need high education for my daughters

Safety is the first reason Rushdi chose to come to the United States as a refugee, but *safety* is directly followed by *peace* and *education*. For him, finding safety and peace is as important as providing opportunities for his daughters through education. For Rushdi, *safety* is not purely the physical safety of his family, but their future prospects.

E: Did something happen that made you feel like unsafe in Iraq? Or was it that just, because for so long you had so many wars that you felt, come to the United States away from, away from so much wartime
N: (translates for Rushdi)
R: Yes yes because the wars and it's very difficult for I told you before when I'm 19 through 52 I'm in the army and I'm in the army for

30 years and (unclear) you know after the Iraqi enter Kuwait you know (speaks to Nadia in Arabic)
N: (speaks to Rushdi in Arabic) Another country with export
R: And everything is hold. Everything
E: Right
R: And I thought in 2003 we can be..
N: Study
R: We can study and learn English and take another experience for me so can I do it... do... ah... get a job

In this segment of the interview, which followed the previous one, I try to elicit the persecution narrative he would have given the immigration officers in order to get his refugee status. However, his reasons extend beyond the *physical safety* of escaping years of war and hint at the *economic safety* of being able to find a job outside of the military. Because he had been drafted into the Iraqi army and was forced to work there for 30 years, finding a job outside of the military is a clear goal in his emigration from Iraq. Also, finding a new job is directly connected to studying and learning English.

Rushdi's ultimate goal is to go to college, learn English, get his US citizenship and build an international business with the help of a US passport. The *physical safety* associated with resettlement in a third country is, for Rushdi, superseded by the transnational economic opportunities a US passport will afford him, as evidenced by his decision to stay in the United States while his wife and daughters return to Iraq. Aihwa Ong (2003) argues that transnationality, in its nature, is 'horizontal', 'relational' and still dependent on national and political–economic structures that control the flows of people, things and ideas. Because refugees have access to the political–economic structures of the US green card and passport, and yet may still have strong ties to their country of origin, citizenship for people like Rushdi becomes 'flexible'.

In a third and final attempt to elicit the story, Rushdi gave to the immigration officials in order to receive refugee status, the following story was recounted:

R: Somebody ask me, what happened to you in Iraq and you need to go to United States or another country. And I told him before, sometime my wife take a call from somebody about my house, not my house, I am rent the house, he tell her you must be leaving from the house. He ask who him you who who
N: She she...

R: She ask him who are you
N: Who are you
R: Who are you? but he does not answer
E: [so you got]
R: [at this time] at this time I think this is not good for us. My wife is afraid, and my daughters, but I am not afraid. I wake up every time and I say 'coming to me, if you want the house coming to me' but nobody answer. Yes yes and that's it. And then no problem, I'm staying in the same house
N: And nobody come to us, nobody come to talk to us
R: Yes and we stay two years two years
N: He say to us if you don't leave in three month
R: One month
N: One month? one month. He say one month but we stay two years
R: two years yes and[we stay two years]
N: [and nobody tell us to leave the house]

The UNHCR definition of *refugee* does not specify that persecution must have happened, just that it was threatened. Their story of a threat to their safety and home is not insignificant, but it is also not one of the more horrifying stories that have been recounted (e.g. Hess, 2010; Ellis, 2009). Although *safety* is not mentioned here directly, the threat to their personal safety, in their home, was what allowed them refugee status to immigrate to a 'safe' country. However, in a study of Sudanese refugees in Canada, it was found that 'increased safety in the country of refuge was perceived as scant comfort considering the loss of customary social support' (Simich *et al.*, 2010: 205), which may be why Nadia and the female members of her family chose to return to Iraq.

Safety has been analyzed up until this point as a keyword that references motivation for coming to the United States. Bashir's narrative of the geographical and emotional spaces where *safety* is found is a traditional sense of what it means to apply for refugee status based on political persecution. Rushdi's sense of *safety* reflects an international *economic safety*, which is interwoven with perceived opportunities that are available by immigrating to the United States. For Nadia, however, *safety* is complicated by her identity as a Muslim woman and the outward indexing of her beliefs through her donning of the *hijab*. The *scarf* or *hijab* became a keyword in the interview with Rushdi and Nadia, functioning beyond just a reference of affiliation to a religion; the narratives in which the word occurs refer to the discrimination against those who wear *hijab*. As Kira *et al.* (2010) have shown, perceived discrimination of Iraqi refugees in the United States negatively affects their physical and mental health.

The introduction of this keyword in the interview was a narrative of discrimination against one of Nadia's sisters, who had orange juice purposefully spilled onto her face while eating lunch at school.

N: My sisters they go to school, high school, so they say it's good for you, you don't go to high school because of they're new to school, they're new students, some of the students make fun of them, because of [the hijab]
R: [scarves]
E: They wear the hijab
N: Yes, they make fun of them, they threw papers at them, one of my sisters, they put drinks in her eyes

In this introduction, Nadia is not the direct recipient of the bullying; however, this story is told as evidence of the ways in which racism has been enacted against her family. Nadia then provides a list of three supporting examples of how her sisters are being bullied: *they make fun of them, they threw papers at them, one of my sisters, they put drinks in her eyes*. Research on bullying shows that the target 'is not merely the individual child, but the entire group from which the child has developed belonging, identity, customs and beliefs' (Scherr & Larson, 2010). Nadia's sisters are experiencing a threat to their identity as young Muslim women, as well as to their religion and culture, and Nadia herself narrates the story as evidence of what she might also suffer. If Nadia and her sisters must translate their identity in a new environment that does not accept the hijab, and bullies them for wearing it, their identities are being challenged and they are being relegated to the 'other'.

What is absent from this discussion of *safety* is the security the United States seeks by admitting only certain Iraqi refugees (mostly Christians or those who worked for the US government or military). It can be assumed, based on the policies governing anti-terrorism restrictions on refugees from the Immigration and Nationality Act, that Rushdi, Nadia and Bashir were allowed into the United States because they were not a security risk, there was a quota to be filled and they had stories of persecution. However, Nadia, her mother and her siblings were confronted with xenophobic attitudes and discrimination after arriving in the United States and responded by taking control of their situation, utilizing their agency and returning to Iraq despite the tenuous security and potential threats to their physical safety upon repatriation.

Keywords in Refugee Accounts   63

Geographical domain, nationality and ethnicity

In this section, geographical domain, nationality and ethnicity are explored through keywords that reference association and belonging to a particular nation and its language(s). For each of the interviewees, their own associations to geographical and ideational spaces are elaborated upon through the performance of their narratives of belonging, and their life stories are analyzed through the key terms of *country* and *language* (specifically Arabic and English). This section will focus first on occurrences of *country* in order to geographically center the discussion of *language*.

In the interviews, the collocation of *my* and *country* was highlighted in Rushdi and Nadia's life stories. *My country* is a common collocation[6] where *my* implicates the country being possessed by the individual, not the individual belonging to the country. The deictic word *my* is used to distinguish between *my country* and *your country*, so it is unsurprising that in an interview with recent immigrants, these words should collocate. However, with every incidence of *my country* from Rushdi, *the same* is also present. Below is every instance of his use of *my country*:

R: Because in *my country* the same thing when you buy a car you must go to insurance company to do registration the same thing in *my country* or go to doctor you must take appointment
R: I think is better for me. The same in *my country*
R: Yes, the best way, the same in *my country*, when I leaving, the right road
R: The same in *my country*, when a girl is not wearing a scarf, why you don't wear scarf?
R: It was the same, in *my country* without scarf

In each instance of *my country*, Rushdi makes explicit connections between Iraq and the United States. This is indicative of the position he has taken in relation to the US society – he feels connected to Iraq but is actively constructing the United States as similar because he plans to stay in the United States (even though his daughters and wife will return to Iraq). In other words, he is creating a means to translate himself from one country/culture to another. These expressions of the similarities between Iraq and the United States allow him to construct a reality in which the cultural differences between the two countries are minimized and he can understand the workings of his new country of residence.

Nadia also uses the collocation of *my country;* however, she does not construct similarities between the countries, but rather lists the ways in which the two countries differ.

N: When I was in *my country* I think I found maybe better things for me
N: In *my country*, I was going to civil engineering college. It's kind of high college in *my country* and not everyone can go to it
N: In *my country*, I can study civil engineering and I don't have to pay any money
N: So if I get sick, I will have to pay so many money, why is that? For *my country* I don't
N: In *my country*, if I get sick I can go to doctor for full description for like 40 dollar

Nadia's construction of differences is reflective of her dissatisfaction with her life in the United States and her plans to return to Iraq. Each instance of *my country* appears in a comparison of how the opportunities for her are better in Iraq, particularly opportunities regarding education and access to healthcare. Ironically, it is opportunities such as those for education which Rushdi lists as the prime motivations to come to the United States. Clearly, however, both identify with Iraq as the country which belongs to them, and neither references the United States as *my country* or even as *home*.

Nadia and Rushdi differ from Bashir in this as he does not refer to Iraq – or any other country – as *my country*. As much as the use of a word (or pair of words) can be meaningful, so is the non-use (Fairclough, 1995). In the case of Bashir, he self-identifies as being more American than Iraqi after having lived and worked with the armed forces in Iraq and subsequently moving to the United States.

B: First of all when I worked with the US army some units didn't like the idea we covered our faces, so many people they saw us and with the US military and it wasn't the best idea to stay in Iraq, especially when we had to live and work with the American army. This is, you know, make us more different than other Iraqis. We can call it we get Americanized, you know. Like become more American than we are Iraqi. Even when I came here, I don't know, sometimes I think I'm Iraqi, sometimes I think I'm American. If I go back to Iraq, definitely I'm not Iraqi, understand me? It's by character you know, I'm not Iraqi. Many things is different, many things changing, changing in me. It's been almost six, seven years, seven years, yeah
E: It's been seven years?
B: I worked with the US army six years, almost six years and one year here. Less than six years, but one year here

Bashir says he has been 'Americanized' and feels torn between his identity as an Iraqi and as an American. For him, the translation between countries/cultures/languages has recast his life in more hybrid terms; he is not entirely Iraqi, but not American either. Interestingly, this change in him occurred before he came to the United States, while he was still working for the US army in Iraq. Geographical location is clearly not a prerequisite for a sense of belonging to a nation; however, neither is it a guarantee that a sense of belonging to the nation of resettlement will develop, as evidenced by Nadia's plan to return to Iraq. Also Bashir did not refer to the United States as *my country*, since as the interviewer and an American I could have misinterpreted it to refer to Iraq. As with any conversation, both speaker and listener (or interviewee and interviewer) influence what is said because the listener/receiver of an utterance is not a passive participant (Bakhtin, 1986).

The relationship between identification with a nation and identification with that nation's language(s) was constructed during the Enlightenment (Bauman & Briggs, 2003), and this constructed link has since been tied to notions and regulations of citizenship, ethno-national identity, colonialism, migrations and related processes (Heller, 2007). Iraq, having been under British control after World War I, still requires that English be taught in schools. However, as Bashir notes, 'English, supposedly every Iraqi should learn it in school, but it's funny, most of them they can't speak it because no one use it'.

As both of the interviews were conducted in English, and one of the goals of the interviews was to reflect on REAP's strengths and weaknesses, the word *English* arose often. *English*, in all of the interviews, collocated with *learning*, but each interviewee associated *learning English* with different facets of their past and future goals. For Nadia, learning English was prohibitive of her attaining her degree quickly because before studying civil engineering in college in the United States she would have to take ESL classes for at least one year. This would not only increase the number of years it would take her to earn her degree, but because she would have to pay for her education here, this necessity would be expensive – an expense of time and money that would be avoided by returning to Iraq and continuing her education in Arabic.

For Rushdi, on the other hand, *learning English* was a means to engage more directly with a globalized world and have access to a better future. For him, *learning English* is one of the reasons why he chose to stay in the United States while the rest of his family returns to Iraq.

E: So, your girls are all leaving you and you're staying here, tell me about your decision to stay here. Why do you want to stay?
R: I told you before, I need more experience. I need to learn English, I need to take education. I think is better for me. When you go to Iraq, when I go to get a job, always ask me, you speak English? What's your education? You know my education is high school

For Rushdi, *learning English* is not only a necessity for finding a job in the United States, it is a prerequisite for desirable employment in Iraq and other countries. In another comment, Rushdi also expresses his desire to learn more about other ways of life, in other countries (including but not exclusive to the United States) and sees *learning English* as the key to achieving this goal.

R: But when I in Iraq without English is, you know, the English is necessary for anybody. I can go any country because everybody talk English, and I think the English (speaks in Arabic to Nadia)
N: Language
R: Language for world. I think that

Rushdi sees English as a world language, and because his primary reason for staying in the United States is to eventually provide for his family better than he would be able to from Iraq, he views *learning English* as a tool for advancement. Here, it is evident that Rushdi's goal is not merely to participate in the US society, but through English he can translate himself into a global citizen.

Bashir also sees *learning English* as an endeavor, which results in access to more jobs as it was a means to find employment in Iraq before the US invasion in 2003, working on cargo ships. International shipping requires that both seamen and officers know English, and Bashir took advantage of his position to practice English so that he could leave Iraq.

B: I worked for almost a year as a seaman on a cargo ship so I had to, sometimes I had to use English to communicate with the other crews, like when we go to Dubai, in the ports, we have to use like some English to communicate to other crews because ship, on ship they...
E: Right, shipping you have to use English
B: So, let's see, it was the first step to improve my dialogue. I was smart also to practice it more, more than others actually because many seamen didn't do that, but I was thinking, hey I need it, because maybe someday I leave Iraq, you know

In this case, *learning English* is not directly stated, but rather implicated by 'improve my dialogue'. This active learning was motivated by a wish to emigrate from Saddam's regime. However, before Bashir could flee to Jordan, the US invasion occurred, and English became a means to help his countrymen by interpreting for the US army. Later, his involvement with the army allowed him access to refugee status and once again English was a tool for survival – this time in the United States. The meaning of *learning English* is to each of the refugees a reflection on their association with their country of origin, their country of current residence and most especially, their goals for the future.

English also collocated often with *speaking,* or synonyms such as *talk,* indicating that *learning English* foregrounded *speaking English*. When I asked about their experiences in REAP, Rushdi responded by explaining the difference between speaking with his tutor in the class and speaking with people outside of this safe environment.

R: The people in the class is understand my situation. Maybe another place I can't talk to
N: They don't understand what [we what we can say]
R: [when I told him] I'm sorry my English is not very well, is he say, I'm sorry I'm not understand and he leave. But in your class (speak to Nadia in Arabic).
N: They're helpful, helpful
R: They're very helpful. Your staff is very helpful. Yesterday the guy he say if you want to talk with me anytime I am here you can talk with me. It's, frankly, it's wonderful. Maybe in the night I go to him to talk something with him

For Rushdi, the opportunity to speak English in the one-on-one tutoring session with a volunteer from the community provided a safe space to practice speaking English. Research has shown that for refugees, often the most difficult aspect of resettlement is not the prior trauma suffered under persecution, but the sense of isolation which results in resettlement to a location that was not of your choosing (Simich *et al.*, 2010). Creating opportunities for people to connect and have conversations is a large part of what refugees need as they settle in their new home, and Rushdi's tutor saying that they can talk anytime, even outside of class, is both common in the class and meaningful to the refugee.

The quote above indicates where it is *safe* to *speak English* because someone will take the time to listen (in the tutoring session) and where it is not (other places). Despite Nadia's proficiency in the English language, she explains that her linguistic knowledge does not equal cultural competence in the United States.

N: We know all people there, we know how to live, we know all laws, we know, I know, everything there. Now I don't know anything. And that's right, I can speak English, but sometimes sometime I think that

some people make funny of me when I speak English, or they want to like (speaks in Arabic to Rushdi)
R: Somebody, when he can't talk English very well, somebody say (speaks in Arabic to Nadia)
N: Try to laugh at me
E: Like make fun of
R: For her, she [feel]
N: [I feel] so bad when things like that happen to me

Linguistic competence is not the only motivating factor for *speaking English*; for these two individuals, *speaking English* is bound up in issues of external survival knowledge and fears of symbolic violence (Bourdieu,1991), such as being laughed at. This issue also correlates with Nadia's sense of being invisible because of the hijab; the issues surrounding silencing from hijab are reflected in her feelings of not understanding the culture of the United States.

Policies granting refugee status to Iraqis who aligned themselves with US objectives, such as aiding the US military, create a population of refugees with culturally more experience with the United States than others. However, those without such experience need more resources to effectively translate themselves into the new country/culture/language. Documentation of the immigrant experience shows that it requires a translation of the self and this takes time (Hoffman, 1989). Policies of refugee resettlement allow eight months of federal help such as Medicaid and welfare to translate oneself into becoming self-sufficient members of society, yet this short time has been shown to be far too little (Christoff, 2010). As educational resources dwindle, community-based programs such as that offered by REAP become even more necessary.

Discussion

Safety, hijab, my country and *English (learning* and *speaking)* are the keywords which emerged from this data. The words themselves are powerless outside of their context, yet are used to indicate the situatedness of the translated speaker in time and space. In the case of Nadia, the lack of safety and opportunity that she found in the United States motivated her return to Iraq and repatriation to Iraq was a means for her to enact an agentive response to a situation which otherwise left her feeling powerless. Rushdi, on the other hand, was able to translate Iraq with the United States, while his goal of learning English for its global opportunities kept him in the

United States. Bashir's translation of the self resulted from experiences in both Iraq and the United States, and this blurred the boundaries between his identification with these two countries. In each case, these life stories were used to express a sense of self and to negotiate group membership and socially constructed norms (Linde, 1993).

The keywords, contextualized in discourse, allow for a critical inquiry into the policies affecting resettlement, especially those which were unsupportive of newly arrived refugees' abilities to translate themselves. The policy to award in-state tuition only after one year of residency makes sense for those US citizens who came from another state, and have not paid into the system; however, this social wrong is not needed for refugees who have just entered the United States, having escaped persecution and for whom an additional cost for education is unjust. The only possible benefit would be higher revenues for the institutions, but if these extra fees are preventing students from entering, the policy is ineffective. The educational policies which made Nadia's goal of getting a degree in civil engineering unattractive should undergo critical re-evaluation. Greater financial support and recognition of foreign studies would help the higher education system attract intelligent and motivated students like Nadia.

On the other hand, policies that restrict refugee status based on broad interpretations of 'material support' and 'terrorist organizations' are necessary to the social order because although their intention is safety the effects are often that those in the worst need, having suffered the most harm and likely having expensive medical (physical and emotional) needs, are not considered for refugee status. This allows for a prejudiced favoritism for those who are wealthy, educated and appear to be future contributing members of the US society. Such an injustice needs to be revised to ensure that humanitarian concerns are balanced with national security and foreign policy. Although there is some level of 'need' for this social structure (preserving safety), the level at which it is practiced is not necessary (Human Rights First, 2009). Nadia's return to Iraq indicates that some who are admitted to the United States are not under such a threat of persecution that they are unable or unwilling to return, a stipulation outlined in the UNHCR's definition of *refugee*. Although policy changes have been proposed (Sridharan, 2008; Acer et al., 2006), these changes have not been incorporated.

In order to have a successful refugee resettlement program in the United States, changes need to happen at the policy level. Until that time, a community-based program where more than language is learned – where social bonds are built between community members and newly resettled refugees and cultural differences can be explored without threats or bullying – is a possible way past this obstacle. Since November 2011, many changes have been introduced to REAP, based on the research documented here. The program now focuses on getting more women and families to participate and encouraging safe, supportive discussions of bullying in schools and instances of discrimination. Creating a social support network in the country of asylum is imperative for the mental and physical health of newly arrived refugees (Kira *et al.*, 2010; Simich *et al.*, 2010), and one of the goals of the newly designed REAP is to provide opportunities to build a sense of community within the local Iraqi diaspora, between Iraqis and other Americans (through the tutoring sessions) and within the program itself. For Iraqis, it is an opportunity to practice speaking English in a safe environment while building a social support system and increasing cultural awareness within their new geographical community.

Notes

(1) I am using this term as Elahi (2006) uses it: to refer to the concept of language as a key element of cultural identity, where the translated self is one which moves towards liminality and de-territorialization. Elahi (2006: 465–6) states, 'those who are forced to learn a new language and are physically displaced by exile, are more likely to realize that their relationship to language is always a matter of displacement... a perpetual metamorphosis that attempts to re-imagine the national or ethno-linguistic self as an in-between entity'. As an example, Hoffman's (1989) *Lost in Translation* is an example of how such discursive activity of translating between languages and cultures are transformative and liminal.
(2) Some examples of refugees who have been denied requests for asylum in the United States are '(1) A nurse from Colombia who was kidnapped, assaulted and forced to provide medical treatment to terrorists; (2) A fisherman from Sri Lanka who was abducted by the Tamil Tigers and forced to pay his own ransom; and (3) A student activist and torture survivor who fled Bhutan and was the victim of Maoist extortion while teaching in Nepal' (Acer *et al.*, 2006: 150).
(3) If the refugee has dependents, the welfare provided to them may be extended.
(4) SIRC is a pseudonym.
(5) All names have been changed to protect the identities of the participants.
(6) According to the Corpus of Contemporary American English, this collocation occurs 1537 times out of 425 million words (http://corpus.byu.edu/coca/).

References

Acer, E., Hughes, A. and Staunton, J. (2006) The United States should help refugees wrongly accused of supporting terrorists. Reprinted in Haerens (ed.) (2010) *Opposing Viewpoints Series: Refugees* (pp. 147–152). Farmington Hills, MI: Greenhaven Press.
Bakhtin, M.M. (1986) *Speech Genres and Other Late Essays* (V.W. McGee, trans.). Austin, TX: University of Texas Press.

Bauman, R. and Briggs, C. (2003) *Voices of Modernity: Language Ideologies and the Politics of Inequality.* Cambridge: Cambridge University Press.
Blommaert, J. (2009) Language, asylum, and the national order. *Current Anthropology* 50 (4), 415–441.
Bourdieu, P. (1991) *Language and Symbolic Power.* Cambridge, MA: Harvard University Press.
Christoff, J. (ed.) (2010) 'Iraqi Refugees and Special Immigrant Visa holders face challenges resettling in the United States and obtaining U.S. government employment'. Report to Congressional committees. Government Accountability Office 10-274.
Delgado-Gaitan, C. (1994) Russian refugee families: Accommodating aspirations through education. *Anthropolgy & Education Quarterly* 25 (2), 137–155.
Eades, D. (2009) Testing the claims of asylum seekers: The role of language analysis. *Language Assessment Quarterly* 6 (1), 30–40.
Elahi, B. (2006) Translating the self: Language and identity in Iranian-American women's memoirs. *Iranian Studies* 39 (4), 461–480.
Ellis, D. (2009) *Children of War: voices of Iraqi refugees.* Toronto, Ontario: Groundwood Books, Ltd.
Fairclough, N. (1995) *Critical Discourse Analysis: The Critical Study of Language.* Essex: Pearson Education Limited.
Fairclough, N. (2009) A dialectal-relational approach to critical discourse analysis in social research. In R. Wodak and M. Meyer (eds) *Methods for Critical Discourse Analysis* (2nd edn, pp. 162–185). Thousand Oaks, CA: Sage Publications Limited.
FY 2010 Refugee Arrivals (nd) *Office of Refugee Resettlement,* accessed 20 December 2011. http://www.acf.hhs.gov/programs/orr/data/fy2010RA.htm
Haerens, M. (ed.) (2010) *Opposing Viewpoints Series: Refugees.* Garmington Hills, MI: Greenhaven Press.
Heller, M. (2007) Introduction. In M. Heller (ed.) *Bilingualism: A Social Approach* (pp. 1–24). New York, NY: Palgrave Macmillan.
Hess, T. (2010) Forced to Flee: Iraqi experiences of displacement in the 2003 Iraq War. Master's thesis, Graduate School of The Ohio State University.
Hoffman, E. (1989) *Lost in Translation.* New York: Penguin Books.
Human Rights First (2009) *Denial and Delay: The Impact of Immigration Law's "Terrorism Bars" on Asylum Seekers and Refugees in the United States.* New York, NY: Hughes, A.
Kira, I.A., Lewandowski, L., Templin, T., Ramaswamy, V., Ozkan, B. and Mohanesh, J. (2010) The effects of perceived discrimination and backlash on Iraqi refugees' mental and physical health. *Journal of Muslim Mental Health* 5 (1), 59–81.
Langness, L.L. and Frank, G. (1981) *Lives: An Anthropological Approach to Biography.* Novato, CA: Chandler & Sharp Publishers, Inc.
Leudar, I., Hayes, J., Nekvapil, J. and Turner, J. (2008) Hostility themes in the media, community and refugee narratives. *Discourse Society* 19 (2), 187–221.
Linde, C. (1993) *Life Stories: The Creation of Coherence.* New York: Oxford University Press.
Margesson, R. Bruno, A. and Sharp, J.M. (2010) Iraqi refugees and internally displaced persons: A deepening humanitarian crisis? In A. Sanchez (ed.) *Iraqi Refugees: A Humanitarian Crisis?* (pp. 71–97). New York: Nova Science Publishers, Inc.
Martin, D.C. and Hoeffer, M. (2009) Refugees and Asyless: 2008. *Annual Flow Report.* From the Office of Immigration Statistics and U.S. Department of Homeland Security. http://www.dhs.gov/xlibrary/assets/statistics/publications/ois_rfa_fr_2008.pdf

Ong, A. (2003) *Buddha is Hiding: Refugees, Citizenship, the New America*. Berkeley: University of California Press.
Ramanathan, V. and Morgan, B. (2007) TESOL and policy enactments: Perspectives from practice. *TESOL Quarterly* 41 (3), 447–463.
Scherr, T. and Larson, J. (2010) Bullying dynamics associated with race, ethnicity and immigration status. In Jimerson *et al.* (eds) *Handbook of Bullying in Schools: An International Perspective* (pp. 223–234). New York: Routledge.
Simich, L., Este, D. and Hamilton, H. (2010) Meanings of home and mental well being among Sudanese refugees in Canada. *Ethnicity and Health* 15 (2), 199–212.
Sridharan, S. (2008) Material Support to Terrorism – Consequences for Refugees and Asylum Seekers in the United States. http://www.migrationinformation.org/usfocus/display.cfm?ID=671
Tollefson, J. (1989) *Alien Winds: The Reeducation of America's Indochinese Refugees*. New York, NY: Praeger Publishers.
Venuti, L. (2000) Introduction. In L. Venuti (ed.) *The Translation Studies Reader* (pp. 1–8). New York: Routledge.
Weick, K.E. (1995) Sensemaking in organizations. In Decker (ed.) *Human Resource Development Quarterly* (pp. 198–201). Thousand Oaks, CA: Sage.
Williams, R. (1976) *Keywords: A Vocabulary of Culture and Society*. London: Collins.
Woods, A. (2009) Learning to be literate: Issues of pedagogy for recently arrived refugee youth in Australia. *Critical Inquiry in Language Studies* 6 (1), 81–101.

5 'The World Doesn't End at the Corner of their Street': Language Ideologies of Chilean English Teachers

Julia Menard-Warwick

The concept of international language means that English is no longer the property of a few countries where it is spoken as the native language, but it belongs to everybody ....If you want to be part of the world you must speak English, otherwise you are out. So integrativeness should be the most important reason to learn English. People who have not understood this yet are the ones who see English only as a way to get a better job or more opportunities to get success.

This chapter examines the language ideologies of English teachers in Chile, a nation whose government is promoting English in tandem with export-oriented economic policies (McKay, 2003). Although ideologies connecting English language teaching (ELT) with success in the global marketplace have been widely critiqued (e.g. Pennycook, 2007), few studies have examined how English teachers position themselves and their work amidst ideological debates. The quote above was taken from an essay written by Rita,[1] a Chilean adult school English teacher, who was working on her Masters in English Teaching at a Chilean university. In her view, English is a key asset, not so much for the marketplace, but rather for global citizenship, if citizenship means participating in a world where 'English belongs to everybody'.

Too often, pronouncements about English as a global language proceed from the 'center' (e.g. US universities) to the 'periphery' (e.g. Chilean English classrooms) (Canagarajah, 1999). This chapter takes the position that the global ELT profession can only understand the full ramifications of its work through dialogue (Bakhtin, 1981, 1984) between ELT scholars and practitioners in a wide range of social and geographic locations. As a US-based academic who has participated in research and teacher training at a small university in northern Chile (I was Rita's professor for her MA class), I try to approach my own work in a spirit of dialogue, and I envision this chapter on the language ideologies of Chilean English teachers as a way to promote further dialogue both about and within the ELT profession.

Language ideologies can be defined as perceptions of language varieties or linguistic practices that are constructed in the interest of specific social groups (Kroskrity, 2000). Often this involves both evaluating a particular language variety *and* connecting this variety to a particular social group (Woolard, 1998). For example, the idea that 'English is an imperialist language' connects English learning to the economic and political interests of English-speaking countries (Canagarajah, 1999), and in so doing serves the interests of non-English speaking anti-imperialists in Chile (Menard-Warwick, 2009), implying a contradiction between English learning and Chilean (or Latin American) citizenship.

Thus, ideologies are beliefs about language varieties and linguistic practices, but they are often unspoken and reproduced through practice rather than explicit inculcation. Ideologies can be hegemonic, but often multiple ideologies compete within particular social contexts (Achugar, 2008; Bakhtin, 1984). Moreover, dominant ideologies can be reinforced as well as counteracted by voices that argue against them, as I discuss below. Specifically, I examine the following: What language ideologies do English teachers in Chile reference in talking about their work? How do they position themselves and their work? What value do they see for English teaching in Chile?

By juxtaposing teachers' varied responses with the 'dominant ideologies' that have been portrayed in the literature on ELT, this chapter attempts to situate itself on 'the borderline of dialogically intersecting consciousnesses... bring(ing) together ideas and worldviews, which in real life (are) absolutely estranged (from)....one another' (Bakhtin, 1984: 91). I conclude by discussing implications of this research for pedagogies of global citizenship in ELT.

Juxtaposing Language Ideologies

In this section, I detail a number of specific language ideologies that are described in the linguistic anthropological literature, including many that could be called dominant or hegemonic, as well as some that tend to counter hegemonic trends.

A prominent ideology in English-dominant environments is monolingual ideology, the belief that knowing or using only one language has significant individual and/or societal benefits; this is related to, but distinct from the idea that English itself is a superior language. For example, Woolard (1989) explores monolingual ideology in the context of San Francisco, California, in the 1980s, through analysis of arguments made in favor of a voter initiative to ban multilingual ballots. In this English-dominant context, it was not necessary to argue that English was intrinsically superior to other languages, but simply that local politics should be conducted in a single language, which 'common sense' decreed to be English. In contrast, Choi's (2003) discussion of parental preferences for English-medium education in Hong Kong casts English as the unique language that can help young people succeed in the global marketplace.

These two ideologies – monolingual ideology and dominant-language ideology – are certainly widespread to the point of hegemony, but do not go unquestioned. For example, a number of individuals, communities and scholars connect particular languages to ethnicity or nationality (Lo, 1999). The use of a non-dominant language in a particular context thus indexes ethnic or national loyalty, as in the promotion of Corsican-medium education where French has long been dominant (Jaffe, 2007) or in the increasingly popular Korean language courses for Korean-American youth (Jeon, 2008).

Moreover, there is considerable ideological contradiction as to why particular languages or language varieties should be valued. Clearly, Pakistani call center workers who interact with US consumers (Rahman, 2009) have an economic incentive for linguistically affiliating with speakers of American English. In Niño-Murcia's (2003) research, the financial motives behind Peruvians' desire to learn English are clear: 'English is like the dollar', as one participant remarked. However, it is apparent from other examples around the world (e.g. Jaffe, 2007) that languages can derive ideological power from sources other than hard currency and many language users see cultural rather than economic value in particular language varieties. In fact, Leeman and Martinez's (2010) exploration of the US Spanish textbooks chronicles a shift in portrayals of Spanish since 1970s from a language of cultural heritage to a language of global business.

Moreover, Shankar's (2008) article about Indian immigrants in California explores some ideological perspectives that contrast with what the literature portrays as hegemonic. In this community, standardized English was valued as one variety among many, and multilingualism was seen as useful for allowing communication with people from other social groups; it was viewed as common sense that the language variety you use should be adapted to your social situation, an ideology also referenced in Godley *et al.*'s (2007) article about conflicts over standardized English in a US high school classroom.

Thus, a wide variety of language ideologies are chronicled in the literature. However, with few exceptions (e.g. Achugar, 2008), articles tend to examine one or two ideologies at a time rather than illustrating how multiple ideologies compete within a social context (Bakhtin, 1984). Moreover, when the literature has portrayed the ideologies of language teachers, it has tended to show them imposing dominant ideologies on their students (Olivo, 2003), rather than exploring their own ideological positioning as multilingual individuals.

To interpret teachers' complex positionings, I find Bakhtin's theories of language and identity development to be helpful (1981, 1984). From his perspective, social individuals, including teachers, are constantly in process of 'ideological becoming' that is, 'assimilating our consciousness to the ideological world' (1981: 341), as we position ourselves between the 'authoritative discourses' dominant in society and the 'internally persuasive discourses' by which we interpret our own experiences (1981: 342). These competing discourses provide language for teachers' ideological struggles to make sense of their work: to themselves, with their colleagues, in dealing with student resistance, and in promoting their own interests as English language teachers in local, national and global contexts.

Chilean History

With Blommaert, I see ideologies and specific instances of language use as 'influenced by the structure of the world system...including the relationships between different societies' (2005: 15) and as 'intrinsically historical' (2005: 18). Thus, in order to discuss ideologies connected to English learning in Chile, it is important to review recent Chilean history. A key event was the 1973 coup against the democratically-elected socialist government of Salvador Allende, which was followed by 17 years of military dictatorship under Augusto Pinochet. For most of those years, the dictatorship was supported by the United States and United Kingdom. At the behest of US economists known (in English) as 'the Chicago Boys', Pinochet implemented a neoliberal economic model, based on the privatization of the economy and the promotion of exports. Chile's return to democracy in 1990 came with the condition that this economic model continue (Drake & Jaksic, 1999; Loveman, 2001).

Nevertheless, democracy brought a significant improvement in the human rights situation and an end to media censorship. Chile describes itself as 'open to the world' (Loveman, 2001): economically since Pinochet, culturally also since 1990 (Menard-Warwick, 2011). English-language media (music, television, film and the internet) has become ubiquitous in Chilean society. The Chilean economy is widely seen as 'successful', but

Chile remains highly stratified, with vast differences between rich and poor (Moulián, 1997; Winn, 2004), including in access to English learning. While English is part of the environment for the Chilean poor (e.g. through songs on the radio), traditionally only the wealthy have had the opportunity to become proficient in the language. In connection with its export-oriented economic model, the Chilean government has promoted English instruction, but the country remains predominantly Spanish speaking.

Methodology

Drawing on ethnographic data collected at a small university in the north of Chile, this chapter explores teachers' evaluations of the English language, its role in their society and their pedagogical reflections. With funding by the US-Chile Binational Fulbright Commission, I first visited the university in 2004. The following year I spent 10 weeks at the university, interviewing English teachers and observing classes. In 2006, I conducted more interviews, and also co-taught and videotaped an intensive course on language and culture in an MA program for practicing English teachers, which included teaching demonstrations from all participants. I also collected final essays from the course.[2] Since then, I have carried out a thematic coding of all data (approximately 25 hours of audio-recorded observations in English language classrooms, 20 hours of MA class video, 17 essays and 21 interviews with 18 teachers). In my thematic coding, I defined language ideologies as evaluations of language varieties or linguistic practices in the interests of a specific social group (see above). In this chapter, I juxtapose and problematize teachers' specific ideological statements, from interviews, classroom comments, essays and teaching demonstrations. Throughout this chapter, the juxtaposition of teachers' views shows how contradictory and untidy the enactment of (dominant) ideologies can be, as teachers' lived experiences both resist and sustain dominant ideologies in complex ways.[3]

Findings

My thematic analysis demonstrates that while teachers at times equated English learning and teaching with economic success, they also called this equation into question based on their own life experiences and student critiques. Some teachers connected English learning not only to social stratification in Chile but also to its possible transformation. Others valued English for the connection they saw it providing to a broader global culture rather than as a means of financial gain. Teachers saw English as a superior language (Choi, 2003) only because it is so 'global'; they saw three principal reasons to learn English: economic (to improve financial standing), cultural (to access English language cultural materials) and intercultural (to communicate with other English-speaking people around the world). They tended to disagree on the relative importance of these three reasons but cultural reasons seemed perhaps strongest overall.

English is 'Universal'

One overarching justification for English instruction in Chile, mentioned by most teachers I interviewed, is the ubiquity of English in global society. When I asked an older teacher, Sofía, what she tells her public high-school students about English, she quoted herself at length:

> 'Although you don't like it, you have to learn [...] It's part of your life, it's part of your environment, it's part of society, if you want to study in university, all the books are written in English....O.K.? If you go to Internet, it's in English, if you listen to music, it's in English, and all the jobs are required a person that's trained in English'.[4]

It is important to note that what Sofía is saying is not literally true; she is overstating her case. Not all the books in the university are in English, the internet has a lot of Spanish content, it is easy to listen to music in Spanish and many Chilean professionals get by with minimal English. Nonetheless, this is a clear statement, in the voice of an individual teacher, of the dominant ideology about the value of English learning in Chile and in other contexts around the world.

Gonzalo, an instructor of Business English, wrote in an essay a similar statement of the dominant ideology with a more explicit focus on economic reasons for learning English and a stronger emphasis on the connections between language and culture:

> English is the universal business language, and we need to know the cultures that come with it. It is not just learning the language; it is learning the cultures behind this beautiful language. Because English is not just anymore American or British, English is universal [...]. We live in a global village with no boundaries and we have English as a common language. [...] English opens doors, but these doors do not mean only

opportunities, [...] they are also the gates to new worlds. By understanding these cultures they will be successful and have good (business)[5] relationships.

However, not all teachers emphasized the value of English as a business language. In the language and culture workshop, Rita contradicted this dominant view:

I realized last night that when I decided to study English, was because I thought, 'Okay, English is going to be the future, right, so let's do it [...]' And I decided to study because of that and now that I can speak English, right? I have noticed, that because of English, I have had the opportunity to experience so many wonderful things, right? Not because of money, not because of jobs, not ( ) because of travel, but because I have had the opportunity to meet so many people. And for me that's so important, right? Because I have the chance to know about other peoples' culture.

Here, Rita constructs an opposition between the dominant ideology's emphasis on the (illusory?) economic value of English and the more concrete cultural and intercultural opportunity that she herself has experienced: 'to know about other peoples' cultures'.

Moreover, despite claims that English is important for success in Chilean society, very few teachers offered concrete examples of times when they had found English actually necessary. The narrative below, recounted in an interview by Maritza, a 5th year undergraduate prospective teacher, is an interesting exception to this trend:

I have a friend that is a making a post grad in physical education, and she asked me, 'Please help me, because all the handouts that the teacher gave me are in English', 'Okay, I'm going to help you', and I translate all the handouts (that) she (sent), and all [her] classmates that day, tell me, 'Oh, you're great, you are fantastic', oh, I was like a queen, ((laughing)) [...] because they said, 'We never have the opportunity to learn English, and now we know that it's very important'. [...] Because even the teacher was going to make the class in English, [...] but they said, 'No, it's awful', they have to ask for the teacher that (they) have to speak in Spanish, and it was difficult for him because he was Chinese, and he speaks Portuguese, ((laughing)) and English, and he has to make the class in Spanish. [...] It was difficult, very difficult, and English, now, it's like uh, it's the language that everybody in the world speak.

This ethnically-Chinese Portuguese-speaking physical education instructor is a good example of the kind of global citizen who depends on English to communicate across national borders; however, the Chilean graduate students described by Maritza see English as 'awful' and 'difficult', and can insist on having their monolingual needs accommodated. Although, here a proficient English speaker is like 'a queen', this narrative does not substantiate Sofía's argument that students will be unable to access university without English. In this way, Maritza's voice contradicts as well as sustains the dominant ideology about the 'necessity' of English in Chile.

Complications of Social Class and Politics

However, if English competence in Chile is not yet necessary or sufficient for academic or professional success, it is still ideologically associated with higher social classes, who have traditionally accessed superior language instruction in private educational venues. While teachers in my study did not for the most part identify with the upper classes, they valued English as part of their own professional competence and as a potential asset for their students. Teachers in elite settings found English easy to 'sell' to their students; the dominant language ideologies in Chile are constructed in the interests of *their* social group (Kroskrity, 2000). As Diego described his private high-school students:

> They know they are going to study in university. I told them if you are going to study in the university, medicine or architecture, you need to speak English. You need to know the language. 'Oh sure, I know that, I know I want to be a doctor…' 'But how about if you are going to study in the United States, you need to know the language'. They know that. They *know* that. Their *parents* know that.

However, students like this were not common in the experiences of the teachers I talked to, and for the most part they themselves had been unable to even travel to an English-speaking country.

Nevertheless, this connection between English and the elite then raises a question: if English is associated with the upper classes, can we work toward social equity by teaching English? As one teacher, Amanda, wrote in an essay:

> English would be the language able to change the relationship between these specific individuals (those from the lowest strata) and the given

social group (Chilean society). But, the most important point is that English could *permeate* in these individuals' very thinking and way of viewing the world. To open their eyes and know other realities and understand that inequality must not be seen as something 'normal'. English would be the weapon against this unequal system.

This idealistic view of the potential of English to promote social change, through 'know(ing) other realities', is an alternative voicing of the dominant ideology about the economic importance of English; by arguing that English should be available to the Chilean poor, Amanda both resists and sustains connections between English and wealth. However, a far more common way for teachers to talk about their lower-class students' relation to English can be seen in the following comments made in the workshop by Hector, an elementary school teacher:

> I have this huge problem with my school. I work with very low social class students, and they see English as an un-useful subject. And it's my everyday struggle, that I am trying to teach them [...] that English could be a plus for them, a cultural plus, because in the society that we are living now [...] a large amount of information [...] is everything. They need to get involved with these changes, and they need English because it's the global language, so to speak. So that's what I have to do almost every day because I come to a classroom for example, and [...] I have 45 students, and 13 students are not motivated to learn language, because they think they are not going to use it, because they think that when they finish high school, they are going to work, I don't know, cleaning houses, being mechanics.

We can note that only a minority of Hector's students complains, but this articulate minority tends to stand out when teachers talk about their work (and even the majority is usually not very successful in learning English, according to the teachers I have talked to). Even in elementary school, the Chilean working class has little reason to think that the dominant language ideologies are constructed in their interests (Kroskity, 2000).

At the same time, teachers reported that many Chilean students negatively associated English with the United States or United Kingdom. Teachers themselves did not ideologically connect English with US politics, but had to confront some students' ideological perspective that speaking English indexes loyalty to the United States and disloyalty to Chile (Menard-Warwick, 2009; Woolard, 1998). While Diego taught private high-school students during the day (see above), he worked at a public adult school in the evening, and found his students' political questions challenging:

I am always trying to be positive about the cultural burden of the language. Because there are many students who feel that English language could be negative. They don't agree, for example…when I say English, they say Bush. Or Iraq. Or the war there. 'No, it's an empire…' OK. So I take the positive things. 'How…what can be good for you about the English language?' This is what I am trying to do with my students [...] [at the] night school. Adult people. So they have lots of prejudice about United States.

These questions of social class and politics were not a problem for all teachers, but created huge difficulties for some. In the following interview narrative, Alán, a university instructor, describes why he stopped teaching public high school after a year in the United Kingdom:

[My students] didn't care about English, they didn't like me, when I came back from England [...] They thought that I was, like I belonged to a higher class or something like that [...] They said that the English people were imperialists, like the Americans, that they were capitalists, they only wanted to conquer us, with their ways and their methods [...] And I'm talking to you about very young people, you know, fourteen, thirteen years old. Or, if they wanted to learn, they wanted to learn about uh bad words, they wanted to learn about rap lyrics, hip-hop lyrics, things that I didn't know [...] I didn't spend much time struggling for finding a solution [...] I talked to the principal, and I talked to our counselor [...] so they said that if I was feeling like that, I should stay till the end of term, and walk away ((laughing)). That's what I did.

A number of teachers told stories like this one about public high schools. Success with this population often involved incorporating the popular music (e.g. hip-hop lyrics) that they appreciated (Menard-Warwick, 2009, 2011), and both Diego and Hector mentioned this strategy.

As the teachers above explain the challenges they have faced with working-class students, they necessarily juxtapose dominant and resistant ideologies to construct their own positions (Bakhtin, 1981). They and other teachers could easily state reasons why English is valuable, frequently repeating the authoritative discourses (Bakhtin, 1981) that connect the language to economic success. However, these vague reasons were not enough to convince their students, so many teachers had to grapple with social class and international politics. Even then, teachers often reported that students saw no use for English. And interviewees rarely shared examples of people actually using English, for example, to get a job.[6]

Thus, Amanda's essay discusses how 'authoritative discourses' about English learning have not proved persuasive for many Chileans (Bakhtin, 1981).

In Chile, to know English is considered 'important' by most of the population. I think most people would agree with that, in an eventual survey. But probably, it is really important for those who have a higher education level [...] As a sign of the low valuation that in Chile common people give to English as linguistic capital, we could mention the fact that even when there are many courses available to learn English, some of them absolutely free, people are not interested in taking them.

In contrast, when I asked Tomás, an undergraduate prospective teacher, about his own aspirations, he referenced discourses around English that he found 'internally persuasive':

I want to say to my students that the world doesn't end in the corner of their street. That's why I wanted to [teach]. Because I realized very young, very child, that the world was very huge [...] Someday I go to travel around the world, and I'm going to know about different cultures. [...] But there are lot of students, lot of young people, that doesn't know that. They think that just, the only city in the world is [this one] and there is no more, I don't know. It's just like they just em blind their eyes and think, 'Well, I live here, and I got some drugs, so I am happy', and that is no good, that is no world [...] but I like to do something for it.

In fact, when teachers talked about their own experiences learning English, they, like Tomás (and Rita's essay at the beginning of the chapter), tended to extol the ways that English had given them a broader outlook on life, had shown them that 'the world didn't end at the corner of their street'. Thus, even those who resisted the dominant ideologies that connect English with financial success nonetheless supported what many critics (including some Chilean students) consider to be the cultural hegemony of English in the world (Kumaravadivelu, 2008). As in Rita's essay, they see English as the one language that gives them access to global citizenship.

English in Chile

In any case, when reflecting on their classroom practice, teachers had to respond ideologically to the general status of English in Chile. Perhaps because Spanish remained dominant in Chile (and in neighboring countries), none of the teachers in my study worried that English might usurp functions from other languages. As Chileans, they could see English promoted by the government and international business; resisted by leftist movements; and consumed (e.g. as music on the radio) but not learned or used by most of the populace.

Positioning themselves as favorably as they could within this ideological context, teachers made use of the 'authoritative discourses' (Bakhtin, 1981) that connect English to the global economy, the upper classes, social mobility and 'the future' – while recognizing that many Chilean students felt disconnected from those phenomena. They valued the opportunities for cultural and intercultural contact provided by English fluency – but recognized that these opportunities are limited in many parts of Chile. Their positionings were complicated by the fact that few teachers had personal experience with economic growth, the upper classes, social mobility or travel outside South America. Nevertheless, they drew upon their identification with English-language culture to differentiate themselves from their students and also to transform students (to show them that 'the world doesn't end at the corner of their street').

To these ends, teachers recognized but contested connections drawn by students between English and US politics. Moreover, because the monetary rewards of English seemed illusory in northern Chile (English teachers had little difficulty finding jobs, but often had to work two or three of them to make ends meet), they tended to redefine globalization to focus on cultural rather than economic aspects. Nearly everyone I interviewed spoke at length about their appreciation of English-language music, television and film, and especially the easy access to English-language popular culture provided by the internet (Menard-Warwick, 2011). Insofar as feasible, they focused English teaching on cultural products enjoyed by themselves and their students, enacting the ideology that the central value of English is cultural. Positioning themselves in this way, and drawing on discourses that they found 'internally persuasive' (Bakhtin, 1981), teachers sought to offer students access to an imagined global citizenship without negating their Chilean national identities.

The Workshop on Language and Cultural Identity

As seen above, some of the data for this chapter came from the videotaped MA course on language and culture for practicing English teachers which I co-taught as an intensive workshop with a Chilean colleague over

25 hours in July 2006. (I taught this workshop again in 2008 and 2010 without collecting further data.) As well as providing research results, the workshop curriculum itself was based on research I had conducted in 2005. For this workshop, I bring in readings to give teachers an international perspective on issues like resistance to English, but mostly I facilitate a dialogue on how they deal with cultural and ideological issues in the classroom. We begin by discussing language and identity; we define 'culture' and note that it is dynamic and heterogeneous; we reflect on recent Chilean history; we discuss English as an international language that can facilitate sharing across borders; we examine the cultural messages in English textbooks in Chile and explore possibilities for the use of Chilean content in English classes; and additionally we share ideas for bringing English- language popular culture into the classroom. The highlight of the workshop is the teaching demonstrations on the last day, which provide a variety of answers to the following question: given our discussions, how would you teach cultural issues in your classroom?

In July 2006, five groups of MA students (3 or 4 per group, for a total of 17 students) conducted videotaped teaching demonstrations at the end of the language and culture course. They were grouped by the level of the students they taught, with two university-level groups, one adult level, one high school and one elementary, with the rest of the MA students and the two professors role-playing the students for each lesson. Each group had 45 minutes, including discussion time. Though the demonstrations did not address language ideology directly, they provide provisional representations of Chilean teachers' ideas of appropriate English-language pedagogies: these demonstrations inevitably, though implicitly, address the purposes of English instruction in Chile and the identities of learners of English. The demonstrations thus enact language ideologies, without referencing them explicitly.

The first university-level group included Diego, who was a university adjunct instructor as well as teaching high school and adult school. This group's lesson was based on a clip from the 2004 Chilean film *Machuca*, which portrays the 1973 military coup through the eyes of an upper-class boy and a working-class boy who both attend an elite English-medium academy. The clip shown in the lesson depicts the first day the working-class scholarship students arrive at the school. The presenters then led a discussion on social change in recent decades in Chile and on current issues of social class and education. This discussion revealed general approbation of efforts to educate the working class, but doubt as to the appropriacy of bringing up political issues (such as the legacy of the dictatorship) even in university classrooms.

The second university-level group, which included Alán, showed a US videotape featuring interviews with immigrants, all of whom were successful in US society. The video was accompanied by commercial English as a second language (ESL) listening-comprehension activities, but the presenters used it to again spark a comparative discussion, this one examining similarities and differences between United States and Chilean immigration. Comparing the US immigrants portrayed in the video with exploited Peruvian workers in Chile, participants concluded that it was easier for immigrants to prosper in the United States despite greater potential for culture shock.

The presenters for the adult-level group, which included Rita and Gonzalo, explained that they taught in varied contexts, their students ranging from professionals to unemployed workers. However, the demonstration lesson targeted adults who might travel to English-speaking countries and thus experience 'culture shock'. It used two audio recordings, Sting's 1987 song 'Englishman in New York' and an account by a Korean student of her difficulties in a US high school. Lesson activities involved listing aspects of life in Chile that might be disconcerting to foreigners as well as possible sources of culture shock for Chileans who travel abroad.

The theme for the high school lesson (9th grade) was 'subcultures'. (This group did not include any of the teachers quoted above.) Many Chilean youths identify with global subcultures connected to musical genres, and this can be a motivation to learn English. The lesson began with audio recordings of songs from the following genres: punk, reggaeton, goth, metal, hiphop, grunge. We were asked to fill out charts based on our knowledge of clothing styles connected with each genre, and to talk about which genre(s) we identified with. This was easy for the Chilean MA students (and they agreed it would be easy for high school students), but proved challenging for their aging US professor.

The elementary school group, which included Amanda and Hector, taught a 5th grade lesson which involved no audio recordings, but rather paper cut-outs of images, some from the internet. An interactive lecture, it featured the adventures of a paper airplane, Little Wing, who visited different continents, and presented basic information in English (which students were expected to already know in Spanish) about each country. For example, Egypt is an African country where Arabic is spoken and pyramids are a national symbol; Chile is a South American country where Spanish is spoken and the araucaria tree is a national symbol. We were then asked in English about which country we hoped to visit and why (participants commented that they would hold this discussion mostly in Spanish in a real 5th grade classroom).

Thus, three out of five lessons used popular culture to spark discussion of social issues; only one of these groups used a Chilean cultural product (the film *Machuca*). However, every group used Chilean content (e.g. an araucaria tree) or included discussion of the Chilean context or both. No group directly addressed economic reasons for learning English, although the adult-level group implied that their students might travel abroad for work. Three groups referenced foreign contexts, but in the university lesson on immigration there was no suggestion that Chileans needed English to live abroad. The children's lesson involved 'fantasy' travel as a way to display geographical knowledge and build English vocabulary. No activities included even pretending to talk to non-Chileans. Overall, lessons enacted the ideological perspective that English is primarily valuable for helping Chileans gain comprehension of the larger world and their own place in global society. In undercutting the economic aspects of the dominant ideology on English as a global language, they reinforced cultural aspects of this same ideology.

Consumers or Citizens?

In a strong piece of social criticism (which we read in the workshop), Moulián (1997) wrote that Chile had become the 'wasteland of the citizen (*páramo del ciudadano*)' and the 'paradise of the consumer (*paraíso del consumidor*)'.[7] Winn (2004) likewise argues that this was one aim realized by the Pinochet dictatorship:

> Pinochet's efforts to replace Chile's culture of solidarity with one of individualism and consumerism finally triumphed in the 1990s ...under democratic governments.... Younger workers...(who) identify with MTV's transnational youth culture .... (are) more likely to act as consumers than as citizens. (2004: 51–52)

Recent discussions with Chilean English teachers confirm that although Chilean society is changing rapidly, consumerism (*consumismo*) remains a dominant ideology, even as new generations of youth forge their own paths to political activism through strikes and street demonstrations (Franklin, 2011). Chilean indigenous and human rights activists maintain an English-language internet presence (e.g. Mapuche International, 2011), but the student movement has not sought international solidarity in the same way – and based on my interviews with teachers, at least some of the protesting students see English as an 'imperialist' language (Menard-Warwick, 2009).

Moreover, the English teachers I interviewed, including prospective teachers who were current students, did not tend to identify with political movements (though while working on this chapter I received an email[8] from one of the university instructors who was participating in current protests against the privatization of education).

In any case, when I write about English as a language of global citizenship, I situate myself, along with my Chilean research participants, within a global society that lacks many of the forms of political participation that have been possible within the democratic nation state (Risager, 2007). Global 'citizens' cannot vote at the worldwide level and have no elected representatives (beyond the nation state) who are obligated to respond to their interests. Thus, societal 'participation' primarily takes place via consumerism. This is especially true on the internet, the premier global institution (Kumaravadivelu, 2008; Menard-Warwick, 2009), which juxtaposes a wide variety of ideologies as well as products, providing space for authoritative discourses to become internally persuasive, and for internally persuasive discourses to become authoritative (Bakhtin, 1981). In contemporary society, environmentalism can be purchased in the form of recycled notebooks, political ideologies as music, social critique through clothing. In this way, *active* consumerism shapes the direction of global and local society through lifestyle choices, just as the ease of posting internet content allows global 'citizens' to attempt to shape global culture in the image of their own internally persuasive discourses (a task facilitated by English proficiency). Thus, to further the dialogue in this chapter, I define 'citizenship' as *full participation*, the capacity to define and promote one's own interests and values.

The Pinochet dictatorship understood the importance of media censorship for its political aims. From its perspective, the free market of goods was an ideological imperative, but could not be allowed to become a free market of ideas. Thus, the end of censorship was the most striking sign of the change from dictatorship to democracy in 1990. Alán, born in the 1970s, saw a striking difference in Chile with the end of censorship:

> There were two [television] channels, and lots of censorship, and movies were cut, the news were like filtered and selected, and all the programs, the language that they used on television was very careful, very formal. [...] Television was very different after, when our first president in democracy was elected. [...] I remember the first day, I was in high school in fourth year, and there was an immediate change on television, different people, different faces, [...] It was yeah, it was like a big, big change.

Although few of the teachers mentioned the end of censorship directly, it was common for them to talk about the ideational content of the media products they enjoyed, such as the anti-discrimination message of Phil Collins' 1989 song 'Another Day in Paradise' (Menard-Warwick, 2011). They found the discourses of popular music 'internally persuasive' (Bakhtin, 1981) and brought songs and video clips into the English classroom when possible. This dialogic practice allows teachers to juxtapose not only depictions of diverse English- speaking cultural contexts but also divergent ideological perspectives (Bakhtin, 1984). In interviews and in the workshop, teachers made it clear that they not only wanted to motivate English study but also to inspire thought on interesting and controversial issues.

For example, Francesca, a 5th year undergraduate, expressed to me the hope that learning English could make her students more 'open-minded'. She then described a lesson she had given while student teaching, based on a pop song by Avril Lavigne:

The music was about a girl, she didn't like the boy that was in love with her, [...] and she was really ( ) shy, you know, and things like that, and she was really pretty. And after, 'Tell me, what do you, how do you think she is?' 'She's pretty'. ( ) I told them, 'Do you think she's intelligent?' 'No', some girls say. 'Why don't, you don't think she's pretty? She's pretty but she cannot be intelligent?' You know, like prejudice, like, 'Oh, you look good, so you can't be intelligent', you know. 'Do you think ( ), so if it's a good-looking guy, he must be a stupid guy?' (Menard-Warwick, 2011)

It is this kind of dialogue, in this case on gender issues, facilitated by popular music downloaded from the internet, that illustrates how participating in global society as a consumer is perhaps not so far, after all, from citizenship – if citizenship is seen as the capacity to define and promote one's own interests and values.

Notes

(1) All names are pseudonyms.
(2) At times in this paper, I will refer to the course as a 'workshop' since it was short-term and workshop style. This was the class for which I was Rita's professor.
(3) I thank volume editor Vai Ramanathan for this insight.
(4) See transcription conventions, final page.
(5) bracket in original essay.

(6) I should mention, however, that short-term interpretation opportunities were available several times a year when cruise ships docked in their city; a number of teachers and advanced students took advantage of these.
(7) These are chapter titles for his book *Chile Actual* (Contemporary Chile).
(8) The email is dated August 3, 2011.

References

Achugar, M. (2008) Counter-hegemonic language practices and ideologies: Creating a new space and value for Spanish in Southwest Texas. *Spanish in Context* 5 (1), 1–19.

Bakhtin, M. (1981) *The Dialogic Imagination: Four Essays* (C. Emerson and M. Holquist trans.). Austin: University of Texas Press.

Bakhtin, M. (1984) *Problems of Dostoevsky's Poetics* (edited and translated by C. Emerson). Minneapolis: University of Minnesota Press.

Blommaert, J. (2005) *Discourse*. Cambridge: Cambridge University Press.

Canagarajah, A.S. (1999) *Resisting Linguistic Imperialism in English Teaching*. Oxford: Oxford University Press.

Choi, P.K. (2003) 'The best students will learn English': Ultra-utilitarianism and linguistic imperialism in education in post-1997 Hong Kong. *Journal of Education Policy* 18 (6), 673–694.

Drake, P. and Jaksic, I. (1999) *El Modelo Chileno: Democracia y Desarrollo en Los Noventa*. Santiago de Chile: Editorial LOM-ARCIS.

Franklin, J. (2011) Chile student protests explode into violence. *Guardian*, August 5, 2011, accessed 17 August 2011. http://www.guardian.co.uk/world/2011/aug/05/chile-student-protests-violence

Godley, A.J., Carpenter, B.D. and Werner, C.A. (2007) 'I'll speak in proper slang': Language ideologies in a daily editing activity. *Reading Research Quarterly* 42 (1), 100–131.

Jaffe, A. (2007) Codeswitching and stance: Issues in interpretation. *Journal of Language, Identity, and Education* 6 (1), 53–77.

Jeon, M. (2008) Korean heritage language maintenance and language ideology. *Heritage Language Journal* 6 (2) 54–71.

Kroskrity, P.V. (ed.) (2000) *Regimes of Language: Ideologies, Polities, and Identities*. Santa Fe, NM: School of American Research Press.

Kumaravadivelu, B. (2008) *Cultural Globalization and Language Education*. New Haven, CT: Yale University Press.

Leeman, J. and Martinez, G. (2010) From identity to commodity: Ideologies of Spanish Heritage language textbooks. *Critical Inquiry in Language Studies* 4 (1), 35–65.

Lo, A. (1999) Codeswitching, speech community membership, and the construction of ethnic identity. *Journal of Sociolinguistics* 3/4, 461–479.

Loveman, B. (2001) *Chile: The Legacy of Hispanic capitalism* (3rd edn). Oxford: Oxford University Press.

Mapuche International, accessed 12 July 2011. http://www.mapuche-nation.org/english/frontpage.htm

McKay, S.L. (2003) Teaching English as an international language: The Chilean context. *English Language Teaching Journal* 57 (2), 139–148.

Menard-Warwick, J. (2009) The dad in the Che Guevara t-shirt: Narratives of Chilean English teachers. *Critical Inquiry in Language Studies* 5 (4), 243–264.
Menard-Warwick, J. (2011) Chilean English teacher identity and popular culture: Three generations. *International Journal of Bilingual Education and Bilingualism* 14 (3), 261–277.
Moulián, T. (1997) *Chile Actual: Anatomía de un mito*. Santiago de Chile: Editorial LOM-ARCIS.
Niño-Murcia, M. (2003) English is like the dollar: Hard currency ideology and the status of English in Peru. *World Englishes* 22 (2), 121–142.
Olivo, W. (2003) 'Quit talking and learn English!': Conflicting language ideologies in an ESL classroom. *Anthropology and Education Quarterly* 34 (1), 50–71.
Pennycook, A. (2007) *Global English and Transcultural Flows*. London: Routledge.
Rahman, T. (2009) Language ideology, identity and the commodification of language in the call centers of Pakistan. *Language in Society* 38, 233–258.
Risager, K. (2007) *Language and Culture Pedagogy*. Clevedon: Multilingual Matters.
Shankar, S. (2008) Speaking like a Model Minority: "FOB" Styles, Gender, and Racial Meanings among Desi Teens in Silicon Valley. *Journal of Linguistic Anthropology* 18 (2), 268–289.
Winn, P. (2004) *Victims of the Chilean Miracle: Workers and Neoliberalism in the Pinochet Era, 1973-2002*. Durham, NC: Duke University Press.
Woolard, K.A. (1989) Sentences in the language prison: The rhetorical structuring of an American language policy debate. *American Ethnologist* 16 (2), 268–278.
Woolard, K.A. (1998) Introduction: Language ideology as a field of inquiry. In B. Schieffelin, K.A. Woolard and P.V. Kroskrity (eds) *Language Ideologies: Practice and Theories* (pp. 3–47). Oxford: Oxford University Press.

Transcription conventions

I leave out backchanneling (e.g. 'Mmmhmmm'), fillers (e.g. 'um'), false starts, self corrections, most repetitions and my questions when they can be inferred from the answers.

....	trailing intonation
[...]	text omitted
(text)	transcriptionist doubt
( )	incomprehensible
((text))	paralinguistic behavior, e.g. laughter
[text]	author comment or explanation

6 A Perfect Storm for Undocumented Latino Youth?: Multi-level Marketing, Discourses of Advancement and Language Policy

Gemma Punti and Kendall A. King

> *¡Estamos creando una cultura de hombres y mujeres libres económicamente! La libertad empieza a dentro de nosotros diciendo, 'Yo valgo. Yo merezco. Yo nací para triunfar. Yo puedo ser rico, sano y feliz. Puedo tenerlo todo porque tengo un Dios que me lo puede dar todo.'*
>
> We are creating a culture of economically free men and women! Liberty begins inside ourselves when we say, 'I count. I'm worth it. I was born to triumph. I can be rich, healthy and happy. I can have it all because I have a God that can give it all to me.'
> Antonio Maldonado, Head of MDE Latino, at an Amway Conference in 2009, SusanaaRamirezz, 2009

This chapter examines one way in which undocumented youth navigate their extremely limited educational and professional opportunities in the United States. For many of these ambitious and hard-working young adults, multi-level marketing (MLM) schemes such as Herbalife and Amway provide a means – or the discourse of a means – to financial, educational and social advancement. Here, we examine MLM language policies and their discourses of advancement as well as their uptake and entextualization by undocumented Latino young adults. To this end, we present case studies of two individuals' engagement with MLM organizations, including how they position themselves and their decisions to invest in an MLM business within their life trajectories. We demonstrate how and why MLM discourses are particularly salient for them, as well as the ways in which these discourses are adapted and personalized. This chapter illustrates how MLM schemes, in conjunction with the dysfunctional US immigration system, create a 'perfect storm' for undocumented Latino youth.

Aspiration and Undocumented Migration

Unauthorized migration in the United States reached its peak in 2007, with estimates of around 12 million undocumented individuals in the country (Hoefer et al., 2010). Since then, this has slightly decreased to 11.2 million (largely due to the falling total number of unauthorized Mexicans[1]) (Passel & Cohn, 2011). Still, about 58% of all undocumented migrants are Mexican (Passel & Cohn, 2011) and more than three-quarters (82%) are Latino (Passel, 2011). Presently, there are more than 2.1 million undocumented youth who have been in the United States since childhood (Gonzales, 2011).

Most adult undocumented immigrants aspire to improve their economic circumstances through waged employment (Chavez, 1998). While economically and politically marginalized from the US mainstream, many of these adults maintain a 'dual frame of reference' that enables them to develop a positive sense of self; that is, although their wages are low (by US standards), they are often higher than in their home countries (Suárez-Orozco & Suárez-Orozco, 1995). However, undocumented young adults who came as minors have limited recollection of their nation of origin. Most enroll in US schools, learn to speak English, socialize with US-born and legal resident peers and expect to have better opportunities than their parents (Gonzales, 2011). To some degree, then, these youth internalize 'American values and expectations that equate academic success with economic rewards and stability' (Abrego & Gonzales, 2010: 147).

Throughout their childhoods and early teen years, many of these youth have limited knowledge of their legal status and its implications. For most, a full understanding of their predicament comes when youth are banned from working legally, obtaining financial aid, voting, and, in most states, driving (Abrego, 2006; Gonzales, 2011) – activities that often symbolize coming-of-age in the United States.

These youth must contend with the contradiction between the predominant discourse – that is, that investment in schooling leads to college acceptance followed by occupational opportunities – and what their legal status implies and what family and friends often tell them: 'you can't go to college' (Abrego, 2006; King & Punti, 2012). While not accurate (i.e. US citizenship is generally *not* an admissions requirement), these statements reflect the fact that undocumented youth *are* ineligible for most forms of federal financial aide. As undocumented youth come-of-age and simultaneously become aware of their limited opportunities, interest in formal schooling often diminishes (Abrego, 2006; Abrego & Gonzales, 2010). This educational disengagement is evident in graduation rates. For instance, an estimated 60% of undocumented youth (ages 18–24) graduate from high school, compared to 85% of legal immigrants and 92% of US-born youth (Passel & Cohn, 2009). Even for graduates of four-year higher-education institutions, professional employment and middle-class wages remains out of reach, as evident in the substantial annual income gap between unauthorized immigrant families ($27,400) and legal immigrant families ($47,800) (Passel, 2005).

Despite these education and income gaps, past research (e.g. Abrego & Gonzales, 2010; King & Punti, 2012) finds that many undocumented youth are ambitious and aspire to professional positions, economic stability and social advancement. In spite of their sharply limited opportunities, these young adults are surrounded by an ideology of achievement (Barnes, 2002) that stresses a causal link between effort and education on the one hand, and life success on the other. As demonstrated in this chapter, these ideologies of achievement, together with the aggressive advertising and recruitment strategies employed by MLM schemes, and the restrictions of the current US immigration system, create a 'perfect storm' for undocumented Latino youth.

Multi-level Marketing (MLM)

MLM is a general term for businesses in which the salesperson is compensated not only for product sales but also for recruitment of additional salespeople who work 'down line' as product distributors. The Direct Selling Association estimates there were 15.8 million MLM salespeople in the United States in 2010. Many MLM companies are household names, including Amway, Avon, Herbalife and Equinox. MLM businesses can be legal or illegal, depending on the extent to which they operate as pyramid or 'endless chain' schemes. Such 'schemes ask people to make an investment and, in return, grant them a license to recruit others who, in turn, recruit still others into the scheme' (Koehn, 2001: 153). These pyramids are illegal and unethical because they are (a) deceptive; and (b) recruitment-centered rather than product-centered businesses.[2]

MLM organizations have been critiqued not only for operating within a tiered structure, which demands distributors recruit others below them in order to make money, but for requiring distributors to purchase products (for re-sale) which are non-competitively priced and for heavy reliance on MLM salespeople's social and familial relationships (Van Druff, 1990). Tellingly, MLM is also known as 'network marketing'. Within this system, recruiters must act as a 'model of trust in the company' since showing any doubt discourages those lower on the hierarchy and thus weakens their own possibilities for moving up the hierarchy (Groβ, 2010: 65).

In fact, in all MLM schemes, relatively few distributors earn a living wage or make a return on their initial investment in products and training. Just one quarter of 1% (0.26%) of Amway distributors earn more than $40,000 a year (O'Donnell, 2011). While Herbalife has a relatively low-startup cost ($87.95), the average distributor earns about $2400 a year (Correal, 2010). In addition, many MLM investors spend significant sums to attend training sessions and purchase 'educational' materials. Those items are MLM schemes' second product line – often sold at a high profit margin (Brodsky, 1998).

MLM businesses such as Amway and Herbalife have made significant in-roads within US Latino communities. For instance, fully 64% of Herbalife's distributors in the United States are Latino (Correal, 2010). Both companies market directly to Spanish speakers in the United States by purchasing Spanish-language commercials and maintaining an all-Spanish-language versions of their websites and bilingual customer service lines. Herbalife has adapted its business model (via innovations by distributors in Zapotecas, Mexico) to fit preferences of its Latino participants. Most significant in this respect are the no-commitment, low-fee Herbalife nutrition clubs where customers and potential future distributors drink teas (for $4.00). In turn, Amway's most aggressive recruitment strategies come from mid-level distributors, known as 'Accreditation PLUS' teams such as MDE Latino, Camino El Exito and Proyecto Libertad. These distributors, many of them functioning exclusively in Spanish, are permitted by Amway to sell motivational and training materials and to host recruitment and training events.

For many MLM recruiters, recent-immigrant Latinos are perceived to be an optimal target. As stated bluntly in a YouTube video entitled, 'Network Marketing: The Hispanic Market' (Glycodoc, 2010), Latinos are an ideal audience for recruiters (and merit Spanish-language materials in particular), given their (a) lack of English skills and preference for Spanish-medium sales exchanges, (b) cultural tradition of face-to-face selling, (c) 'entrepreneurial spirit', (d) interest in science-based products related to health and beauty and (e) strong and dense community networks. Some of these claims are in fact supported empirically. For instance, focus-group research finds that Latino internet users prefer buying from websites that highlight Latino families and communities, show respect to US Latinos and have Latino role models as inspiring successful figures (Singh et al., 2008). And psycholinguistically oriented research suggests that advertisements in consumer's first language are better retained (relative to second-language ads) (Luna & Peracchio, 2001). Yet while Spanish-language advertising seems to increase Latino consumers' interest in the target product, there is also evidence that Spanish-language advertisements potentially promote feelings of inferiority among Latino targets given the association of Spanish in the United States with communities that are perceived to be low-class and poor (Koslow *et al.*, 1994; Luna & Pericchio, 2005). Further, with respect to MLM advertising in particular, survey research suggests that Latinos and lower-income consumers (defined here as self-reporting less than $35,000 in annual income) are more likely than the general population to mistake pyramid schemes for legitimate businesses and as an effective means of providing supplemental income (National Consumer League, 2009).

While the practices of US Latino communities are undoubtedly complex and varied, for ambitious, hard working, and undocumented young adults, MLM schemes can be highly appealing, providing the discourse of a means to financial, educational and social advancement. Through engagement with MLM texts (at training events, via written promotional materials), MLM recruits are motivated to invest and participate, begin to adopt an MLM worldview of success and acquire the shared MLM discourses of advancement. Below we examine MLM organizations' language policies and their discourses of advancement, as well how these discourses are entextualized by undocumented Latino young adults. Specifically, we ask: (1) how do MLM discourses and language policies attract the undocumented young Latinos? and (2) how are these discourses interpreted and entextualized by Latino recruits relative to their own life circumstances?

Data and Analysis

To address these questions, the remainder of this chapter examines the nature of the intersection between undocumented youth and MLM schemes by profiling two young adults, Noberto and Patricia. These youth were part of a broader study of undocumented youth and academic engagement (King & Punti, 2012). The broader project surveyed, interviewed and observed 13 undocumented young adults about their experiences with the US legal, educational and occupational systems, and collected and analyzed narrative accounts of legality, finding that immigration status is experienced and understood largely in racial terms.

For the present analysis of Noberto and Patricia's engagement with MLMs, we collected data via informal conversations, unstructured interviews and participant observations at MLM trainings, sales and recruitment events over 18 months. These events were free with the stated intention of recruiting new participants (but fee based for members who are expected to attend both weekly [at $5 per session] and larger, monthly gatherings [at $30 or more]). We also examined MLM texts that were accessed by our participants, including brochures, videos, websites and training materials.

Rather than focusing exclusively on the language and images of advertisements (cf. Cook, 2001), our analysis sought to identify the processes through which participants adopted MLM discourses of advancement. We take discourse here to mean 'a socially accepted association among ways of using language, of thinking and of acting that can be used to identify oneself as a member of a socially meaningful group' (Gee, 1989: 18), in this case, as part of Herbalife or MDE Latino (Amway). Discourse, then, refers not just to talk, but to an '"identity kit", which comes complete with appropriate costume and instructions on how to act and talk so as to take on a particular role that others will recognize' (Gee, 1989: 7). Our close analysis of texts here (e.g. talk in interviews, at meetings, Spanish-language promotional materials) aims to reveal the ways in which Amway and Herbalife discourses of advancement were entextualized by participants, and in doing so, took on new meanings salient to their own experiences as undocumented Latino youth in the United States.

At the most general level, entextualization (Silverstein & Urban, 1996) refers to the process through which chunks of discourse are perceived, and thus treated, as independent from the processes through which they were produced. As a result, these discourse chunks 'come to seem autonomous, operating as free-flowing encapsulations of what social actors take as shared, transmittable meaning that circulate in written and spoken form across social boundaries' (Urciuoli, 2010: 49). Crucial to our analysis here is the fact that these chunks of discourse are not neutral; to the contrary, entextualization entails 'producing particular types of texts in the service of social and political agendas' which aim to sustain, and/or challenge power relations through employment of specific 'tactics, strategies and discursive constraints' (Briggs, 1993: 390). Our analysis here focuses on how broader MLM discourses of advancement are entextualized within context of life experiences of undocumented young adults. We show how these discourses take on specific and very powerful meanings for recent immigrants.

MLM schemes recruit and maintain participants through regular weekly and monthly meetings. These events have a fixed, repetitive organization; set participant structures and roles; and recurrent topics, themes and arguments. In this sense, these events function as rituals as they are repeated actions of a symbolic nature (Du Bois, 2003). As Kapchan (1995) notes, rituals are 'multi-semiotic modes of cultural expression' in which performances of communicative events are processes of group and individual transformation (1995: 480). For instance, MLM events require participants to demonstrate enthusiasm in defined ways (e.g. repeated chanting of *¡éxito!* ['success!'] and *¡campeón!* ['champion!']), and to follow a 'successful' dress code (e.g. MDE Latino men wear black suits and red ties). Through these events, participants are socialized into MLM discourses of advancement, and begin to construct an individual identity as a successful entrepreneur and a collective identity as a supportive, dynamic business community.

Of particular interest here is how MLM discourses of advancement are entextualized by Latino participants, and how the metapragmatic value of these discourses varies across contexts (Vigouroux, 2009). For instance, Amway has long promoted itself as a mean of achieving 'the American dream'. (Indeed, the name is short for 'the American way'). For US citizens, this connotes wealth and financial independence; however, for immigrants, 'the American dream' suggests this as well, but also a transnational narrative of mobility, sacrifice and family separation (Chavez, 1998). Likewise, a recurrent Amway argumentative thread contrasts the limitations of being an employee with the advantages of being a business owner. For undocumented Latinos, who are barred from legal employment, this distinction serves a much more specific rhetorical function, as illustrated below through our case studies of Patricia and Norberto.

Noberto

Noberto, a 19-year-old Indigenous Guatemalan, and speaker of Mam (a Mayan language), came to the United States at 16, leaving his widowed mother and younger siblings behind. In the United States, he was reunited with his older brother and uncle. Following his brother's advice, he started to work at a fast-food restaurant and attend high school. After about a year, he was introduced to Amway's Latino branch MDE Latino 'by an Ecuadorian undocumented friend who actually backed off [from Amway]'. The message he received from MDE Latino leaders was that *puedo ser millonario.... [y] cuando empiezo a ganar más de seis mil dólares en adelante, el gobierno me va a buscar para que me dé una visa empresarial* ('I can be a millionaire...[and] when I start earning more than six thousand dollars [every month], the government will look for me and to give me a business visa') (Noberto, interview, June, 2010). Noberto left high school in late 2010, at age 18, to dedicate his time to business, church and hourly fast-food work. In Fall, 2011, with encouragement from the church youth pastor, he enrolled in a GED (General Educational Development) program. Since then, he has attended GED test preparation class every weekday morning and participated in bible classes twice weekly, while working 20 hours per week at the fast-food restaurant and attending weekly MLM meetings. After more than three years with MDE Latino, Noberto still struggles economically. Nevertheless, he maintains his hopes of becoming wealthy, gaining a US visa, attending a Christian college, and becoming a Christian leader.

Patricia

Patricia, is a 22-year-old Mexican woman with two young children. She came to the United States from Acapulco, Mexico at age 10 with her mother to be reunited with her father. As Patricia explained, around the age of 16, she began *a ver la realidad de un ilegal ... cuando yo quise trabajar, dijo mi papá, los papeles [falsos] cuestan tanto dinero... y yo lo pagué* ('to see the reality of an illegal individual...when I wanted to work my dad told me that the [fake] papers cost money ... and I paid them') (interview, June, 2010). With these documents, Patricia was able to work in a fast-food restaurant, and around that time, she became pregnant. After the birth of her child, Patricia, her boyfriend and her baby moved to Texas to search for better job opportunities, but were deported after a routine traffic stop. Patricia soon returned to the United States, and in Minnesota she gave birth to her second child and enrolled in a high school for teen mothers. She successfully attended high school while working part time at a restaurant and caring for her two children, and graduated in June 2010 with no specific plans.

Roughly a year after graduation, a cousin recruited her to Herbalife by inviting herself to Patricia's house to prepare *licuaditos* ('smoothies'), a common beverage in Mexico. Patricia reports that she was initially hesitant about these costly drinks, but her father started to use them and a month later the entire family believed that Herbalife was effective. Since July 2011, Patricia and her father have enrolled as Herbalife supervisors, investing more than $4000 and working daily at the Herbalife club. Patricia also works at a factory part time *para más producto [Herbalife], comprar inversión* ('to buy more [Herbalife] product, to buy investments'). She trusts and believes in Herbalife and as she says, *na más me falta ganar más – buscar más gente* ('all I need is to earn more – to look for more people') (interview, November, 2011).

MLM Language Policy and Discourses of Advancement

Across both MLM schemes (Herbalife and Amway) and both of our study participants (Patricia and Noberto), we find a shared set of discourses, what we characterize as discourses of advancement. These embody MLM companies' stated value on personal wealth and self-improvement, but also on helping one's family and community. As suggested above, MLM recruits take on, and through mandatory ritualized meetings, are socialized into, very particular identities and discourses. These discourses, as Gee (1989) reminds us, are inherently ideological, that is they depend on viewpoints one must speak and act, in this case, free market and Christian values. They are also resistant to scrutiny as the discourse itself defines what counts as acceptable criticism; in these MLM contexts, for instance, any doubts about the organizations are framed as personal failings and negative thinking. Further, discourses are formed in part in opposition to other discourses (e.g. that education is essential for financial success) and put forth certain viewpoints at the expense of others (e.g. being a business owner vs. being a lowly employee). Finally, as will be apparent below, these discourses are ultimately related to the social distribution of power and social hierarchies.

MLM discourses of advancement are powerful and effective in part because they are in Spanish, and thus accessible to Spanish-dominant recruits. As noted above, all of the materials (websites, training seminars, brochures and videos) are available in Spanish. In this regard, MLM language policies are more adaptive and responsive to the needs and preferences of immigrants than most other US institutions, including schools. As noted above, there is evidence suggesting that Latinos prefer websites showcasing Latinos as role models and focusing on their communities (Singh *et al.*, 2008), qualities that MLM companies actively strive for. Perhaps even more significant than MLM Spanish language policies are the ways in which MLM discourses reflect participants' life experiences. Not only are training and sales pitches provided *in a language* that participants best understand, but they are also framed within a shared cultural context that validates participants' experiences (Korzenny & Korzenny, 2005). For instance, in one training event we attended, a regional leader of Herbalife testified to his own early immigration experiences, explaining that when he first arrived to the United States: *Yo no tenía nada. Tenía que trabajar todo el día por nada, por un 'muy bien muy bien trabaja trabaja' y con suerte no te gritaban, y vivía amontonado en el sótano con otras siete personas.* ('I didn't have anything. I had to work all day for nothing, for 'very good, very good work, work' and with luck they didn't yell at you, and I lived cramped in a basement with seven other people') (training session, December 2011). Similar shared immigration experiences were highlighted at an MDE Latino training session (November 2010). To a room of 25 enthusiastic distributors in a suburban chain hotel, the speaker began by asking – rhetorically – why everyone came to the United States. He then went on to answer: *aquí en los Estados Unidos...hay mayores oportunidades de ganar dinero, de prosperar. Nadie se viene por el frío. Nadie se viene por la nieve... Ini siquiera porque les gusta!* ('here in the United States...there are higher opportunities to earn money, of prospering. Nobody comes for the cold. Nobody comes here for the snow...not even because they like it!')

This rhetoric establishes a shared experience of immigration and common motivations for migrating. Within this constructed in-group space, participants can be frank about the fact that they would prefer to be elsewhere and that they are here in the United States to earn money. These shared vantage points are referenced in each meeting, and function to promote a sense of trust and cohesiveness amongst the recruits, but more importantly, between these recruits and MLM leaders.

Through the medium of Spanish and with these shared experiences as a starting point, MLM discourses are entextualized by participants with reference to their own lives and circumstances. Below we highlight how three threads of this discourse are articulated within official MLM texts, and then interpreted and entextualized by Patricia and Noberto.

Hard work results in success

The first and perhaps most prominent MLM discourse of advancement is that *hard work results in success*, and in particular, that financial success depends on one's effort, *not* on one's legal status or formal education. Amway's Spanish-language website emphasizes that *Amway cree que el trabajo arduo debe ser recompensado* ('Amway believes that hard work should be rewarded') (http://www.amway.com). Likewise, an Amway motivational speaker (November 2011) told participants: *el éxito de tu negocio depende de ti, de que tan duro trabajes* ('the success of your business depends on you, on how hard you work'). Similarly, Herbalife's website stresses that as an independent distributor, *se gana lo que se merece* ('one earns what one deserves') (http://www.herbalife.com). Further, Spanish-language recruitment materials for both companies highlight that *no se necesitan papeles* ('one does not need papers'). Overall, these messages convey to recruits the valued and rare sentiment 'of being treated in a fair way [by] having a fair chance to succeed individually' (Groβ, 2010: 70).

Patricia fully embraced this work ethic as she labored daily in the Herbalife nutrition club. Seven days a week, she woke at 5.30 am to serve teas at the club at 6.00 am. Her responsibilities entailed preparing the teas and cleaning the rented space. Working this many early hours in addition to attending regular training sessions and passing out flyers in public areas was challenging given that she also was primary caretaker for two young children as well as a factory employee. As evident in Excerpt 1 below, Patricia's commitment to Herbalife is partly due to her alignment with the MLM discourse of hard work. She seems to embrace Herbalife's promise of 'fair system' and the premise that financial success is not dependent on formal education or legal status.

Excerpt 1 Interview with Patricia (November 2011) (See Appendix for transcription conventions)

01	**Gemma:**	y ahora ya no piensas sobre el hecho de tener papeles?
02	**Patricia:**	esto+/...esta compañía no pide papeles. hay mucha gente que yo he visto+/... hay gente
03		que no sabía leer ni sabía ni escribir, y Herbalife no les cierra la puerta-> no necesita
04		colegio-> ni necesita high school-> si es ilegal o no es ilegal-> por eso me IDENTIFICO
05		con Herbalife. SI::: me gusta Mucho
06	**Gemma:**	o sea no impORTA tu situación legal. no les importa. tu puedes trabajar con ellos
07	**Patricia:**	y por ejemplo si me deportan, yo puedo hacer Herbalife en México

01	**Gemma:**	and now you don't think about the fact of having papers?
02	**Patricia:**	so+/...this company doesn't ask for papers. There are a lot of people that I've seen+/...there are people
03		who didn't know how to read or write, and Herbalife doesn't close the door to them-> you don't need
04		college-> nor you need high school-> if one is illegal or is not illegal-> for that reason I IDENTIFY
05		with Herbalife. YE::S I like it a LOT.
06	**Gemma:**	so it doesn't MAtter your legal situation. they don't care. you can work with them
07	**Patricia:**	and for example if I am deported, I can do Herbalife in Mexico

Patricia expresses the meritocratic idea of 'no papers needed' in the first person, noting that she, personally, has seen individuals from a wide range of backgrounds do well (lines 2–4). She aligns herself with Herbalife explicitly because the company opens the door to everybody: 'for that reason I identify with Herbalife' (lines 4–5). Further, she extrapolates this notion of hard work to her own life circumstances, which include the possibility of deportation (line 7). In this way, Herbalife discourse of advancement provides a means for Patricia to imagine a successful life, one which is dependent on hard work, *not* on legal status or even place of residence.

Excerpt 2 Interview with Noberto (Sept. 2010)

01	Gemma:	ha habido alguna situación en que no tener documentos ha sido un problema en los meses pasados?
02	Noberto:	en alguna situación pero ya no me interesé.
03	Gemma:	qué significa?
04	Noberto:	que una vez me dice un amigo "hay trabajo donde estoy. trabajo por 13 dólares en una empresa y
05		está bien. 13 dólares la hora está bien" y me dice "tienes papeles?" "no" le digo. y me dice
06		"lo siento mi amigo" me dice "pero no se va a poder" y yo dije "tengo un negocio donde
07		nadie me dice cuanto tengo que ganar y puedo ganar la cantidad que yo quiera!" le digo. o sea::
08		no me puse frustrado si me explico? no me puse a pensar "AY si tuviera papeles-> si yo tuviera
09		papeles" no. NAda de eso. fuera de la mente-> como que no existió nada. esa oportunidad la perdí
10		porque no tenía papeles pero no me desanimé porque en primer lugar tenía mi negocio->
11		yo puedo ganar la cantidad que yo quiera! no 13 dólares la hora, sino 20 dólares la hora.

01	Gemma:	there has been any situation in which not having documents has become a problem in the last months?
02	Noberto:	in some situation[s] but it didn't interest me
03	Gemma:	what does that mean?
04	Noberto:	that once a friend told me "there is work where I am. I work for 13 dollars in a company and
05		it's ok. 13 dollars per hour it's ok" and he tells me "do you have papers?" "no" I tell him. and he tells me
06		"I am sorry" my friend tells me "but it won't be possible" and I said "I have a business where
07		no one tells me how much I have to earn and I can earn the quantity that I want!" I told him. so::
08		I didn't get frustrated do I explain myself? I didn't start thinking "AY if I had papers-> if I had

Excerpt 2 Interview with Noberto (Sept. 2010) (*continued*)

09	papers" no. Nothing like that. out of the mind-> like it didn't exist at all. I lost that opportunity
10	because I didn't have papers but I didn't get discouraged because in first place I had my business->
11	I can earn the amount I want! No 13 dollars per hour, but 20 dollars per hour.

Noberto also seemed to believe that his work would be rewarded and to value his investment in Amway because his legal status would not limit his earnings nor his position in the company. He relayed many stories, such as the one below, which suggested that Amway success would make his visa status irrelevant.

Noberto's small story (Georgakopoulou, 2007) entextualizes several 'chunks' of stock MLM discourse. Noberto's story relates a conversation between Noberto and a friend in which the friend tells Noberto about a factory job that pays a desirable wage of $13 per hour. His friend then tells him that because of Noberto's legal status he is ineligible for the job. Noberto relates this exchange in order to share insights on his internal thought process and to make a broader argument about his social and economic position. As he notes, rather than feeling sorry for himself, he refuses to be discouraged. To justify this positive take on occupational exclusion, he draws from the MLM discourse of being able to earn whatever he wants (line 7). He frames the advantages of being an Amway entrepreneur here in the first person: 'I have a business where no one tells how much I have to earn' (lines 4–7). Thus, the discourse of earning what one is worth provides him with a means of saving face, maintaining positive self-esteem and an optimistic stance in the face of disappointment and job ineligibility.

These excerpts illustrate how for undocumented young adults, the MLM discourse of *hard work* = *success* has particular appeal and is entextualized by them with reference to their own life circumstances and legal status. Further, and perhaps equally appealingly, MLM organizations promise not only economic advancement but also professional training and self-improvement.

Access to education, training and self-improvement

An additional MLM discourse of advancement is that MLM schemes provide *access to education, training and self-improvement*. For instance, Amway's website promises that *desde capacitación específica sobre productos hasta educación comercial, capacitación para mejorar y programas con mentores, tendrás acceso a recursos que te ayudarán a generar negocios de Amway* ('from product-specific training, to business education, self-improvement training, and mentoring programs, you'll have access to resources to help you build a successful Amway business'). Herbalife's Spanish-language promotional magazine (Herbalife Today en Español, 2009) promotes Herbalife's *capacitación que apoya el crecimiento de su compañía a través de reuniones y eventos para los Distribuidores junto con materiales y herramientas avanzadas de mercadeo...* ('training system that supports the growth of your business through meetings and events for Distributors, together materials and advanced marketing tools...'). For Patricia and Noberto, this notion of self-improvement and education was an important investment and attraction, and connected to their life experiences.

Patricia regularly attends the weekly training sessions to learn about Herbalife products. As she explains: *Bueno cada jueves se habla de diferentes cosas. Como que dan ideas de cómo hacer ventas. Hablan sobre la compañía, de los productos... hay diferentes cosas todos los jueves, diferentes maneras que te dicen como aprender a vender, la ética de Herbalife, lo que es Herbalife, como hacer un club.* ('Well, each Thursday they talk about different things. They give ideas about how to make sales. They talk about the company, about the products... there are different things each Thursday, different ways to tell you how to learn to sell, the ethics of Herbalife, what Herbalife is, how to make a club') (interview, December 2011).

Mandatory weekly training sessions are common within MLM schemes (Fitzpatrick & Reynolds, 1997). Yet while these sessions are billed as 'trainings' (Patricia refers to them as *capacitaciones*), a central function is to keep distributors motivated and engaged, but also to recruit new members. As suggested above, these sessions have ritualistic features, including chants, formal dress code, and first-person testimonials. These trainings in fact seemed integral in convincing Patricia and Noberto to commit their time and energy to their MLM businesses.

Amway training sessions often include Evangelical themes and rhetoric, as Evangelism and business success are tightly linked within MDE Latino (see chapter's opening quote). Amway leaders advocate bible study, church attendance and the study of self-improvement Christian books with business themes (e.g. by authors such as Dale Carnegie and John C. Maxwell). Noberto valued and took very seriously the training component of Amway. Indeed, he perceived the Amway training to be of higher quality than formal education. As Noberto explained,

... ahorita estoy aprendiendo más sobre la organización. es una organización mucho más grande. para mí, para mí en todos los respetos es un+/... es una organización mucho más grande que un college. porque en primer lugar, te enseñan cómo ganar dinero. el college lo hace. te enseña a aprender los principios y valores de la vida. el college te enseña a lo mejor un 70 o 80% creo. pero un paso más grande te enseña a tener una relación con Dios. el college no lo hace. esta es la diferencia. esto me enseñó a mí yo no era cristiano antes. decía que creía en Dios pero no sabía quién era Dios. entonces cuando me metí en esta organización me enseñaron cómo hacer dinero, cómo socializarme con la gente, comportarme bien, no maltratar a nadie, así. cosas importantes de la vida.

...right now I am learning more about the organization. it is an organization much bigger. for me, for me in every respect it is a+/... an organization much bigger than a college. because in the first place, they teach you how to earn money. in college they do. they teach you to learn the principles and the values of life. in college they teach you perhaps 70 or 80% I think. but a bigger step is to teach you to have a relationship with God. in college they don't do this. this is the difference. they taught this to me and I was not a Christian before. I said I believed in God but I did not know who God was. so when I entered this organization they taught me how to make money, how to socialize with people, how to behave myself, how to not mistreat anyone; things like this which are important in life (interview, December 2011).

For Noberto, Amway training was more meaningful than traditional schooling because it taught him how to earn money, but also how to be a better person. Here Norberto personalizes a common Evangelical conversion discourse. A central component of conversion is accepting Christ (being 'reborn'); this entails establishing a personal relationship with God (as Noberto notes here), but also of rejecting one's former (inferior, sinful) self (Engelke, 2004; Santos, 2012). In this excerpt, Norberto contrasts his former self (who was a Christian in name only) with his current self (who 'knows God', who knows how to make money, and how to treat others). Notable here is the way Noberto's description of his conversion, and the discontinuity between current and former selves, relates conversion not just to Christian beliefs, but to knowledge about making money and capitalist norms.

Building strong communities and families while helping others

While a central thrust of MLM discourses is personal advancement, MLM texts also promote a model for success that includes family and community advancement. The weekly training sessions, for instance, routinely present examples of MLM families and stress the importance of family involvement and community support. In this vein, Amway's website emphasizes that *juntos, continuamos teniendo éxito al construir una comunidad fuerte, brindando capacitación y apoyo, y ayudando a los empresarios en cada paso del camino* ('together, we continue having success by building a strong community, bringing training and support, and helping the entrepreneurs step by step'). Claims such as these on their websites, and even more directly in face-to-face training sessions, illustrate Amway's strategic use of discourses that are powerful and attractive for potential Latino recruits (Singh *et al.*, 2008).

This sort of MLM community support is important for Noberto given that most of his family is in Guatemala and the only relatives living in the United States (uncle and brother) have distanced themselves from him due to his MLM involvement. MDE Latino provides a support network for Noberto that he lacks in other contexts. For instance, he has stated multiple times that he feels ostracized by his fast-food co-workers as well as by his school peers. The family support he receives within the MLM organization (and in church) motivates him to continue with MDE Latino.

Patricia, in contrast, already had a strong family life prior to Herbalife. Most of her family lives in the same US city and she resides with her two children, her parents, and her husband. For Patricia, Herbalife is attractive not as a quasi-extended family, but as business model that gives her flexibility to attend to family needs. This flexibility is prominent on both Amway and Herbalife sites. For instance, the Herbalife website asks: *¿Qué tal si quisiera ganar algún dinero extra, ser su propio jefe, disfrutar de horarios flexibles o viajar por el mundo?* ('How about earning some extra money, being your own boss, enjoying flexible hours, and traveling the world?') (http://www.herbalife.com). Likewise, Amway's website promises that if you are a distributor, *tú decides cuándo comenzar a trabajar. No necesitas el permiso de nadie para asistir al partido de fútbol de tu hijo.* ('you decide when you want to start work. You don't need permission from anyone to attend your son's football game.').

In Patricia's case, all of her close family members drink the teas, and her father is also a supervisor in Herbalife. In this way, Herbalife makes porous the line that divides family and work life. With Herbalife, Patricia can work from home, at the tea club – where she takes her children – and distribute Herbalife materials at local malls. This has given her a sense of autonomy she has not experienced with any other job, and which is more common to professional positions to which she aspires.

Furthermore, MLM discourses not only promote a strong sense of community (and thus a sentiment of family-like relationships), but also stress the importance of bringing one's family in the business. Most Amway and Herbalife success stories showcase married couples who work together happily and productively. For example, Pam Shoffler, in an Amway testimony, explains how 'our AMWAY business has helped us develop a solid marriage and has blessed our kids and a lot of other people' (Achieve Magazine, 2012). Therefore, MLM businesses promote the notion that collective family investment results in a *blessed,* stronger and happier family.

Yet, while MLM texts promote themselves as a means to family stability and security, these same materials encourage people to begin by selling to their parents and family members. For instance, Herbalife magazine showcases successful leaders such as *Juan Carlos..... [quien] haciendo clientes entre sus amigos y familiares, logró generar mensualmente el dinero que tanto buscaba* ('Juan Carlos...[who] making as clients his friends and relatives, he was able to monthly generate the money he was so much looking for') (Herbalife Today en Español, 2009: 29). There is of course an unmentioned contradiction here: that one can build strong families and communities while simultaneously making money off of those same individuals.

For this reason, 'helping others' is rhetorically complex. Rather than stressing the need to recruit others to enrich oneself (the central mechanism of all pyramid schemes), the focus is on recruiting others to help them to be successful too. For instance during an MDE Latino training session (November 2010), the wife of the presenter, Julia, highlighted the help they are offering to other people:

> *Cada día ayudamos a la gente a conseguir su libertad. de no depender de un empleo porque un empleo está bien pero únicamente para ayudar para las necesidades básicas. pero cuando una persona tiene deseos más grandes necesita de ingresos adicionales. y normalmente cuando la gente piensa en un ingreso adicional piensa en el part-time y nosotros enseñamos a la gente que no es otro empleo sino es tener un negocio!*

> Each day we help people achieve liberty. to not depend on a job because a job is good but only for the basic necessities. but when a person has bigger desires one needs additional incomes. and normally when people think of additional income they think of working part-time and we teach people that it's not another job but it's having a business!

MDE Latino promotes the idea that they help others achieve 'liberty' – a word which invokes both residency rights and equal opportunity. Within this discourse, *help* starts with educating others. As Julia states, 'we *teach* people that it's not another job [what they need] but it's having a business'. Through this 'education', MDE Latino posits that it can *transform* (Spanish-speaking) people into liberated business owners. A central aspect of this process, according to MDE Latino leaders (and subsequently, Noberto), is leaving behind the Latino mentality of an impoverished wage earner (see Excerpt 3).

A Perfect Storm for Undocumented Latino Youth? 109

Excerpt 3 Interview with Noberto (June 2010)

01	**Gemma:**	...pero en la comunidad latina de Minnesota, cuál crees que son los problemas que más
02		comúnmente viven?
03	**Noberto:**	yo diría que el problema de la gente hispana. porque ellos desde su país traen una mentalidad de
04		pobreza. llegan aquí y se salvan porque la educación es gratis pero después de la high school se
05		quedan atascados. en primer lugar están de acuerdo con un empleo y con el resultado con un
06		empleo y lo que hacen con sus hijos. "lo siento hijo pero tienes que trabajar". segunda generación
07		que va a hacer-> trabajar. tercera generación trabajar-> cuarta generación trabajar trabajar trabajar y así
08		se mantiene mi cultura hispana. y así este papel ((folleto de MDE Latino)) dice creando una nueva
09		cultura-> estamos dando luz en el camino del hispano. hoy en día viven en oscuridad no
10		saben dónde ir y con la economía de hoy en día no saben qué hacer. algunos ya se van a sus países
11		es como estar en un cuarto oscuro y nosotros estamos dando luz. hay un camino que recorrer-> un camino
12		que agarrar-> este es el problema de los hispanos que vienen de una mentalidad de pobreza y se lo creen.
13		yo también vengo de una comunidad de pobreza pero decidí romper esa mentalidad. romperla porque
14		eso no me va a ayudar. la dejo a un lado y agarro otra mentalidad.

01	**Gemma:**	...but in the Latino community of Minnesota, what do you think are the problems that they most
02		commonly live?
03	**Noberto:**	I would say that the problem of the Hispanic people. Because from their country they bring a mentality of
04		poverty. they arrive here and they get saved because education is free but after high school they
05		get stuck. In the first place they agree with an employment and with the consequences of an

Excerpt 3 Interview with Noberto (June 2010) *(continued)*

06	employment and what they do with their kids. "I am sorry son but you have to work". second generation
07	what will they do-> work. third generation work-> fourth generation work work work and this way
08	the same Spanish culture continues. and this paper ((pamphlet of MDE Latino)) says creating a new
09	culture-> we are giving light in the path of the Hispanos. Nowadays they live in the darkness they don't
10	know where to go and with today's economy they don't know what do to. some are living to their countries
11	it's like staying in a dark room and we are giving light. there is a path to cover-> a path
12	to take-> this is the problem of the Hispanos that come with a mentality of poverty and they believe it.
13	I also come from a community of poverty but I decided to break such mentality. to break it because
14	this won't help me. I leave it aside and I take another mentality.

Noberto articulates MDE Latino leaders' stated intentions to educate and liberate (lines 8-9) and uses them to make sense of his own life choices and his own mission. Here, Noberto includes himself as an educator, using first person plural 'we' (line 9). Further, Noberto uses his own experience of coming from a poor community to support MDE Latino's claims that (1) there are options (e.g. poverty, darkness and dependency vs. light and liberty) and (2) that one has the capacity to choose one over the other.

Within Herbarlife 'helping others' is also central message; however, the emphasis is on *ayudar a las personas a llevar una vida activa y más saludable* ('helping people live healthier, active lives'). Patricia embraces this aspect of the business, and recounted many specific instances in which Herbalife products had helped others around her (e.g. cured her husband of sleep apnea, her daughter of the flu and her mother of headaches), thus avoiding expensive professional medical care.

Discussion and Conclusion

MLM involvement was a powerful experience and resulted in some undeniably positive changes in our participants' lives. For instance, Noberto returned to school to complete his GED as a result of his Amway-related church involvement, and Patricia now eats healthily and exercises regularly. These shifts were the direct result of participation in MLM networks, and via those interactions, MLM organizations were more effective than traditional education or medical interventions in influencing behavior and maintaining participation.

Of even greater significance is that both Patricia and Noberto reported feeling markedly more motivated, valued, and optimistic about their futures as a result of their MLM involvement. This is in part because MLM schemes, in some respects, promote personal agency and independence under the guise of 'entrepreneurship'. As a result, within these organizations, both Patricia and Noberto felt respected as capable individuals and up-and-coming professionals. For instance, Patricia was deeply impressed by the dinner offered at one monthly meeting, raving about the elegant tablecloths, water glasses and table service, noting she had never been to such an event in her life. Noberto, in turn, feels highly valued as an entrepreneur when he can teach aspects of the business to new recruits and when he travels to out-of-state Amway conventions. Involvement in MLM companies has allowed them both, for the first time, to feel confident in their business skills and in control of their lives.

Yet these positive changes do not alter the fact that the hierarchical structure of all MLM schemes demands ongoing recruitment of individuals 'downstream' in order to make money and to move up. And despite Amway's claims that one earns what one deserves, the average monthly income for distributors such as Noberto is $115 (Amway, 2011). Further, although MLM schemes promise autonomy and independence, distributors in fact are tightly controlled 'via a particular organizational identity and ideology' (Groβ, 2010: 61). As Whitsell summarizes, 'the primary product is opportunity. The strongest, most powerful motivational force today is false hope' (O'Donnell, 2011).

Thus, despite MLM texts' stated intentions of 'helping' the US Latino community, the primary goal of all leaders is to recruit more 'down line' distributors. MLM discourses of advancement are powerful mechanisms to that end. Noberto, for instance, fully embraced expectations of hard work, Christian commitment, and self-improvement for three years. In June of 2010, he optimistically stated: 'Now I am earning just a bit, but by the end of this year [2010] my goal is to start earning $4000 per month'. However, at the start of 2012, Norberto was still very short on cash, still working in a fast-food restaurant, but also fasting and praying regularly for business success. Similarly, when Patricia started in July 2011, she stated 'I can earn a lot of money in the business....I have just started but there are people who have been there for one year and they are already making $1000 per month'. By January 2012, after seven months with Herbalife, she took a third job to pay the bills and to invest more in Herbalife products. She worried that this extra job meant even less time with her children – a concern that contrasts sharply with MLM claims about greater family time.

As illustrated here, MLM discourses of advancement are powerful, and, they can be particularly persuasive for undocumented Latinos. MLM discourses of advancement are highly effective in part because they are in Spanish (Koslow *et al.*, 1994; Luna & Peracchio, 2001), but also because they recognize participants' life experiences, which often include hardship and sacrifice. The central threads of MLM discourse – i.e. that hard work results in success (independent of one's background), that MLM schemes provide access to education, training and self-improvement while also allowing for family and community advancement and service to others – resonate with Latino participants. As demonstrated above, participants adapt these discourses as they are socialized into MLM culture, but they also modify them to fit their personal experience and life narrative. For individuals with extremely limited educational and professional opportunities, MLM schemes provide the discourse of a means to financial, educational, and social advancement. These schemes – in conjunction with the dysfunctional US immigration system – form a 'perfect storm' for undocumented Latino youth.

Ultimately, MLM discourses, like all discourses, are about power and reflect inequalities in the distribution of social capital. At the most basic level, these discourses serve to attract and entice recruits into the scheme, and in the process convert them to the MLM Christian-free-market worldview. Poignantly, this pro-free-market ideology and ethic of hard work is often embraced by precisely those who are excluded from legal employment and mainstream economic advancement. MLM discourses assert equal opportunities and success for all; yet the foundation of all MLMs is structural inequity that promotes extreme financial disparities. Hypocritically, the MLM leaders who espouse these meritocratic values are, in fact, promoting a system designed to enrich themselves.

Perhaps most troubling is the not-so-subtle rhetoric of personal failure for unsuccessful recruits given that more than half of all MLM distributors quit within their first year (Fitzpatrick & Reynolds, 1997). Indeed, the personal, financial and social costs of MLM investment (and failure) can be high as participation entails changing one's belief systems, aggressively selling to family and friends, thus putting those relationships at risk. For undocumented young adults, dense and supportive social networks can be one of their mostly powerful resources in negotiating the myriad demands of life in the United States. In light of the fact that comprehensive immigration reform seems unlikely for the near future, one can only hope that MLM involvement will not do lasting damage to this most valuable resource.

Notes

(1) In 2007, there were an estimated 7 million unauthorized immigrants from Mexico. In 2010, the number of Mexican unauthorized immigrants had declined to 6.5 million. While the number of Mexicans voluntarily leaving the country has not increased, the inflow has decreased, and the number of Mexican deportation has clearly increased. In the past decade deportations have doubled, and more than 70% of deportees were Mexican in 2009 (Passel & Cohn, 2011).

(2) As defined by US courts, in order to operate legitimately in the US, MLM companies must: (a) 'monitor performance of independent agents to ensure that they really are making retail sales; (b) have buy-back policies in place so that independent contractors do not get stuck with excess product; (c) charge low upfront-fees for the right to market the MLM product; and (d) make purchases of sales training materials completely voluntary' (Koehn, 2001: 156). MLM businesses frequently have faced legal challenges for failing to meet these guidelines. For instance in 2010, Amway was charged with operating as a pyramid scheme in which distributors rarely sell products to outside customers, but only to other new distributors they bring in. In the face of this major class-action lawsuit, Amway agreed to pay $55 million to former distributors as well as to closely oversee high-level distributors who run training businesses.

References

Abrego, L.J. (2006) 'I can't go to college because I don't have papers': Incorporation patterns of Latino undocumented youth. *Latino Studies* 4 (3), 212–231.

Abrego, L.J. and Gonzales, R. (2010) Blocked paths, uncertain futures: The postsecondary education and labor market prospects of undocumented Latino youth. *Journal of Education of Students Placed at Risk* 15, 144–157.

Achieve Magazine (2012) *Glenn and Pam Schoffler*, accessed 6 January 2012. http://www.achievemagazine.com/glenn-and-pam-shoffler.html

Amway (2011) *Business reference guide.* http://www.amway.com/en/ResourceCenter-Documents/Visitor/ops-amw-gde-v-en--BusinessReferenceGuide.pdf

Barnes, S. (2002) Achievement or ascription ideology? An analysis of attitudes about future success for residents in poor urban neighborhoods. *Sociological Focus* 35 (2), 207–225.

Briggs, C. (1993) Metadiscursive practices and scholarly authority in folkloristics. *The Journal of American Folklore* 106 (422), 387–434.

Brodsky, N. (1998) Multilevel mischief. *Inc*, accessed 1 June 1998. http://www.inc.com/magazine/19980601/941.html

Chavez, L.R. (1998) *Shadowed Lives: Undocumented Immigrants in American Society* (1992, 1st edn). New York: Harcourt Brace College Publishers.

Cook, G. (2001) *The Discourse of Advertising* (revised edn). London: Routledge.

Correal, A. (2010) Latino immigrants embrace Herbalife. *Feet in 2 Worlds*, accessed 24 May 2010. http://news.feetintwoworlds.org/2010/05/24/latino-immigrants-embrace-herbalife/

Direct Selling Association (2010) *Fact sheet US direct selling in 2010.* http://www.dsa.org/research/industry-statistics/10gofactsheet.pdf

Du Bois, J.W. (2003) Ritual language. In W.J. Frawley (ed.) *International Encyclopedia of Linguistics* (2nd edn, Vol. 3, pp. 463–465). Oxford: Oxford University Press.

Engelke, M. (2004) Discontinuity and the discourse of *conversion*. *Journal of Religion in Africa* 34 (1), 82–109.

Fitzpatrick, R.L. and Reynolds, J.K. (1997) *False Profits: Seeking Financial and Spiritual Deliverance in Multi-level Marketing and Pyramid Schemes*. Charlotte, NC: Herald Press.

Gee, J.P. (1989) Literacy, discourse, and linguistics: Introduction. *Journal of Education* 17, 5–25.

Georgakopoulou, A. (2007) *Small Stories, Interaction and Identities*. Amsterdam: John Benjamins.

Glycodoc (2010) *Network marketing: The Hispanic market*, accessed 12 January 2012. http://www.youtube.com/watch?v=Cvugp_gts5A

Gonzales, R.G. (2011) Learning to be illegal: Undocumented youth and shifting legal context in the transition to adulthood. *American Sociological Review* 76 (4), 602–619.

Groß, C. (2010) Spiritual cleansing: A case study on how spirituality can be mis/used by a company. *Management Revue* 21 (1), 60–81.

Herbalife Today en Español. (2009) Juan Carlos Igartua. *Herbalife Today Edicion EUA, 142*, 1–44. https://bo.myherbalife.com/Content/es-BO/pdf/home/HOY_CONTENIDO.pdf

Hoefer, M., Rytina, N. and Baker, B.C. (2010) Estimates of the unauthorized immigrant population residing in the United States: January 2009. *Department of Homeland Security*. http://www.dhs.gov/xlibrary/assets/statistics/publications/ois_ill_pe_2009.pdf

Kapchan, D.A.(1995) Performance. *Journal of American Folklore* 108 (430), 479–508.

King, K.A. and Punti, G. (2012) On the margins: Undocumented students' narrated experiences of (il)legality. *Linguistics and Education* 23, 235–249.

Koehn, D. (2001) Ethical issues connected with multi-level marketing schemes. *Journal of Business Ethics* 29, 153–160.

Korzenny, F. and Korzenny, B.A. (2005) *Hispanic Marketing: A Cultural Perspective*. Burlington, MA: Elsevier Butterworth-Heinemann.

Koslow, S., Shamdasani, P.N. and Touchstone, E.E. (1994) Exploring language effects in ethnic advertising: A sociolinguistic perspective. *Journal of Consumer Research* 20 (4), 575–585.

Luna, D. and Peracchio, L.A. (2001) Moderators of language effects in advertising to bilinguals: A psycholinguistic approach. *Journal of Consumer Research* 28 (2), 284–295.

National Consumer League (2009) More bad economic news: Recession putting consumers at increased risk of being duped by pyramid schemes, accessed 26 February 2009. http://www.nclnet.org/newsroom/press-releases/260-more-bad-economic-news-recession-putting-consumers-at-increased-risk-of-being-duped-by-pyramid-schemes

O'Donnell, J. (2011) Multilevel marketing or 'pyramid'? Sales people find it hard to earn much. *USAToday* (Gannett Company), accessed 10 February 2011. http://www.usatoday.com/money/industries/retail/2011-02-07-multilevelmarketing03_CV_N.htm

Passel, J.S. (2005) Background briefing prepared for task force on immigration and America's future. *Unauthorized Migrants: Numbers and Characteristics*. Pew Hispanic Center. http://pewhispanic.org/files/reports/46.pdf
Passel, J.S. (2011) Demography of immigrant youth: Past, present, and future. *The Future of Children* 21 (1), 19–41.
Passel, J.S. and Cohn, D. (2011) *Unauthorized Immigrant Population: National and State Trends, 2010*. Washington DC: Pew Research Center.
Passel, J.S. and Cohn, V. (2009) *A Portrait of Unauthorized Immigrants in the United States*. Washington, DC: Pew Hispanic Center.
Santos, J. (2012) *The spider will follow you: Evangelical Salvadoran perspectives on US immigration*. Talk at the University of Minnesota, Global REM Seminars, Minneapolis, MN.
Silverstein, M. and Urban, G. (eds) (1996) *Natural Histories of Discourse*. Chicago: University of Chicago Press.
Singh, N., Baack, D.W., Kundu, S.K. and Hurtado, C. (2008) U.S. Hispanic consumer e-commerce preferences: Expectations and attitudes toward web content. *Journal of Electronic Commerce Research* 9 (2), 162–175.
Suárez-Orozco, C. and Suárez-Orozco, M. (1995) *Transformations: Immigration, Family Life, and Achievement Motivation Among Latino Adolescents*. Stanford, CA: Stanford University Press.
SusanaaRamirezz (2009) *Antonio & Juanita Maldonado…diamantes*, accessed 15 January 2012. http://www.myspace.com/video/susanaaramirezz/antonio-juanita-maldonado-diamantes/59594760
Urciuoli, B. (2010) Entextualizing diversity: Semiotic incoherence in institutional discourse. *Language & Communication* 30, 48–57.
Van Druff, D. (1990) What's wrong with multi-level marketing? accessed 2 January 2012. http://www.vandruff.com/mlm.html
Vigouroux, C.V. (2009) The making of a scription: A case study on authority and authorship. *Text & Talk* 29 (5), 615–637.

Appendix: Transcription conventions

CAPS	spoken with emphasis (minimum unit is morpheme)
.	falling intonation at the end of words
,	rising intonation at the end of words
?	rising intonation in clause
->	continuing or flat intonation (as in lists)
!	animated tone, not necessarily an exclamation
[ ]	implicit information
+/…	interruption (self or other)
::	elongated sound
" "	reported speech
(( ))	transcriber's comment

7 Education Policy, Citizenship and Linguistic Sovereignty in Native America

Teresa L. McCarty

> A sovereign nation defines itself and its citizens, exercises self-government and the right to treat with other nations, applies its jurisdiction over the internal legal affairs of its citizens..., claims political jurisdiction over the lands within its borders, and may define certain rights that inhere in its citizens....American Indian tribes are sovereign nations.
> (Wilkins & Lomawaima, 2001: 4)

What does it mean to participate fully as a 'citizen' in Native America, and what are the implications for access and rights to language and education? How do language policies – formal and informal – influence these rights, and how do those policies interface with the exercise of tribal sovereignty? This chapter explores these questions, critically examining the contours of the contested terrain of citizenship, sovereignty and language-in-education policies in Native American communities. I begin with the premise that these issues cannot be understood separately from the understanding that Native American peoples 'occupy a distinctive political/legal status' within the United States (Wilkins & Lomawaima, 2001: 8). Unlike other US ethnolinguistic groups, Native Americans possess a unique nation-to-nation relationship with the federal government. That relationship dates back to the European invasion, is both constitutional and extra-constitutional and recognizes the inherent sovereignty of Native nations. As we will see, the tribal–federal relationship has frequently been one of colliding interests; it is, as Wilkins and Lomawaima (2001) write, 'uneven ground'.

The second premise is that the conjoined projects of language policy and education have been (and are) principal sites in which the battle over sovereignty has been waged. Nearly 40 years ago legal scholar Arnold Leibowitz argued that language is not merely a means of communication but is more fundamentally a means of social control. Reflecting on the history of US language policy, Leibowitz contended that its basic purpose has been to 'exclude from access to power' and 'control by exclusion and limitation' those deemed to be 'irreconcilably alien' and linguistically 'dissident' (1974: 3).

I come to this discussion as a vested outsider, a native English-speaking educator, anthropologist, and 'allied other' (Kaomea, 2004). My earliest encounters with these issues, some 30 years ago, landed me squarely on the 'uneven ground' of American Indian community-controlled schooling, described later in this chapter. An outgrowth and expression of a growing American Indian self-determination movement, this then-radical education project shattered centuries of exclusionary education practices, promising full and equal access to an uplifting, quality education based on pedagogic practices that valorize Indigenous knowledges and languages in their own right and as tools for student empowerment. I quickly came to appreciate, however, the gloved and strangulating hand of the federal bureaucracy, as it sought to police this revolutionary movement (McCarty, 2002). In the years that followed, I have worked closely with Native American educators and communities on the self-determination initiatives that inhere in tribal sovereignty – in particular bilingual-bicultural education and the repatriation of endangered mother tongues through community-driven language revitalization.

In the pages that follow, I explore the tensions and possibilities within this rough and rutted linguistic, cultural, political and pedagogic terrain. The chapter begins with a brief overview of the confounding forces underlying citizenship and sovereignty in Native America, focusing on language policy in education. I then introduce safety zone theory, a framework formulated by Lomawaima (2002, 2012) and developed in our work together (Lomawaima & McCarty, 2002, 2006), which helps us understand the tug and pull between sovereigns – Native nations and the US government – as that contest has been waged in the field of Native American education. Using safety zone theory, Lomawaima and I propose that these political processes construct a social, psychological and pedagogic space intended to domesticate Native American cultural difference, using educational language policy as a mechanism of social control. As will be discussed, these processes continue in current English-only standardizing regimes. I then examine two language-in-education projects – Native American community-controlled schooling and Indigenous language revitalization – drawing on my long-term work with Navajo (Diné) communities and schools. The Navajo case illuminates the ways in which safety zone boundaries have been ruptured as Indigenous communities have carved out new spaces for the exercise of linguistic and education rights. However, equally the data presented here spotlight what Foucault (1991) called the problems of governmentality: the power-linked bureaucratic structures and discourses that manipulate, manage and patrol the exercise of those rights. These contested power relations, Luke et al. (1990) observe, foreground fundamental questions of whose language is being planned, '"for whom", "by whom" and "by what"', leading us to larger issues of identity, self-determination and decolonization (1990: 41; see also Blum Martinez, 2000). I conclude with a discussion of these issues and their implications for 'full citizenship', access through equitable policy processes, and the realization of Indigenous linguistic and educational sovereignty.

Tribal Sovereignty and the Multiple Citizenships of Native American Peoples

The term Native American encompasses diverse American Indian, Alaska Native and Native Hawaiian peoples. As peoples, each group has encountered the US sociopolitical and educational system in distinct ways, but all are descendants of the original inhabitants of what is now the United States, and, 'irrespective of their legal status, retain some or all of their own social, economic, cultural and political institutions' – the internationally recognized definition of Indigenous peoples (International Labour Organization [ILO], 2009: 9).

There are certain internationally recognized rights to language and education that attend the ILO definition above, most notably Articles 13 and 14 of the 2007 United Nations *Declaration on the Rights of Indigenous Peoples*:

> Indigenous peoples have the right to revitalize, use, develop and transmit to future generations their histories, languages, oral traditions, philosophies, writing systems and literatures...[and] to es*tablish and control their educational systems and institutions providing education in their own languages.* (United Nations General Assembly, 2007, Articles 13[1] and 14[1, 3]; emphases added)

This is a clear statement of language education policy. Even more germane to the present analysis is the principle of tribal sovereignty: the 'right of a people to self-government, self-determination and self-education', including the right to linguistic and cultural expression according to local languages and norms (Lomawaima & McCarty, 2006: 10). Like the sovereignty of US states and the federal government, tribal sovereignty is not absolute; the political realities of tribal-federal-state relations, 'competing jurisdictions, local histories, circumscribed land bases and overlapping citizenships' all constrain, but do not negate, the exercise of sovereignty (Wilkins & Lomawaima, 2001: 5). Examples of tribes' sovereign powers include 'the right to determine their membership, administer justice through tribal courts, govern their citizens and regulate the use of their land base' (Lomawaima & McCarty, 2006: 10).

Sovereignty is inherent, and therefore predates the US constitution (Wilkins & Lomawaima, 2001). Tribal sovereignty is also recognized in treaties, case law, and the US Constitution, which grants Congress the power to regulate commerce with foreign nations and tribes, and authorizes the US President to negotiate treaties with foreign nations and Indian nations. Between 1779 and 1871, the US government signed more than 400 treaties with American Indian tribes, of which 120 had education stipulations. Through those treaties, Native peoples relinquished certain rights and possessions – most critically, land – in exchange for certain federal guarantees (e.g. education and other social services). This is the basis of the tribal-federal relationship; it is a legally and morally codified relationship of binding *trust responsibility* on the part of the federal government. The trust responsibility is both voluntary and contractual, and entails 'the notion of federal responsibility to *protect or enhance* tribal assets (including fiscal, natural, human and cultural resources) through policy decisions and management actions' (Wilkins & Lomawaima, 2001: 65; emphasis in original). The reality underlying this singular political relationship, Wilkins and Lomawaima emphasize, 'is the transfer of land from tribes to the United States. The United States did not "give" tribes rights or lands. Tribes possessed both' (2001: 250–251).

Over the years, the federal government has repeatedly violated its trust responsibility, and tribal and federal powers have frequently been at odds. For example, the Civil War-era Reconstruction Congress voted to exclude American Indians from the citizenship clauses of the 1866 Civil Rights Act and the Fourteenth Amendment on the grounds that, in one US senator's words, 'Our dealings with the Indians are with them as…separate nations.…[The Fourteenth Amendment] is not intended to include them' (cited in Anderson, 2007: 250). Through discursive practices such as this, Native people were produced as 'dis-citizens' (Ramanathan, 2010: 7) – a non-White-normative citizenship embodied in their indigeneity and justifying their exclusion from federal citizenship guarantees.

It was not until 1924 that Native Americans were officially declared US citizens, but the federal legislation through which this occurred (the Indian Citizenship Act of 1924) did not guarantee suffrage rights, including the right to vote. The State of Maine, for example, did not extend voting rights to Native Americans until 1953; Arizona withheld voting rights from Native people until 1948 and Utah withheld those rights until 1957. Even as thousands of Native Americans were serving in the US military during World War II, including the famed Navajo Code Talkers whose use of Navajo to relay Allied military strategies secured the Allied victory in the Pacific, many were legally prohibited by their state of residence from voting. Eventually, as Native people became 'naturalized' as US citizens, state and federal citizenship 'were "layered" onto their tribal citizenship'; Native Americans thus possess multiple, overlapping citizenships (Wilkins & Lomawaima, 2001: 147).

Further pitting the uneven ground of tribal sovereignty is the fact that not all tribes are recognized as sovereigns by their resident states; conversely, some are recognized by states but not by the federal government, and some – such as many Native California peoples – have been denied recognition as sovereigns by both states and the federal government, thereby disenfranchising them from trust-related government services. Native Hawaiians, whose internationally recognized sovereign kingdom was illegally overthrown by the US government in 1893 and who were not officially incorporated into the US system until Hawaiian statehood in 1959, are still fighting for federal recognition of their sovereign status.

That the trust responsibility has been abrogated by the trustee does not invalidate its binding legality and morality, nor does it vitiate the principle of tribal sovereignty. Native American peoples have in the past and continue to vigorously exercise their inherent sovereign rights. 'This is the essence of an indigenous vision of trust', Wilkins and Lomawaima maintain (2001: 97). It is nevertheless the case, as Brayboy (2005) points out, that this vision is frequently ignored, misunderstood or assaulted by dominant social actors: 'The racialized status of American Indians appears to be the main emphasis of most members of US society; this status ignores the legal/political one, and is directly tied to notions of colonialism, because the larger society is unaware of the multiple statuses of Indigenous peoples' (2006: 433).

Language Education Policy as an Arbiter of 'Safe' vs. 'Dangerous' Cultural Difference

Nowhere has the push and pull of sovereigns – Native nations and the US government – been more apparent than in the linked domains of language and education. Beginning in the early 19th century, Native students were subjected to a federal policy that forcibly removed them from their homes and communities to distant boarding schools where they endured 'the continual verbal assault and denigration' of their home languages and cultures (Benally & Viri, 2005: 90). 'While trust responsibility and sovereignty were supposed to be the guiding principles of Indian education', Brayboy notes, '"appropriate" education was assumed to be that which eradicated Indianness or promoted Anglo values and ways of communicating' (2005: 437). Federal Indian schools literally operated on the backs of Native students, whose manual labor in the kitchens, boiler rooms, and fields allowed the government to feed students on a budget of 11 cents per pupil per day ('the minimum standard of health and decency for growing children was determined to be 33 cents' at the time, Lomawaima observes [personal communication, 4/5/12; see also Meriam *et al.* (1928)]). The prescribed *Uniform Course of Study* was 'filled with minutiae calculated to fit Natives to the right level in America's laboring classes' (Lomawaima & McCarty, 2006: 53).

Lomawaima and I (2006) propose a theory of the safety zone to explain these policy processes and their pedagogic entailments. We conceive of the safety zone as a physical, social, psychological and pedagogic space in which the federal government and other colonizing agents have deliberately and systematically sought to distinguish 'safe' from 'dangerous' Indigenous cultural beliefs and practices:

Drawing the boundaries between safe and dangerous cultural difference and illuminating the safety zone of [US] national culture lie at the heart of [the] history of American Indian education....Which Native beliefs and practices might be judged safe, innocuous, and tolerable? Which Native beliefs and practices are too dangerous, different, and subversive of mainstream values? How best to manage or eradicate dangerous cultural expression? (Lomawaima & McCarty, 2006: 5)

Specifically, when Indigenous linguistic and cultural differences have been viewed by dominant interests as instrumental or non-threatening – as they were during early colonial encounters when European missionaries found knowledge of Indigenous languages to be essential to achieving their evangelizing aims – those differences have been tolerated and even supported in official and unofficial ways. 'Dangerous' expressions of Native difference – manifest, for example, in the presence of thousands of Native-speaking children in 19th and early 20th century federal schools – have been systematically repressed. So, in the case of the boarding schools –

Native individuals...were being fitted into an American 'safety zone' of obedient citizenry and innocent cultural difference. Parameters of the safety zone corresponded to relations of power: safe citizens were part of a subservient proletariat, and safe cultural differences were controlled by non-Native federal, Christian and social agencies that could proclaim themselves benefactors dedicated to 'preserving' Native life. (Lomawaima & McCarty, 2006: 49)

Safety zone theory is graphically represented in Figure 7.1. With few exceptions, the aim of federal Indian education policy has historically been to circumscribe and contain Indigenous cultural and linguistic difference within the manageable boundaries demarcated by the metaphoric safety zone. For example, whereas earlier mission schools, with their overriding aim of Christianization by whatever means possible, often taught in the Native language, prohibitions against speaking Indigenous languages in federal boarding schools were fiercely enforced. 'The language issue, which had received little [prior] attention, now was mentioned in almost every [federal] report concerned with Indian education', Leibowitz observes (1974: 17; for an example, see the 1887 report of then-Commissioner of Indian Affairs J.D.C. Atkins, 'Barbarous Dialects Should Be Blotted Out' [Atkins, 1887]). 'Language became a critical element' in federal Indian education policy, and 'English-language instruction and the abandonment of the native language became complementary means to the end' (Leibowitz, 1974: 17).

But it would be a gross misrepresentation to portray Native American language education solely from a colonialist, top-down perspective; this direction of influence is only part of the story (cf. Erickson, 2004: 190). Native peoples have never been passive recipients of oppressive federal policies; like all social-political processes, the interactions between tribes and

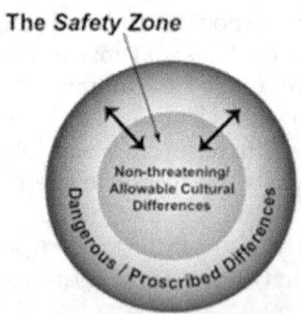

Figure 7.1 Safety zone theory applied to Native American language education

the federal government operate through complex, situated networks of agency and power. These agentive processes are depicted in Figure 7.1 by the fuzziness of safety zone boundaries and by arrows signifying the push-and-pull of sovereign agents from within and without. In the remainder of this chapter, I interrogate the architecture of the safety zone, focusing on two complementary language-in-education projects: American Indian community-controlled schooling and the movement to reclaim endangered Indigenous mother tongues.

'Control of Education is a Natural and Inherent Right': American Indian Community-controlled Schooling

One unintended consequence of the boarding school system was the forging of an alliance of Native American peoples from diverse cultural communities, who grew up together in the schools and who, in the context of the 1960s–1970s Civil Rights Movement and the American Indian Movement (a national movement demanding restoration of abrogated treaty rights), joined with tribal leaders and other activists to press for tribal sovereignty: 'self-government, self-determination and self-education' (Lomawaima & McCarty, 2006: 116; see also Lomawaima, 2012). During the latter part of the 20th century, this Civil Rights activism led to a constellation of federal policy victories, including the 1964 Civil Rights Act, the 1964 Economic Opportunity Act, the 1965 Elementary and Secondary Education Act (ESEA), the 1968 Bilingual Education Act, the 1972 Indian Education Act and the 1975 Indian Education and Self-Determination Act. (For a detailed discussion of these laws as they relate to Native American education, see Lomawaima and McCarty, 2006; McCarty, 1993, 2002; and Reyhner & Eder, 2004). Among other transformations in tribal-federal relations, out of these political conquests came the first American Indian community-controlled schools.

In this context, the Navajo (*Diné*, The People) Nation emerged as the epicenter of the late-twentieth century American Indian community-controlled school movement. With 300,048 enrolled citizens, the Navajo Nation today comprises nearly 7% of the American Indian/Alaska Native population (Donovan, 2011). The US Census Bureau (2010) reports almost as many speakers of Navajo (170,822) as all other Native American languages combined (203,127). The Navajo Nation also controls the largest Indigenous land base in the United States: 27,000 square miles of high plateau, canyonlands and forested mountain ranges stretching across northern Arizona and New Mexico and into southern Utah.

In the mid-1960s, the majority of the Navajo Nation remained largely Navajo speaking, with Spolsky's (1975) Navajo Reading Study reporting 90% of 3500 six-year-olds to be Navajo-English bilinguals or monolingual speakers of Navajo. As Spolsky summarized the study's findings: 'our survey showed that over two-thirds of the children would be in serious trouble faced, as nearly all were, with a monolingual English teacher' (1975: 348).

On September 12, 1966, the situation of monolingual English schooling for Navajo students began to change when, in the small (population 1300) reservation-interior community of Rough Rock, Arizona, the first American Indian community-controlled school opened its doors to 220 elementary students (McCarty, 2002: 83). An outgrowth of Civil Rights initiatives and a unique contract between a locally elected all-Navajo school board, the Bureau of Indian Affairs (BIA), the Office of Economic Opportunity and a tribal nonprofit organization called DINÉ, Inc. ('Demonstration in Navajo Education'), the Rough Rock Demonstration School (*Tsé Ch'ízhí Diné Bi'ólta'* – Rough Rock The People's School) was explicitly positioned as an agent of community empowerment. Its mission combined economic development, bilingual-bicultural instruction and Navajo control of Navajo education (for more on the school's beginnings, see Collier, 1988; Johnson, 1968; McCarty, 2002; and Roessel, 1977). Soon, other Navajo communities began pressing the federal government to run their own schools. As Kathryn Manuelito explains this political process for Ramah, a small Navajo 'satellite' reservation on the eastern edge of the main Navajo reservation: 'A few courageous, nonformally educated Navajo elders and a recent high school graduate traveled to Washington, D.C. to request funding for a school in their community' (Manuelito, 2005: 77). Manuelito, a native of Ramah who taught in and directed the school's bilingual-bicultural program, describes what happened next:

> When their demands were ignored, Bertha Lorenzo, a frail elder, threw her blanket down in the doorway of the BIA building and said she wouldn't leave until they were granted aid. Thus, on April 20, 1970 [the US Commissioner of Indian Affairs] approved funding for the Ramah Navajo High School, the first Navajo community-controlled secondary school. (2005: 77)

Within a few years there were six Navajo community-controlled schools, sparking a flurry of 'counterpoised' top-down and bottom-up language planning and policy initiatives (cf. López, 2008). Working at the national level, school leaders at Rough Rock and other community-controlled schools pushed successfully for passage of the 1972 Indian Education Act and the 1975 Indian Self-Determination and Educational Assistance Act (discussed above), which authorized, respectively, American Indian bilingual-bicultural education programs (including curriculum development, teacher preparation and parent involvement), and the legal mechanism by which tribes and Native communities could contract to run their own schools and social services. With this legislation in place, new 'implementational space' (Hornberger, 2002, 2006) opened for other Native American communities to establish community-based schools. During this time the first tribally controlled college, Navajo Community College opened 15 miles from Rough Rock (it is now called Diné College and was relocated to Tsaile, Arizona, about 50 miles from Rough Rock), prying open further implementational space for passage of the Tribally Controlled Colleges and Universities Assistance Act in 1978. Today, there are 35 tribal colleges/universities and 122 community-controlled schools.

As these projects got under way, in each case 'there...needed to be material and curriculum development and the use and training of...native speakers' (Spolsky, 1974: 62). With the goal of producing a thousand Navajo bilingual teachers in five years, the newly established Navajo Division of Education (initially headed by Rough Rock's second director, Dillon Platero) began delivering university-accredited courses at reservation schools and providing graduate training for Navajo school administrators (Read *et al.*, 1975: 5). Rough Rock educators established the Diné Bi'ólta' Association (Navajo [The People's] School Association), out of which 'came many materials on Navajo language and culture and much refinement on Navajo-related curricula' (Silentman, 1995: 10). In 1967, Rough Rock founded the Navajo Curriculum Center, the first Native American publishing house. A few years later, a consortium of Navajo community-controlled schools established the Native American Materials Development Center. Together, these and other 'bottom-up' language planning efforts (Hornberger, 1996) produced hundreds of high-quality language teaching materials, many of which are still in use today.

The radical challenge to safety zone boundaries represented by these projects cannot be overstated. 'People were shocked when we suggested using Navajo...in the school to learn', said Agnes Dodge Holm, cofounder of one of the first Navajo literacy projects (McCarty, 2002: 113). 'Before Rough Rock', explained her husband Wayne Holm, also a leader in the movement, 'the notion that you have to have community-responsive curricula, or...some form of [community] empowerment...it was just literally unthinkable'

(McCarty, 2002: 123). 'We planted the seeds...of Indian self-determination', former Rough Rock school board president Ernest Dick reflected in a 1997 interview (McCarty, 2002: 195). Those seeds came to fruition in what Agnes and Wayne Holm have described as a 'four-fold empowerment' consisting of new forms of community leadership, a corps of Native educators, the active participation of parents in their children's schooling, and the academic success of students 'who came to value their Navajo-ness and to see themselves as capable of succeeding because of, not despite that Navajo-ness' (Holm & Holm, 1990: 182–184).

Taken together, these emancipatory processes expanded safety zone boundaries in multifarious ways, even as those processes collided with monumental safety zone barriers. Chief among the latter was a federal bureaucracy and school funding system that stifled self-determination at every turn. Unlike off-reservation public schools, Indigenous community schools must rely on congressional appropriations for virtually all their funding. This obligation is entailed by the federal trust relationship, but is equally a consequence of economic injustice and marginalized reservation economies. Also unlike more affluent, off-reservation school districts, Indigenous community-controlled schools operate as independent units, providing all education services – from transportation to paper and pens to employee salaries – from a single local budget. The costs of these largely rural schools are significantly higher yet their infrastructure support is much more limited. And their budgets are highly volatile, dependent upon annual congressional appropriations, which are deeply politicized.

For years, community-controlled schools were enmeshed in protracted, time- and labor-intensive budget negotiations. It was typical for school budgets to be finalized months after the school year began, stalling staff hiring and even the purchase of basic school supplies, and keeping school leaders at distant federally orchestrated budget meetings instead of at school when the academic year began. These realities forced school leaders to knit together instructional programs from disparate and often conflicting federal programs, resulting in chronic programmatic volatility and staff turnover, and contributing to ongoing academic inequities for Native students (for an extended discussion, see McCarty, 2002: chap. 5).

According to official government rhetoric, these volatile conditions were to be ameliorated by a forward-funding provision introduced in the 1988 Elementary and Secondary School Improvement Amendments to the ESEA. Yet this legislation contained a crucial 'catch': Eligibility for forward funding (called 'grant status') required community-controlled schools to tailor their instructional programs to externally imposed standards, locking these schools into a system of federal constraint and control (McCarty, 2002: 164). In recent years those requirements have been dramatically intensified with the 2001 ESEA reauthorization known as No Child Left Behind (NCLB, discussed later in this chapter).

Thus, Indigenous community-controlled schools have been forced onto the rocky ground of high-stakes English-only 'accountability'. For a time at Rough Rock, this resulted in the near elimination of its seminal, academically proven bilingual-bicultural education program. But Rough Rock has not been alone; as Wyman *et al.* (2010a) document in their work with Alaska Native communities, NCLB acts as a de facto language policy, intensifying hegemonic ideologies that the Native language 'will "hold children back" from academic achievement in English' and wreaking 'damaging effects on [Indigenous] language programs' (2010a: 44; see also McCarty *et al.*, 2012; Menken, 2008; and Wyman *et al.*, 2010b). Analyzing the cascading negative consequences of this policy for Indigenous communities whose languages are already endangered, Wyman and her colleagues note that, 'In...some cases, these effects are extending out of schools into family life, disrupting processes of intergenerational language maintenance' (2010a: 44).

The community-controlled school movement has thus proven to be a testing ground for the impact of formal and informal language policies on Native American linguistic and educational sovereignty. As I have described elsewhere (McCarty, 2002), it has been a 'two-faced' movement: On the one hand, community-controlled schools represent a grass roots revolution in which the unimaginable 'became doable' (Pfeiffer, 1993), empowering Native American parents, educators, students and communities. On the other hand, the schools' financial survivability pits them and their personnel against relentless federal surveillance, the most recent manifestation of which is the NCLB Act of 2001. This raises what Luke *et al.* call the 'kernel issue' in language-in-education planning: '"Whose language" is...taken as a norm for teaching and use, and to what end?' (1990: 31).

Yet there can be no doubt that Native American community-controlled schools remain one of the most significant and resilient education counter-movements of the past century. As Dorothy Small, a member of the Rocky Boy (Montana) Community School Board, testified to a national commission charged with investigating federal Indian education policy in 1976, 'Our people believe that control of education is a natural and inherent right' (American Indian Policy Review Commission, 1976: 261). Though still embattled, more than three decades after the commission filed its report, that right stands as a concrete embodiment of tribal sovereignty.

'It is the *Students*' Language, Culture and Heritage': Language Reclamation and Public Schooling

When I began working at the Rough Rock Demonstration School (now called Rough Rock Community School) in the 1980s, virtually all of Rough Rock's 600 students entered school speaking Navajo as a primary language. Today, despite a long history of bilingual education, Rough Rock teachers estimate that as few as two or three in 10 of their students enter school with conversational proficiency in Navajo.

Language endangerment is a growing crisis facing Indigenous and minoritized communities around the world. (For more on this, see Austin and Sallabank, 2011). At the turn of the 21st century, the linguist Michael Krauss (1998) estimated that of the 210 Native North American languages still spoken in the United States and Canada, only 34 were being acquired as primary languages by children. Recent US census data indicate that only 5.4% of individuals living within American Indian/Alaska Native residential areas (reservations and villages) self-identify as speakers of a Native American language; of these speakers, most are elderly (Siebens & Julian, 2011: 3).[1] The disquieting reality is that even as more Native children enter school speaking English, they are subjected to school labeling practices that stigmatize their English as 'non-standard' and in need of remediation. As we have seen, this subtractive view of children's cognitive and linguistic abilities has a long and ugly history in Native American education and is a prime cause of both language loss and academic disparities.

In this ideological and pedagogical environment, the US Congress enacted the only extant official federal language policy: the Native American Languages Act (NALA) of 1990/1992. NALA upturns past federal Indian policy, authorizing programs to 'encourage and support the use of Native American languages as media of instruction in order to encourage and support Native American language survival, educational opportunity, increased student success and performance,…and increased student and community pride' (NALA, 1990, Sect. 104[3]). Was NALA simply a fortuitous 'swing' in federal Indian policy? Or was it, as some suggest, merely a symbolic gesture of little consequence now that Native American languages are no longer perceived as 'dangerous' or threatening to the White English-speaking status quo?

As Lomawaima and I have written, the latter interpretation is both inaccurate and misleading, for NALA represents a crucial breakthrough in a larger fight for self-determination and linguistic human rights (Lomawaima & McCarty, 2006: 136–137). Drafted and propelled through Congress by citizens of diverse Native American communities, 'NALA was the product of Indigenous vision, intent, and design' (Lomawaima & McCarty, 2006: 136). The result 'was a new resource for language revitalization that... embodies the voices of Native peoples' (McCarty & Warhol, 2011: 136). In 2006, NALA was augmented by the Esther Martinez Native American Languages Preservation Act (EM-NALPA), which provides for Native-language immersion preschools and early education programs, language classes for parents, language survival schools and programs to prepare language teachers and instructional materials (EM-NALPA, Sec. 2[C][iv]).

The remainder of this section takes up the grass roots revitalization movement embodied in NALA and EM-NALPA. Revitalization projects have taken many forms, depending upon community histories, extant sociolinguistic resources, and the desires and needs of diverse Native peoples (for a sample of these projects, see Hinton and Hale, 2001; McCarty & Zepeda, 2006; Reyhner & Lockard, 2009; and Romero-Little et al., 2011). School-based revitalization is but one option among many, and among school-based projects there is tremendous heterogeneity in pedagogy and curriculum design (see, e.g. Coronel-Molina & McCarty, 2011 and McCarty, 2013: chap. 5). Here I explore two Navajo public school projects, one within the Navajo Nation and the other in a city of moderate size not far from the reservation. Each is traversing new ground in negotiating language policies in schools (cf. Menken & García, 2010), as well as new ground for what it means to be a citizen of a Native American nation, the United States, and the world. I begin with Tséhootsooí Diné Bi'ólta', The Navajo School at the Meadow Between the Rocks, or the Fort Defiance Navajo Immersion School.

'Navajo Immersion Gave Students Navajo Pride': Tséhootsooí Diné Bi'ólta'

A century-and-a-half ago, Fort Defiance, Arizona was the epicenter of Anglo-American violence perpetrated against Navajo people. Prior to Anglo intrusion, this place, which Navajos call *Tséhootsooí* – Meadow Between the Rocks – was traditionally a popular grazing area for Navajo horses and sheep. By 1851 it had become the first US military post in what is now the State of Arizona (Lapahie, 2001). For the next decade, Navajo families and US troops co-existed there uneasily. Then, in the fall of 1863, Colonel Kit Carson and his companies occupied the fort as a base for carrying out a scorched earth campaign, destroying Navajo corn and wheat fields, inciting other tribes to raid Navajo livestock, and forcing Navajo families to flee their homes.

By the following spring, starvation and desperate circumstances led thousands of Navajos to give themselves up to the troops at Fort Defiance, and from there to trek by foot and ox cart to a concentration camp 300 miles eastward at Fort Sumner, New Mexico (Lapahie, 2011; Underhill, 1956). Hundreds of people died on the Long Walk to Fort Sumner (called *Hwéeldi* by Navajos), and, during their incarceration there, thousands more succumbed to starvation and foreign-borne diseases. To speak of this place still brings tears to people's eyes (for personal accounts of the Long Walk period, see Johnson & Roessel, 1973). Finally, in 1868, a treaty was signed, promising, among other things, a schoolhouse and teacher for every 30 Navajo children between the ages of six and 16 (Link, 1968: 7). Four years later, the first federal boarding school for Navajos opened at the original Fort Defiance military base (Link, 1968: 19).

Fort Defiance is both a physical site and a symbol of genocide – quite literally the center of the federal safety zone. It is also 'crushing proof' of the federal abrogation of trust (Wilkins & Lomawaima, 2001: 87). The historic significance of this place makes contemporary language reclamation efforts there equally symbolic and momentous.

By the mid-1980s – just a few generations after the treaty-signing – Fort Defiance had grown into a small town whose location adjacent to the tribal headquarters at Window Rock, Arizona and 30 miles from the reservation border town of Gallup, New Mexico regularized contact with English speakers. These social and physical transformations, alongside the legacy of compulsory English-only schooling, are reflected in children's linguistic repertoires; increasingly, children growing up in border town situations such as Fort Defiance speak English as a primary (and sometimes only) language.

In response to the loss of Navajo speaking ability among younger generations, in 1986 the Window Rock Unified School District launched a voluntary Navajo language immersion program at Fort Defiance Elementary School. At the time, fewer than one in 20 kindergarten and first grade students were considered 'reasonably fluent' in Navajo; a third were judged to have passive knowledge of the language (Arviso & Holm, 2001: 204; Holm & Holm, 1995: 148). According to program cofounders Marie Arviso and Wayne Holm, 'even those children who spoke some Navajo were reluctant to do so in public' (2001: 204–205). At the same time, many Fort Defiance students had been labeled 'limited English proficient' on the basis of their performance on English standardized tests. 'We said that in an environment which tended to devalue Navajoness, we wanted to help these children experience success in school *through* Navajo', Arviso and Holm write; '[w]e said that by the end of the fifth grade, these students not only would be doing as well academically as those children instructed only in English, but they would also have come to talk, understand, read, and write Navajo' (2001: 205)

In 2003, the district's Navajo immersion classrooms were consolidated at a single school, now called Tséhootsooí Diné Bi'ólta' (hereafter TDB). In kindergarten and first grade, all instruction, including initial literacy, takes place in Navajo. English is introduced in second grade and gradually increased until a 50-50 distribution is attained by grade 6. Florian Tom Johnson and Jennifer Legatz, who were instrumental to the program's expansion, explain that it affords 'maximum exposure to the Diné language...to provide for the greatest effect on acquiring (and instilling) the Diné language (heritage language) as a second language' (Johnson & Legatz, 2006: 27). Parents enroll their children at TDB, Johnson and Legatz say, 'in hopes that the Diné language could be revitalized within their families through these children' (2006: 30). TDB's curriculum integrates Navajo tribal standards for language and culture with those required by the state, and the school as a whole emphasizes a 'Diné language and culture rich environment...including lunch room, playground, hallways and the bus' (Johnson & Legatz, 2006: 30).

Longitudinal data from TDB show that the benefits to language revitalization have not come at the cost of children's English language learning or academic achievement. To the contrary, Navajo immersion students consistently outperform their peers in English-only classrooms on local and standardized assessments of English reading, writing, and mathematics, while also developing strong Navajo oral language and literacy skills (Holm & Holm, 1995; Johnson & Legatz, 2006; McCarty, 2003; Romero-Little & McCarty, 2006). Moreover, adds Wayne Holm, 'What the children and their parents taught us was that Navajo immersion gave students Navajo pride' (2006: 33).

'We're fighting for our kids to have the right to learn their language!': Puente de Hózhǫ́ Trilingual Magnet School

In the fall of 2009, with Arizona State University Professor Bryan M.J. Brayboy, I began a two-year ethnographic study of a trilingual K-5 public magnet school in northern Arizona.[2] Part of a larger national study investigating the role of Native languages and cultures in Native American students' academic achievement (McCarty, 2012), we were drawn to this school because of its unique Diné-Spanish-English program and its successful record of meeting state and federal policy mandates. Called Puente de Hózhǫ́, the school's name combines the Spanish *puente de* ('bridge of') and the Navajo *hózhó*, meaning beauty or harmony. In English, this is Bridge of

Beauty School. According to school cofounder Michael Fillerup, the name 'mirrors the vision of the school: to build bridges of beauty between the rich languages and cultures of the American Southwest' (2008, para 1).

To do this, the school offers a conventional dual immersion program in which native Spanish-speaking and native English-speaking students are taught jointly for a half-day in each language, and 'one-way' Navajo immersion in which English-dominant Navajo students are taught in their heritage language. In the latter program, kindergartners receive approximately 80% of their instruction in Navajo, with English instructional time gradually increased until a 50/50 balance is attained in grades four and five. All required state standards are taught in either Navajo and English or Spanish and English. In a school district in which 26% of students are American Indian (mostly Diné) and 21% are Latino/a, 'local educators were searching for innovative ways to bridge the seemingly unbridgeable gap between the academic achievement of language-minority and language majority children', Fillerup explains (2005: 15). The goal is to create an environment in which children from diverse language and culture backgrounds can 'learn harmoniously together' while learning to speak, read and write proficiently in two languages:

> On a grander scale, the vision was to create a school where each child's language and culture was regarded not as a problem to be solved but as an indispensable resource, the very heart and soul of the school itself.... English speakers would learn Spanish, Spanish speakers would learn English, Navajo children would acquire their tribal language, and all students would interact harmoniously and achieve academically. (Fillerup, 2008: para 3)

On our first visit to the school, we heard this vision articulated in Diné teachers' words: 'We're fighting for our kids to have the right to learn their language and culture!' (field notes, 1/13/09). Over the two-year study, we witnessed how this was being accomplished through the implementation of school-based language policies representing small and large acts of educational and linguistic sovereignty. This de facto language-in-education policymaking begins with a stunning visual statement that greets all who enter the school: expansive exterior wall murals created by the student 'artists of Puente de Hózhǫ́' depicting the Navajo girls' puberty ceremony (*Kinaaldá*) and the multihued topography of *Diné Bikeyah* (Navajo Country or Navajoland). Throughout the school, the print environment displays vivid images of academic content in Navajo, Spanish, and English.

Puente de Hózhǫ́ (hereafter PdH) educators explicitly reject the remedial labels historically associated with federal language education policy in the US. According to these educators, the way to ameliorate long-standing academic disparities is to create a school culture in which 'diverse languages and cultures [are] regarded as assets rather than deficits, as things to be desired and augmented rather than eliminated or suppressed' (Fillerup, 2011: 149). Instruction in Navajo language and culture shares equal status with English and academic content in English. 'This school is predicated on [the assumption] that learning more than one language is a *good thing*', an administrator emphasized during one of our site visits; [t]here is a belief in this school that all three languages should be treated equally (field notes, 1/12/10). 'We have to tell the parents, this is not what they were used to in their own schooling', a Diné teacher pointed out (field notes, 1/12/10). Explicit in these pedagogic practices is the 'shedding [of] the remedial label that has dogged American Indian...children for over a century' –

> Students in the Navajo immersion program are viewed not as problems to be solved but as an educational elite – the ones who are learning Navajo, that most difficult language [used by the Code Talkers] during World War II. It is *their* [the students'] language, program, school, culture, and heritage. (Fillerup, 2005: 16)

During the study period, every Diné-language classroom displayed a poster-size song script, *Shí Naashá* (literally, 'I Walk About' but translated culturally and historically by teachers as 'I'm Alive').³ The song is a constant reminder and commemoration of the Navajo people's survival and return to Diné Bikeyah from Hwéeldi, the federal concentration camp at Fort Sumner, New Mexico. Teachers speak of their implicit and explicit language policies as a reversal of past pedagogic practices, including their own. As one Diné teacher acknowledged when asked if her children spoke Navajo:

> When I was a young parent, I really didn't know what it meant...to value the language that you were raised in...we were just barely getting over the shame of being Native American...that we were minorities and we were not of value – we were just healing from that....I think working as a bilingual teacher here at Puente de Hózhǫ́ really opened my eyes to how important my language and culture are. (Interview, January 12, 2010)

This is a school community that, in its everyday practice, aims to conquer what Luis Enrique López (2008) calls the 'subaltern condition' of bilingualism, indigeneity and difference.

Like students at TDB, PdH students consistently outperform comparable peers in monolingual English programs (Fillerup, 2005, 2011). 'This became our unofficial goal', Fillerup writes – 'to score high enough on [standardized tests] to appease the powers that be' (2005: 15). But the program's impacts extend beyond test scores. As one teacher noted, '[H]earing parents comment on how much their kids have learned, or that their child may be the only one of all the cousins that [is] speaking to their grandparents – this tells us that we are doing something [worthwhile]' (interview, 11/3/09).

Keeping the 'NCLB wolves from the door': Challenges to school-based language revitalization

Like other school-centered revitalization projects, TDB and PdH face significant constraints in achieving their goals. At PdH, for example, our research team spent considerable time documenting teachers' corpus planning – in particular, the development of language and literacy standards in Navajo (and Spanish) that would satisfy state mandates. Every school year, Fillerup states, PdH educators 'hold their breath' that standardized test scores will be 'respectable enough to keep the NCLB wolves from the door' (2005: 15). 'The bottom line [is] this', he says: 'We need to ensure that our [test] scores [are] at least on par with the scores of students in English-only programs....As long as our scores [are] competitive, outsiders [cannot] accuse our school of being educationally unfit...' (2011: 159).

Moreover, both PdH and TDB have had to justify their school programs in the face of an Arizona English-only mandate that states that, 'All children in Arizona public schools shall be taught English by being taught in English and all children shall be placed in English language classrooms' (Arizona Proposition 203: Sec. 3.1, 752). In both cases, school personnel have pointed to the voluntary, enrichment emphasis of their programs; TDB, a reservation-based public school, has also cited NALA's protection of 'the right of tribal communities to teach Native languages in public schools' (Combs & Nicholas, 2012: 114). Both the Navajo Education Code and the 2005 Navajo Sovereignty in Education Act (NSIEA) further affirm the Navajo Nation's 'inherent right to exercise its responsibility to the Navajo people for their education by prescribing and implementing educational laws and policies applicable to all schools serving the Navajo Nation', including the teaching of Diné language and culture (NSIEA, 2005: Sec. 3.1). Implementation of the NSIEA, however, has been challenged by Arizona's state education agency on the grounds that it and its superintendent of public instruction have authority over all public schools in the state, regardless of whether those schools are located on Native lands. The Navajo Nation has nevertheless begun full implementation of its tribal law. In a state in which ethnic (i.e. non-White) studies has recently been banned in public schools,[4] these tensions continue unabated, foregrounding the racialized and neocolonial political environment in which Native nations assert their sovereign rights.

Reclaiming Rights 'in the Midst of Oppression'

The Diné examples profiled here represent just a few of many Native American language and culture recovery projects. As Lomawaima (2012: 18) notes, brief profiles such as these mask 'years poured into the effort' by Indigenous educators and their non-Indigenous allies. What the examples clearly show is that linguistic and educational sovereignty operate in linked policymaking domains; they are co-entailed, in theory and practice. 'An essential dimension of educational sovereignty', Moll and Ruiz point out, 'is the extent to which communities feel themselves to be in control of their language behaviors' (2005: 209). As we have seen, that control requires that Indigenous and minoritized communities reclaim their language rights 'in the midst of their oppression' (Moll & Ruiz, 2005: 300).

The community school at Rough Rock provides a final telling illustration of these political, linguistic, and educational processes. After having been nearly silenced by the strictures of NCLB, Diné language and culture have been re-established as the core curriculum through the joint efforts of Diné educators, parents, and students. As described by Dr Monty Roessel, the Diné educator under whose leadership the changes were effected, 'we decided to create a Navajo language immersion program...aligning our Navajo curriculum to our traditional ways of thought' (2011: 20). The goal is to enable Rough Rock students to cultivate the multiple citizenships that inhere in their indigeneity: 'We are creating students who know their place in the world as a Navajo and as an American', Roessel maintains (2011: 21).

In the same way that tribal sovereignty, as a legal-political status, is not without limits, linguistic and educational sovereignty operate in constant interaction with overlapping sovereignties, citizenships, and interests. That Native American nations and educators recognize this is evident from their sustained efforts to develop parallel educational standards such as those created by the schools serving Diné students documented here (for additional examples, see the standards and guidelines for culturally responsive schools produced by the Assembly of Alaska Native Educators, 1998 and by the Native Hawaiian Education Council and Ka Haka 'Ula O Ke'elikōlani College of Hawaiian Language, 2002). This complicates but does not contradict the right to and the exercise of linguistic and educational sovereignty.

Control of language and education 'doesn't have to be a one-way choice', Roessel stresses; 'done correctly, it is a BOTH-AND' (2011: 23; emphasis in original).

Present US education policy, which, as has been noted, is also a language policy (Menken, 2008), attempts to force a 'one-way choice', pitting academic achievement in English against the linguistic and cultural continuance of Indigenous and other minoritized communities. In states such as Arizona, this either-or dichotomy is exacerbated by policies designed to erase from the curriculum linguistic and cultural difference deemed 'dangerous' and threatening to dominant interests; in this instance we see acutely the use of language as a means of social control (Leibowitz, 1974; see also Lomawaima, 2012). Yet, as evidenced in the cases presented here – just a few among many that could be cited – these are false and ultimately profitless dichotomies. 'Native American parents want their children to do well in school', Blum Martinez insists in an analysis of language and tribal sovereignty among the Pueblos of New Mexico, 'and they want their children to have all of the opportunities that other children have' (2000: 217). This does not negate the fact that parents 'also recognize that their children will need to lead their communities' in the future (Blum Martinez, 2000: 217). Preparing children for full participation in their communities requires that they have access to local Indigenous knowledge, including the community language through which that knowledge is acquired.

This vision of conjoined linguistic and educational sovereignty is best articulated by the Indigenous educators who navigate its parameters each day. I close with the reflections of one such educator – a Diné teacher at Puente de Hózhǫ́ School. Asked to reflect on her aspirations for her students, she replied that she hoped they would leave PdH prepared for the 'real world' – a world of multiple languages, cultures, and citizenships. At PdH, she noted, 'English is taught,...Spanish is taught,...Navajo is taught' –

> And that really is how the world is....There are many different languages spoken and there are many different types of people...and when the children leave the classroom they know out there, there will be children speaking [different languages] and it's OK. It's OK to be different, and...that is what...the spirit of the school is. (Interview, 1/12/10)

That is also the spirit of a just and equitable language-in-education policy, and the concrete reality of Indigenous linguistic and educational sovereignty: a sovereignty secure in its own cultural and linguistic moorings yet mature and expansive enough to respect and reciprocate the sovereign rights of others.

Acknowledgements

I thank Vaidehi Ramanathan for inviting me to contribute to the important scholarly conversations she has initiated with this volume. I am also indebted to Vaidehi Ramanathan and K. Tsianina Lomawaima for invaluable feedback on an earlier draft of this chapter. Parts of this chapter are adapted from McCarty (2013) and used with permission of Multilingual Matters.

Notes

(1) As discussed by many scholars, counting languages and speakers is problematic, not only because sources such as the self-reports in census data are suspect, but because the project of enumeration is an ideological one (Hill, 2002). As Moore *et al.* (2010) point out, linguistic enumeration privileges a concept of languages 'as neatly bounded, abstract, autonomous grammatical systems', obscuring the complex dynamics of 'actual language-in-use' (2010: 2). Enumeration also calls into question issues of dialect difference (what counts as a 'language' versus a 'dialect'?) and 'speakerhood' (what constitutes a 'fluent' or 'proficient' speaker?) (Moore *et al.*, 2010: 11). Readers should use the numbers with caution, recognizing that they are but one index of language diversity and endangerment.

(2) The Puente de Hózhǫ́ study was part of a national study of promising practices in American Indian/Alaska Native education commissioned by the US Office of Indian Education Programs under contract to Kauffman Associates, Inc., of Spokane, Washington. Dr Bryan Brayboy led the national study group. In addition to Brayboy and myself, the PdH research team included graduate research assistants Erin Anacortez Nolan and Kristin Monahan Silver. Although no individual teacher names are used in the reporting of data from that study, the school and the district gave permission to use the school's actual name.

(3) I thank Irene Silentman for invaluable assistance with the literal and figurative translation of this song script.

(4) Arizona's ethnic studies ban is part of a constellation of recent state legislation targeting Mexican Americans and Spanish-speaking immigrants, and is *prima facie* evidence of the state's intent to protect metaphorical safety zone boundaries. In April 2010, the Arizona legislature approved Senate Bill 1070 ('Support Our Law Enforcement and Safe Neighborhoods Act'), an anti-immigrant measure that a federal judge later ruled encourages racial profiling and violates federal law (the US Supreme Court subsequently struck down significant portions of the law). On the same day, the legislature approved House Bill 2281, a ban on (non-White) ethnic studies (specifically, Mexican American Studies) in public schools, on the grounds that such classes 'promote resentment toward a race or class of people' and 'promote the overthrow of the United States government' (Hull, 2010: para 8). The latter claim, made by then-state superintendent of public instruction Tom Horne (and directly cited in section 1.15-112 of the bill), would seem ridiculous were it not for the fact that he subsequently ran a successful campaign for state attorney general on a 'Defending Arizona!' platform that discursively linked his support for banning bilingual education with bans on ethnic studies and immigration. The week that S.B. 1070 and

H.B. 2281 were approved, Horne instructed school districts to remove teachers with (Spanish) 'accents' from English language arts classrooms. The ethnic studies ban, which to date has impacted only Mexican American Studies classes in the Tucson Unified School District (notably, Native American and African American Studies classes in the district remain 'safe' from the ban), is also under appeal.

References

American Indian Policy Review Commission (1976) *Report on Indian Education*. Washington, DC: U.S. Government Printing Office.

Anderson, J.A. (2007) Race-conscious education policies versus a 'color-blind constitution': A historical perspective. *Educational Researcher* 36 (5), 249–257.

Arizona Proposition 203 (2000) *English Language Education for Children in Public Schools*. An amendment to Arizona Revised Statutes Title 15, Chapter 7, Article 3.1, accessed 11 August 2010. http://www.ade.az.gov/oelas/PROPOSITION203.pdf/

Arviso, M. and Holm, W. (2001) Tséhootsooídi Ólta'gi Diné bizaad bihoo'aah: A Navajo immersion program at Fort Defiance, Arizona. In L. Hinton and K. Hale (eds) *The Green Book of Language Revitalization in Practice* (pp. 203–215). San Diego, CA: Academic Press.

Assembly of Alaska Native Educators (1998) *Alaska Standards for Culturally Responsive Schools*. Anchorage: Alaska Native Knowledge Network.

Atkins, J.D.C. (1887) 'Barbarous dialects should be blotted out...' Excerpts from the 1887 Report of the Commissioner of Indian Affairs, accessed 23 March 2012. http://www.languagepolicy.net/archives/atkins.htm/

Austin, P.K. and Sallabank, J. (eds) (2011) *The Cambridge Handbook of Language Endangerment*. Cambridge, UK: Cambridge University Press.

Benally, A. and Viri, D. (2005) *Diné bizaad* (Navajo language) at a crossroads: Extinction or renewal? *Bilingual Research Journal* 29 (1), 85–108.

Blum Martinez, R. (2000) Languages and tribal sovereignty: Whose language is it anyway? *Theory Into Practice* 39 (4), 211–219.

Brayboy, B.M.J. (2005) Toward a tribal critical race theory in education. *The Urban Review* 37 (5), 425–446.

Collier, J., Jr. (1988) Survival at Rough Rock: A historical overview of Rough Rock Demonstration School. *Anthropology and Education Quarterly* 19 (3), 253–269.

Combs, M.C. and Nicholas, S.E. (2012) The effect of Arizona language policies on Arizona Indigenous students. *Language Policy* 11 (1), 101–118.

Coronel-Molina, S.M. and McCarty, T.L. (2011) Language curriculum design and evaluation for endangered languages. In P. Austin and J. Sallabank (eds) *The Cambridge Handbook of Endangered Languages* (pp. 354–370). Cambridge, UK: Cambridge University Press.

Donovan, B. (2011) Census: Navajo enrollment tops 300,000. *Navajo Times*, July 7, accessed 24 March 2012. http://navajotimes.com/news/2011/0711/070711census.php/

Erickson, F. (2004) *Talk and Social Theory: Ecologies of Speaking and Listening in Everyday Life*. Cambridge, UK: Polity Press.

Esther Martinez Native American Languages Preservation Act (EM-NALPA) (2006) H. R. 4766. *Esther Martinez Native American Languages Preservation Act of 2006*. Washington, DC: 109th Congress of the United States of America.

Fillerup, M. (2005) Keeping up with the Yazzies: The impact of high stakes testing on Indigenous language programs. *Language Learner* (September–October), 14–16.
Fillerup, M. (2008) Building bridges of beauty between the rich languages and cultures of the American Southwest: Puente de Hózhǫ́ Trilingual Magnet School, accessed 22 March 2012. http://puentedehozho.org/puenteschool.htm/
Fillerup, M. (2011) Building a 'bridge of beauty': A preliminary report on promising practices in Native language and culture teaching at Puente de Hózhǫ́ Trilingual Magnet School. In M.E. Romero-Little, S.J. Ortiz, T.L. McCarty and R. Chen (eds) *Indigenous Languages Across the Generations – Strengthening Families and Communities* (pp. 145–164). Tempe: Arizona State University Center for Indian Education.
Foucault, M. (1991) *Discipline and Punish: The Birth of a Prison*. London: Penguin Books.
Hill, J. (2002) 'Expert rhetorics' in advocacy for endangered languages: Who is listening, and what do they hear? *Journal of Linguistic Anthropology* 12 (2), 119–133.
Hinton, L. and Hale, K. (eds) (2001) *The Green Book of Language Revitalization in Practice*. San Diego, CA: Academic Press.
Holm, A. and Holm, W. (1990) Rock Point, a Navajo way to go to school: A valediction. *Annals of the American Association of Social and Political Science* 508, 170–184.
Holm, A. and Holm, W. (1995) Navajo language education: Retrospect and prospects. *Bilingual Research Journal* 19 (1), 141–167.
Holm, W. (2006) The 'goodness' of bilingual education for Native American children. In T.L. McCarty and O. Zepeda (eds) *One Voice, Many Voices – Recreating Indigenous Language Communities* (pp. 1–46). Tempe: Arizona State University Center for Indian Education.
Hornberger, N.H. (ed.) (1996) *Indigenous Literacies in the Americas: Language Planning from the Bottom Up*. Berlin: Mouton de Gruyter.
Hornberger, N.H. (2002) Multilingual language policies and the continua of biliteracy: An ecological approach. *Language Policy* 1 (1), 27–51.
Hornberger, N.H. (2006) *Nichols* to *NCLB*: Local and global perspectives on US language education policy. In O. García, T. Skutnabb-Kangas and M.E. Torres-Guzmán (eds) *Imagining Multilingual Schools: Languages in Education and glocalization* (pp. 223–237). Clevedon: Multilingual Matters.
Hull, T. (2010) Arizona teachers claim law against Mexican-American studies unconstitutional. *Courthouse News Service*, October 21, accessed 22 June 2011. http://www.firstamendmentcoalition.org/2010/10/arizona-teachers-claim-law-against-mexican-american-studies-unconstitutional/
International Labour Organization (ILO) (2009) *Indigenous and tribal peoples' rights in practice: A guide to ILO Convention No. 169*. Geneva: International Labour Standards Department, accessed 23 March 2012. http://www.ilo.org/wcmsp5/groups/public/@ed_norm/@normes/documents/publication/wcms_106474.pdf/
Johnson, B.H. (1968) *Navaho Education at Rough Rock*. Rough Rock, AZ: Rough Rock Demonstration School.
Johnson, B.H. and Roessel, R. (eds) (1973) *Navajo Stories of the Long Walk Period*. Tsaile, Navajo Nation, AZ: Navajo Community College Press.
Johnson, F.T. and Legatz, J. (2006) Tséhootsooí Diné Bi'ólta'. *Journal of American Indian Education* 45 (2), 26–33.
Kaomea, J. (2004) Dilemmas of an indigenous academic: A native Hawaiian story. In K. Mutua and B.B. Swadener (eds) *Decolonizing Research in Cross-cultural Contexts: Critical Personal Narratives* (pp. 27–44). Albany: State University of New York Press.

Krauss, M. (1998) The condition of Native North American languages: The need for realistic assessment and action. *International Journal of the Sociology of Language* 132, 9–21.
Lapahie, H., Jr. (2001). *Fort Defiance (Tséhootsooí – Meadow in Between the Rocks)*, accessed 18 July 2008. http://www.lapahie.com/Fort_Defiance.cfm/
Leibowitz, A. (1974) Language as a Means of Social Control: The United States Experience. Paper prepared for the Annual Meeting of the World Congress of Sociology, Toronto, Ontario, accessed 21 March 2012. http://www.eric.ed.gov/ERICWebPortal/contentdelivery/servlet/ERICServlet?accno=ED093168/
Link, M. (1968) *Navajo – A century of progress, 1868-1968*. Window Rock, AZ: The Navajo Tribe.
Lomawaima, K.T. (2002) American Indian education: *By* Indians vs. *for* Indians. In P.J. Deloria and N. Salisbury (eds) *A Companion to American Indian History* (pp. 422–440). Malden, MA: Blackwell.
Lomawaima, K.T. (2012) Speaking from Arizona: Can scholarship about education make a difference in the world? *Journal of American Indian Education* 51 (2), 3–21.
Lomawaima, K.T. (in press) Education. In R. Warrior (ed.) *World of Indigenous North America*. New York: Routledge.
Lomawaima, K.T. and McCarty, T.L. (2006) *'To Remain an Indian': Lessons in Democracy from a Century of Native American Education*. New York: Teachers College Press.
López, L.E. (2008) Top-down and bottom-up: Counterpoised visions of bilingual intercultural education in Latin America. In N.H. Hornberger (ed.) *Can Schools Save Indigenous Languages? Policy and Practice on Four Continents* (pp. 42–65). Houndsmills, Basingstoke, UK: Palgrave Macmillan.
Luke, A., McHoul, A.W. and Mey, J.L. (1990) On the limits of language planning: Class, state, and power. In R.B. Baldauf, Jr. and A. Luke (eds) *Language Planning and Education in Australasia and the South Pacific* (pp. 25–44). Clevedon: Multilingual Matters.
Manuelito, K. (2005) The role of education in American Indian self-determination: Lessons from the Ramah Navajo Community School. *Anthropology and Education Quarterly* 36 (1), 73–87.
McCarty, T.L. (1993) Federal language policy and American Indian education. *Bilingual Research Journal* 17 (1 and 2), 13–34.
McCarty, T.L. (2002) *A Place to be Navajo – Rough Rock and the Struggle for Self-determination in Indigenous Schooling*. Mahwah, NJ: Lawrence Erlbaum.
McCarty, T.L. (2003) Revitalising Indigenous languages in homogenising times. *Comparative Education* 39 (2), 147–163.
McCarty, T.L. (2012) Indigenous languages and cultures in Native American student achievement – Promising practices and cautionary findings. In B. Klug (ed.) *Standing Together: Indigenous Education as Culturally Responsive Pedagogy*. Manassas, VA: Association of Teacher Educators.
McCarty, T.L. (2013) *Language Planning and Policy in Native America – History, Theory, Praxis*. Bristol: Multilingual Matters.
McCarty, T.L., Nicholas, S.E. and Wyman, L.T. (2012) Re-emplacing place in the 'global here and now' – Critical ethnographic case studies of Native American language planning and policy. *International Multilingual Research Journal* 6 (1), 50–63.
McCarty, T.L. and Warhol, L. (2011) The anthropology of language planning and policy. In B.A.U. Levinson and M. Pollock (eds) *A Companion to the Anthropology of Education* (pp. 177–196). Malden, MA: Wiley-Blackwell.

McCarty, T.L. and Zepeda, O., with V.H. Begay, S. Charging Eagle, S.C. Moore, L. Warhol and T.M.K. Williams (eds) (2006) *One Voice, Many Voices – Recreating Indigenous Language Communities*. Tempe: Arizona State University Center for Indian Education.
Menken, K. (2008) *English Learners Left Behind: Standardized Testing as Language Policy*. Clevedon, UK: Multilingual Matters.
Menken, K. and García, O. (eds) (2010) *Negotiating Language Policies in Schools: Educators as Policymakers*. New York: Routledge.
Meriam, L., Brown, R.A., Roe Cloud, H., Dale, E.E., Duke, E., Edwards, H.R., McKenzie, F.A., Mark, M.L., Ryan, W.C. and Spillman, W.J. (1928) *The Problem of Indian Administration*. Baltimore, MD: Johns Hopkins Press for the Institute for Government Research.
Moll, L.C. and Ruiz, R. (2005) The educational sovereignty of Latino/a students in the United States. In P. Pedraza and M. Rivera (eds) *Latino Education: An Agenda for Community Action Research* (pp. 295–320). Mahwah, NJ: Lawrence Erlbaum.
Moore, R.E., Pietikäinen, S. and Blommaert, J. (2010) Counting the losses: Numbers as the language of language endangerment. *Sociolinguistic Studies* 4 (1), 1–26.
Native American Languages Act (NALA) (1990). Public Law 101-466 – October 30, 1990. *Title I – Native American Languages Act*, accessed 21 March 2012. http://www.access.gpo.gov/congress/senate/pdf/108hrg/87260.pdf/
Native Hawaiian Education Council and Ka Haka 'Ula O Ke'elikōlani College of Hawaiian Language (2002). *Nā Honua Mauli Ola: Hawai`i Guidelines for Culturally Healthy and Responsive Learning Environments*. Honolulu, HI: Native Hawaiian Education Council.
Pfeiffer, A. (1993) American Indian educational issues. Panel presentation at the Quarterly Regional Meeting of the Bilingual/Multicultural Personnel Training Alliance, BUENO Center for Multicultural Education, University of Colorado, Boulder.
Ramanathan, V. (2010) *Bodies and Language: Health, Ailments, Disabilities*. Bristol: Multilingual Matters.
Read, J., Spolsky, B. and Neundorf, A. (1975) Socioeconomic Implications of Bilingual Education on the Navajo Reservation. Paper presented at the Annual Meeting of the American Educational Research Association, Washington, DC.
Reyhner, J. and Eder, J. (2004) *American Indian Education: A History*. Norman: University of Oklahoma Press.
Reyhner, J. and Lockard, L. (eds) (2009) *Indigenous Language Revitalization: Encouragement, Guidance and Lessons Learned*. Flagstaff: Northern Arizona University College of Education.
Roessel, M. (2011) 'Preserving the past to secure the future': The Center for Indian Education – The next 50 years. *Journal of American Indian Education* 50 (2), 13–23.
Roessel, R.A.R., Jr. (1977) *Navajo Education in Action: The Rough Rock Demonstration School*. Chinle, AZ: Navajo Curriculum Center Press.
Romero-Little, M.E. and McCarty, T.L. (2006) *Language Planning Challenges and Prospects in Native American Communities and Schools*. Tempe: Arizona State University Education Policy Studies Laboratory.
Romero-Little, M.E., Ortiz, S.J. and McCarty, T.L., with Chen, R. (ed.) (2011) *Indigenous Languages Across the Generations – Strengthening Families and Communities*. Tempe: Arizona State University Center for Indian Education.
Siebens, J. and Julian, T. (2011) *Native North American Languages Spoken at Home in the United States and Puerto Rico: 2006–2010*. American Community Survey briefs. Washington, DC: U.S. Department of Commerce, Economics and Statistics Administration, U.S. Census Bureau.

Silentman, I. (1995) Navajo bilingual education in the 1970s: A personal perspective. Unpublished manuscript.
Spolsky, B. (1974) *American Indian bilingual education*. Navajo Reading Study Progress Report No. 17. Albuquerque: University of New Mexico College of Education.
Spolsky, B. (1975) Linguistics in practice: The Navajo Reading Study. *Theory Into Practice* 14 (5), 347–352.
Underhill, R.M. (1956) *The Navajos*. Norman: University of Oklahoma Press.
United Nations General Assembly (2007) *United Nations Declaration on the Rights of Indigenous Peoples*. Paris: United Nations General Assembly 61st Session, Agenda Item 68, accessed 22 March 2012. http://www.un.org/esa/socdev/unpfii/documents/DRIPS_en.pdf/
US Census Bureau (2010) Table 1. Detailed languages spoken at home and ability to speak English for the population 5 years and over for the United States: 2006-2010. Washington, DC: U.S. Census Bureau, accessed 24 March 2012. http:www.census.gov/hhes/socdemo/language/
Wilkins, D.E. and Lomawaima, K.T. (2001) *Uneven Ground: American Indian Sovereignty and Federal Law*. Norman: University of Oklahoma Press.
Wyman, L., Marlow, P., Andrew, F.C., Miller, G.S., Nicholai, R.C. and Rearden, N.Y. (2010a) Focusing on long-term language goals in challenging times: A Yup'ik example. *Journal of American Indian Education* 49 (1 and 2), 28–49.
Wyman, L., Marlow, P., Andrew, C.F., Miller, G., Nicholai, C.R. and Rearden, Y.N. (2010b) High-stakes testing, bilingual education and language endangerment: A Yup'ik example. *International Journal of Bilingual Education and Bilingualism* 13 (6), 701–721.

Part 2
Education and Citizenship: Creating (and Constraining) Spaces for Language, Learning and Belonging

8 Citizenship as Social, Spiritual and Multilingual Practice: Fostering Visions and Practices in the Nishkam Nursery Project

Gopinder Kaur Sagoo

Setting the Scene

It is a Saturday morning in January 2010, in Birmingham, Central England. A new nursery is about to have a civic opening ceremony with a visit from the Lord Mayor. We are on a busy main road in the inner city area of Handsworth, leading to the city centre on one side and a motorway interchange on the other. The local linguistic diversity is reflected in the many shops, centres and places of worship which line it, revealing largely South Asian, Afro-Caribbean, Eastern European – as well as multidenominational Christian[1] – influences contributing, in part, to the official representation of Birmingham as 'A Global City with a Local Heart'.[2]

The nursery is located at one corner of a crossroads. A grade-II-listed building, newly renovated to conserve its Georgian features, it neighbours three buildings which are part of Handsworth's 'heritage trail'[3]: a still functioning church, a girls' grammar school and a historic home-turned-museum and former meeting place for pioneers of the industrial revolution. At the same time, the nursery forms part of a new local heritage being created by a Sikh faith-based organisation known widely as 'Nishkam'.[4] This includes a landmark gurdwara[5] developed from the late 1970s, with its domed parapet design, receiving daily streams of Sikh and non-Sikh visitors (such as school groups) and serving an estimated 1 million free meals[6] a year. On its right is a builders' merchant, formed as a self-help community cooperative during the economic recession of the 1980s, and on its left – directly in front the nursery – the drum-shaped, glass-walled Nishkam Centre for Civic

Engagement. Constructed in 2004 to extend local and global connectivity, it brings people from many backgrounds and organisations to use its adult learning, conference and wellbeing facilities[7] and provides a base to collaborate around various social projects.

Reflecting different architectural styles and evoking multi-layered identities, the above developments have emerged out of ideas integrating Sikh faith-derived concepts with more widely circulated citizenship concepts, linking them also to Birmingham's 'Civic Gospel'[8] legacy (see Green, 2008). These include: *nishkam sewa* ('selflessly serving others') and 'active volunteering'; imbuing 'secular regeneration with spiritual values'; combining 'heritage conservation' with 'social innovation' and working towards *sarbat da bhalla*, 'the common good', based on the threefold Sikh ethic of living 'meditatively, industriously and generously' (Nesbitt, 2005: 28).

Outside the nursery's front door, in preparation for today's civic ceremony, a commemorative brass plaque has just been polished. A nursery mother, who works and volunteers on site, hangs a small curtain over it, cleans the steps and arranges the hanging basket of flowers, while the pavement outside the Nishkam Centre is swept by the turbaned centre director. Inside, the final touches of an exhibition are put together and space made for serving a celebratory, vegetarian lunch prepared by the nursery chef.

Soon the Lord Mayor, an emeritus professor from a city university, will arrive with the Lady Mayoress. They will be greeted by Bhai Sahib (a title of esteem denoting a 'brotherly leader'), the chair and spiritual successor[9] of the Nishkam organisation, joined by his wife, 'Mata Ji' (denoting an affectionately respected 'mother'). In attendance will be three generations of South Asians aligned in different ways to Sikh tradition, bringing together eastern and western styles of dress. They include the nursery staff, its children and their families, Nishkam's network of volunteers involved in its various educational projects, such as a complementary school which has run for three decades.

Guests from local government, education, voluntary and business sectors will bring Birmingham's wider social mix to the reception. Following a ribbon-cutting ceremony across the road at the nursery, the unveiling of the plaque and the release of red and white balloons into the sky, plus a tour of the building inside, the Lord Mayor will return to the Nishkam Centre to give a speech about the nursery's contribution to value-led education and care of young children, integrating as it does the national framework for early childhood provision in England, a locally agreed framework of 'dispositions' extrapolated from Birmingham City Council's multi-faith syllabus for Religious Education and concepts derived from Sikh heritage. The nursery staff will be presented awards in recognition of their care and commitment, whilst the children and their families move between a specially created play area and the main proceedings.

* * * * *

This glimpse into a very public moment in the early history of the 'Nishkam Nursery' introduces it as a site for developing ways of conceiving, practising and nurturing citizenship. In this chapter, I draw on my ethnographically oriented doctoral research, examining the discursive and interactive processes through which the nursery's visions and practices were fostered. I do so to offer insights into how citizenship can be understood as a state of becoming and being 'able to participate fully', rather than as a status that is inherited, acquired or achieved. The possibility of such citizenship depends on a range of available (as well as accessible and constructible) contexts, conditions, visions, motivations, dispositions, traditions of knowledge – and the dynamics of their interplay. Ethnographic work is uniquely able to identify these dynamics and provide a grounded perspective.

In this chapter, I will first introduce the socio-historical and philosophical foundations of early childhood education, referring to work underlining its ethical and political dimensions in local and global contexts. I will then introduce my study, touching on some of the orienting theories and describing the nature of the ethnographic work undertaken. I will then provide an account of how the vision for the Nishkam nursery was developed, showing how it was rooted in a particular faith tradition (the Sikh *dharam*). After this, I will show how the vision was gradually developed in and through practice and how it is being sustained and extended in the ebb and flow of day-to-day communicative practice in the nursery. My concluding discussion will point to some of the wider implications of this localised study.

Contextualising British Early Childhood Education and Care

Historical influences from Europe and North America

Stearns (2005, 2006) provides a global, social history of childhood, introducing the sedimentation, circulation, adoption and adaptation of ideas and practices across societies over broad epochs of human history. In industrialising Britain, class divisions and national and colonial imperatives created different expectations for the care and education of children of the elite and the masses. The first public nurseries were founded by Christian socialist pioneers, such as Robert Owen (Scotland) and the McMillan sisters (England), as part of wider endeavours to establish a model community and uplift the poor. In France, the *crèche* movement provided support for underprivileged working mothers in Paris (La Berge, 1991), whilst Froebel's religiously-inspired vision of human wholeness (McLaughlin, 1996; Weston, 2002) initiated the German *kindergarten* movement, the emphasis on play, activity and closeness to nature extending earlier ideas articulated by Pestalozzi and Rousseau. In the United States, nurseries affiliated to universities served as 'laboratories' (Beatty, 2005) for the burgeoning science of child development (stimulated by Piaget), whilst Dewey's interest in enabling democratic citizenship foregrounded the nurturing of dispositions through co-operative, process- and project-oriented learning. This was echoed in the work of Freinet in France (Starkey, 1996). Bronfenbrenner's (1979, 2005) focus on human development, through fluid processes of interaction with micro- to macro-level 'ecological' systems, built on Vygotsky's work in the Soviet Union, engendering a shift in focus from decontextualised, individual learning to the socio-cultural dimensions of learning. These examples sketch out some of the standpoints which have informed public provision, from supporting children's welfare and development to providing a service for parents and the state, and fulfilling a philosophical vision of childhood and society.

Policy developments in England

For most of the 20th century, pre-school provision in England remained largely informal, based on child-centred, experiential learning (Eaude, 2006; Kwon, 2002). The end of wartime funding for nurseries led to the 'playgroup' movement, started by parents and volunteers. A subject-based National Curriculum for schools introduced in 1988 increased interest in fostering school-readiness in the under-fives. Professional training and academic research in early childhood was stimulated over the 1990s and, in 2000, *Curriculum Guidance for the Foundation Stage* (Qualifications and Curriculum Authority, 2000) was introduced. Renewed concern for child welfare led to the *Every Child Matters* policy document (Department for Education & Skills, 2004), requiring interagency collaboration to support six wellbeing outcomes. In 2008, the *Early Years Foundation Stage Framework* (Department for Children, Schools & Families, 2008) consolidated previous initiatives, its four principles being: 'a unique child; positive relationships; enabling environments; learning and development'. Reporting to government on the crucial role of social and emotional nurture, Allen (2011) set out the long-term social benefits of strategizing to invest in early intervention.

The institutionalisation of daycare has prompted alternative visions, advocating one-on-one or multi-aged, collaborative care and a reframing of national values to guide provision (as seen in media articles by Palmer, 2007 and James, 2011).

Contesting and re-imagining local and global discourses

The pervasive, normalising power assumed by an 'Anglo-American' (Dahlberg & Moss, 2005) early childhood discourse has been contested from a range of perspectives. Dahlberg and Moss (2005) and Moss (2007) critique its mass production of sites for 'technical practice', positioned as commodities for parents-as-consumers, presuming objectivity and universality as they are rolled out to local and global markets. Potential is highlighted for pre-schools to be 'forums, spaces or sites for ethical and political practice' (Dahlberg & Moss, 2005: 1–2) as exemplified in the 'local cultural project of childhood' developed in the Italian city of Reggio Emilia (2005: 157) and in Sweden's decentralised state nurseries, guided by a clear framework of democratic values. Cleghorn and Prochner (2010) and Cottrell (2010) consider tensions, as well as opportunities for the 'global reimagining of schools' (Cottrell, 2010: 223), arising from the forces of globalization and legacy of colonialism on the one hand, and increased recognition of the validity of local, indigenous epistemologies and cultures on the other (Cleghorn & Prochner, 2010: 1). Such perspectives are extended by ethnographic studies of urban pre-schools by Gupta (2006) in India (discussed below) and Tobin *et al.* (1989, 2009) in Japan, China and the United States. Tobin (2009: 430) points to a phenomenon of 'internal colonialism' arguing that, in a heterogeneous society such as the United States, notions of quality and standards cannot presume 'a one-size-fits-all' solution to questions of practice (2009: 434); they 'should arise out of conversations in local communities among early childhood educators and parents' (2009: 421).

David *et al.* (2010) consider what can be learnt from New Zealand's early childhood curriculum, *Te Whariki*, developed to articulate and integrate values from Maori heritage through its principles of 'holistic development, empowerment, family and community relationships' (2010: 40). Whilst nurseries have been researched as sites for reclaiming linguistic rights and promoting language revitalisation, for example in Wales (Jones & Martin-Jones, 2004) and Scotland (Stephen *et al.*, 2012), Dahlberg and Moss (2005) see one purpose of pre-school projects as being to '*vitalise* the place of ethics, making it explicit and central to the life of the pre-school – something that is openly and knowingly practiced' [their italics] (2005: 12). As I will show in this chapter, this stance underpins the linguistic, cultural, philosophical and epistemological 'border crossings', which have characterised the Nishkam nursery project.

My Study: Theoretical Framing and Research Approach

The writing of Biesta and colleagues (Biesta, 2006, 2009; Lawy & Biesta, 2006; Osberg & Biesta, 2010) on educational philosophy and democratic citizenship provides an apt theoretical framing for my study at three levels. The first concerns the purpose of education, situating it beyond aims to reproduce, or enable functioning within, an existing social order, anticipating new possibilities that children (as 'newcomers') bring (Biesta, 2006). The second emphasises the social conditions we create for nurturing *citizenship-as-practice*, over and above teaching of *citizenship-as-achievement*, in terms of knowledge transmitted or status acquired (Lawy & Biesta, 2006). The third recognises society as complex and plural, suggesting that 'inclusive education' in a democracy involves more than the inclusion of difference (again, as a newcomer) within a predetermined, dominant curriculum order; rather, it creates scope to engage with difference and bring transformation to shared orders (Biesta, 2009; Osberg & Biesta, 2010).

These ideas find resonance in longstanding work from the fields of ethnography, sociolinguistics and cultural studies. Levinson *et al.* (1996) examine the 'cultural production of the educated person', reviewing international research on the convergences and tensions between dominant systems of schooling and local practice. Erickson (1987), discussing low school achievement of minority and working-class students in the United States, demonstrates how analyses of communicative classroom interaction can outline possibilities for 'culturally responsive pedagogy' to engender pupil success. In the United Kingdom, Martin-Jones and Saxena (2003) reveal the communicative resources and 'funds of knowledge' (González *et al.*, 2005), which bilingual classroom assistants draw upon to facilitate the processes of children's learning in linguistically diverse classrooms. Gupta (2006) brings to the surface implicit concepts and values of early childhood educators in urban India, arising from their communal cultural and religious heritage, thus questioning the exclusive focus on individual western theorists in their higher education training in India. Beyond a commitment to cultural responsiveness, she proposes reciprocity and interaction between culturally contrasting educational frameworks as vital for evolving education in a postcolonial, globalised world.

Ethnographic research encourages a movement from the observation of concrete, day-to-day realities to broader socio-historical and cultural processes, including spiritual and moral concerns which shape them. I draw on Holland et al.'s (1998) concept of 'figured worlds', examining the formation of identity and exercise of agency in culturally produced, socially organised worlds, creating contexts of meaning and significance for 'artefacts', activities and roles within them. Individuals come to understand and 'figure' who they are, and expand the possibilities of who they are, through participation in these contexts and processes, and relating to others within and outside these worlds (see Urrieta, 2007).

The ethnographically oriented nature of my study enabled me to conduct an analysis of the naturally occurring discursive and interactive processes underpinning the nursery project. My own positioning as a researcher is that I am a British-born Sikh, one of the early nursery parents and helpers, involved for just over a decade in the life of the Nishkam campus as it has evolved. In the sections which follow, I draw on field notes, documentary and interview data, and audio recordings of interactions inside the nursery. I outline the notions of citizenship and other funds of knowledge, which have informed the creation of the nursery and contributed to the development of its day-to-day practices.

Conceptualising and Doing 'Dharmic' Citizenship to Create the Nishkam Nursery

This section contextualises the nursery as part of the Nishkam organisation's wider project of articulating and demonstrating what citizenship can mean from a particular standpoint in the world, encompassing visions for both childhood and society. I draw here on interviews with key social actors involved in the initial conceptualisation of the nursery project and on field notes from key events.

Since being entrusted to lead Nishkam's work, Bhai Sahib (interviewed in Sagoo, 2008) has taken the organisation through local and global civic, inter-faith and intra-faith engagement projects, building on his own transnational background, professional expertise as well as contemplative faith commitment.[10] This has given rise to a multilingual discourse on faith-inspired citizenship, which helps to frame and set a tone for the developments glimpsed at the start of the chapter. Take, for example, explicit inclusion of the Punjabi word *'dharam'* to indicate 'religion' or 'faith', for its ability to conceptualise and, in Bhai Sahib's words, evoke a 'loving responsibility' and 'sacred duty towards all creation' as well as denote an identifiable faith tradition (e.g. 'the Sikh *dharam*'). This he described as 'spiritual citizenship', based on rights and responsibilities assumed by virtue of being 'domiciled... as a human citizen' on the planet. A view of dharam as a 'heritage of values', lived 'breath-to-breath, moment-to-moment', emphasised the application of an ethos in new contexts – combining 'heritage conservation' with 'social innovation' (to guide, for example, strategic planning for the Nishkam Centre). At the same time, visible markers of Sikh identity (e.g. the turban and five *kakkar*)[11] were cherished as gifts historically 'bestowed' to evoke values such as ethical living and social responsibility guided by spiritual wisdom. Fear of terrorism and extremism had accentuated their potential, as carriers of meaning, to be 'misinterpreted, misused and hijacked', as Bhai Sahib put it. Social projects to make the ethos more evident could thus be seen as an endeavour to reveal or recover understandings which lie beneath the surface of what Erickson (2001: 39) describes as the visible 'tip of the iceberg' of culture.

Shared values were often explored by recalling several centuries of multilingual, inter-faith exchange preserved in Sikh sacred text.[12] Bhai Sahib often used the word 'resonance' to link them with contemporary notions in government, corporate and third sector discourse of 'the common good', 'good governance' or 'active volunteering', as well as to describe a palpable quality of mutually responsive, value-sensing interaction between people. In his speeches, established social values were given a spiritual identity – e.g. 'social cohesion' based on finding 'cohesion within the self' – and customary personal values a social identity – e.g. identifying a search for 'social compassion, social forgiveness' alongside social justice. Justice as a form of payback and 'a culture of despondency, condemnation and blame' were to be avoided and 'respect to be earned, not demanded'. The need to cultivate a long-term, sustainable vision and consider broader social and historical impact was regularly stressed, summed up in an often-used phrase about connecting 'whole to part'. Such ideas were reiterated in his emphasis on the need to recognise and foster 'interdependence', alongside 'self-confidence', 'responsibility' and 'accountability', as some of the key dispositions for the practice of citizenship.

The idea of a nursery arose, both pragmatically and philosophically, as part of a vision to establish a Sikh ethos, multi-faith school and to influence the wider processes involved in the regeneration of communities and fulfilment of social responsibilities towards children. Whilst Bhai Sahib articulated an overall framing, his leadership style encouraged what he often described as grassroots 'soul searching', when a small team was invited to meet and begin a period of reflection, research and planning. R. Singh (interviewed in Sagoo, 2008) was involved in the longer-term education project.

Explaining this process to a producer of educational films who was one of many external visitors to the nursery, he stressed the importance of this stage as a means to enable *'simple, deep conversations'*, especially amongst parents, so that *'you feel you are amongst friends, that we are not talking about a school, but we are talking about your child'*. The rationale was not to create a system to *'teach or sell'*, but to stimulate a reflective process, which of itself might offer insights to others.

Blue-sky thinking about young children's most important needs led the planning group to prioritise wellbeing, love and attention. This ran in parallel with Bhai Sahib's emphasis on 'an abundance of love and good nourishment' as the most vital ingredients for nurturing the under-fives. The question then asked was how to (re)configure provision, given changes in the structures, roles, routines and pressures of family and working life, and taking account of gains and losses following migration to and settlement in Britain. The group was also concerned to ensure that the core needs identified would not be neglected amidst aspirations for a good mainstream and heritage education. As British-born Sikh parents weighing up their own childhood experiences of heritage education, they imagined a space to build, in the words of one mother who was a key player (B. Kaur interviewed in Sagoo (2008)), *'pyaar'* or love for it from a young age, rather than didactically imposing it, seeing the culture emanating from the gurudwara, with its spiritual and social dimensions, as an ideal shared resource.

On my visits to the education office at the Nishkam Centre, having been invited to join the project, I would see printouts of reports about the state of childhood in national and international contexts (Children's Society, 2006; UNICEF, 2007), historical references to education in pre-British India (explored in Sagoo, 2008) and histories of schools and approaches to learning with a distinctive ethos. As the project team began to draft written accounts of an ethos underpinning the envisaged nursery, I was struck in discussions reviewing the emerging text, by the emphasis that was put on 'where' particular values and practices might be fostered for and around children (rather than what outcomes were to be expected in them) and by the keen sense of place that was being engendered. The word *nishkam* was talked about, not only in terms of 'selflessness' but also an attitude of hard work accompanied by trust and openness to unexpected possibilities, both in children's capabilities and the grace of a Creator. The concept of *sangat,* as well as describing a static 'congregation', was used to highlight processes of cooperative, intergenerational learning, bringing *'intangible'* benefits and *'blessings'*. The word *'dispositions'* also came up in discussions. This had gained currency through its use in a locally agreed multi-faith syllabus for Religious Education (Birmingham City Council,

2007), produced with Nishkam as one of the collaborating organisations.[13] This emphasised ways of 'learning from' religions, beyond simply 'learning about' them (Grimmitt, 1987).[14] This seemed to me to complement Bhai Sahib's references to the human as an 'agent' gifted with 'originality', to *dharam* as resource which can be accessed to 'uplift the human condition', and mention given to the 'social' and 'cumulative' power of dispositions as they gain momentum through practice.

In 2007, the gurudwara provided resources to set up a small in-house parent and child group (in which my then two-year old daughter and I participated). B. Kaur (quoted above) who played a lead role in conceptualising and running the group, reviewed some of the learning from this interim, experimental phase in written reports. She noted parents' appreciation – in the contexts of day-to-day pressures and constraints – of the creation of a space to give creative attention to bilingual learning with their children and a culturally attuned environment, within which the contrasting challenges of raising children in extended, nuclear or single-parent life could be addressed. This revealed to her a need to support to parents and carers negotiating multi-layered worlds, as well as the children entering them. She also identified the value of adopting particular styles of interaction with the children. For example, use of a quiet, firm tone and respectful terms like '*nehi ji*' ('no', plus '*ji*' as a marker of respect) to index a 'loving boundary', as B. Kaur put it, instead of shouting at children or behaving in abruptly negative ways.

This small play group project helped to forge some clear ideas about the nature and day-to-day practice of an envisaged local pre-school provision. But what was still needed was a dedicated site for longer term nursery. In 2008, a dilapidated former council nursery, located opposite the Nishkam Centre, was purchased. Its 'listed' status required conservation of its heritage features. This prompted a period of enthusiastic renovation and refurbishment by a multi-skilled network of volunteers, including grandparents and parents, students and professionals, contributing their time outside of work. In some cases, a number of key volunteers on the Nishkam campus had taken a career break, extending a familiar mainstream tradition of setting off to engage in volunteer work overseas to include involvement in local project development. This level of community investment in the project stemmed from the well-established culture of '*kar sewa*', community-scale, hands-on volunteering to maintain or enhance social (traditionally religious) institutions, motivated by a sense of shared ownership, belonging and solidarity. Its completion before the nursery first opened in September 2009 was marked with a religious inauguration of prayers and singing before dawn. This event, together with the civic opening described earlier, reflects the spiritual and secular, Sikh and

Citizenship as Social, Spiritual and Multilingual Practice 155

British heritage identities of the nursery which research participants made reference to in interviews.

Nurturing citizenship as day-to-day practice: Inside the nursery's 'figured world'

This section introduces the fluidly interconnected 'figured worlds' of the nursery by taking readers inside and glimpsing the ways in which everyday life unfolded within these worlds. Two extracts of multilingual interactions in the hallway will be analysed to discuss how the nursery ethos was revealed and co-constructed through day-to-day practice.

It is 9am in the nursery as a practitioner routinely guides a small group of pre-schoolers from the playground (after morning drop-off by their parents) upstairs to their classroom. We are in the hallway where, as in all the rooms, the walls are an expanse of white, simply embellished with a pale golden dado rail and a few framed areas to display children's art and class work or information. A wrought iron chandelier set in the high ceiling, and a stained glass window on the staircase landing, echo the building's heritage. This is detailed in a specially designed timeline displayed by the front door entrance, recording the property's history since 1875, as a private home, a professional practice, a wartime nursery and council-run community nursery until 2006, hinting an on-going history after becoming the Nishkam Nursery in 2009. A hallway plasma screen enables parents to observe children still settling in, and functions as a notice board. One ground floor door leads to the baby room, another to a toddler room, while another lead into to the kitchen. This is much valued as the hearth of the nursery, where vegetarian meals are freshly prepared each day on site, to the background sound of devotional music combining eastern and western traditions. The head chef is an aunty-like figure, insistent on flavoursome, home-style and culturally varied cooking, emphasising 'love' as a key ingredient and sometimes involving children in the preparation of food.

Right now in the hallway, with coats on and plastic book bags still in their hands, six or so pre-schoolers, all from Punjabi families,[15] have started to climb the staircase. The practitioner standing by to guide them is B. Kaur (whose interview and written reports are discussed above), a Scottish-born Sikh in her early thirties. A founding nursery staff member, she is continuing her professional early childhood training whilst being keen, as an early interview with her revealed, to research and draw on approaches from her Sikh and South Asian heritage. Like other female staff she is addressed as 'Masi Ji' (a kinship term meaning mother's sister) and she wears a white *kurta-pajama* (Punjabi tunic and trousers) and a red *chuni* (scarf) draped over her head (the two turbaned male practitioners in the nursery, who also wear white, are addressed as 'Mama Ji', meaning 'mother's brother', a term which was chosen by the children themselves). The first extract begins just as the practitioner praises one of the children for taking her first step.

Extract 1

1. Masi:		Well done, and what do we hold on to?
2.		Let me see. *[Girl 1 holds on to bannister]*
3.		*[Masi addresses girl 1]* Good girl.
		[slight raising of voice as Masi addresses group on stairs]
4.		Slowly walking.
5.		Looking where you're going.
6.		Taking time.
7.		Not pushing.
8.		*[Masi calls to girl 2 who is not holding the bannister]* Jaspreet Kaur.
9.		*[Masi softens voice]* Have you forgotten something?
10.		Hold on to the….
11.		What's it called?
12. Girl 2:		Bannister.
13. Masi:		Bannister. Well done!
		[Masi addresses other children climbing stairs]
14.		Well done, Jaipal.
15.		Have you got your arm (?) on there?
16.		Good listening, Gursev.
17.		Well done, Harnam Singh Chana.

In a retrospective interview about the event, 'Masi Ji' explained that her immediate aim was to ensure that the children, who until recently were accustomed to being brought in by their parents to the ground floor toddler room, were supported to climb the stairs safely and competently. She managed this interactionally in a number of ways. Indexing her professional 'British-practitioner' identity, she used classic teacher questions (lines 1, 9 and 11) and ample, inclusive positive feedback (lines 1, 3, 13, 14 and 16), while softening directives, through tone of voice (line 10) selecting present continuous instead of imperative tense (lines 4–7). Her interview revealed her acknowledgment of the child's perspective to elicit a positive response; by explaining her conscious use of *'two word level'* instructions (lines 4–7) readily understood by all the children, especially during a practical task demanding significant concentration, and her strategy to keep a girl from losing focus on the task (lines 8–9): *'So she's met a friend and got excited. So, rather than stop her and say, "Hold on, what are you doing?", it was just to remind her to get back into focus.'* This stance is also revealed in the interaction which immediately followed (code switches into Punjabi are indicated with bold font):

Extract 2
[Girl 3 looking anxious, asks Masi an inaudible question, pointing to her book bag]
18. Masi: **Haan ji** *(Yes)*
19. Girl 3: *[inaudible]*
20. Masi: **Haan ji** *(Yes)*
21.   Because... **Pata ki si** *(You know what)*
22.   **Eh...eh** book **da haiga hai** five book
            (This...this book is a level five book)
23.   **Jidhaan** Spot book **vala, hana, oh** five **hounda hai.**
            (Like the Spot book, you know, it is a level five book)
24.   **Eh jehra aapna, oh** hard **hai**
            (This one of ours, it's a hard[er] one)
25   **Te mai chauhundi si ke tusi** done **parleho**
            (And I was hoping you could try and read both)
26. Girl 3: *[inaudible]*
27. Masi: **Achha ji, tuhanu pasand sigai?**
            (OK, did you like them?)
28.   **Tuhanu ik hee davaan, kai do davaan?**
            (Should I give you just one, or should I give you two?)
29. Girl 3: **Do... Ik...** *(Two...one...)*
30. Masi: **Achha, ttheek hai**
            (OK, that's fine)
31.   **Mai siraf ik dou'ngi**
            (I'll only give you one.)
32.   OK. Thank you **ji** *['ji' as marker of respect]*

Commenting on the above interaction in her interview, the practitioner explained that her switch to Punjabi meant that her response was more reassuring for this particular girl, who has a tendency to become anxious.

As a Punjabi-dominant speaker it was easier for her to digest in a moment of stress. Code switches back to English in the extract, relating to book resources and reading levels (lines 22 and 23) show how Punjabi is used to mediate the English-dominant world of the pre-school classroom curriculum. The use of Punjabi fostered closeness with and respect for the child, in turns of phrase such as *'pata ki si'* (you know what) (line 21), *'hana'* (isn't it) (line 23), signalling a style shift into a more informal and reassuringly familiar interactional context. In addition, the use of the respectful second person plural (*'tusi'*; *'tuhanu'*) (lines 25, 27 and 28) is used to address the child, alongside the reiteration of *'ji'* a marker of respect (lines 27 and 32), indexes the kind of relationship that exists between adult and child. Other examples of daily hallway interactions involving this practitioner include code switches to Hindi for some young children, for whom Hindi is a dominant home language and style-shifting in English to address children as 'darling'. These examples reveal her instinctive use of communicative resources in ways that were inclusive and sensitive to each child.

I have focused here on just one moment in the nursery day, but in other moments of interaction that I observed and video-recorded during this study, B. Kaur and the other practitioners working in the nursery made similar uses of the communicative resources available to them, within the daily rounds of communicative life with the children. The main language of teaching and learning was English but the practitioners moved in and out of different languages, genres and styles as they fostered calm, safe stair-climbing routines (or other similar routines); as they reassured children who were more comfortable in Punjabi or Hindi or as they established relationships of mutual respect with the children, making liberal use of fictive kinship terms, like Masi Ji and Mama Ji, to create a world reminiscent of home and family. As I have also suggested in this account, the use of verbal resources was combined with other semiotic resources like the use of gesture and tone of voice, the adoption of particular forms of dress, the serving of vegetarian food, accompanied by shared rituals around the lunch table. Practitioners and parents saw the use of music and the creation of a homely environment, without excessive displays evidencing classroom work, as contributing to an atmosphere of calm, ease and focus. A regional journalist covering the opening of the nursery reported it to be 'a little school of calm' (Ind, 2010).

The nursery had clearly become a space between the children's home environment and public nursery education as currently conceived within the contemporary educational policy context in England, as well as one being shaped through locally generated values. Talking about the daily morning nursery 'drop off', one father commented favourably to me, as follows, on how the use of terms of address helped to create a seamless transition between home and school: 'Now he just goes "Dada! *[father gestures his son waving goodbye to him]* Masi! *[father gestures his son welcoming the practitioner]*"'. He added that, as a couple, they chose the nursery because: 'it felt homely... I could see that my son was going to be relaxed when he was here'. This, both parents felt, had contributed to his enjoyment and ability to learn well. The felt sense of the place was summed up for me when, on a visit to the nursery, I discovered that a large framed poster of the dispositions framework from Birmingham's multi-faith syllabus, which usually hung in the office, had been taken away for repair. When I questioned the nursery manager (a Sikh with extensive experience of running mainstream nurseries in the region) he replied, half-humorously, that the dispositions had 'dissolved all around into the nursery!'

Concluding Comments

My intention in this chapter has been to contribute to the growing number of ethnographically oriented studies of urban pre-schools and to show, with close attention to ethnographic and textual detail, how particular, local pre-school projects can and are creating spaces where citizenship-as-practice can be nurtured, underpinned by the construction and practice of a distinctive vision of community-based responsibility and action, and of culturally responsive pedagogy. Recognised in 2011 by the school inspection body as 'outstanding' for its support of children's wellbeing and 'spiritual, moral, social and cultural development',[16] at the time of writing, the nursery has a year-long waiting list. It has led to the development of a sister project to create a visionary local primary school, emerging from similar orienting principles (this opened as a state-funded institution in 2011, extending the cultural diversity of the school population). One of the ingredients of the success of the project is that described by Bhai Sahib: the nursery is 'more than bricks and mortar'. It has an 'ambience' and, as he puts it, 'a fragrance', in which particular dispositions can be fostered. Moreover, his reflections on dharmic heritage suggests that communicative resources such as 'gaze and touch', and the more 'intangible' aspects of communicative exchange, are as important as the verbal resources employed in the daily rounds of the nursery's communicative life.

Thinking through the whole trajectory of a child's education, R. Singh, one of the original nursery project members now shaping the school development, had the following to say about the way in which citizenship education can be embedded in educational spaces for young learners (rather than being instituted as a distinct area of the curriculum). 'because you have the right environment, because you have the right atmosphere, because you have the right support, this idea of their responsibilities as a citizen will actually blossom in a way, without having to be taught...' Recalling his past involvement in educating marginalised groups about their citizenship rights, he described how his understanding evolved, inspired by the concept of *dharam*, to recognise that 'the starting point should be our responsibilities, not what we are owed by institutions or other people, but what can we do for ourselves and other people, and for society as well'. This continuum of concern begins to link with the idea of rights when the need arises 'to create those structures, the institutions, the support mechanisms, for us to fulfil those responsibilities'. In this way, the network of people involved in the creation of the Nishkam nursery can be seen as what Cornwall and Gaventa (2001) describe as 'makers and shapers' rather than 'users and choosers' of social policy and social provisioning.

Dahlberg and Moss (2005) raise similar concerns in the context of pre-school provision, arguing for the creation of 'children's spaces' instead of simply 'children's services', where functional and therapeutic notions of 'care' are transformed into ones that foreground 'attentiveness, responsibility, competence, responsiveness' (2005: 92). Such a stance is suggested in the interactional data I have presented in this chapter. It is also reflected in ideas circulated in the early childhood press on how citizenship, while not an explicit theme in the national framework, may be fostered through features of it, such as 'dispositions and attitudes; self-confidence and self-esteem; relationships; behaviour and self-control; sense of community; language for communication; language for thinking' (Telfer-Brunton & Thornton, 2004).

Contextualising early childhood education and care in Britain, I outlined the historic interchange of ideas, approaches and movements across Europe and North America. This present research contributes to a growing number of studies which identify scope for including knowledge from heritages arising geographically further afield and which argue for moving forward such an interchange, as both ethical responsibility and a shared benefit (echoing the stance on linguistic rights outlined by May, 2005: 327). Building on historical research (Day Ashley, 2008, forthcoming; Dharampal, 1983; O'Connell, 2003) about the exchange and interplay of educational ideas between Europe and South Asia, it journeys forward into today's coexistence of multiple understandings, aspirations and identities in the internal landscapes of social actors.

The founding of the Nishkam nursery has encompassed highly local and contemporary, as well as global, historical and existential concerns. Connecting these, the conceptual and practical unpacking of *dharam* can be seen to engender citizenship as a social, spiritual and multilingual practice. This makes way for new possibilities brought about by human agency emerging from overlapping figured worlds within a plural society, and the possibilities brought by children and adults as newcomers to existing social orders. Linking up examples of data I collected, this chapter has sought to shed light on some of the ways in which this concept of citizenship was played out in the discursive and interactional processes underpinning the nursery's creation and unfolding of its day-to-day world.

Acknowledgement

I would like to gratefully acknowledge the helpful feedback and assistance given by Marilyn Martin-Jones and Vaidehi Ramanathan in the writing of this chapter.

Notes

(1) From the 17th century in England, Birmingham's reputation for supporting religious freedom encouraged the migration of non-conformists to the area, from the non-Anglican churches e.g. Baptists, Quakers, Unitarians and Methodists, who influenced the emergence of Birmingham's 'Civic Gospel', linking social activism and civic pride to spiritual growth (Green, 2008). See note (8).
(2) See, for example, the vision for Birmingham 2026 at http://www.birmingham.gov.uk/2026 (accessed 2012).
(3) See http://handsonhandsworth.info/handsworth-heritage-trail/ (accessed 2012).
(4) The full title is 'Guru Nanak Nishkam Sewak Jatha', an organisation (*jatha*) founded to promote 'selfless service' (*nishkam sewa*) in the name of the founder of the Sikh faith, Guru Nanak. Its increased regional profile has given rise to an abbreviated, local reference to the organisation as 'Nishkam'. Its origins go back to the migration of Sikhs from the Punjab, India, to British East Africa at the turn of the 20th century. Its saintly founder, Sant Puran Singh, is recognised for his contribution to municipal developments in his Kenyan home town of Kericho and for revitalising the faith practice of Sikhs settled in new places outside of India. This work was continued in post-war Britain, with Birmingham becoming its headquarters. Since Sant Puran Singh, two consecutive successors, addressed as 'Bhai Sahib', have led the organisation in an unremunerated role of lifelong commitment.
(5) A *gurdwara* is a Sikh place of worship, understood as a gateway ('*dwar*') to the 'Guru', referring to the Sikh sacred text, the Guru Granth Sahib, a copy of which is enthroned inside in a hall known as the Guru's *darbar* or court. This reflects the reverence it receives as a spiritual sovereign and perpetual guide, after ten consecutive human Gurus founded the faith between 1469 and 1708. Its verses are shared and internalised largely through oral and musical transmission (see Sagoo (2008)).
(6) Integral to every gurdwara is the *langar*. This is the area where volunteers prepare and serve vegetarian meals, as well as the name given to the meal itself. It is founded on an ethos of welcoming and offering hospitality to visitors of all religious, cultural and social backgrounds; of recognising human equality by inviting all to sit at the

same level; and providing a practical opportunity for undertaking *sewa* or service to others.
(7) The Nishkam Centre and its Civic Association have been publicly recognised through awards including a regional 'Built in Quality' Award in 2006 from Birmingham's Building Consultancy and a national 'Queen's Award for Voluntary Service' in 2010.
(8) Reference to the 'Civic Gospel' (see note (1)) has been made at a number of events where key drivers have presented the work of the Nishkam Centre, as well as on its home page http://www.ncauk.org/ (accessed 2012).
(9) See note (4). 'Bhai Sahib' is also a rare, official title given by the global Sikh apex organisation, in recognition of his historic leadership and service. His civic and interfaith work is recognised in honorary doctorates from two of Birmingham's universities and several international awards.
(10) Bhai Sahib was born in British East Africa and trained as a civil and structural engineer, with a period of study and work in the United Kingdom. He went on to project-lead national rural and urban housing developments in Zambia for twenty years. Association with Sant Puran Singh, initiation to become a practising Sikh, the decision to leave his job, migrate to the United Kingdom and commit himself to sewa, linked him to the emergence of the Nishkam organisation, his appointment to lead it in 1995 accelerating the pace and scope of local and international engagement. On a personal note, he has identified the loss of his mother as a young child, and subsequent nurture within a supportive step family, as factors prompting greater reflectivity on the perspectives of a child and a deeper exploration of his faith heritage.
(11) Sikh minority rights activism is often associated with safeguarding a highly visible faith identity, which includes the *dastar,* or turban along with five 'articles of faith' known as the *kakkar*. See, for example, the *First Global Sikh Civil Rights Report* (2008), published online at http://unitedsikhs.org/rtt/sikhconf/FirstGlobalSikh-CivilRightsReport.pdf (accessed 2012).
(12) Guru Granth Sahib includes compositions of saintly figures in Northern India between roughly the twelfth and seventeenth centuries, spanning different social classes and Hindu and Muslim religious traditions. Their inclusion by the Sikh Gurus is seen to encourage a conversation about shared values, based on linking spiritual growth to humanitarianism, social responsibility and transformative action.
(13) My involvement, as a Sikh representative of the Nishkam organisation, on the multi-faith committee participating in the revision of Birmingham's locally agreed syllabus for Religious Education (see note (14) below), stimulated discussions with Bhai Sahib and Nishkam colleagues, notes from which provided early inspiration and data for the current research.
(14) These two official attainment targets are set out in the national non-statutory framework for Religious Education (Qualifications & Curriculum Authority, 2004), drawing on earlier work linking Religious Education to human development (Grimmitt, 1987). Religious Education in England is a statutory, non-confessional, academic school subject. Instead of a nationally agreed curriculum, syllabi are locally agreed through a network of Standing Advisory Committees on Religious Education (SACREs) to respond to local visions, demographics and needs.
(15) The nursery has had an open admissions policy and initially marketed extensively in the local area. Its promotion as a 'faith-inspired' nursery, evidently close to the gurdwara, was seen by staff to encourage interest from South Asian families with

an affinity for Sikh and Punjabi culture. Some such enquirers raised concerns about social integration, which itself was seen as a longstanding Sikh value, and many initial applicants were not from the core congregation of the gurdwara or initiated faith practitioners. The nursery served an Afghani Muslim family, for whom some concern about religious and cultural difference was outweighed by the level of care offered. Newer local migrants enquiring from other communities were not in a position to afford the private day care fees or claim state subsidies, and there was an absence of young English Caucasian families living locally.

(16) The national inspection body for schools is OFSTED, the Office for Standards in Education. Its inspections include assessment of 'spiritual, moral, social and cultural development', a legislated aim of education in England (Education Act, 1992). This requirement shaped some of the initial rationale for my doctoral study. Two inspection reports (2010 and 2011, published at http://www.ofsted.gov.uk/, accessed 2012) currently exist for the Nishkam Nursery, the latter reflecting its registration as an independent primary school in anticipation of a state-funded phase in autumn 2011. This was enabled through a new government policy for 'Free Schools', which are state-funded and run independently, rather than by a local authority.

References

Allen, G. (2011) *Early Intervention: The Next Steps. An independent Report to Her Majesty's Government*. London: Cabinet Office.

Beatty, B. (2005) The rise of the American nursery school: Laboratory for a science of child development. In D.B. Pillemer and S.H. White (eds) *Developmental Psychology and Social Change*. Cambridge: Cambridge University Press.

Birmingham City Council (2007) *The Birmingham Agreed Syllabus for Religious Education*. Birmingham: Author.

Biesta, G. (2006) *Beyond Learning: Democratic Education for a Human Future*. Boulder, CO: Paradigm Publishers.

Biesta, G. (2009) Sporadic democracy: Education, democracy and the question of inclusion. In M.S. Katz, S. Verducci and G. Biesta (eds) *Education, Democracy and the Moral Life*. Dordrecht: Springer Science & Business Media B.V.

Bronfenbrenner, U. (1979) *The Ecology of Human Development*. Cambridge: Harvard University Press.

Bronfenbrenner, U. (2005) *Making Human Beings Human: Bioecological Perspectives on Human Development*. Thousand Oaks, CA: Sage Publications.

The Children's Society (2006) *The Good Childhood: A National Inquiry*. London: Author.

Cleghorn, A. and Prochner, L. (2010) *Shades of Globalization in Three Early Childhood Settings*. Rotterdam: Sense Publishers.

Cornwall, A. and Gaventa, J. (2001) *From Users and Choosers to Makers and Shapers: Repositioning Participation in Social Policy*. Institute of Development Studies Working Paper 127. Sussex: Institute of Development Studies.

Cottrell, M. (2010) Indigenous education in comparative perspective: Global opportunities for reimagining schools. *International Journal for Cross-Disciplinary Subjects in Education* 1 (4), 223–227.

Dahlberg, G. and Moss, P. (2005) *Ethics and Politics in Early Childhood Education*. Abingdon: Routledge Falmer.

David, T., Powell, S. and Goouch, K. (2010) The world picture. In G. Pugh and B. Duffy (eds) *Contemporary Issues in the Early Years* (5th edn). London: Sage.

Day Ashley, L. (2008) *Creating and connecting local and global communities: Tagore's university and rural reconstruction experiments at Santiniketan*. Beyond the Lecture Hall Conference of University of Cambridge Faculty of Education and History of Education Society UK, Homerton College, Cambridge (unpublished conference paper).

Day Ashley, L. (forthcoming) A study of Indian influences on progressive education in Britain during the early twentieth century and their subsequent impact. For details of research in progress see http://www.birmingham.ac.uk/research/activity/education/domus/research/index.aspx

Department for Children, Schools & Families (2008) *Statutory Framework for the Early Years Foundation Stage*. London: Her Majesty's Stationary Office (HMSO).

Department for Education & Skills (2004) *Every Child Matters: Change for Children*. London: HMSO

Dharampal (1983) *The Beautiful Tree: Indigenous Indian Education in the Eighteenth Century*. New Delhi: Biblia Impex Private Limited.

Erickson, F. (1987) Transformation and school success: The politics and culture of educational achievement. *Anthropology & Education Quarterly* 18 (4), 335–356.

Erickson, F. (2001) Culture in society and in educational practices. In J. Banks and C. McGee Banks (eds) *Multicultural Education: Issues and Perspectives* (4th edn). New York: John Wiley & Sons, Inc.

Eaude, T. (2006) *Children's Spiritual, Moral, Social and Cultural Development: Primary and Early Years*. Exeter: Learning Matters.

González, N., Moll, L. and Amanti, C. (eds) (2005) *Funds of Knowledge: Theorizing Practices in Households, Communities, and Classrooms*. Mahwah, NJ: Lawrence Erlbaum Associates.

Green, A. (2008) *Civic Gospel: Networks for Social Change*. Part of the Birmingham Stories Research Project. Accessed from the Connecting Histories website at http://www.connectinghistories.org.uk/birminghamstories/guides/downloads/bs_rg_civic_gospels.pdf

Grimmitt, M. (1987) *Religious Education and Human Development: The Relationship Between Studying Religions and Personal, Social and Moral Education*. Great Wakering: McCrimmons Publishing Co.

Gupta, A. (2006) *Early Childhood Education, Postcolonial Theory, and Teaching Practices in India: Balancing Vygotsky and the Veda*. New York: Palgrave Macmillan.

Holland, D., Lachiocotte, W., Skinner, D. and Cain, C. (1998) *Identity and Agency in Cultural Worlds*. Cambridge, MA: Harvard University Press.

Ind, J. (2010) Birmingham Sikh nursery is a little school of calm. *Birmingham Post*, accessed 2012. doi: http://www.birminghampost.net/2010/02/26/birmingham-sikh-nursery-is-a-little-school-of-calm-65233-25922675/3/

James, O. (2001) Children Need Love Not Warehousing. *The Independent*, accessed 2012. http://www.independent.co.uk/opinion/commentators/oliver-james-children-need-love-not-warehousing-2278097.html

Jones, D.V. and Martin-Jones, M. (2004) Bilingual education and language revitalization in Wales: Past achievements and current issues. In W. Tollefson and A. Tsui (eds) *Medium of Instruction Policies: Which Agenda? Whose Agenda?* NJ: Lawrence Erlbaum Associates.

Kwon, Y. (2002) Changing curriculum for early childhood education in England. *Early Childhood Research & Practice* 4 (2), 1–25.
La Berge, A.F. (1991) Medicalization and moralization: The crèches of nineteenth-century Paris. *Journal of Social History* 25 (1), 65–87.
Levinson, B., Foley, D. and Holland, D. (1996) *The Cultural Production of the Educated Person.* Albany: State University of New York Press.
Lawy, R. and Biesta, G. (2006) Citizenship-as-practice: the educational implications of an inclusive and relational understanding of citizenship. *British Journal of Educational Studies* 54 (1), 34–50.
May, S. (2005) Language rights: Moving the debate forward. *Journal of Sociolinguistics* 9 (3), 319–347.
Moss, P. (2007) *Bringing politics into the nursery: Early childhood education as a democratic practice.* European Early Childhood Education Research Journal 15 (1), 5–20.
Martin-Jones, M. and Saxena, M. (2003) Bilingual resources and 'funds of knowledge' for teaching and learning in multi-ethnic classrooms in Britain. *International Journal of Bilingual Education and Bilingualism* 6 (3/4) Special Issue, 267–282.
McLaughlin, T. (1996) Education of the whole child? In R. Best (ed.) *Education, Spirituality and the Whole Child.* London: Cassell.
Nesbitt, E. (2005) *Sikhism: A Very Short Introduction.* Oxford: Oxford University Press.
O'Connell, K.M. (2003) *Rabindranath Tagore on education.* Accessed 2012 from The Encyclopaedia of Informal Education website at http://www.infed.org/thinkers/tagore.htm
Osberg, D.C. and Biesta, G. (2010) The end/s of education: complexity and the conundrum of the inclusive educational curriculum. *International Journal of Inclusive Education* 14 (6), 593–607.
Palmer, S. (2007) How we forgot the art of child-rearing. *The Independent*, accessed 2012. doi: http://www.independent.co.uk/opinion/commentators/sue-palmer-how-we-forgot-the-art-of-child-rearing-436288.html
Qualifications & Curriculum Authority (QCA) (2000) *Curriculum Guidance for the Foundation Stage.* London: Author.
Qualifications & Curriculum Authority (2004) *Religious Education: The Non-statutory National Framework.* London: Author.
Sagoo, G.K. (2008) A Sikh-inspired vision for learning: The discursive production of an ethos by members of the GNNET education trust. M. Res. dissertation, University of Birmingham.
Starkey, H. (1996) *Freinet and citizenship education.* Based on Osler, A. and Starkey, H. (1996) *Teacher Education and Human Rights.* London: David Fulton. Accessed 2012. http://www.educacionenvalores.org/spip.php?article819
Stearns, P. (2005) *Growing Up: The History of Childhood in a Global Context.* Waco, TX: Baylor University Press.
Stearns, P. (2006) *Childhood in World History.* New York: Routledge.
Stephen, C., McPake, J. and McLeod, W. (2012) Playing and learning in another language: Ensuring good quality early years education in a language revitalisation programme. *European Early Childhood Education Research Journal* 20 (1), 21–33.
Telfer-Brunton, P. and Thorton, L. (2004) Little Citizens. *Nursery World Magazine*, accessed 6 May. doi: http://www.nurseryworld.co.uk/news/717210/Little-citizens/?DCMP=ILC-SEARCH

Tobin, J., Hseuh, Y. and Karasawa, M. (2009) *Preschool in Three Cultures Revisited: China, Japan and the United States*. Chicago: Chicago University Press.

Tobin, J., Wu, D. and Davidson, D. (1989) *Preschool in Three Cultures: Japan, China, and the United States*. New Haven, CT: Yale University Press.

United Nations Children's Fund (UNICEF) (2007) *Child Poverty in Perspective: An Overview of Child Wellbeing in Rich Countries*. Florence: Innocenti Research Centre.

Urrieta Jr., L. (2007) Figured worlds and education: An introduction to the special issue. *The Urban Review* 39 (2), 107–116.

Weston, P. (2002) *The Froebel Educational Institute: The Origins and History of the College*. London: University of Surrey Roehampton.

9 Re-imagining Citizenship: Views from the Classroom

Jacqueline Widin and Keiko Yasukawa

In this chapter we explore the highly contested notions of citizenship and dis-citizenship through the experiences of teachers and learners in four very different classroom settings: a literacy and numeracy program for young people disengaged from learning, a vocationally oriented class for speakers of English as an additional language, a numeracy class for adults and a flexible learning centre for adult basic education (ABE) students. The settings bring learners from various intersecting communities within Australia. We take the classroom (in its broadest possible sense) as the point of departure to illustrate citizenship as something generative and collectively created in a shared space. We present a more critical interpretation and different possibilities of citizenship than what is defined by dominant discourses and that which underpins the content of programs designed for people seeking to be accepted as 'worthy citizens'. We show the teacher's role as pivotal in creating a collaborative space where the society's power relations are acknowledged, but where students' agency to achieve their own goals in and beyond their classrooms is affirmed and addressed. We argue that teachers can work with their learners to create these new spaces of belonging and being.

Our studies have led us to acknowledge citizenship as a powerful notion that includes and excludes. Pothier and Devlin (2006) discuss the broad ranging views of citizenship from a formal definition of holding a passport to what is seen as a more 'substantive' understanding of citizenship which recognises one's capacity to participate in all institutions in society. In their view, citizenship is not only a noun but a practice inseparable from the broader societal power relations which position people in a society. Pothier and Devlin, in their critical examination of the construction of disability, discuss the notion of dis-citizenship as applicable to people with disabilities, who because of not being able to meet the supposed criterion of 'capacity to participate or be productive' are denied access to society's institutions and rights, and consequently, they cannot claim their status as citizens. The learners or students in each of the classes occupy positions typically categorised as marginalised, excluded or disadvantaged: Indigenous students, recent and long-term immigrants, job-seekers, people with learning disabilities, those who live under the 'regime of dis-citizenship' (Pothier & Devlin, 2006: 2) in a deeply unequal society.

In this chapter we focus on a dimension of teaching alluded to in our opening paragraph: where the teaching space provided opportunities for development of a mutually negotiated sense of place, belonging and rights in this society. In this space, the students and teachers built a shared ethics of 'mutual respect and civility' within diversity, rather than reproducing the assimilation of the dominated to the dominant culture (Singh, 2007: 7).

Discourses of Citizenship Outside the Classrooms

In 2007, at the time of conducting our research in the (English) language, literacy and numeracy (LLN) classrooms (Widin *et al.*, 2008) the Australian Federal Government proposed to introduce a citizenship test for immigrants who wanted to become Australian citizens (see http://www.citizenship.gov.au/learn/cit_test/background/ for a brief history). It proposed a multiple choice question test with the content based on a particular view of Australian history. The many critics of the test saw it as xenophobic; the test could include questions on topics such as the country's flora, fauna and sports people and was seen as 'a superficial filter based on a very narrow reading of what Australia's culture actually is' (http://ipsnews.net/news.asp?idnews=39473). Those who challenged this proposal included unions, human rights groups, teachers of migrants and other educational organisations (see http://www.aph.gov.au/senate/committee/legcon_ctte/completed_inquiries/2004-07/citizenship_testing/submissions/sublist.htm for the submissions received by Government). We (the authors) were similarly struck by the way 'a citizenship test' is based on an exclusionary definition of who should belong and who is worthy; this formed our initial impetus to think about ways that critical pedagogy can engage learners in ways that challenge the assimilationist and integrationist push of such measures. In this chapter we opt to discuss and showcase pedagogies that include rather than discriminate or impose a particular way of seeing the world. The citizenship test is an ongoing issue; others in this volume have also referred to the gate-keeping role of this type of test.

The current Labor government, while not publicly pursuing such an overtly assimilationist agenda as the previous government, has maintained a watered down version of a citizenship test and in its paternalistic management of Indigenous communities has suspended human and land rights legislation and has maintained control of day to day running of once independent Aboriginal communities. While these issues are of utmost concern to us and underpin the fabric of Australian society, our purpose in this paper is to critique assimilationist policies through the lens of adult learners' experiences in LLN classrooms and to show ways that classrooms can become sites of dynamic citizenship.

Australia is a highly relevant site of exploration, it has a recent and ongoing history of colonisation and since European invasion has had very high levels of immigration; it is estimated that more than one in four Australians were born overseas (Australian Bureau of Statistics [ABS], 2011). While notions of citizenship and dis-citizenship have been mainly used in reference to issues to do with immigration, colonisation has been a major force in determining whether people belong or not; for example Australian Aboriginal people were not recognised as Australian citizens and were not included in the census until 1967; this is another feature of our context, if not the main one.

The Politics of LLN Education

Teachers (particularly LLN teachers) are increasingly recognised for their pivotal role in creating the spaces and processes for learners to productively negotiate their rightful place in their society, and in some sense their 'global citizenship' (Birch, 2009). Birch (2009) describes this role as being at the centre of 'important socio-cultural networks' which in turn facilitates a different kind of space for citizenship.

In exploring the dynamics of the classrooms, we are also located in a particular social and policy context which focuses on the students' employability and other aspects of workforce participation; in this context, there is a sharp delineation between citizenship and dis-citizenship. The current challenge to teachers and learners is to counter the identities imposed by policy and the institutions: 'student as potential employee', 'student as test taker', 'student as aspirant citizen'. In our analysis of the case studies we examine how (and whether) the teachers and learners successfully counter these more dominant discourses of citizenship and build more mutually negotiated identities of citizenship (Simpson, 2011).

Some adult education policy researchers (Walker, 2009; Gibb & Walker, 2011; Hamilton & Pitt, 2011) have applied critical discourse analysis to analyse and uncover the ideological underpinnings of recent life-long learning statements and policies from the Organisation of Economic Co-operation and Development (OECD) and adult literacy policies in the United Kingdom. Walker (2009) analyses key OECD documents on life-long learning, and concluded that through these documents 'a worthy citizen is constructed as having a moral imperative to engage in learning to help their country grow in terms of GDP, to prevent the need for a broad social welfare system and to avert widespread social exclusion' (2009: 336). She claims that the recent OECD policy discourse is imbued with a philosophy of 'inclusive liberalism' that engenders a conditional form of social inclusion based on a 'moral quasi-religious imperative to activate individuals to undertake citizenry duty to learn, and in so doing, adopt certain values, behaviours and personality traits' (2009: 336).

In the United Kingdom, Hamilton and Pitt (2011) examine the *Skills for Life* adult literacy, language and numeracy policy and observe that it is also underpinned by 'a discourse of conditionality in the social contract between the individual and the state, expressed through the theme of exclusion and duty' (2011: 368). Furthermore, Hamilton and Pitt identify the existence of 'orders of discourse' (2011: 368) where national policies are influenced by policies made at transnational levels such as the OECD or the EU. Walker makes the related observation that the OECD's influence in education policies has increased since the 1970s, and there is an increasing standardisation of policy in lifelong learning through 'policy transfer' and 'policy borrowing' (2011: 337). This is also visible in Australian LLN policy (cf. DEEWR, 2011; Skills Australia, 2010).

In spite of this policy context, LLN teachers are often strategically placed to exercise judgment and make professional decisions that affect curriculum and pedagogy. As Ramanathan and Morgan (2007: 451) demonstrate, teachers are no longer the 'passive recipients' of the whims of changing policies but rather they have the potential to be agents of change in even the most constricting setting. Thus they can buffer the penetration of the dominant policy discourses into the classroom, and consequently, reflect contrasting concepts of citizenship, one which we call 'top down' (imposed), serving society's narrow economic interests and the other, which is generative, serving to create collaborative spaces. One illustration of this is by incorporating norms of pro-social communicative competence (Birch, 2009) (pro-social 'refers to attitudes and behaviours benefitting others in a societal relationship and environmental context'; 2008: 11) into curriculum and pedagogy. LLN teachers are also placed at the intersecting point of the global and the local, between global civil society and local civil society, and between global civic culture and local civic culture. We demonstrate how teachers take up this mantle of 'pro-social' approaches which embody a 'shared ethos of respect and civility' (Singh, 2007) that we referred to earlier.

Dominant Constructs of Citizenship: Deficit, Assimilation and Integration

Citizenship programmes proliferate in countries with past and present colonial/immigration histories, particularly in language and literacy education and lifelong learning contexts. In the United Kingdom and its former colonies, alongside the emphasis on English language and literacy, the programs propose to impose certain socio-political and cultural mores. They seek to replace participants' language and cultural practices. Guo (2010) critiques most lifelong learning opportunities in the United Kingdom as vehicles for assimilation, which fail to integrate productive notions of cultural difference and diversity. He wonders how this approach can build towards the government rhetoric of cohesiveness and instead proposes 'transnational lifelong learning for recognitive justice and inclusive citizenship' (Guo, 2010: 150). Ng and Shan (2010), also from the United Kingdom, are concerned about the increasing focus on the production of human capital and blatant economic interests inherent in lifelong learning programs, where much of the supposed citizenship programs are located. Their analysis shows how lifelong learning, as an ideological frame, is naturalised and becomes a mechanism of neo-liberal control to produce ideal workers and learners for the knowledge-based economy. They also show how it reproduces inequalities of gender, race and class.

In his critique of the dominant discourse of lifelong learning, Rogers (2006) identifies learning for citizenship as one of the two foci of lifelong learning discussions and policies (the other being learning for work), but he says that while 'inclusion' is a favourite keyword of those involved in discussing lifelong learning '... the process involved consists of that form of participation which leads to the co-option of individuals within existing structures; it does not engage in critical analysis of those structures' (2006: 127). Thus, like Guo, Rogers sees lifelong learning as a process of assimilation into the status quo. He further critiques the use of the terms such as *marginalisation* and *social deprivation* as a way to avoid naming the act of *oppression* as the root of the problem, and similarly the reference to *social inclusion* rather than *liberation* from the oppressive forces that are the dominant status quo. Thus, according to Rogers, the possibilities of social change through extending citizenship are not contemplated by the dominant paradigms of lifelong learning.

Dominant discourses concerning English language and literacy and numeracy education circulate around the notions of testing and assessment, employability (as stated beforehand) and responsible citizenship in Australia (Walker, 2009; Skills Australia, 2010). The increasingly narrow understanding of ESOL and literacy and numeracy, which is seen in Australia, is reflected in other OECD countries (Simpson, 2011) and referred to above, where LLN education is seen as a service to the economy, accompanied by more rigid qualifications frameworks and positioning of learners as potential employees and test takers (Simpson, 2011). Learners in LLN contexts are once again positioned as 'deficient'; in particular, ESOL learners' multilingual skills are seen as a hindrance and consequently invalidated. The ideology of the monolingual nation dominates and in the case of bi- or multilingual people their language skills are surrendered as the price they need to pay for membership to the new society (Miller, 2010).

Very often the proponents of citizenship courses and tests are concerned that immigrants get to know about their new country's culture, what they as newcomers can have access to. Teachers, like the one in Han et al.'s (2010) recent study, agree that it is vital for people coming to live in Britain, to learn about British culture; however, this begs the question, 'which British culture will they get to know about?'. Britain, similar to Australia and other countries of high immigration, has a diverse and multilingual culture (Jackson, 2010). The students in Han et al.'s study, like students in our study, were keen to learn English; their priorities were instrumental, creating a 'sense of belonging' through learning the dominant language.

Societies such as United States, United Kingdom and Australia are in a contradictory position regarding cultural diversity, multiculturalism, multilingualism; on the one hand there is a public preoccupation with these matters and a growing perception that today's society is much more open to and accepting of Indigenous and immigrant communities sustaining and growing their first languages and cultures (Griswold, 2010). On the other hand, the push towards assimilation, in countries such as the United States, United Kingdom, Australia and many more countries, which receive high numbers of immigrants (Griswold 2010), is still strong. At the same time, the research shows that there is a persistent idea that acquiring citizenship is concomitant with embracing the dominant language, culture and the political ideals of the accepting country (cf. Griswold, 2010 for further references; Baynham & Simpson, 2010; Ramanathan & Morgan, 2007; Scarino & Papdemetre, 2001). Language proficiency and language ideologies have become a particular focal point for examining an immigrant's cultural and political loyalty; the assumption is that accepting countries are monolingual and mono-cultural and that immigrants are only welcomed if they are prepared to assimilate (Cooke & Simpson, 2008). However, there is no research that has established links between language proficiency and civic engagement.

Third Space – The Classroom as a Productive Space of Citizenship

Many adult language and literacy learners, for example those who are learning English as an additional language, literacy learners who have a learning disability or younger learners who left school early, are often viewed as coming from some marginalised space, as people who are not quite able to participate fully as citizens of the dominant society. But, like all people, adult learners who are categorised in this way bring with them rich personal, social and cultural histories that they can draw on as literacy resources to make sense of their world; these resources are not always legitimated within the official curriculum. Gutiérrez (2008) and Moje *et al.* (2004) discuss the need for teachers to create a 'Third space' that enables learners to negotiate their experiences of the institutional space and their lived experiences in their communities, as a way of increasing academic engagement and learning.

The work of Gutiérrez (2008) and Moje *et al.* (2004) reports on their work with middle and high-school students from ethnic minority groups in the United States. Gutiérrez's work theorises the Third space using the lens of activity theory, in particular Engestrom's expansive learning model, and sees the Third space as offering students to develop historically new forms of activity that are different to what dominant discourses prescribe as legitimate ways of being and acting. Moje *et al.* explain that there are different theoretical perspectives on Third space, including those from different geographic and discursive perspectives (e.g. Soja, 1996); post-colonial and discursive perspectives (e.g. Bhabha, 1994); and educational and discursive perspectives, including Gutiérrez's work. These perspectives all share the aim of destabilising the binaries between different discursive spaces (for example school and home), and of examining the possibilities of creating a new or hybrid space that productively engages participants in new ways.

We draw on Moje *et al.*'s (2004) distillation of the views of Third space as a productive learning space. One view is that the Third space is a way to 'build bridges' from often marginalised knowledges and discourses to the academic and conventional discourses (2004: 43); this view aligns with Gutiérrez's views of Third space. The second view sees the Third space as 'a navigational space' where students find ways of exploring and negotiating their 'funds of knowledge' from different discourse communities that they engage in (as marginal or core participants). The Third view of the this space is

> a space of cultural, social, and epistemological change in which the competing knowledges and Discourses of different spaces are brought into 'conversation' to challenge and reshape both academic content literacy practices and the knowledges and Discourses of youths' everyday lives. (2004: 44)

The third view aims to challenge, destabilise and expand school literacy practices by bringing into the frame the different kinds of knowledges that students have in their lives. Moje *et al.* (2004) acknowledge that some aspects of this view are more aspirational rather than real.

In our study, the students are younger and older adults who are studying in a variety of adult learning contexts for different purposes. The discursive spaces that these learners are negotiating cannot be simply summarised as those of their academic and the home and/or community discourses. However, in very broad terms, they are all negotiating the dominant human capital discourse of education that marginalises the linguistic, cultural and individual histories that the students bring. What we examine is the teachers' roles in working with the learners to create a Third space that helps to create a space in which the learners see as places worth belonging to (rather than the established place that judges them as worthy or not worthy citizens), and the pedagogical approaches teachers use to make this a productive learning space for their learners.

We discuss perspectives on pedagogies that help us see and explain the ways in which the teachers and learners in our studies created a Third space within their respective classrooms that enabled them to work and act productively. We draw on Kumaravadivelu's (2003, 2006) dimensions of practice to provide a lens for analyzing the teaching and learning in the sites below.

In the hope of reaching mutually meaningful notions of citizenship, civility and/or ethics in the classroom, Kumaravadivelu (2003, 2006) believes teachers need to do more than base their teaching on a particular methodology, rather teachers need to devise a personal theory of practice based on the context of learning, the needs and particularities of the learners and possibilities for transformation. His broader teaching framework rests on three pedagogic parameters: particularity, practicality and possibility. The parameter of particularity takes into account the particular needs and particular context of the learners when making decisions how and what to teach. That of practicality recognises and acknowledges the teacher's sense-making, the teacher generated theory of practice which informs and is informed by teaching. This sense-making sees the classroom walls as permeable, the learners are situated within the context that exists outside of the classroom. The third parameter of possibility takes account of the socio-political world and is the dimension which is concerned with identity and social transformation. The teacher cannot fulfil their pedagogic obligations without at the same time fulfilling their social obligations. They must be aware of both the socio-political and cultural reality that shapes their lives and of their capacity to transform their own and their students' realities.

The Teaching Sites

The aspects of responding to the particularity of the policy and learner contexts were exhibited in different ways in the four sites. Overall, a striking characteristic of the teachers was the way they provided space for the students to negotiate and make sense of their experiences in the external world. In the earlier section, we outlined three views of Third space that were distilled in the work of Moje *et al.* (2004), namely, the space that scaffolds the formal learning; a navigational space for learners to negotiate their different funds of knowledges; and a space where dominant knowledges and discourses may be questioned, challenged and perhaps even transformed. Priya, an ESOL teacher, found herself working in an increasingly vocationally focused environment where language and literacy teaching and learning was integrated into the teaching of vocational knowledge and skills. Peter and Jean, literacy and numeracy teachers, were working with people who are often spoken about as 'at risk' students in a community youth centre. Here they were involved in team teaching as a way to provide greater degrees of responsiveness to learners with multiple learning needs, and working with volunteers who provided further support and enabled each learner's individual goals to be negotiated and achieved. At the third site, the teacher, Ann, was clear in her philosophy of teaching. She showed that teaching was about knowing and responding to the learners' individual goals and needs. What was specified in the syllabus was important, but it had to be balanced against the needs and abilities of the learners. Tania taught in a Flexible Learning Support Centre where she facilitated and mentored students to accomplish and complete their courses. In all four sites the teachers demonstrated how they were attuned to the changing circumstances of their learners, how they gained, a sense of (a particular) reality.

What follows are some selected observations from the sites to illustrate the manifestations of the aspects of particularity, practicality and possibilities in the teachers' pedagogy and how this practice in turn created spaces for the learners to reconceptualise their relationship to the wider society. We also point to the ways the teachers acted contingently by bringing in the learners' external worlds and encouraging student agency.

Bridging academic, vocational and community practices

We start with a program that illustrates the collective Third space as a richly interactive space that attends to a repertoire of literacy practices to engage learners from non-dominant communities (Gutiérrez, 2008) in a vocational course for newly arrived migrant women. In this program, 22 women from a range of cultural and linguistic backgrounds including south and east Asia, the Middle East and eastern Europe study together to gain a qualification in children's services. All of the students are concurrently enrolled in an English language certificate course. Two teachers, Ann and Priya team, teach these students: Ann as the vocational teacher and Priya as the ESOL teacher. Integrated LLN support in vocational education is in many ways a difficult teaching environment for the LLN teacher. By definition, integrated LLN creates a hybrid space where there is: the concurrent development of literacy and numeracy and vocational competencies, seeing these 'as interrelated elements of the one process' (Courtenay & Mawer, 1995: 2)

However, a recent national study found that, with a few exceptions, there is a prevalence of a 'deficit model' where there is a strong emphasis on assessment of LLN skills, the teaching of LLN is treated as a remediation of students' deficits and the role of the LLN teacher has a lower status compared to the vocational teacher's (Black & Yasukawa, 2011). This program would be one of the exceptions where Priya is regarded by both the students and the vocational teacher Ann as having a pivotal role in enabling the learners to succeed in their course.

In one part of the session, we see a student recounting an instance in her work experience site where she learned the English word 'benchtop'. She explains that the supervisor at the childcare centre told her that they had left her work 'on the benchtop', but she didn't know what the benchtop was. She explains how she eventually figured out 'ah, that's the bench top' through asking questions and trial and error. This experience of solving a workplace problem that emerged for not knowing an 'everyday' English word was treated respectfully by Priya and the rest of the class. During this lesson it was clear that all of the learners in the room have experienced similar situations. Priya further validates the student's experience by emphasising to the whole class: *'Never feel scared or worried or not confident of seeking clarification because that's the best way you're going to learn. It's better to ask than to do something wrongly because you are learning.'*

Learning English – whether it is the technical language of children's services or the 'everyday' language – is normalised and valued as an integral part of their vocational learning. Thus Priya normalises the particularities of the learner groups, and legitimises the time spent in teaching and learning a range of 'everyday' language and cultural knowledge that will enable the learners to succeed in their vocational goals. As one student explains to us that, *When I don't understand something – a word, a situation – the teacher can explain in very detail to us – very, easy to understand.*

And another student says about Priya and Ann: *They listen to us patiently and attentively, encourage discussions listen and encourage us to express our opinion.* The students draw on and learn a repertoire of practices in Priya and Ann's class. One student says that in the course, she is learning: *Australian culture, English and how to get a job.*

And we see the students using a number of language and literacy resources including their own languages, electronic dictionaries, and computers to seek information and clarify meanings. Gutiérrez (2008) talks about the Third space attending to boundary crossing between different spaces that in which students belong and the ways a boundary can 'reinforce, extend and conflict with individuals' dispositions and repertoires of practice' (2008: 152). Over the day in which their lessons were observed, Priya is both individually and collectively with the whole class, supporting the learners negotiate the different kinds of cultural and language demands they are experiencing in their academic study at the college, their work experience sites, settlement in Australia – moving house, and starting a family. As Priya says in her interview with the authors:

> *My awareness of the Chinese culture, the Indian culture, other cultures has helped me greatly. When I teach the language aspects, I can always relate them to the cultural aspects. ... We have actually seen them grow a lot. The language is taught, I encourage them to use it.*

Thus among the learners who one student describes in the following way:

> *We have different clothes, food, languages*

The teacher's acknowledgement and efforts to turn the classroom space into an affirming, supportive space results in one student being able to say:

We are like a family.

Building bridges to new conceptions of citizenship

In this section we illustrate how the students and teachers work in the collective Third space to begin to re-conceive who they are, what positions they occupy inside and outside the classroom and what they might be able to achieve academically. In this space, teachers and students are oriented to a form of 'cosmopolitanism' (Appiah, 2006) and is described by Gutiérrez (2008:149) as having: ideals and practices of a shared humanity, a profound obligation towards others, boundary crossing and intercultural interchanges which celebrate differences without essentialising. The exchanges we discuss here privilege and are contingent upon students' socio-historical lives (Gutiérrez, 2008).

The ABE class consisted of five men and one woman who the teacher, Ann, described as being very weak in their literacy and numeracy skills, some with mild learning difficulties, and who had experienced disrupted school learning. Ann's response to what she was learning about her learners: *The main thing really is to know my students, to really know and understand where they're coming from, what their learning difficulties are, where their weaknesses and their strengths are.*

In this numeracy class the lesson is focussing on telling time (24 hour vs. 12 hour time; digital watches vs. analogue watches) when a learner brings out his father's watch ostensibly to provide an example of an analogue watch. After showing his watch and gaining the teacher's confirmation that this indeed was an example of an analogue watch, the learner continues to say: *'This was a present from my dad a long time ago ... I keep it good ... I don't even wear it because I don't want to lose it ... Maybe one day I'm gonna give it to my son'.* The teacher listens giving him full attention and showing respect to and acknowledgement of the personal pride and significance that the learner attaches to this watch.

The learner, Oman, is a refugee from Guinea-Bissau who had settled in Australia and is now involved in developing his English language and literacy and numeracy. Later on, in an interview with one of the researchers, Oman talks about how the learning in this class and the people are so important for him. He says:

My classmates [are] really friendly person[s] ... they [are] very good people. So since I come to this class I meet all these people – like so good for me. Like three months, something like that, but I'm getting really better for reading and writing and I know these people they're my friend when I come to school I'm happy you know. So it's quite nice. It's very nice.

and adds:

... everywhere you go, you need people Now I'm here like five years, nearly five years in Australia. I didn't come here with my family with my mum and dad and brother and sister. I have to make my own friends.

While establishing a life and a new social network in a new country, Oman's past life and family in Guinea-Bissau are shown in this classroom moment to be not far away from his thoughts. By allowing time for him to tell his story about the watch, the teacher provides an opportunity for his outside world and his history to enter the classroom, and in so doing, enables him to reveal something more about who he is. Oman becomes not just a learner with numeracy needs, but a person with a history and a future. The attention that the teacher and the other learners afford Oman as he tells his story suggests that there is something in the story that resonates for each of them – perhaps it is a new understanding that some have gained about him, a connection with their own history, or a shift in how they want to relate to this learner in this social space. In this instance Oman's position is transformed, his socio-historical life is presented, he moves from the margins into the centre, challenging his position under the 'regime of dis-citizenship'.

Another illustration of how learners take up new positions and re-conceive of themselves as citizens is shown in the Flexible Learning Centre in a vocational college. This centre supports the learning needs of a very diverse group of students who are enrolled in a trades or technical courses or English language programs, the centre focuses on the students' literacy and numeracy learning needs. Both the students and the teacher highlighted how the students exercise their agency in deciding what and how they will learn; the teacher discusses the individual student's needs and works with them to develop a four weekly schedule where they jointly plan what will be covered. The teacher sees her role as that of a facilitator and mentor, of moving each learner towards becoming a more independent learner:

My role is to stand back, it's really not to impose myself too much on the decisions that students are making. When students ask me 'what am I going to do?' I kind of shrug my shoulders and say, 'well okay, what is it you would like to do?'

I think it is being a facilitator, a mentor, rather than the teaching being directed by me all the time. I think it is the students making choices about what it is they want to do, what is the focus for them. (Tania, literacy teacher)

The space created within this class is interesting, learning support is often seen as a fairly instrumentalist type of intervention where students are seeking to correct problems they are having with their mainstream courses. The students' learning is far from an instrumentalist approach of learning literacy as a set of skills. The teacher and learners create a Third space where the learners' engagement which is mediated by a range of tools, giving rise to 'socio-cultural literacy' (Gutiérrez, 2002) incorporating and contingent upon students socio-historical lives.

Ben, a young man in his early 30s is keen to talk openly about how the centre has provided a liberating opportunity; at first he describes what he hopes being able to spell will allow him do and feel: 'through all the years of not being able to spell it would just be a luxury to be able to write what I think'. He later repeats that his learning of this skill will be able to (gestures to his head) 'get the thoughts from here to on paper', he is smiling and clearly says this in a way which signifies some enormous change for him. He also addresses the way the centre, and approach of the teacher Tania, has developed his own sense of agency in undertaking this work. As Tania describes above, the students need to identify what they want to work on and how, Ben comments that this approach, 'allows you to do what you want, leads you to being responsible, not slacking off, and to take full advantage while you've got the opportunity'. Another student, Josef, was wanted to let us know

Tania seems passionate, look (pointing to the teacher) she kneels down beside you, you can see that she is really absorbed, she likes to see us blossom.

Bridging dis-citizenship

If we take the status of 'dis-citizenship' to mean being denied access to social, cultural, economic and political rights which are subsumed under the more 'substantive' (Pothier & Devlin, 2006) notion of citizenship then many of the students in our programs live under this regime. Our explorations of bridging 'dis-citizenship', albeit a shaky structure, takes us to a community youth centre where an ABE teacher, Jean, worked with an Outreach coordinator, Peter, and learners who had been excluded from the formal education system. Both Jean and Peter are highly experienced in teaching literacy and numeracy to a range of young and older adult learners. The teachers and learners worked together in a learning space negotiated within and across the particularities of the learners and their goals, the practicalities of the teachers, their 'sense making' and the possibilities for transformation.

The learners are young people, aged 15 to 18 years, many of whom are Aboriginal people. These learners have dropped out of school, and have not been linked into any further education, training or employment. Most have experienced difficulties with school-based learning, often as a result of significant gaps in their school literacies and numeracies. In addition to being socially excluded from learning and disconnected from school-type education, many of the young people are struggling with various behavioural issues such as anger and finding it hard to concentrate. A number have minor physical difficulties that have never been addressed, such as being unable to read effectively because their eye-sight has never been tested. Others have ongoing alcohol and drug issues. Several are on juvenile justice orders, while others have served time in juvenile detention.

Their socio-economic context is an inner city public housing estate, where the young people are often in precarious or chaotic home situations. They also have little financial security. The youth centre provides a safe and easily accessible space where they can meet, make friends and take part in a range of activities and programs that are supported by a mix of paid and volunteer staff. It is also a place where they are encouraged and able to learn at their own pace. The Outreach teacher, Peter, sees the centre as a place where the learners are able to re-connect with teachers and school learning in different and positive ways and where they are able to achieve successes with formal learning, for the first time. Significantly for most of the young people the program was often the first time that they had worked in groups. Within the centre there are a number of other spaces that learners can go to, to work alone or in pairs.

When asked about what they needed out of a learning program, the young people attending the centre said that among their main concerns, a primary one was, how to 'get a piece of paper to help them move on with their lives'. One of the ways of addressing this concern was to develop a program that provided a way for them to work towards a school qualification, this involved working on their literacy and numeracy proficiency and attending to and completing the school subjects they had missed out on.

The learners, like all learners, live complex lives in which different forms of literacy and numeracy are practiced. While their academic literacy and numeracy have gaps, they are not 'empty vessels' that wait to be filled with literacy and numeracy skills and knowledge. However, in the practices of teachers in this program, we did not see a constant referral to the learners' everyday experiences as a starting point in the way many literacy and numeracy pedagogies might suggest. What was more noticeable was a focused attention on the work outlined in the standardized distance learning materials. Does this mean that rich life experiences and prior knowledge and skills are not being given recognition and validity in this program? Close observations and interviews with the teachers suggested otherwise.

The teachers were closely aware of the lives that the learners faced as soon as they stepped outside the youth centre. They were aware of the chaos and uncertainty that surrounded meeting basic needs, such as housing and food. For some of the learners uncertainty was present on a day-to-day basis. Some might argue that as survivors of these challenging situations they would have very sophisticated 'street' literacy and numeracy skills and experiences from which the classroom literacy and numeracy teachers could draw. However, there was no sign of the teachers eliciting the learners' out of school experiences in this program. But neither were the teachers making any value judgments about the learners' street literacy and numeracy.

What was evident in the way the teachers were working was the very strict observance of a 'contract' between the learners and them. Within the boundaries of the youth centre, the teachers would provide almost unlimited support for the learners to achieve their own stated goal of completing the school curriculum. Peter, the Outreach teacher, commented on how the students are able to go off and work independently in different areas of the centre but they are keenly aware that the teachers are close by to help at any time. And far from denying the learners' histories and cultures, the physical environment of the centre was that of strong affirmation of the diversity of the learners' cultures. There was acknowledgement of the undeniable economic, social and educational disadvantages that these learners had faced in their lives through the historical tensions between Aboriginal and 'white' Australia with which this country is still struggling to come to a satisfactory and genuine reconciliation. The teachers both acknowledge that they '*do need to be aware of the social world they are coming from because that's what is really impacting on their learning*' (Peter, Outreach teacher). However, the teachers did not draw explicitly on either the personal issues of the learners or the social histories of Aboriginal people to explain or justify the challenges that the learners had experienced in school. Rather, the teachers focused on the goals that the learners had identified for themselves: achieving the formal school credentials. The difference between how the learners experienced the teaching at the youth centre and their previous schools was that at the youth centre, the teachers were there to help the learners achieve their stated goal(s). By contrast, in their previous schools the learners were there more for the school, so that they could satisfy the rules of a system in which the learners were feeling marginalized. Peter (the Outreach teacher) was keenly aware of how the program needed to differentiate itself from formal schooling: *'I think one of the key ingredients for maintaining the program has been not to come with a model that has failed them before, such as a typical school model.'*

The teachers, working as a team, were able to focus on the particular needs and goals of the students and to maintain connections with the students through all many seemingly disruptive elements. The teaching and learning dynamic provided a space for the learners to exercise their agency to ask for what they wanted, to engage in the work under terms which they had negotiated with the teachers. The teachers, highly aware of the challenges the students faced, were committed to appropriately providing educational opportunities for the learners and to enabling learners to achieve some success at each session. For Outreach teacher, Peter, it meant:

> If we sense that they feel that they are failing on the day, then we redesign what we are doing, so that they can always leave here [feeling] wow I had a day there and I did well.

It was not always easy, by revisioning what counts as teaching and learning for youth excluded from the formal sector, the teachers faced many challenges. At times the behaviours they experienced from some young people severely tested their ability to keep the learners connected with the program. But the teachers still found ways to keep reconnect with the learners and keep them engaged:

> there are times I know that when a student is angry ... we have little cues. We have that sense of when to jump in and when to get out.... its being able to navigate around all of these students and around their issues that come in with them. (Peter, Outreach teacher).

We saw that the teachers' practices embodied the strong philosophies and beliefs of their role in helping the learners achieve success by creating an environment of trust and safety. The learners described their learning in the centre as 'fun', that the teachers were there to 'help' them through any difficulties with their particular studies and that the teachers complemented each other and worked together. They felt strongly supported in their learning. Both teachers commented a number of times on this aspect of working in the program. They worked well together, seamlessly negotiating a 'division of labour' with the students and keeping in constant contact with each other: *I suppose that's how we work ... there's a lot of communication that goes on outside of the room in between the breaks... during class and after class.* (Jean, ABE teacher)

The teachers here demonstrated how knowing one's learners takes on a special dimension and where the context and particularities of the learners are paramount to the success of the program.

Both teachers expressed a strong commitment to helping the learners overcome the negative experiences that most of them had encountered during their school years:

> *... we actually offer an opportunity for students to come here and maintain or renege without the necessity of meeting the traditional year 7 or year 8 scheduling ... so we would then say OK we have a student who has walked in who doesn't want to be out there on the street, who cannot survive in the normal school environment. What we will do is just facilitate their learning and promote their learning. ... Our key ingredient for success is you can walk in eight months into the year and we will take you in and look at your literacy, numeracy and your vocation pathway, try and establish a firm footing from which to rebuild.* (Peter)

The teachers explained that sometimes they had to throw away the methods or theories they had learned in their teacher education diplomas '*and react in a certain way to a certain situation*'. (Peter)

Conclusion: Creating Spaces for Re-conceptualising Citizenship

We have highlighted four teaching contexts which we regard as examples of where teachers are pivotal in creating spaces for learners to reconceptualise their sense of place and belonging. The learners in these examples may otherwise be characterized by dominant discourses, defined in assimilationist and economic productivity terms, as deficient in key citizenship skills. The teachers illustrated abilities to work with the particularities of their students' needs and goals and their own sense-making; showed practicality, in response to the students and context; and identified possibilities for transformation. The teachers whose practices and classrooms we studied illustrate Ramanathan and Morgan's (2007) observations cited at the beginning of this chapter that the values and beliefs about possibilities for transformative learning are a powerful challenge to a restrictive policy environment (2007: 453).

Dominant discourses of citizenship, even those that wish to account for broader understandings than just holding documents such as a passport, still have a reliance on instrumentalist ideas of being 'productive' (Pothier & Devlin, 2006). These discourses speak of a one-way process of new migrants or those excluded from formal institutions learning to become citizens in a pre-figured world; there is no talk about a two way process, for example from those already 'so-called' citizens learning about what newcomers bring nor about our possibilities for shaping, rather than fitting into imposed meanings of global citizenship.

In the classrooms discussed in this paper, we see a potential microcosm of our broader society: we see a dynamic process where people are learning about each other, and learning to belong to a new community. The concept of the Third space enabled us to analyse the pedagogic space as a place that the learners and the teachers co-create, using what they have brought with them and the relationships they form with each other through learning together. We reported on how learners speak about the relationships they formed with fellow students as 'a family', how a teacher draws on her own experiences in different cultural and language settings to inform her pedagogy with learners from diverse backgrounds, how two teachers create a learning environment in which the learners could experience security and stability in ways that are not currently possible in their lives outside their classroom. Some of these learners may never achieve the kinds of human capital outcomes that 'count' in the dominant discourses of who is a worthy citizen (although there are others who most likely will use the LLN learning they acquire for employment). However, the Third space that these learners and their teachers have created expands the space within which people can exercise citizenship, from the world where entry is permitted on the basis of English proficiency and capacity to contribute to economic productivity, to one that embraces and indeed invites the influence of different cultures and languages and seeks to extend social capital within and outside the classroom walls. We pose this question: Why can't this process be replicated in the wider community? Why can't citizenship be more dynamic and responsive to the changing demographic and cultural mix in society – a collaborative and cooperative project. As Ramanathan and Morgan (2007), Birch (2009), Simpson (2010) and Burns and Roberts (2010) remind us, teachers, educators and policy makers are in a prime position to challenge and make changes to how notions such as citizenship maintain the power to exclude and assimilate. The teachers whose classrooms and practices we have studied exemplify this role.

References

Appiah, K.A. (2006) *Cosmopolitanism: Ethics in a World of Strangers*. New York: Norton & Co.
Australian Bureau of Statistics (ABS) (2011) 3412.0 – *Migration, Australia 2009–2010*, Canberra: ABS.
Baynham, M. and Simpson, J. (2010) Onwards and upwards: Space, placement and liminality in adult ESOL classes. *TESOL Quarterly* 44 (3), 420–440.
Bhabha, H.K. (1994) *The Location of Culture*. New York: Routledge.
Birch, B. (2009) *The English Language Teacher in a Global Civil Society*. New York: Routledge.
Black, S. and Yasukawa, K. (2011) *Working Together: Integrated Literacy and Numeracy Support in VET*. Sydney: University of Technology. http://www.rilc.uts.edu.au/projects/working-together.html
Burns, A. and Roberts, C. (2010) Migration and adult language learning: Global flows and local transpositions. *TESOL Quarterly* 44 (3), 409–419.
Cooke, M. and Simpson, J. (2008) *ESOL: A Critical Guide*. Oxford, England: Oxford University Press.
Courtenay, M. and Mawer, G. (1995) *Integrating English Language, Literacy and Numeracy into Vocational Education and Training: A Framework*. Sydney: TAFE NSW.
Department of Education, Employment & Workplace Relations (DEEWR) (2011) *National Foundation Skills Strategy for Adults: Consultation Paper*. Canberra: DEEWR.
Gibb, T. and Walker, J. (2011) Educating for a high skills society? The landscape of federal employment, training and lifelong learning policy in Canada. *Journal of Education Policy* 26 (3), 381–398.
Griswold, O. (2010) Narrating America: Socialising adult learners into idealised views of the United Sates during citizenship preparation classes. *TESOL Quarterly* 44 (3), 488–516.
Guo, S. (2010) Toward recognitive justice: Emerging trends and challenges in transnational migration and lifelong learning. *International Journal for Lifelong Education* 29 (2), 151–167.
Gutiérrez, K. (2008) Developing a sociocritical literacy in the Third space. *Reading Research Quarterly* 43 (2), 148–164.
Hamilton, M. and Pitt., K. (2011) Challenging representations: Constructing the adult literacy learner over 30 years of policy and practice in the United Kingdom. *Reading Research Quarterly* 46 (4), 350–373.
Han, C., Starkey, H. and Green, A. (2010) The politics of ESOL (English for speakers of other languages): Implications for citizenship and justice. *International Journal for Lifelong Education* 29 (2), 63–76.
Jackson, S. (2010) Learning through social spaces: Migrant women and lifelong learning in post-colonial London. *International Journal for Lifelong Education* 29 (2), 237–252.
Kumaravadivelu, B. (2003) *Beyond Methods: Macrostrategies for Language Teaching*. New Haven: Yale University Press.
Kumaravadivelu, B. (2006) TESOL methods: Changing tracks, challenging trends. *TESOL Quarterly* 40 (1), 59–81.
Miller, E.R. (2010) Agency in the making: Adult immigrants accounts of language learning and work. *TESOL Quarterly* 44 (3), 465–487.

Moje, E.B., Ciechanowski, K.M., Kramer, K., Ellis, L. Carrillo, R. and Collazo, T. (2004) Working toward third space in content area literacy: An examination of everyday funds of knowledge and discourse. *Reading Research Quarterly* 39 (1), 38–70.
Ng, R. and Shan, H. (2010) Lifelong learning as ideological practice: An analysis from the perspective of immigrant women in Canada. *International Journal for Lifelong Education* 29 (2), 169–184.
Pothier, D. and Devlin, R. (eds) (2006) *Critical Disability Theory: Essays in Philosophy, Politics, Policy and Law*. Vancouver: UBC Press.
Ramanathan, V. and Morgan, B. (2007) TESOL and policy enactments: Perspectives from practice. *TESOL Quarterly* 41 (3), 447–463.
Rogers, A. (2006) Escaping the slums or changing the slums? Lifelong learning and social transformation. *International Journal of Lifelong Learning* 25 (2), 125–137.
Scarino, A. and Papdemetre, L. (2001) Ideologies, languages, policies: Australia's ambivalent relationship with learning to communicate in 'other' languages. In J. Lo Bianco and R. Wickert (eds) *Australian Policy Activism in Language and Literacy* (pp. 305–323). Melbourne: Language Australia.
Simpson, J. (2011) Telling tales: Discursive space and narratives in ESOL classrooms. *Linguistics and Education* 22, 10–22.
Singh, D. (2007) *Our Shared Future*. West Yorkshire: Commission on Integration and Cohesion.
Skills Australia (2010) *Australian Workforce Futures: A National Workforce Development Strategy*. Canberra: Commonwealth of Australia.
Soja, E.W. (1996) *Thirdspace: Journeys to Los Angeles and Other Real-and-Imagined Places*. Maiden, MA: Blackwell.
Walker, J. (2009) The inclusion and construction of the worthy citizen through lifelong learning: A focus on the OECD. *Journal of Education Policy* 24 (3), 335–351.
Widin, J., Yasukawa, K. and Chodkiewicz, A. (2008) *Making Connections: Adult Literacy and Numeracy Practice*. Canberra: Department of Education, Science and Training.

10 Classroom Meanings and Enactments of US Citizenship: An Ethnographic Study

Ariel Loring

Introduction

Citizenship is a term with various nuanced interpretations in a context that is often high-stakes, political and official. To government officials citizenship is the acquisition of a certified document, to district judges administering the naturalization swearing-in ceremony it is a petition to be granted and to citizenship teachers it is often a process of test preparation. When discussed in the media it is something that can be *sought, promised* and *questioned*.

There is no more appropriate time to study the meaning of citizenship; it is frequently mentioned in news stories at the global, national and local levels. In just a two-week period in 2011, citizenship was discussed in *The New York Times* in terms of President Obama's birth certificate (Stelter, 2011), inspections of students' immigration status (Semple, 2011), presidential promises of immigration law overhauls (Calmes, 2011) and even Superman's renunciation of American citizenship (Gustines, 2011).

While citizenship continues to find ground in the media, services and assistance to potential new citizens has only declined. Budget constraints in Sacramento, California, the city in which this study takes place, have caused many adult schools in the area to close their citizenship classes, and the city's monthly naturalization swearing-in ceremony of over 1500 new citizens has terminated. The juxtaposition of increasing public interest with waning resources creates a fertile ground for an investigation of citizenship meaning.

Thus, the larger questions investigated are: (1) In what ways do citizenship instructors enact citizenship in their classrooms? and (2) What are the implications of sustaining different meanings of citizenship? These questions are important to ask because local understandings of citizenship are diverse and proceed from teachers' differing philosophical approaches. This research aligns itself with other work that takes a bottom-up, politically oriented approach to language policy (Blommaert, 2009; Canagarajah, 2005; McCarty, 2011; Ramanathan, 2005).

Meanings of Citizenship

The definition of citizenship has evolved both historically and theoretically. The Oxford English Dictionary (OED)'s first defined the word *citizen* in the year 1330 as 'an inhabitant of a city or (often) of a town; especially one possessing civic rights and privileges' (Citizen, 2012). The term *citizenship*, first used in 1611, meant, 'the position or status of being a citizen, with its rights and privileges' (Citizenship, 2012).

This attention to *rights and privileges* is reiterated in the US Constitution, which decrees, 'the citizens of each state shall be entitled to all privileges and immunities of citizens in the several states' (US Constitution, Art. 4, § 2, cl. 1). Official discourse of USCIS (United States Citizenship and Immigration Services, hereafter referred to as *CIS*) reinforces citizenship in this light, mandating that citizenship means being 'rewarded with all the *rights and privileges* that are part of US citizenship' (*Citizenship*, 2011, my italics). Becoming a new citizen is accomplished by passing the naturalization test: answering six of ten history/civics questions correctly from a published list of one-hundred questions and their answers, successfully reading and writing one of three basic English sentences, and orally using English to discuss the submitted N-400 application. The citizenship test and discourse exemplify a minimalist view of citizenship that limits its meaning to the legal level,[1] the most basic in Banks's (2008) typology of citizenship stages. Citizenship according to the OED and CIS does not include active, transformative possibilities such as protesting and demonstrating, giving public speeches, promoting social justice or challenging existing laws (Banks, 2008). Additionally omitted is the reality that citizenship is not stable and has not always been conferred on residents equally (Kerber, 1997).

Political theorists define citizenship with the same notion of rights and responsibilities (Marshall, 1950; Soysal, 1994), but also underscore notions of membership (Castles, 1998; Marshall, 1950; Soysal, 1994), community (Bauböck, 1994; Castles, 1998), participation (Dahrendorf, 1994; Touraine, 1997) and shared values (Cogan & Morris, 2001). Recently, scholars have brought attention to other facets of citizenship not traditionally considered, such as spatial rights (Yuval-Davis, 2006), gender rights and cultural rights (Castles, 2000). Scholars have argued that globalization has challenged what citizenship traditionally embodies, such as the role of the nation state (Kuisma, 2008) and narratives of nationhood (Glick Schiller *et al.*, 1995).

Historical, theoretical and official underpinnings of citizenship undoubtedly influence teachers of prospective citizens in their course curriculum. Australian educators in DeJaeghere's (2008) study reference themes of privilege and power, a sense of belonging, involvement in issues and access to knowledge and resources, even though they teach citizenship as an inculcation of ideals, rather than actual lived experiences and critical thinking. In Singaporean secondary schools, citizenship teachers' views range from a *minimalist interpretation* of citizenship, where knowledge is standardized, answers are predetermined, and information is mastered, to a *maximal interpretation* of citizenship, where comprehension is emphasized, different views are explored and content is linked to students' experiences (Sim & Print, 2009).

Few studies have analyzed adult school citizenship classes. This arena encompasses a host of additional teaching hurdles, such as a student population with a wide range of abilities, open registration dates and reduced funding. Additionally, citizenship takes on a high-stakes, bureaucratic meaning for adults who enroll in citizenship classes to prepare for the naturalization interview, resulting in curriculum designed to 'teach to the test'. Teachers' instructional narratives, while helpful for teaching students with limited English proficiency, transmit particular ideological views, such as the United States being an ideal, individualist democracy with a glorified history (Griswold, 2010). An analysis of one teacher's tendency to predominantly correct the most perceptible student language errors exemplifies the position that it is more important to *appear* proficient than to develop deeper grammatical and discursive competency (Griswold, 2011). While the current study investigates a similar setting and student population as Griswold (2010, 2011), it centers on a comparison of different teaching approaches and what this implies about the range of existing citizenship meanings.

Methodology

Site descriptions

The data for this chapter comes from ethnographic observations and interviews with four classroom teachers at three educational sites offering adult citizenship classes. Two of the classes are held at adult schools (Ford

School for Adults and Wilson Adult School), and one is offered at a community center (Asian American Community Center).[2]

Ford School for Adults, along with its sister branch, boast 1640 students,[3] of which 61 have attended at least one citizenship class at Ford School during my period of observation. The instructor, Mr Morris, has helped over 3000 students become naturalized citizens in his 15 years of teaching citizenship. The student demographic is mostly women, around 40 to 65 years old and is predominately Chinese, Hmong and Mexican, although over 15 nationalities are represented. Teaching material includes a frequent distribution of CIS-produced, supplemental, and English as a second language (ESL) handouts[4] (an average of 6.3 a class). Handouts are used to present a reduced number of test questions in various formats (multiple choice, matching, fill-in-the-blank, word search) and provide practical instruction on multilingual voting guides, voter registration and passport applications.

The Wilson Adult School citizenship class is primarily composed of 15 middle-aged, Russian-speaking students. Their teacher, Ms Lara, is a native Russian speaker and naturalized American citizen who uses Russian translations in class as a pedagogic tool. Unlike Mr Morris's system of distributing new handouts to each class, Ms Lara initially supplies a handout packet, which consists of the N-400 application for citizenship, the 100 history and government test questions in either English or English-Russian bilingual, civics and conversational English sample writing sentences and sample questions for the oral interview. Each class progresses by learning a handful of new questions and sentences, in order, from each source. These handouts are not the most recently published versions, and while there are no major adjustments, some of the questions have been deleted or amended in the current edition.[5] Ms Lara also uses electronic resources in class; students are taken to the computer lab to practice test questions from a website that scores their multiple choice test instantaneously.

Founded in 1980 and now employing 25 paid and volunteer staff, the Asian American Community Center (AACC) is a non-profit organization that provides assistance to the community's immigrant, refugee, low-income, and limited English-speaking population, of which citizenship assistance is one component. The center distributes a citizenship workbook, available in English, Mandarin, Vietnamese and Tagalog, which includes all relevant publications by CIS in addition to application instructions and a sample-completed application. The citizenship class consists of approximately 17 middle-age and senior Chinese and Vietnamese students. Ms Maria is the regular instructor, who has worked for the agency as a community service worker for 19 years, teaching ESL and citizenship for the last year. She gathers material from citizenship and ESL websites, in the form of true/false, multiple choice, matching and letter-tracing handouts, which usually corresponds to the naturalization test questions but also includes additional factual content. Ms April is the occasional substitute teacher, and also one of the co-founders of the AACC. She relies less heavily on handouts and written student work, and instead holds a continuous oral conversation with the class, which reinforces concepts about civics and daily life while integrating actual test questions into the discussion.

The following chart, continued in an endnote, summarizes crucial distinctions between the citizenship classes:[6,7]

	Teaching materials & activities		Classroom layout	Teacher background
Ford School for Adults	CIS, ESL, & supplementary handouts, CIS & ESL flash-cards, former students' test sharing, mock-interviews, classroom games		Desks in pods, citizen-ship-themed images, wall of graduates' photos	High school principal, community service volunteer
Wilson Adult School	CIS handouts, CIS flash-cards, writing practice, computer quizzes		Desks in rows, ESL-themed images	Naturalized US citizen, former full-time teacher
Asian American Community Center	CIS book-let	ESL handouts, reading & writing practice	Desks in rows, citizen-ship-themed images	Community service worker
		CIS DVD, oral practice		Social worker, center's co-founder

Data analysis

In total, qualitative data collected from these venues entail 28 field note entries, 3 teacher interviews, 5 student interviews from Mr Morris's class, over 100 handouts and booklets and classroom photographs and maps.

Approaching data analysis from the constant comparative method (Glaser & Strauss, 1967), I jointly coded and analyzed my data. Broad, open coding categories (Strauss, 1987) were first pursued, leading to more specific, emergent themes as data collection continued. Burgeoning categories were constantly grounded in concrete pieces of evidence from field notes.

Interviews were conducted in a non-scheduled (questions were asked in a flexible order) and standardized style (all interviewees were asked variants of the same questions) to enable a comparison of teacher and student responses to the same set of questions, which were grouped thematically into key topics. Interviews were transcribed and passages were coded as they are related to the indexed field notes categories. As new themes emerged from selective coding (Strauss, 1987), all materials were further analyzed in the TAMS Analyzer coding program (http://tamsys.sourceforge.net/) to facilitate comparisons and distinctions between codes. To the extent possible, data collection ceased at the point when coding categories became thoroughly saturated (Glaser & Strauss, 1967); at Ford School the conclusion of data collection coincided with a significant shift in student attendance, at the AACC this occurred at the end of a semester, but at Wilson Adult School the data collection end date was outside researcher control. The value of this data is that it comes from varied sources and was analyzed from a close, critical standpoint.[8]

Findings

Three broad themes emerge from the data, concerning classroom enactments of citizenship: (1) what is believed, (2) what is taught and (3) what isn't taught. I divide each category into two respective subdivisions: teacher and student understandings, surface and peripheral meanings, and assumed and neglected knowledge.

What is believed: Teacher and student understandings of citizenship

Teacher understandings

While the four classroom teachers demonstrate varied approaches to teaching citizenship, it is noteworthy that all who were interviewed responded in similar fashions when asked what citizenship means to them:[9]

Mr Morris: 'We forget, *we take this country for granted*. These are dreams that they've had since they were little kids'.
Ms April: 'Being able to have the freedom and those rights that *we take for granted*'.
Ms Maria: 'I appreciate being a citizen more than you'll ever know because of the fact that being a citizen or growing up born a citizen here is something that *so many people take for granted*'.

At this philosophical level, citizenship involves the notion of native-born citizens taking certain aspects of citizenship for granted. Mr Morris's perspective is that native-born citizens do not recognize the advantages they have as Americans. He prefaced this statement by describing his teaching decision to discuss the shooting of Congresswoman Gabrielle Giffords three days earlier, 'I was reluctant to bring up this whole assassination thing that occurred in Arizona because they start to look at this country: "boy what kind of place is this?"' Mr Morris does not want to spoil his students' idealistic images of America by disclosing negative events.

Ms April's answer is in terms of native-born citizens not acknowledging, or even *knowing* the rights and freedoms they possess. She believes that students in citizenship classes 'understand what it means to have these rights much more than we do'. This is because in a class primarily composed of Chinese immigrants and Vietnamese refugees, the majority of the students have experience living without rights such as the freedom of expression and assembly. Ms Maria teaches the same group of students, and for her, becoming a citizenship instructor led her to reflect on what it means to be a citizen. She appreciates the rights she always had now that she is a first-hand observer of those who live without these rights.

All four teachers additionally believe that the most difficult part of attaining citizenship is passing the English-proficiency requirement. Despite sharing this view, their classroom enactments of English instruction differ. As a monolingual English speaker, Mr Morris nonetheless knows a few words in Spanish, and will use them, albeit infrequently, to try to facilitate comprehension and demonstrate his limited knowledge of Spanish. He mentions that a US passport costs *'mucho dinero'* [a lot of money], defines the pledge of allegiance as 'a promise to be *leal'* [loyal], and describes the length of time students wait for their interview date as, 'it takes five *mes'* [months]. Thus, while his objective is for students to use and understand English well enough to pass the oral interview, he is not a staunch believer in English-only in the classroom. An additional strategy is to use fragmented *teacher-English* (related to Bourdieu's (1991) strategy of condescension) to try to simplify his utterances, such as 'how you doing', 'lot of Mexican and Filipino people democrats' and 'most of them passed first time'. His presumed intent is to construct easily understandable utterances.

Ms Maria also uses English-only in the classroom, but never ventures from monolingual instruction. Unlike the other teachers who encourage students to use their L1 in the classroom, Ms Maria reprimands a Chinese couple for speaking to each other in their L1: 'you're supposed to speak English'; in response to the student's proclamation that his English is only 'so-so', she concludes, 'it won't be if you practice in class with teacher, with your wife'. By omitting the determiner before *teacher*, Ms Maria is also participating in simplified teacher-English.

Ms April, a native English speaker who predominately uses English in the classroom, is also proficient in Mandarin and Cantonese. However, she utters only four non-English phrases in a total of two hour-long class periods. Even when a student sustains multiple interactional turns in a language other than English, Ms April responds in English. She also uses teacher-English, advising students to 'write to newspaper' and asking, 'how long you been here?' Her view of English learning is that exposing students to multiple English accents is not only typical, but optimal since interacting with a teacher who is hard to understand better replicates actual experiences outside of the classroom.

In contrast to these three teachers, Ms Lara uses her (and the majority of her students') L1, Russian, as a tool for classroom instruction. She translates individual words, entire sentences, and sets of instructions in Russian while she teaches. Even though she is proficient in English, she does not see herself as an 'authentic' speaker compared to a native-English speaker such as myself. She encouraged me to pronounce English words for her students due to her ideology of native English teachers as the most suitable candidates for language instruction.

Student understandings

Students interviewed from Mr Morris's class expressed certain views of citizenship that coincided with their teacher's views (as well as tropes from government discourses). When asked why they want to become US citizens, students responded with the following answers:

'I've been living in the States for ten, eleven years… but you want to be a *part* and you want to mix. I want to *vote* 'cause I live here I want to be active in the social life'. (Lucio)
'I want citizen because I want follow America law' (Feng)
'I want the policy of the government, like freedom and work, and receiving benefits for especially like me- the elderly- for the medicine… the government give fifteen percent another additional for my monthly pension benefit-- spouse benefit'. (Viola)
'Because my parents, they still in my country. I want to visit there sometime'. (Yi)

While the themes of integration, following, and respecting the law closely align with CIS's view of citizenship, students also mention *benefits*. In particular, the benefits mentioned distinguish citizens from permanent residents, such as receiving non-deducted social security payments and obtaining a US passport. Mr Morris teaches his students about benefits, including living without the threat of deportation, which highlights a view of citizenship that focuses more on practical and immediate benefits rather than responsibilities and cultural assimilation. Other teachers also acknowledge student objectives in these terms; Ms April mentions 'family reunification' and a fear of losing rights as a permanent resident, and Ms Maria notices students wanting to vote. This suggests that instead of conceptualizing naturalized citizens as uprooted, assimilated immigrants, many should be seen as transmigrants (Glick Schiller *et al.*, 1995), who desire *flexible citizenship* (Ong, 1999) for its economic, global and familial benefits.

Another dimension of citizenship involves the belief in a specific type of linguistic integration, what I term *phonotactic assimilation*. This is evident in students wanting to change their given name to something that 'sounds American', meaning that it adheres to English phonotactics. For those interested, completing a name change during the naturalization process is a relatively simple task, hence multiple discussions of this possibility ensued in citizenship classes. One student in Ms Lara's class voiced a desire to shorten her Russian name to only its first syllable because she was told her real name is too difficult to pronounce. While fictitious, an equivalent of this student's name change is from 'Natalya' to 'Nate'. This student expressed hesitancy that this shortened version constitutes a 'real' name, and asked how it would be spelled.

A similar incident occurred in Mr Morris's class, where a Chinese woman who had given herself an American name to ease pronunciation for American acquaintances, planned to change her name a third time when told her that her American name sounded 'lonely'. While she ultimately decided to keep her chosen American name, the flexibility in naming possibilities she exhibited, and the willingness to accept native English speakers' views of a 'good name', (mine included), demonstrated an eagerness to assimilate.

	Mr Morris			Facilitating comprehension in the classroom is the most important goal
Teacher meanings	Ms April	Native-born citizens take rights for granted	English is the hardest part of the test, therefore:	Exposing students to different English accents supports comprehension
	Ms Maria			English-only is the appropriate classroom policy for students
	Ms Lara			Native-English speakers are the most helpful language teachers
Student meanings	Importance of citizenship benefits (besides obligations) (Some) desire phonotactic assimilation			

What is taught: Surface and peripheral meanings of citizenship

Turning to how citizenship is taught in the classroom, two main themes emerge. There is a predominant focus on preparing students for passing the test at the expense of engaging in deeper learning. Additionally, peripheral meanings of citizenship are transmitted to students, beyond the scope of the test.

Surface meanings

As evidenced by the type of citizenship curriculum taught and the type of learning promoted, a surface-level understanding of citizenship is the main goal of most citizenship instructors. For Mr Morris and Ms Lara, the majority of class time is spent reviewing the different components of the citizenship test, with little to no attention given to additional content. Ms Lara never deviates from the citizenship interview material, and her teaching strategy is memorization of the test content. When initially introducing a test question, she will attempt to explain it in context: when teaching the civics question 'What is freedom of religion?' she responds with a practical example, 'no one is going to follow you and ask what church you go to'. Once explained, she reinforces that students should memorize the exact wording of the CIS published answer, 'you can practice any religion, or not practice a religion' by announcing, 'it's a long sentence and you don't have a choice you have to memorize it'.

Mr Morris distributes numerous handouts to practice the preferred answer choices as well, but will occasionally introduce a lesson that provides background information on a particular concept. In one class he supplies students with a two-page summary on Martin Luther King Jr. in the form of a simplistic comic strip. However, he concludes this lesson by stating, 'now I'm going to ask you one question from the one-hundred questions: who was Martin Luther King Jr.?' After students respond, he reiterates, 'civil rights leader, that's all you need to know'. Thus, even when a deeper lesson is initiated, his final goal is providing the three-word answer that satisfies the test question. Mr Morris and Ms Lara's teaching practices exemplify the banking model of education in which the instructor 'makes deposits which the students patiently receive, memorize and repeat' (Freire, 2000: 72). Concepts and meanings are not transmitted, only context specific 'packets' of information are acquired.

In the above example, it could be argued that a greater knowledge of Martin Luther King Jr. and the civil rights movement, while important to US history, is not necessary for successful daily interactions as a US citizen. However, in the following example of promoting a surface meaning of citizenship, Mr Morris's priority that his students pass the test prevents him from capitalizing on an opportunity for teaching conversational English:

> Mr Morris asks Qing if she is going to take her purse to the interview. He demonstrates in the front of the room, with the chair, that the interviewer might say to you, 'put your purse on the chair, listen to that because I had one student... right away it was a problem'. Mr Morris says, 'don't take a purse'.

In this field note excerpt, Mr Morris is encouraging students to *avoid* potential interactive situations during their interview, by leaving routine items at home, rather than teaching the root of the issue, which is the need for more English instruction. He believes that his students have already demonstrated good citizen-like behavior and that prolonging their time spent in class delays their rights as US citizens (further elaborated in the Implication section).

The AACC citizenship teachers are less concerned with teaching only the information required to pass the citizenship test, but for different reasons. Ms Maria is the teacher who routinely introduces additional history and government content, including lessons on Washington D.C., the bald eagle, and the Statue of Liberty. She uses handouts that involve simple recall of information which suggests that her objective is not necessarily to teach supplemental content, but to develop ESL skills through civics-based content. For example, one class period is spent entirely of students reading aloud a descriptive paragraph for each of the 100 history/civics questions. As she knows her students do not fully understand what they are uttering, Ms Maria's purpose is reading fluency and pronunciation practice; at this level a deeper understanding of citizenship is not attained.[10]

Ms April is the sole teacher to actively discourage memorization of test questions. She purposefully asks the history/civics questions thematically, and not in their published order, cautioning students, 'all the questions are a guide but if you only memorize [question numbers] one, two, three, you won't remember because they don't ask you in order'. For example, in asking students the following questions, Ms April addresses the CIS questions: (#50) Name one right only for US citizens?, (#27) In what month do we vote for President?, (#28) What is the name of the President of the United States now? and (#26) We elect a President for how many years?:

'If you're a US citizen what do you have a right to do?'
'In 2012 we will have an election, in what month is it?'

'Who is our president now?'
'How long can President Obama serve?'
'When was he elected?'
'When will the next president election come up again?'

The questions Ms April asks flow logically, and are not the verbatim-published questions. Consequently, students are required to comprehend the questions and apply their answers to real-life situations (calculating the year of the next presidential election). Thus, Ms April takes the farthest step from teaching citizenship at a superficial level.

There is evidence from classroom observations that students are in fact receiving only a shallow understanding of citizenship and are not fully synthesizing what they are learning. A common occurrence is for students to answer questions with incongruous responses that happen to be published answers to different, albeit similar questions. For instance, in Mr Morris's class, Viola responded to the question 'what stops one branch of government from becoming too powerful?' with the name of a branch itself, and Raul answered '435' to the question, 'who does a US representative represent?'[11] In Ms Maria's class, one student admits that she doesn't understand the words she is reading and writing, explaining, 'I just copy, feel bad'.

One component of the citizenship test is answering personal eligibility questions, which are obviously unique to each applicant. However, some students in Mr Morris's class believe that there are 'correct' answers to such questions as 'why did you come to the United States?' and will change their response to mimic one that the teacher endorses. This further suggests that many students are learning the minimal amount of civics and English required to pass the test, as their teachers both explicitly and implicitly encourage.

Peripheral meanings
When teachers educate students about certain types of information not directly provided in the CIS-produced study material, they are teaching peripheral components of citizenship. Mr Morris, Ms Lara and Ms April all provide students with practical information for citizenship, either for the application and interview process or for more successful experiences in their daily lives.

Students in Mr Morris's class observe and track fellow students' application processes, and buoyed by Mr Morris's running narrative about each student's progress, they learn about the length of the application process and how to solve problems that may arise. When one student wrote on her application that she had been arrested, referring to a traffic ticket, Mr Morris turned this into a teaching lesson for the entire class. Mr Morris also shares practical test-day information with the students, such as parking options and cell phone policies. These details increase the transparency of the naturalization process so that applicants have a better sense of what to expect on their interview day.

The type of practical information Ms Lara provides is with regards to application term definitions. She spends class time applying a term like 'maiden name' to each female student, making sure they understand the word's specific bearing on them. Ms April informs her students about practical aspects of life in the United States, such as the fact that Californian residents pay taxes on clothes and equipment but not on food, and that buses operate on a limited schedule on holidays. As will be explained, this is because Ms April's view of citizenship includes knowing more knowledge than just passing the test.

To some extent, all three of these teachers' practices reflect their value that community is an aspect of citizenship. The government does not address this peripheral dimension of citizenship, either in the language of the test or in its official discourse (although scholars do, see Bauböck, 1994; Castles, 1998). If anything, naturalization applicants are encouraged to integrate with the existing American community, but not with each other as an immigrant population. However, in some fashion, Mr Morris, Ms Lara and Ms April all create a community-like atmosphere in their classrooms.

As discussed in the section on Site descriptions, various visuals around Mr Morris's classroom depict the students as part of their own community of naturalization applicants. In addition to the wall of recent 'graduates', the white board in the classroom also lists each current student's name next to his/her naturalization application stage. Community is also built during the day-to-day classroom routines. Each week Mr Morris engages in a status check, identifying which student has the next scheduled interview by asking, 'who's the most nervous person in the room?' After students pass the naturalization test, they are encouraged to return to class to share their experience with their remaining classmates. When they return, Mr Morris announces their achievement: 'I'd like to introduce to you a new citizen'. They relay specific interview details with their fellow students, and students are encouraged to ask questions, even in their shared L1 if applicable.

Mr Morris's class is also unique in that he encourages students to share information about their native cultures. He asks students from different backgrounds if they are allowed to carry a gun in their home country, urges a Hmong student to describe her culture's traditional dating ritual, and distributes handouts on the Chinese New Year. This suggests that citizenship for him is more than a one-directional absorption of American information by students; he is interested in integrating students' cultures into the classroom curriculum as well.

Not only does Mr Morris create a classroom environment in which community membership is promoted, but the students themselves indicate their sense of collegiality. Viola, after attending class for a few months, facilitated a class picture because she wanted a souvenir to remember the class. This reaffirms her positive view of the class as expressed in her interview: 'I decide to start the class here so that I can enjoy... and you know what [for] the old like me is better to go around so that you not boring inside the house'. Even Lucio, a very advanced English student, described one of his reasons for applying for citizenship: 'I want to be active in the social life'. Mr Morris even conjectured, 'he keeps coming [because] I think he likes being with the people'. This suggests that students are attending class not only to learn factual information but also to participate in shared experiences.

To a lesser extent, Ms Lara's classroom is also a community in that the majority of her students share an L1. Due to the fact that students enroll at the same time and progress through the citizenship curriculum at the same pace, a shared goal with a similar learning arc unites the students. Ms April herself acknowledges that not all of the students at the AACC come to class to obtain citizenship. For the elderly students, she believes US citizenship is not feasible due to their low levels of English proficiency. However, the reason they attend class is 'for the camaraderie, they come here and they are together and it's kinda like a good social network for them, too'.

The fact that citizenship teachers encourage a sense of community suggests that what is taught in citizenship classes is broader than what the citizenship test is assessing. Attendees of adult citizenship classes participate in a shared endeavor, and teachers can enhance this notion by developing a supportive community for their students.

Surface & Peripheral meanings	Mr Morris	Attempts supplemental lessons but focus is on passing the test, practical information provided eases fear of process, actively fosters classroom community
	Ms Lara	Teaches minimum required to pass test and practical information to complete application, classroom community formed due to student similarities
	Ms April	Oral teaching style requires student *comprehension*
	Ms Maria	Teaches beginning ESL through civics content

What isn't taught: Assumed and neglected knowledge

Equally important as meanings of citizenship that are taught, is what is not taught. This includes knowledge that is taken for granted and knowledge that is overlooked.

Assumed knowledge

There are certain types of classroom knowledge that teachers assume students possess. This is primarily centered around knowledge of academic conventions necessary for class participation and comprehension, what we can think of generally as 'literacy', following Gee's (2003) depiction of literacies as multiple, broad and domain-specific, which much be learned to be 'read'. Accordingly, there is a realm of 'classroom literacy' in which students must learn how to interpret instructions for various handouts and classroom activities: multiple choice, fill in the blank, and matching, to name a few. For example, during Shaheen's first day in Mr Morris's class, she was confused by a matching handout which required students to match possible interview questions (such as 'When were you born?' and 'Have you ever been arrested?') with potential answer choices (such as 'July 3, 1968' and 'No I haven't'). She first believed she needed to write out the entire answer instead of marking the corresponding letter (typical of a matching activity). She additionally expressed confusion because the column of answer choices contained answers not true for her, such as the 'correct' answer '36' to the question 'How old are you?' Thus, she has not yet acquired the type of literacy required to complete this activity, but the teacher assumes otherwise.

This is also evident in Ms Maria's classroom, in which the students' academic literacies conflict with her expectations of their capabilities. She distributes a particularly difficult handout to one class, which consists of a set of eight factual statements about Presidents George Washington and Abraham Lincoln, followed by directions and a Venn diagram, reproduced below.

The intention is for students to read and comprehend the statements, and then copy the given phrases into the correct circle, depending on whether the statement is true for Washington, Lincoln, or both. However, the students do not understand the handout's content, and furthermore, do not possess the required academic literacy to complete the task (similar to Blommaert's (2009) arguments about a Rwandan refugee's literacy). Ms Maria soon abandons her intended strategy of showing students where relevant information exists in the text, and resorts to giving them technical instructions, 'please put "owned slaves" in the box... in the circle... write down "great president" in the second circle...' This is an example of a lesson's objective turning into one of 'procedural display' (Bloome et al., 1989),

B. Directions: Fill-in- the circles with the correct words.

Father of our country
great president
owned slaves
bron in 1809

Wealthy family
16th president
lawyer
monument in U.S. capital

Bron in february
poor family
bron in 1732
civil war

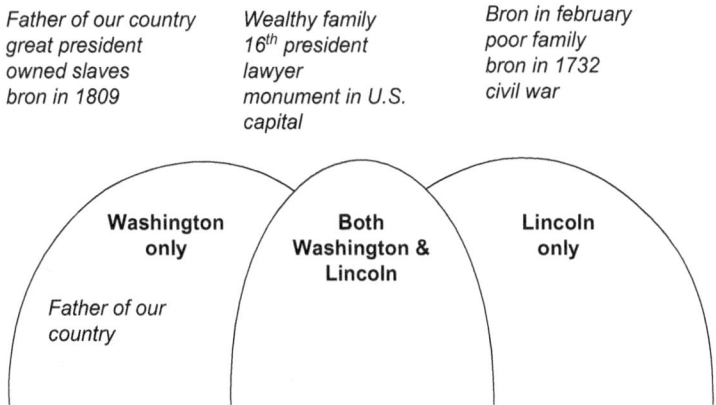

in which the goal is for students to display correct lesson behavior instead of achieving academic learning. Even this goal does not result in successful handout completion; one relatively strong student wrote '16th president' as a characteristic of both Washington and Lincoln, demonstrating her lack of academic literacy in regards to this graphing technique.

A different type of literacy is taken for granted in Ms Lara's class: computer literacy. Her class can utilize a computer lab on school grounds, and each student has access to a computer website that gives a sample multiple choice history/civics ten-question test. Students were initially unsure how to begin the test, and once they finished many students were not able to negotiate the 'certificate' page they were presented with, which listed their correct and incorrect answers to each question. Some students were not able to use a mouse to scroll down the webpage, and one student missed several answers by leaving them blank, presumably due to a mistake in clicking the correct button. A significant population of students in this class is elderly and lack the technical literacy to successfully navigate this assignment. Consequently, their learning experience is hampered due to a mismatch of teacher expectations and student abilities.

Neglected knowledge

Citizenship classes tend to ignore the issue of modality in classroom instruction. For two of the teachers it is a regular tendency for written language exercises to supplant oral practice. Mr Morris and Ms Maria make the most use of handouts that require students to mark correct answers or write in answers, and while they review the handout orally, only the most vocal students participate. Therefore, many students do not receive practice in oral English until immediately prior to their interview date, when they are included in more specialized practice. Ms April, on the other hand, only focuses on the oral medium and does not practice reading and writing with her students. Ms Lara is the sole instructor who delivers instruction and practice specific to the modality in which the content is tested. These teaching practices have significant consequences for students, who likely do not have equal productive abilities in each language mode.

Through looking at common practices of citizenship education, the predominant strategy is to focus on memorizing historical facts and question responses. What this ignores is a completely separate realm of citizenship knowledge, such as thinking critically, questioning expected answers and identifying societal inequalities. These are aspects of *transformative citizenship education* (Banks, 2008), also called *critical citizenship education* (DeJaeghere, 2007), and none of the citizenship classes observed follow this approach. Nor have these classes moved beyond teaching ideals of citizenship to discuss 'the lived experience' of the population of citizenship applicants (DeJaeghere, 2008: 372). Thus, citizenship education in these classes seems to neither question the government's representation of citizenship nor endeavor to foster critical dispositions in its naturalized citizens.

Assumed & Neglected knowledge	Mr Morris	Academic literacy	Modality	Critical citizenship
	Ms Maria			
	Ms April			
	Ms Lara	Computer literacy		

Implications

Addressing the question of teacher enactments of citizenship, it has been demonstrated that the four classroom instructors possess shared, yet often contrasting meanings of citizenship. For Mr Morris, legal citizenship coincides with being a *good citizen*: 'They're guys that have just worked their *butt* off for 20 years – building homes, and you know picking fruit, and been good guys and paid their taxes'. Since he believes his students already possess the necessary qualities for US citizenship, his main priority is assisting his students in passing the test. The study materials he distributes in class therefore focus on memorization of terms and phrases at the expense of deeper content learning.

The instructors at the AACC possess extended interpretations of citizenship as well. Ms Maria acknowledges that her students continue to attend ESL classes at the center even after they become citizens, suggesting that citizenship is a temporal *process* and not a finite status. Ms April's definition of citizenship entails successfully living in the United States and becoming familiar with practical daily information. That is why she not only teaches the minimum answer to a test question, but teaches *all* the national holidays when only two are required.

Ms Lara is the sole instructor whose classroom practices demonstrate a strict adherence to the governmental depiction of citizenship. She only teaches the minimum amount needed to pass and is not concerned with correcting mistakes on her handouts if they fall in the realm of 'extra information'. In terms of a handout that incorrectly identified one of California's two senators, her response was, 'it doesn't really matter, they only have to learn one'.

Teacher perspectives and practices demonstrate a range of meanings and classroom enactments of citizenship. This indicates that citizenship cannot be viewed in exclusively legal and political terms of membership, shared values, and rights and responsibilities. For CIS, citizenship is achieved by passing the naturalization test, and the behaviors and learning that precede this event are irrelevant. For three of the four citizenship teachers observed, citizenship meanings occupy a larger scope than officially recognized. Mr Morris and Ms April are the two instructors whose philosophy and classroom practices go the furthest towards addressing the complex and multifaceted nature of citizenship. Ms Lara, Ms Maria, and to some extent, Mr Morris, teach a minimalist view of citizenship. When the classroom environment is centered on teaching towards the test, information worth knowing is standardized, with all other knowledge, including critical notions of citizenship, ignored. Furthermore, when teachers only focus on English language instruction, ignoring the linguistic capital (Bourdieu, 1991) of students' native languages, linguistic assimilation is promoted. Multiculturalism and multilingualism are often not commemorated in a citizenship/ ESL class, even though this opportunity could be taken when discussing immigrants' cultures and contributions throughout US history.[12]

The population of adult school citizenship class attendees is obviously a select sample of all naturalization applicants. It is likely the case that many immigrants who desire citizenship have learned English in their home country, have not lived with a fear of deportation, understand the system of government bureaucracy and are familiar with accessing online test preparation. These conditions are not true for most of those who attend citizenship classes, and for many the English-proficiency requirement still remains an insurmountable challenge even after living in the United States for over a decade. In the current climate of decreased funding for citizenship classes, it must be recognized that there is a population of immigrants who rely on these classes for assistance in passing the test, for the opportunity to participate in a community of test-takers, and to gain more complex understandings of what citizenship entails.

Notes

(1) It is arguable that 'privileges' refers to the privilege of voting, a more active role of citizenship, but while encouraged, it is not required to be a citizen (and in the 2010 Congressional election it is estimated that 37% of the voting-age population cast votes (US Census Bureau, 2012)).
(2) School names as well as site participants' names are pseudonyms.
(3) As of January, 2011.
(4) Such as 'The Human Body', 'What Does Sue Do?' and 'Where is the Dog?'
(5) An example is students who practiced the sentence 'Citizens have the right to vote' must now correctly write, 'They want to vote'.
(6) The AACC row is divided by teachers, when applicable: Ms Maria (top), Ms April (bottom).
(7) Additional points of comparison

	Fees	Registration	Approx. class size	Student population
Ford School for Adults	$20 a semester or subsidized	Open enrollment, high turnover	14.9 (afternoon); 10.4 (evening)	Chinese, Hmong, Mexican; 20s–40s (afternoon), 30s–60s (evening)
Wilson Adult School	$25 for class	Set enrollment date, low turnover	15.5	Russian; 40s–70s
Asian American Community Center	free	Open enrollment, low turnover	17.8	Vietnamese, Chinese; 40s–70s

(8) Under the critical ethnographic perspective it is essential to acknowledge that a researcher has vested interest in the topic and can never be a completely neutral observer (Bredo & Feinberg, 1982). My involvement in each class ranged from a silent observer, to participant observer, to participant, depending on the teachers' wishes. My own positionality shifted over the course of study, resulting in the belief that citizenship classes are assets for immigrants navigating a confusing, bureaucratic system with an absence of practical information supplied by CIS.
(9) While Ms Lara wasn't interviewed, the fact that she is the only one of the four teachers who is a naturalized American citizen herself suggests that she is also familiar with experiencing daily life with and without US citizenship.

(10) An example of what students are reading: 'After an amendment has passed in Congress or by a special convention, the amendment must then be ratified (accepted) by the legislatures of three-fourths of the states'.
(11) This is the answer to the question 'The House of Representatives has how many voting members?'
(12) As mentioned in the Section Peripheral meanings, a few of Mr Morris's lessons are the exception to this tendency.

References

Banks, J.A. (2008) Diversity, group identity, and citizenship education in a global age. *Educational Researcher* 37 (3), 129–139.
Bauböck, R. (1994) *Transnational Citizenship: Membership and Rights in International Migration*. Brookfield, VT: Elgar.
Blommaert, J. (2009) Language, asylum, and the national order. *Current Anthropology* 50 (4), 415–441.
Bloome, D., Puro, P. and Theodorou, E. (1989) Procedural display and classroom lessons. *Curriculum Inquiry* 19 (3), 265–291.
Bourdieu, P. (1991) *Language and Symbolic Power*. Cambridge, MA: Harvard University Press.
Bredo, E. and Feinberg, W. (1982) The critical approach to social and educational research. In E. Bredo and W. Feinberg (eds) *Knowledge and Values in Social and Educational Research* (pp. 271–291). Philadelphia: Temple University Press.
Calmes, J. (2011) In border city talk, Obama urges G.O.P. to help overhaul immigration law. *The New York Times*, pp. A17.
Canagarajah, S.A. (ed.) (2005) *Reclaiming the Local in Language Policy and Practice*. Mahwah, NJ: Lawrence Erlbaum Associates.
Castles, S. (1998) Globalization and the ambiguities of national citizenshp. In R. Bauböck and J. Rundell (eds) *Blurred Boundaries: Migration, Ethnicity, Citizenship*. (pp. 223–244). Brookfield, VT: Ashgate.
Castles, S. (2000) *Ethnicity and Globalization: From Migrant Worker to Transnational Citizen*. Thousand Oaks, CA: Sage.
Citizen (2012) In *Oxford English Dictionary*. oed.com.
Citizenship (2011) *U.S. Citizenship and Immigration Services*. http://www.uscis.gov/portal/site/uscis/
Citizenship (2012). In *Oxford English Dictionary*. oed.com.
Cogan, J. and Morris, P. (2001) The development of civics values: An overview. *International Journal of Education Research* 35 (1), 1–9.
Dahrendorf, R. (1994) The changing condition of citizenship. In B. van Steenbergen (ed.) *The Condition of Citizenship*. London: Sage.
DeJaeghere, J.G. (2008) Citizenship as privilege and power: Australian educators' lived experiences as citizens. *Comparative Education Review* 52 (3), 357–380.
Freire, P. (2000) *Pedagogy of the Oppressed* (30th anniversary edn). New York: Continuum.
Gee, J.P. (2003) *What Video Games have to Teach us About Learning and Literacy*. New York: Palgrave Macmillan.
Glaser, B.G. and Strauss, A.L. (1967) *The Discovery of Grounded Theory: Strategies for Qualitative Research*. Chicago: Aldine.

Glick Schiller, N., Basch, L. and Szanton Blanc, C. (1995) From immigrant to transmigrant: Theorizing transnational migration. *Anthropological Quarterly* 68 (1), 48–63.

Griswold, O. (2010) Narrating America: Socializing adult ESL learners into idealized views of the United States during citizenship preparation classes. *TESOL Quarterly* 44 (3), 488–516.

Griswold, O. (2011) The English you need to know: Language ideology in a citizenship classroom. *Linguistics and Education* 22, 406–418.

Gustines, G.G. (2011) Superman renounces his U.S. citizenship. *The New York Times*, pp. C2.

Kerber, L.K. (1997) The meanings of citizenship. *The Journal of American History* 84 (3), 833–854.

Kuisma, M. (2008) Rights or privileges? The challenge of gloablization to the values of citizenship. *Citizenship Studies* 12 (6), 613–627.

Marshall, T.H. (1950) Citizenship and social class and other essays. Cambridge, MA: Cambridge University Press.

McCarty, T.L. (ed.) (2011) *Ethnography and Language Policy*. New York: Routledge.

Ong, A. (1999) *Flexible Citizenship: The Cultural Logics of Transnationality*. Durham: Duke University Press.

Ramanathan, V. (2005) Rethinking language planning and policy from the ground up: Refashioning institutional realities and human lives. *Current Issues in Language Planning* 6 (2), 89–101.

Semple, K. (2011) U.S. warns schools against checking immigration status. *The New York Times*, pp. A14.

Sim, J. B-Y. and Print, M. (2009) Citizenship education in Singapore: Controlling or empowering teacher understanding and practice? *Oxford Review of Education* 35 (6), 705–723.

Strauss, A.L. (1987) *Qualitative Analysis for Social Scientists*. Cambridge, MA: Cambridge University Press.

Stelter, B. (2011) In trying to debunk a theory, the news media extended its life. *The New York Times*, pp. A16.

Soysal, Y.N. (1994) *Limits of Citizenship: Migrants and Postnational Membership in Europe*. Chicago: University of Chicago Press.

Touraine, A. (1997) *What is Democracy?* Boulder, CO: Westview Press.

US Census Bureau (2012) *Voting Age Population: Reported Registration and Voting by Selected Characteristics: 1996 to 2010*. www.census.gov

US Constitution, Art. 4, § 2, cl. 1.

Yuval-Davis, N. (2006) Belonging and the politics of belonging. *Patterns of Prejudice* 40 (3), 197–214.

11 (Dis)Citizenship or Opportunity? The Importance of Language Education Policy for Access and Full Participation of Emergent Bilinguals in the United States

Kate Menken

In this chapter, I argue that language education policies restricting the use of immigrants' languages in schools are a form of dis-citizenship. I adopt here the definition of 'dis-citizenship' that is promoted in this volume, in which citizenship moves beyond identification with a certain nation-state and is extended and also used to mean 'being able to participate fully' (Ramanathan, this volume). As enacted in US schools, restrictive English-only policies marginalize emergent bilingual students and the languages they speak, bar these students from reaping the benefits of their bilingualism and limit their future opportunities. This chapter moves explorations of dis-citizenship in this volume into the ambiguous world of schools and classrooms within the United States, and specifically in New York City, where language policies are implicit and must therefore be exposed. In so doing, findings highlight how schools and educators typically regard the bilingualism of their students as disadvantageous within the current test-based accountability system, and respond by eliminating bilingual education programs altogether. Yet for many students, failure to support and use their home languages in school comes at a great academic and emotional cost. Moreover, doing so stems from (mis)conceptualizations of citizenship rooted in monolingual and monocultural ideologies, which serve to marginalize and minoritize students learning English in school.

Although written policy statements have historically been supportive of bilingual education in New York, this orientation towards language has shifted in recent years, as evidenced in school practices. Bilingual education, in which the home languages of emergent bilingual students are used in their instruction, has been mandatory in city schools for emergent bilingual students since the 1970s (Menken, 2011; Reyes, 2006). Yet New York City has borne witness to a significant loss of bilingual education programs since 2002, such that the proportion of emergent bilinguals in city schools enrolled in bilingual education has decreased from 40% to 22%, while the number in English as a second language (ESL) programs has increased from 53% to 70% (New York City Department of Education, 2011). Thus the vast majority of the 154,466 emergent bilinguals attending city schools are receiving instruction in English only.[1] Not only does this limit prospects for a bilingual and biliterate citizenry of the future, it also has a negative impact on emergent bilinguals attending city schools today.

This chapter examines the loss of bilingual education programs in city schools and the impact of these restrictive language education policies on emergent bilingual students, and specifically those labeled 'long-term English language learners' (LTELLs), drawing on data from two different but complimentary qualitative research studies. Taken together, these studies highlight how restrictive language education policies serve as a gatekeeper for citizenship, barring many emergent bilinguals from full participation.[2]

The Importance of Bilingual Education for Academic Success and Full Participation

In defining dis-citizenship to describe the treatment of people with disabilities, Pothier and Devlin (2006) write:

[C]itizenship is not just an issue of individual status; it is also a practice that locates individuals in the larger community. As such, the substantive approach raises questions of access and participation, exclusion and inclusion, rights and obligations, legitimate governance and democracy, liberty and equality, public and private, marginalization and belonging, social recognition and redistribution of resources, structure and agency, identity and personhood and self and other (Kabeer, 2002). Building on Hammar's (1990) concept of denizens to describe guest workers, who have some social rights but no political rights, in countries such as Germany, we want to suggest that because many persons with disabilities are denied formal and/or substantive citizenship, they are assigned to the status of 'dis-citizens', a form of citizenship minus, a disabling citizenship. (1990: 1–2)

While Pothier and Devlin (2006) applied this broad conception of citizenship to people with disabilities, Ramanathan (2009 and this volume) links the term to language. Following their lead, dis-citizenship is used here to offer a critical analysis of the experiences of emergent bilinguals attending US schools where the medium of instruction is increasingly English only.

The vast majority of immigrants to the United States receive instruction in English only, without the use of their home languages as a resource in their instruction, in spite of the fact that these programs likely result in monolingualism over time, diminish the academic performance of many students, and often come at great emotional cost in terms of a student's identity, connections to family, feelings about school and personal growth (Baker, 2011; García, 2009). English-only programs are found to be subtractive, in that the students' home language skills over time are eventually replaced with English, as clarified in the following definition of subtractive bilingualism and schooling:[3]

When monoglossic ideologies persist, and monolingualism and monolingual schools are the norm, it is generally believed that children who speak a language other than that of the state should be encouraged to abandon that language and instead take up only the dominant language... In this model, the student speaks a first language and a second one is added while the first is subtracted. (García, 2009: 51)

Because US schooling is rooted in such monoglossic ideologies, as characterized by an emphasis on English at the expense of home language development, the vast majority of immigrant groups in the United States will lose their home languages and shift entirely to English by the third generation (Fishman, 1991, 2001), if not sooner (Fillmore, 1991; Wright, 2004).

The home languages of emergent bilinguals are often misperceived as counterproductive impediments to learning, and excluded from educational policies, programming, and the formal curriculum (Menken, 2008; Nieto & Bode, 2008). Valenzuela (1999) examines subtractive schooling and documents how school decisions and monolingual policies result in the academic under-achievement of US-Mexican students.

School subtracts resources from youth in two major ways. First, it dismisses their definition of education which is not only thoroughly grounded in Mexican culture, but also approximates the optimal definition of education advanced by Noddings (1984) and other caring theorists. Second, subtractive schooling encompasses subtractively assimilationist policies and practices that are designed to divest Mexican students of their culture and language. (Valenzuela, 1999: 20)

Moreover, failure to incorporate students' languages and cultures in school creates a barrier to their full participation in all the institutions of US society.

These school practices rebuff the persuasive research base that now exists in bilingual education, which provides evidence that emergent bilinguals who are able to develop and maintain their home languages in school through bilingual education are likely to outperform their counterparts in English-only programs and experience greater academic success (Baker, 2011; Krashen & McField, 2005; Thomas & Collier, 1997, 2002). This is because, as Cummins (2000) has demonstrated, the academic language and literacy skills students acquire in their home languages are found to transfer to English. His interdependence hypothesis, or theory of linguistic transfer, maintains that students who have developed their home language literacy skills 'will tend to make stronger progress in acquiring literacy in their L2 [second language]' (Cummins, 2000: 173). Research is conclusive that teaching students to read in their home language promotes higher levels of achievement in English reading (August & Shanahan, 2006; Goldenberg, 2008). Moreover, sustained use and development of both languages is associated with a range of academic, linguistic and cognitive advantages (Bialystok, 2007; Cummins, 2000; Mohanty, 1994).

On the other hand, when the home languages of emergent bilinguals are not developed in school, they cannot benefit from their bilingualism in the same ways. As Cummins (2000: 75) states, 'continued academic development of both languages conferred cognitive/linguistic benefits whereas less well-developed academic proficiency in both languages limited children's ability to benefit cognitively and academically...' Baker (2011) argues that home language literacy skills cannot be transferred to the dominant language if they have not been developed sufficiently. The significant role that the home language plays in literacy learning is particularly salient later in this chapter when I describe the case of 'long-term ELLs', emergent bilinguals who have attended US schools for seven or more years.

Given that most emergent bilinguals do not receive home language instruction, it is therefore not surprising when Short and Fitzsimmons

(2007) refer to a 'literacy crisis' among emergent bilinguals at the secondary level, many of whom arrive in secondary schools without well-developed literacy skills, in spite of years attending US schools. Thonus (2003) clarifies how subtractive schooling can result in limited academic language and literacy skills when describing older emergent bilinguals who are US born or arrived in the United States at school age:

> Because of the lack of maintenance bilingual education and the push towards cultural assimilation, these US-educated students have lost or are in the process of losing their home language(s), without having learned their writing systems or academic registers. (2003: 18)

Thonus (2003) illustrates the correlation between the educational programming an emergent bilingual receives and eventual language loss, when a student's home language is neither maintained nor developed in school.

The Research

New York City is the most multilingual and multicultural city in the United States, and in spite of the extreme diversity of the city's school system and its many years of experience educating emergent bilinguals through a wide range of programming options, in recent years unofficial policy has grown increasingly restrictive as large numbers of bilingual education programs have been dismantled (as described above). Thus there are fewer spaces in city schools where the bilingualism of its students are being built upon in instruction. This chapter presents findings from two studies conducted in New York City public schools within this period of language restriction; while these studies were not intentionally related to one another when they began, their findings intersect in important ways that are presented in this chapter.

One study involves qualitative research gathered from 2009 to 2011 in ten city schools that have recently eliminated their bilingual education programs and replaced them with ESL programs. The purpose of this research is to determine the factors that administrators within these schools cite as having had the greatest impact on their school's language policy. Accordingly, school principals, assistant principals and teachers were interviewed to better understand the decision to adopt English-only instruction in these schools. These findings are contrasted to data from an additional seven schools involving interviews of administrators and educators who are supportive of and involved in implementing bilingual education. A total of 25 educators participated in this research and were interviewed in depth (see Menken & Solorza, in press, for more detailed methodology).

The other study focuses on the educational experiences of a specific population of emergent bilingual students, namely students labeled LTELLs by the city school system, as part of a three-year research study involving interviews of 15 educators and 43 LTELL students conducted from 2006–2009 (methodology further detailed in Menken & Kleyn, 2010). Findings from this research indicate that the schooling experiences of these primarily US-educated students can be described as 'subtractive', in that their home language practices have not been supported in their schooling and instead largely replaced with English. We found that this failure to use and develop the students' home languages has been a significant contributing factor to their becoming 'long-term ELLs' over time (Menken & Kleyn, 2010). Moreover, these studies are connected in that one probes the climate of language restrictionism that has produced the population of students described in the other.

Pressures of Accountability and Testing in English

In their interviews, school administrators and teachers in New York City all identified high-stakes testing and the corresponding pressures of accountability as a primary cause for the decreasing number of bilingual programs in city schools. Due to the city's decentralized leadership and control, school principals are the ones called upon to determine language programming for the emergent bilinguals in their buildings, and they are required by city and state policy to provide bilingual education and/or ESL. Although bilingual education is actually mandatory in city schools that have the population to support it (i.e. enough speakers of the same home language per grade for the program to be viable), as delineated in local policy (see Menken, 2011 and Menken & Solorza, in press), the exacting pressures of testing and accountability under federal education legislation contradict and overpower local policy statements and have been a factor in shifting perceptions of bilingual education. Accordingly, principals increasingly favor English-only programming in an effort to raise test scores and improve the performance of their school on accountability measures. In so doing, without long-term consequences in mind, these educators effectively deny a citizenship comprised of full access and opportunity to their emergent bilingual students.

In specific, the following two main findings emerged: first, school leaders are eliminating their bilingual programs due to the enormous pressure they are under in the United States today to constantly improve school-wide performance, and particularly standardized test scores, in compliance with federal and local accountability mandates. Second, school leaders typically have no formal preparation in the education of emergent bilinguals. As such, they believe that English-only instruction will improve performance on tests administered in English and immediately blame bilingual programs for poor test scores, with the belief that bilingual teachers in these programs use the students' home languages too much and that bilingual programs fail to teach English. Many principals see emergent bilinguals as threatening their school's overall performance and ability to meet the accountability requirements, and prefer not to admit these students or offer programs such as bilingual education that would attract them. In the sections that follow, I offer examples from interview data to support these themes.

In the following passage, Ms P[4] conveys the pressure she personally feels due to the current accountability system:

School administrators – we're the ones accountable. In the news, on the report cards really it's the administration that has the responsibility not only with our bosses but with the community. (Ms P, Junior High School Principal, interview transcript)

In New York City, school leaders must contend with federal and local layers of accountability. Specifically, US educational policy entitled *No Child Left Behind* requires that students make adequate yearly progress in academic content areas, including English and math. In New York City, all students must meet performance goals on city and state exams, as well as other measures such as attendance and graduation rates. Because it is impossible to truly divorce language from content knowledge when an emergent bilingual takes a standardized test administered in English, it is not surprising that these students usually score far below English proficient students, and that schools serving large numbers of emergent bilinguals are disproportionately likely to be labeled low performing or 'in need of improvement' and risk sanctions such as restructuring and/or closure in accordance with federal accountability policy (Menken, 2008, 2010, 2011).

When I asked a high school principal in an interview why he had eliminated the bilingual program at his school, he offered the following reply (note here that educators typically use the term 'English language learners' or 'ELLs' to describe the students referred to in this chapter as emergent bilinguals):

The state data, not enough kids were passing English Regents. That was one of the factors. This school was cited for years, from what I can see, for years the school was cited for not meeting the performance index for ELLs. (Mr A, high school principal, interview transcript)

The English Regents is the statewide English language arts exam for high school students, which all students in New York must pass in order to graduate from high school. As Mr A explains in this quotation, he eliminated the school's bilingual program in an effort to improve student test performance and meet the federal and local accountability requirements. The majority of the schools participating in this study had dismantled their bilingual education programs in an effort to turn around poor performance by emergent bilingual on high-stakes tests.

These views are echoed in elementary schools in New York City, where the pressures of testing in English have also encouraged English-only instruction. This point is discussed during an interview with two elementary school teachers (Ms D and Ms T) in a school serving large numbers of Spanish speaking emergent bilinguals:

Ms D: [I]t's getting very difficult to find bilingual programs in the city because they don't want to fund them. If you look at all the assessments we have, right now everything is in English. There's nothing in Spanish...

Ms T: Right. Everything we receive is in English...[S]o then parents get nervous because their child has to pass the ELA [English Language Arts exam]. How many years do they have to be here before they have to take the test?

Ms D: None. The day they come in.

Ms T: So they have to take the test regardless. So again, another reason why the parents are nervous, the child is going to take a test – the same test that a monolingual takes. (Ms D and Ms T, elementary school teachers, interview transcript)

In this discussion, these teachers also point to the link between the decreasing numbers of bilingual programs in the city and testing in English. As they clarify, even emergent bilinguals who have just arrived in the United States must take high-stakes exams, and their scores are factored into accountability performance reports. This places great pressure not only on schools and educators, but also on students and their families.

In the interview excerpts that follow, two principals who support bilingual education and have a background in educating emergent bilinguals explain why accountability translates into English-only testing for many principals who do not share the same background (my voice in italics).

> So I'm just wondering, what are the factors that have influenced administrators deciding to offer other kinds of programming besides bilingual education, like more English-only programs?
> Testing. Testing is a big thing there. They seem to think that, many principals seem to think that if kids are going to take this English test they have to push the English. Of course they don't necessarily look at the research. They don't understand this whole idea of transfer. And so I find that since *No Child Left Behind* had said that the kids have to be, all this testing has to be taking place and we now do this, it's gotten worse. (Ms G, elementary school principal, interview transcript)

> I think generally speaking, there is a backlash against bilingual education and I think it's a matter of educating them... I think people feel that the only way to ensure that students do well is to teach them in English, and I think we are an example of that that's not true (Ms L, elementary school principal, interview transcript)

In both quotations, principals in schools that have maintained their bilingual programs in spite of the pressures for accountability under *No Child Left Behind* point out why testing in English can be a catalyst for language policy changes in schools. For principals and others unfamiliar with bilingual education theory, it seems counterintuitive that supporting students' home languages in school will help emergent bilinguals to learn English and academic content better. Yet the principals quoted above also show that this is true, in that they both lead schools that are high performing on tests and other measures of accountability; these leaders attribute their students' high performance to their bilingual programs. In these schools, where the principals are knowledgeable about bilingual education, the home languages of the students are regarded as part of the solution rather than as a problem in meeting the federal and local policy demands.

The principals who eliminated their school's bilingual program do not share this point of view. Findings reveal how a deficit paradigm shapes principals' perceptions of emergent bilingual students, in that principals were highly cognizant of the fact that these students usually do not perform well on high-stakes tests and threaten to pull down schoolwide scores and performance reports because they are in the process of learning English. Many school leaders even deny admission to emergent bilinguals for this reason, in overt violation of these students' legal rights in the United States. As one high school principal explains:

> We send them to the region and they move to another school.
>
> *Do you know where they go?*
>
> Well they have a lot of schools now that offer the bilingual programs, the dual programs. I know the ['A'] High School around here... Most of the students go there and ['B'] High School. They go to 'B' too because they still offer the bilingual programs. (Mr R, Acting High School Principal, interview transcript)

Alarmingly, this principal states in no uncertain terms that emergent bilinguals who arrive in his school are rejected and sent back to the student placement office to enroll elsewhere, with the belief that admitting them will make meeting the unforgiving state and federal requirements more difficult. He mentions in this passage that many schools now offer bilingual education programs when in fact, as detailed above, the number of these programs is dwindling. As a result, the number of emergent bilinguals at the high schools that admit them, and particularly those still offering bilingual education, has exploded in recent years.

This point is elaborated in the following, when a high school assistant principal was asked why her principal eliminated the school's bilingual program:

> [A] lot of schools weren't taking bilingual students at all. They were being pushed at my school and it was an enormous amount of need and students...And then I think it was numbers. There was a perception, real or not, that they were bringing the numbers down. Like having the bilingual program he felt kids were not learning English as quickly as maybe they could have if they were in an English-only program. (Ms A, high school assistant principal, interview transcript)

Like the principal quoted above, the principal of this school has chosen not to provide bilingual education out of fear that doing so would attract more emergent bilinguals to his school, which he perceives as a threat to the school's accountability reports. Monoglossic ideologies and the trope of citizenship as English monolingual that undergirds how the accountability system is enacted legitimizes this denial of equal educational opportunities to emergent bilinguals and contributes to the framing of these students as deficient, lesser, dis-citizens.

No Place for Home Language Use: Spanish as a 'Crutch' and Anti-'Assimilation'

The preceding section showed how emergent bilinguals are framed as a liability within the test-driven accountability system where English is what counts, and this section shows how usage of the home language in school is regarded as threatening a student's emerging bilingualism – in spite of research such as that cited above which argues the opposite is true. The following passage offers an example:

> There are some teachers who will only speak to the students in English, and there are some teachers that are easily roped into going back to Spanish. The kids are very, they don't, a lot of them don't see the immediacy of needing to learn English...And the kids kind of joke. They know that if they come up and ask me a question I'm not going to answer them in Spanish. (Ms E, junior high school principal, interview excerpt)

Ms E regards using a student's home language as a teacher's weakness, and something that will get in the way of a student learning English. She also perceives of students who speak their home language in school as unmotivated to learn English, implying that her emergent bilingual students believe English is unimportant.

This point is taken a step further by a high school principal during an interview.

> I go to meetings and I feel pressured to do bilingualism when I know it doesn't work. The students need to learn English and be assimilated but we're holding them back because of some bureaucrat in the state... It becomes like a crutch, they keep learning Spanish and don't move to English. My experience is they need to learn English. They won't compete if they don't know English. (Mr A, high school principal, interview transcript)

In the interview, this principal describes his opposition for bilingual education with the belief that home language usage will impede upon the students' English acquisition. He goes beyond this to say that home language usage will prevent students from assimilating into US society, and will act as a barrier to their identity as Americans – as if it poses a direct threat to citizenship. Ms A is the assistant principal in the school where Mr A is principal, and in this excerpt she describes how his views on this issue translate into his interactions and leadership of the students:

> Like, he had a student gathering, you know I think by grade levels, so an assembly. And he said, like, you know [yelling], 'English language learners! You have to learn English!' And so a lot of the non-ELLs, there's this friction between our black students and our Hispanic students. So a lot of our non-ELL black students were like, 'Yeah, that's it!' It was weird. It was really, like, what are you doing?... He's an assimilationist. He really is... I think his view is the purpose of school is to integrate them fully into American society, the American dream. (Ms A, high school assistant principal, interview transcript)

Ms A describes here an instance during a school assembly when the principal chastised emergent bilinguals, urging the students to learn English, and how this ignited tensions between African American students and Latinos (the vast majority of this school's emergent bilinguals are Latinos). While Mr A's goal may be to improve his students' test scores and assimilate emergent bilinguals into US society, his efforts to do so appear to be having the opposite effect. In fact, in the years since he eliminated the bilingual program at his school, test scores have actually decreased and the school is currently slated for closure and restructuring.

Rooted in the language ideologies and beliefs presented above, bilingual education programs are immediately blamed when emergent bilinguals do not perform well on high-stakes tests in English. This point is addressed in the field notes from my interview with Ms N, a junior high school assistant principal who worked with her school's principal to eliminate the bilingual program:

> When Ms N arrived a few years ago, testing data revealed ELLs not doing well. Whenever she observed the Chinese bilingual teachers she felt they weren't using enough English and nor were they proficient enough in English, and she felt the students were too segregated. Two-thirds of ELLs were in ESL only, but she felt they too were segregated.

To improve test results she eliminated the bilingual program – even though two-thirds were in English only. When I asked about this she couldn't remember how those in ESL only compared in test performance to those in bilingual. It was because of the data, but more based on feeling/ideology and a sense of wanting to include or assimilate ELLs more. (Ms N, junior high school assistant principal, interview field notes)

Like other administrators, Ms N's decision to dismantle the bilingual education program was galvanized by the poor performance of emergent bilinguals on the tests used to evaluate city schools, and her belief that use of the home language in school was hindering rather than facilitating English acquisition. Although this school previously had both ESL and bilingual programs, the performance of emergent bilinguals in the bilingual program was not compared to that of their peers in ESL. In this way, the decision by Ms N and her principal to dismantle the bilingual program was data driven, though not actually data based.

As these cases highlight, the way that bilingual education is being pitted against English acquisition in schools and integration into US society has caused its elimination as an educational programming option within many schools. Bilingual education directly opposes monolingual notions of citizenship. As detailed in the section that follows, however, monolingual instruction to promote a monolingual citizenry fails to provide access to full citizenship, in that subtractive schooling is generating growing numbers of emergent bilinguals who enter secondary schools struggling to attain the academic language and literacy skills that schooling and future opportunities demand.

Subtractive Schooling Limiting Possibilities for Participation: The Case of 'Long-Term ELLs' and Education for Dis-Citizenship

The case of 'long-term ELLs' exemplifies how citizenship, in its metaphoric sense, can be denied to emergent bilinguals through schooling that neither supports nor utilizes their home languages, and then regards these students as deficient for failing to become English monolinguals. Long-term ELLs are emergent bilinguals at the secondary level who have attended US schools for seven years or more, yet whose schooling experiences have been subtractive (Menken & Kleyn, 2010). Although these students have strong oral skills in English and their home language when using language for social purposes, they have limited academic literacy skills in either of the languages they speak. As a group, they are typically low performing in school, characterized by high course failure and grade retention rates, and at great risk of dropping out or being unable to graduate from high school. Yet these students currently comprise one-third of all emergent bilinguals in New York City high schools (New York City Department of Education, 2008), and their numbers exceed 50% of the secondary emergent bilinguals in certain areas of California (Olsen, 2010). The number of emergent bilinguals who become long-term ELLs over time will undoubtedly increase as more schools eliminate their bilingual education programs (Menken & Kleyn, 2010).

When asked to describe the long-term ELLs (LTELLs) at her school, a high school assistant principal stated the following:

> I think the challenge lies in the reading and writing. You'll find the students are verbal but when it comes to academic language, that's where the problem lies. If you examine the writing scores in the [English proficiency exam], this is the most challenging part. For speaking, the social speaking part is their strength so you wouldn't recognize they're even ELLs when you see them... [T]hey haven't developed the reading and writing in either language. You speak to them in Spanish it's the same thing, they speak well but they can't read and write. (Ms J, high school assistant principal, interview transcript)

As shown in this quotation, emergent bilinguals labeled 'long-term ELLs' struggle to attain the academic language that secondary school requires.

Many administrators and teachers attribute the challenges these students face to failure on the part of the school system to support and develop the students' home languages in school. A high school principal was informed which students at her school were labeled 'long term' and stated the following:

> [W]e said, 'Ah, no wonder! These are the ones that we're struggling with. These are the kids that will take longer to graduate. And we suspect based on exams that they were not targeted early enough to work on those areas where they needed work... So if these students would have been targeted early on and worked with, in terms of a holistic language approach in the native language and then to help them to transition into English. Because you need to work with the students' native language the same way you work with the culture to get them to understand and then say, 'You know what? I can transition this, I know how to do it in my language'. (Ms M, high school principal, interview transcript)

As Ms M clarifies, this student population lags behind other emergent bilinguals and struggles to meet the graduation requirements. Ms M attributes the challenges they face to the schools these students have attended in the past, for neither supporting nor developing the students' home languages.

This point is further developed by one of the teachers interviewed, who lamented the elimination of the bilingual education program at her school for the impact of doing so on LTELLs.

> Some of them are even born here and only educated here, but in both languages their vocabulary is extremely limited, it's never been increased anywhere. And so you would be giving them the words in Spanish, so if they had a really good native language arts class and they were really, you know, working with their language and improving it at a grade level capacity they would have something to transition from, to transfer from Spanish to English. So this is the thing. (Ms Y, high school ESL teacher, interview transcript)

Like Ms M, in this quote Ms Y argues for the need to provide emergent bilinguals with home language instruction to promote their English acquisition. According to recent data from the New York City Department of Education (2011), 72% of long-term ELLs are US born and all are primarily educated in US schools. Without home language instruction in schools, it becomes extremely difficult for emergent bilinguals to acquire the academic language needed to succeed.

What follows is an interview with a high school principal (Mr M) and assistant principal (Ms C) about 'long-term ELLs', which exemplifies how LTELL status is immediately associated with school failure and how language education policies serve as a gatekeeper for full participation and citizenship, when restrictive policies limit students' future opportunities.

Mr M: And it can be several years and then, what do you call them? Long-term?

Ms C: Long-term means they have been in our system for many years and because they can speak very well, but can't pass the test....

Mr M: There's a huge dropout rate with long-term ELLs and it's just a really unfortunate situation because they stay in that category for a really, really long time. (Mr M and Ms C, high school principal and assistant principal, interview transcript)

As the interview excerpts in this section bring to light, US schools steeped in ideologies of monolingualism have created populations of students who struggle with the academic language and literacy skills needed to succeed, and who are then labeled 'long term' over time, and regarded as deficient for their failure to achieve English monolingualism. As teachers explained, the pejorative to describe these students in high school is 'lifers'; such deficit views of this population are reproduced in their schooling experiences. Moreover, these students have received an education for dis-citizenship that limits rather than expands, and disables rather than enables, their lifelong opportunities.

Voices of Bilingual Educators on Language Education Policy as Gatekeeper for Citizenship

In addition to interviewing school administrators and teachers who participated in the elimination of bilingual education programs, bilingual educators were also interviewed for purposes of comparison. All of the bilingual educators who participated are experienced teachers and administrators, ranging from 6 to 32 years educating emergent bilinguals in city schools. All evidence resistance against restrictive, monolingual language education policies and are actively engaged in what Hornberger and Johnson (2007) call 'carving out ideological and implementational spaces' in which bilingual education can occur.

Several educators pointed out the value of building on the prior knowledge and experiences that students bring with them to school, and all regard the language and culture of emergent bilinguals as a resource that is crucial to their success in school.

Why is bilingual education/home language instruction important for the current and future academic success of emergent bilinguals and their lifelong opportunities?
Bilingual education more than being an approach or a 'program' is a stance towards educating children. It represents a view that the most effective way to educate children is by placing their educational needs first. In other words, educating students departs from a deep understanding of what they already know and how to facilitate learning based on those strengths. (Ms Z, elementary school supervisor, written transcript)

Students need a place to develop their native language skills to help them access prior knowledge. Working in their native language helps them develop their English skills as well as helps bring them up to speed on the content that they are learning... If they are not literate in their native language, becoming literate in another language becomes much more challenging! (Ms LJ, high school lead teacher, written transcript)

These views of students offer a marked departure from deficit views of the students, whereby linguistic and cultural diversity is seen as a problem; instead, these educators' words show how they see the students for what they bring, not what they lack.

A number of educators note how this acknowledgement is not only essential for academic reasons, but also in terms of their students' sense of identity, connections with family, and self-esteem.

What are the negative consequences, if any, for emergent bilinguals if they do not receive bilingual education (e.g. in terms of their academic success and lifelong opportunities)?
Negative self worth, isolation from the total person they are, inability to communicate fully with the culture and language of students' families, inability for children to return to the place of their families for future employment, possible rejection of students' culture, and perhaps less facility of the brain. (Ms H, elementary school assistant principal, written notes)

Bilingual educators who have also worked in English-only contexts were able to offer comparisons of the students' educational and emotional outcomes, as in the following:

In the middle school I taught at in [region], I worked for two years in an English-only setting until I began teaching in the dual language program... I worked with the same students in both settings in terms of the neighborhoods and schools they came from. What I noticed was that the children who had consistently been given the opportunity to use their home language in school outperformed the other students in terms of academics, and tended to be more cooperative and outgoing in classroom settings. They seemed to have better expectations of themselves in terms of what they should achieve academically, and motivated to progress in both languages... Many of my students in the monolingual setting reported preferring English because they 'didn't like' or 'didn't understand' Spanish – even when this was the only language spoken by their mother or father or both. (Ms K, middle school teacher/program coordinator, written transcript)

In these excerpts, Ms H and Ms K note the importance of home language instruction as a way to meet the needs of emergent bilinguals both academically and emotionally. Students quickly perceive and absorb the messaging of schools with regard to the value placed on their home language and, as exemplified by Ms K's observations, quickly begin to reproduce those messages through negative attitudes towards their home language.

These educators regard bilingual education as an essential part of resisting monolingual and monocultural definitions of citizenship and at the same time giving students the skills they need to participate fully in all institutions of US society.

> [B]ilingual education begins with knowledge that students enter classrooms with and builds on their strengths. This provides a bridge for students to develop fluid ethnolinguistic identities that accommodate the dominant culture while re-appropriating it to fit their purposes. In short, bilingual education offers the possibility for students to master the dominant discourses without having to 'sell out'. This will increase their engagement with school and their engagement with society. (Mr F, high school teacher/supervisor, written transcript)

In this quote, Mr F notes how bilingual education opens possibilities for full participation without students having to give up who they are in order to do so.

In the following quote, Ms Z takes this point a step further, to think about the impact not just on the students but on society as a whole:

> [B]eing bilingual in a way can change what it means to be a US citizen or in US society. Fully participating as a US citizen may mean a lot of things to different people and won't change to incorporate bilingual students unless bilingual US citizens define what fully participating in US society means to them. (Ms Z, elementary administrator, written transcript)

In this excerpt, Ms Z notes how students' re-appropriation of citizenship and assertion of their place within wider society holds the potential to change what it means to be American altogether. In her view, students hold agency and power not only in determining their own lives but also in influencing society as a whole. Moreover, for these educators, bilingual education offers an essential pathway towards attaining citizenship, and a means to do so that does not entail giving up one's own identity in the process.

Moving Forward

This chapter has shown how emergent bilinguals are constructed as liabilities for schools within the current testing and accountability framework, and how many educators reproduce this construction in seeing emergent bilinguals solely through a deficit lens. Accordingly, many school administrators have dismantled their bilingual education programs and behind closed doors barred admission to students learning English. As a result of attending subtractive schools with increasingly restrictive language education policies that neither support nor expand their home language practices, the data presented above shows how many students entering secondary school struggle to acquire the necessary academic language and literacy skills that unforgiving English-medium tests and courses demand; thus, many students face limited chances for success. As such, schools today are offering up citizenship minus to emergent bilinguals, an education for dis-citizenship, a citizenship that is less than the one that is promised to English monolinguals.

The bilingual educators quoted above draw on their experiences and remind us of the importance of bilingual education to give students the skill set they need to not only participate in all institutions of US society, but also to resist the monolingual ideologies that frame citizenship today. Because the use of students' home language practices in school supports their acquisition of academic language and literacy skills in English, bilingual education fosters greater participation and also enables students to reap the full benefits of their bilingualism in an increasingly global society. Equally importantly, bilingual education does not erase who the students are in the process, but rather builds on it. In this way, bilingual programs provide students with the ability to create a new definition of citizenship that makes sense for them – a citizenship plus, even. And this alone is subversive, as it not only draws into question what citizenship is and who defines it, but holds the potential to change altogether what it means to be an American and what US society is during this period of record immigration.

Moreover, as more immigrants arrive in the United States within an increasingly globalized economy, the provision of an education for dis-citizenship is no longer viable and will have to change. This has even been recognized by policymakers in New York, who – in a promising turn of events – have recently mandated the expansion of bilingual education programs in city schools. While the city and state are unable to disobey the top-down federal accountability mandates that have driven the elimination of many bilingual programs over the past decade, they can work to support bilingual programs, prepare principals, and reassure school administrators that bilingual education will actually help their emergent bilingual students meet the testing and accountability requirements. In this way, the city school system seeks to rectify the recent loss of bilingual education programs and resulting damage to emergent bilinguals and their communities, and turn restrictive language education policies into the more expansive and dynamic ones that the 21st century requires. What now remains to be seen is whether this local form of resistance is enough to restore bilingual education programs and improve the extent to which US schools provide emergent bilinguals with access and opportunity.

Notes

(1) While the home languages of students can and should be incorporated in ESL classes (García, 2009; Wright, 2010), this is not traditionally done.
(2) It is important to note at the outset that many emergent bilingual students are undocumented, in which case citizenship according to its traditional definition could not be stripped away, given these students do not have legal status to begin with. What I address in this chapter with regard to emergent bilinguals – those with documents and without – is citizenship in its metaphoric sense, and the extent to which schools provide students the possibility to participate fully in all institutions of US society.
(3) It is worth noting that García (2009) in her work is rightly critical of overly simplistic terms used to describe bilingualism, such as subtractive and additive, contributing more nuanced representations of language usage such as 'dynamic' and 'recursive'.
(4) All names of people and schools are masked pseudonyms.

References

August, D. and Shanahan, T. (eds) (2006) *Developing Literacy in Second-language Learners: Report of the National Literacy Panel on Language-Minority Children and Youth*. Mahwah, NJ: Lawrence Erlbaum Associates.

Baker, C. (2011) *Foundations of Bilingual Education and Bilingualism* (5th edn). Bristol: Multilingual Matters.

Bialystok, E. (2007) Cognitive effects of bilingualism: How linguistic experience leads to cognitive change. *International Journal of Bilingual Education and Bilingualism* 10 (3), 210–223.

Cummins, J. (2000) *Language, Power, and Pedagogy: Bilingual Children in the Crossfire*. Clevedon: Multilingual Matters.

Fillmore, L. (1991) When learning a second language means losing the first. *Early Childhood Research Quarterly* 6 (3), 323–346.

Fishman, J. (1991) *Reversing Language Shift*. Clevedon: Multilingual Matters.

Fishman, J. (ed.) (2001) *Can Threatened Languages be Saved?* Clevedon: Multilingual Matters.

García, O. (2009) *Bilingual Education in the 21st Century: A Global Perspective*. Malden, MA: Wiley-Blackwell.
Goldenberg, C. (2008) Teaching English Language Learners: What the Research Does—and Does Not—Say. *American Educator* Summer 2008, 8–44, accessed 18 July 2008. http://www.aft.org/pubs-reports/american_educator/issues/summer08/goldenberg.pdf
Hammar, T. (1990) *Democracy and the Nation State: Aliens, Denizens and Citizens in the World of International Migration*. Aldershot: Avebury.
Hornberger, N. and Johnson, D. (2007) Slicing the onion ethnographically: Layers and spaces in multilingual language education policy and practice. *TESOL Quarterly* 41 (3), 509–533.
Kabeer, N. (2002) Citizenship and the boundaries of the acknowledged community: Identity, affiliation and exclusion. Working Paper 171, Institute of Development Studies, Brighton.
Krashen, S. and McField, G. (2005) What works? Reviewing the latest evidence on bilingual education. *Language Learner* 1 (2), 7–10, 34.
Menken, K. (2008) *English Learners Left Behind: Standardized Testing as Language Policy*. Clevedon: Multilingual Matters.
Menken, K. (2010) NCLB and English language learners: Challenges and consequences. *Theory into Practice* 49 (2), 121–128.
Menken, K. (2011) From policy to practice in the multilingual apple: Bilingual education in New York City. Editorial Introduction. *International Journal of Bilingual Education and Bilingualism* 14 (2), 123–133.
Menken, K. and Kleyn, T. (2010) The long-term impact of subtractive schooling in the educational experiences of secondary English language learners. *International Journal of Bilingual Education and Bilingualism* 13 (4), 399–417.
Menken, K. and Solorza, C. (in press) No child left bilingual: Accountability and the elimination of bilingual education programs in New York City schools. *Educational Policy*.
Mohanty, A. (1994) *Bilingualism in a Multicultural Society: Psycho-social and Pedagogical Implications*. Mysore, India: Central Institute of Indian Languages.
New York City Department of Education, Office of English Language Learners (2008) *New York City's English Language Learners: Demographics and Performance*. New York: Author.
New York City Department of Education, Office of English Language Learners (2011) *The 2010-11 Demographics of New York City's English Language Learners*. New York, NY: Author.
Nieto, S. and Bode, P. (2008) *Affirming Diversity: The Sociopolitical Context of Multicultural Education* (5th edn). Boston, MA: Allyn and Bacon.
Olsen, L. (2010) *Reparable Harm: Fulfilling the Unkept Promise of Educational Opportunity for California's Long term English Learners*. Long Beach, CA: Californian's Together.
Pothier, D. and Devlin, R. (eds) (2006) Introduction: Towards a critical theory of dis-citizenship. In D. Pothier and R. Devlin (eds) *Critical Disability Theory: Essays in Philosophy, Politics, Policy, and Law* (pp. 1–22). Vancouver: University of British Columbia Press.
Ramanathan, V. (2009) *Bodies and Language: Health, Ailments, Disability*. Bristol: Multilingual Matters.

Reyes, L. (2006, Fall) The Aspira consent decree: A thirtieth-anniversary retrospective of bilingual education in New York City. *Harvard Educational Review* 76 (3), 369–400.

Short, D. and Fitzsimmons, S. (2007) Double the work: Challenges and solutions to acquiring language and academic literacy for adolescent English language learners. A report to Carnegie Corporation of New York. New York: Carnegie Corporation of New York.

Thomas, W. and Collier, V. (1997) *School Effectiveness for Language Minority Students*. Washington, DC: National Clearinghouse for Bilingual Education.

Thomas, W. and Collier V. (2002) A national study of school effectiveness for language minority students' long term academic achievement: Final report: Project 1.1. CREDE, accessed June 2005. http://crede.ucsc.edu/research/llaa/1.1_final.html

Thonus, T. (2003) Serving generation 1.5 learners in the university writing center. *TESOL Journal* 12 (1), 17–24.

Valenzuela, A. (1999) *Subtractive Schooling: U.S. Mexican Youth and the Politics of Caring*. Albany: State University of New York Press.

Wright, W. (2004) What English-only really means: A study of the implementation of California language policy with Cambodian American students. *International Journal of Bilingual Education and Bilingualism* 7 (1), 1–23.

12 English Learning without English Teachers? The Rights and Access of Rural Secondary Students in Nicaragua[1]

Rosemary Henze and
Fabio Oliveira Coelho

Introduction

This chapter is about English language teaching and learning in rural Nicaragua and the relationships among national educational language policy, local implementation and local realities. After providing some background information, we raise a series of questions and responses that reflect critically on our experience as US university partners of Nicaraguan teachers, students and NGO leaders. We ask, why is it that a foreign language education policy, when local leaders faithfully attempt to implement it, can in fact result in the disempowerment of local teachers and local students? How applicable is this national educational language policy to rural, low-income communities, given their lack of access to basic resources, technology and trained English language teachers? Does the assumed model of standard English language learning and teaching with a fluent, trained teacher necessarily have to be maintained? What are the alternatives to this assumed model? And lastly, what have we learned about how foreign partnerships can best support an alternative model of foreign language study?

Historical background

To help our readers understand the basis for these questions, we provide some brief historical and contextual background. Nicaragua is currently the poorest country in Central America and second poorest country in the Western hemisphere, after Haiti (CIA Factbook, 2011). During Nicaragua's revolutionary war against the Somoza regime (1978–1979) followed by the Contra War (1981–1990), which was funded by the CIA, nearly 50,000 citizens lost their lives, approximately 3% of the population (Booth & Walker, 1999). In addition to the devastation caused by these wars, Nicaragua has also suffered three earthquakes in the past three decades – Hurricane Joan in 1988, Hurricane Mitch in 1998 and Hurricane Felix in 2007.

Despite the bold socialist agenda of the Sandinistas, who took over the government after the war ended in 1979, Nicaragua has in recent years moved more to a centrist and corporate friendly government, led by former Sandinista leader Daniel Ortega, who in 2011 was elected to a third term as president. Searing lines of inequality exist between urban and rural people as well as between poor and middle to upper class people. Those living in the rural north experience the 'double whammy' of being both rural and poor. Women and girls are subordinate to men and boys, and women's reproductive rights are taking a backward step in recent legislation which outlaws abortion of any kind.

Public education at the secondary level is still not a right or a requirement of every citizen. Mandatory education is provided through 6th grade, and after that, public secondary education is available only if one resides in an urban area or if one is fortunate enough to live within walking distance or bus transportation to a secondary school. The majority of Nicaragua's rural population does not have access to secondary education. In fact, only 17% of rural adolescents attend secondary education in Nicaragua (IPADE, 2010: 53). Literacy beyond the 6th grade level remains low, and consequently, the power of rural people to shape their own destinies, to have a voice in the local, regional, national and global events that affect them, is limited.

The discourse of globalization is as pervasive in Nicaragua as elsewhere. This discourse frequently references the need for Nicaraguans to learn English so that they can participate in the global marketplace, communicate across borders, etc. As Rajagopalan (2005: 85) states, 'almost everyone agrees that knowledge of English is a must for those who aspire to climb a few rungs up the social ladder'. The Nicaraguan Ministry of Education (MINED) requires students in secondary schools to take three hours a week of English during the five years of *secundaria*, a policy rationalized by the belief that those who know English will have increased access to jobs and a higher standard of living. The official MINED website phrases the requirement as *'Idioma exstranjero (Inglés)'* – Foreign language (English) – indicating that among the many possible foreign languages, English is the only choice and therefore the requirement (MINED, 2012). However, the preparation of English language teachers at the university level is extremely poor both in numbers (not enough to meet the demand) and in quality (Cerezál, 2000; Red MEIRCA, 2011). As a result, Nicaraguan secondary schools face a situation that is almost impossible to resolve: they must provide five years of English language classes (three hours a week), yet the number of qualified teachers is scant at best, and of those who are qualified, few are willing or able to teach in remote villages in the rural areas. Absent a massive infusion of newly qualified English teachers and great expense to the government, it is hard to imagine how the policy can be implemented. At the present time, the English language policy privileges those who live in urban areas where more qualified English teachers live and work, and further marginalizes the children of the rural poor. In Ramanathan's words, 'English still divides' even when it is appropriated as a tool of localized identity and nationalism (2005: 33).

Theory and conceptual framework

In framing this chapter, we draw first on critical theory and critical pedagogy. Friere (1973) left us with a legacy that is more relevant than ever today. His notions of critical consciousness and problem posing continue to resonate with educators who seek to create conditions for self-empowerment in rural, low-income communities that have traditionally remained outside the scope of formal educational alternatives. One might say that although rural Nicaraguans are formally citizens of their country, in practice they are routinely disenfranchised from participating in many of the institutions of the society (Devlin & Pothier, 2006) because without a formal education beyond sixth grade, and lacking access to jobs, technology and transportation, they are in large measure cut off from modernization efforts that are taking place in more urban areas. Devlin and Pothier use the term 'dis-citizenship' to describe similar marginalization of citizens with disabilities. However, even when formal education is provided to rural populations, it should not necessarily be seen as a proxy for empowerment. As Murphy-Graham (2010) points out in her studies of Honduran women's empowerment through education, it is important to look inside the 'black box' of education and examine the specific practices that lead toward greater empowerment. Not all forms of education equally emphasize such concepts as the capacity for self-determination, self-confidence and the critical awareness of gender inequality.

Into the already unequal provision of education to Nicaragua's rural poor compared to the urban middle class, the government's requirement of five years of English adds another wedge. English language teaching can be a slippery slope in a postmodern world where English is both a legacy of colonial power and a useful tool of wider communication (Edge, 2006; Ramanathan, 2005; Tupas, 2008). As Edge puts it, 'The continuing challenge to TESOL professionals is to find ways to have our contributions somehow serve the goals of liberation more than those of domination' (Edge, 2006: xiv).

Challenging the static model of this either-or conundrum, some scholars have asserted the importance of agency and resistance on the part of teachers as well as youth. Ramanathan (2006) asks '[H]ow are each of us in our different TESOL realities being constructed by the discipline and how are we constructing it in turn?' (2006: 145). Furthermore, some scholars recognize that these local realities do not 'simply replicate or instantiate macro structures and ideologies of state and society' (Ramanathan & Morgan, 2007: 449, citing Moore, 2002 and Pennycook, 2002, 2006). Rather, local realizations of broad policies at the national level often look quite different from how those policies were originally crafted; this may be quite positive in the long run because policies that are blindly implemented with no connection to local realities will often be short-lived and ineffective. However, getting from the level of broad policy to on-the-ground implementation practices requires savvy teachers and youth who are willing and able to question, adapt and resist if necessary. Not all teachers and youth are equally positioned to do this without negative consequences. Risks are involved for anyone who resists policies made by those with more power or status, and so we need to ask what resources people bring – discursive, personal and social – to be able to exercise their agency (Davis, 2009, 2011a, 2011b).

Another way to look at the either-colonist-or-liberator conundrum is to try to decouple the traditional linkage of language acquisition and cultural assimilation (Schumann, 1978). Many language learners these days have purposes in learning English that do not involve acculturation to American or British culture as part and parcel of that learning. The relationship between cultural globalization and language education is, according to Kumaravadivelu (2008, 2012) more nuanced and complex than the portrayal we hear in the media. Using English as a tool of wider communication, he argues, does not necessarily mean that the speaker or the educational organization embraces the cultures of native English-speaking countries and the colonizing baggage of English. He cites the example of TESOL practitioners in Muslim countries, who recognize the usefulness of learning English but also take a critical stance, promoting English language teaching 'in ways that best serve the socio-political, socio-cultural and socio-economic interests of the Islamic world' (2008: 139). This example suggests that the forces of globalization do not require us to accept an all-or-nothing package deal. In fact, between the homogenizing force of globalization and the heterogenizing force that resists it (Appadurai, 1990), there exists a third alternative, which some scholars call 'glocalization'. Glocalization involves 'a two-way process in which cultures shape and reshape each other directly or indirectly' (Robertson, 1990, cited in Kumaravadivelu, 2008: 44).

Most foreign language education policies, including the one implicit in MINED's website, do not specify the variety of the language to be taught; this leaves educators to fall back on language ideologies that are largely unspoken – for example, the assumed superiority of American or British English. But recent scholarship on varieties of English shows us that the privileged Englishes of England, The United States, Australia and New Zealand are in fact dramatically receding in terms of number of speakers, giving way to nativized varieties used in places where English is an official language (among them Singapore, India, Nigeria, Hong Kong) as well as varieties used with varying degrees of fluency in places where English has no official status, yet it is used as a lingua franca by those who speak it as a second language (e.g. China, Japan, Korea, Taiwan, Brazil, etc) (Kachru, 1986). Crystal estimated in 2003 that there were three non-native English speakers for every one native speaker. Of course, he added that such estimations vary widely depending on how one measures mastery of the language. It is worth noting that a simplified variety of spoken English, almost like a new pidgin, is also in evidence throughout Asia and may be developing in other areas of the world as well, with local linguistic influences shaping its structure and lexicon. Vittachi (2010) calls this 'Globalese'.

The scholarly literature we have discussed above raises important considerations and questions. With these in mind, we close this section with a quote from Cornell West, who in his graduation address at Wesleyan University in 1993, made a distinction between hope and optimism that is relevant here: 'Optimism is a notion that there's sufficient evidence that would allow us to infer that if we keep doing what we're doing, things will get better. I don't believe that. I'm a prisoner of hope, that's something else. Cutting against the grain, against the evidence'. In this chapter we hope to cut against the grain, against the evidence, to raise the possibility of a different way to look at English language teaching and learning in the rural communities of Nicaragua, and perhaps in other places where similar dynamics are at play.

The Unfinished Story of an International Educational Partnership

Partnership history

In 2008, the leadership of a Nicaraguan non-governmental organization, which we will call Puente al Conocimiento (Bridge to Knowledge), reached out to one of the faculty members at San José State University to see if it might be possible to establish a partnership. Specifically, San José State University (SJSU) faculty and graduate students were invited to assist Puente al Conocimiento in enhancing their English language program, which is a recent add-on to a well established rural secondary education program called Sistema de Aprendizaje Tutorial (SAT). In response, a team was set up at SJSU consisting initially of two faculty members and three graduate students. Later, another faculty member and a recent graduate were added to the team. The original team was associated with the University's Writing Center. They created an online needs assessment in Summer 2008 and sent it out via Puente al Conocimiento staff members to the tutors who were teaching English. As a preliminary step, the needs assessment made a number of issues visible to the SJSU team: many of the tutors lacked English proficiency themselves, yet were expected to teach English nonetheless. Most had no technology such as CD or DVD players in the classroom, and only a few schools had internet access. Some tutors raised critical questions about whether outsiders who didn't know the situation could really provide any meaningful assistance, as the following quote from a volunteer indicates: 'Without experiential knowledge of what it is like to teach and work in [specific location], I have trouble believing that anyone can really offer us much assistance that wouldn't boil down to tired theories and tired ideas'.

Over its three-year history, the SJSU team has gained a richer understanding of local contexts and needs through visits to Nicaragua as well as through ongoing communication with Puente al Conocimiento leaders and teachers via email, Skype and Facebook. The visits have also allowed us to offer professional development workshops and demonstration classes, develop relationships with local teachers and other key personnel and meet with local and international organizations within Nicaragua such as Peace Corps, public and private universities, US Embassy and others.

During the first two years of the partnership, the bulk of the SJSU team's effort went to grant writing. We were initially optimistic that we would be successful in garnering resources for activities such as bringing Nicaraguan teachers to SJSU, enlisting SJSU students and faculty members to volunteer in Nicaragua, creating a culturally responsive curriculum, etc. When, two years later, we had still not received any grants, we recognized that our energies for more grant writing were flagging and that we still had only barely begun to address the original issues and requests that had brought us into contact with Puente al Conocimiento.

During the third year, several of the SJSU team members decided to renew their efforts to support Puente al Conocimiento's[2] educational focus, of which English language teaching is a part, and to do so through a more grassroots approach. This approach can be described as collaborative curriculum development and a return to a more humble, homegrown form of service. We realized that while we had no grant money, we still had many resources that could be mobilized to accomplish some of the original goals. One such resource is the students in the MA TESOL program at SJSU. We were able to arrange for seven graduate students to receive independent study credit in Fall 2011 to assist us with collaborative program planning and curriculum development. Inquiry is a natural part of this process, and it is this continuing, reflective and critical stance that yields the insights we share in this chapter.

The observations and reflections that follow are based on field notes taken during SJSU team members' visits to Nicaragua (five visits altogether), classroom observations, interviews, email, Facebook, and Skype conversations with Nicaraguan teachers and curriculum leaders, responses to a needs assessment questionnaire and review of documents.

Puente al Conocimiento and the SAT curriculum

Today, Puente al Conocimiento serves approximately 10,000 students altogether. Some services are offered through what are known as *oratorios* – before and after school centers that are attached to MINED primary schools. These services include before-and after-school tutoring and school support for students attending MINED primary schools, free hot lunch and school supplies. In addition, a small but growing number of communities in the rural north have secondary schools that are run by Puente al Conocimiento and licensed by MINED. When we visited in 2009, there were five such schools. By 2012, two more had been established.

One of the distinguishing features of Puente al Conocimiento's secondary schools is their use of the SAT curriculum (SAT stands for *Sistema de Aprendizaje Tutorial* or Tutorial Apprenticeship System) (FUNDAEC, 2008) across all content areas. This curriculum plays a central role in supporting rural students' access to participate in their society, and therefore, it is important for readers to understand its key tenets. Originally developed by FUNDAEC in Colombia, SAT has been enriched over the years by several other organizations that have adopted it. The curriculum is also being used in Honduras and Guatemala. In Nicaragua, it is being used for the first time, with very promising initial results. The first cohort of SAT graduates was honored in 2011, five years after the inception of the SAT program in Nicaragua.

SAT aims at providing secondary education to youth and adults in rural communities without forcing them to abandon their production activities or their communities. It utilizes a pedagogical model according to which the pursuit of knowledge is 'applicable to the lives of the rural population'. The curriculum has a spiritual basis in the Bahai religion, which approaches human beings as integral beings, and thus focuses on their material, intellectual, and spiritual dimensions (FUNDAEC, 2008). SAT is delivered in modules that range from 8 to 10 weeks each. Lessons are not taught by subjects, but by thematic books on five central, interdisciplinary themes: Themes such as 'sustainable development' and 'communication' and others may address topics in Math, Physics, Biology and Language, among others, depending on the theme. The teachers are local community members who are in the process of working towards their teaching degrees. They are called *tutores* (tutors)[3], and they operate from a model of apprenticeship in which the tutor '*actua como guia, orientador, animador y facilitador del aprendizaje*' (acts as a guide, orienter, animator and facilitator of learning). Typically, the tutor is someone who has completed his or her *bachiller* (secondary diploma) and is in the process of further professional development (FUNDAEC, 2008).

In a few of the countries where SAT has been used, particularly in Nicaragua and Honduras, the organizations that have adopted SAT have partnered with their national governments to recognize it as a valid curriculum. While the Ministries of Education in these two countries have accepted the idea, they have also requested that SAT incorporate particular subjects taught as part of the national curriculum, but that were not originally part of SAT. This is the case of English and how it became a requirement for SAT students in Nicaragua.

However, Bayán and Puente al Conocimiento, the organizations in Honduras and Nicaragua, respectively, which have been faced with this requirement, soon noticed that English is very detached from the reality of the population they serve in rural areas. This reality forced them to seek cooperation with organizations abroad to help design and implement an English curriculum that fits harmoniously with the other SAT materials. In the case of Puente al Conocimiento, they contacted SJSU for assistance.

The main goal of the SAT curriculum is to change the status quo of traditional rural poverty. SAT does this by promoting students and tutors as change agents who understand the conditions facing rural populations, the resources they have at their disposal and the process of change. SAT supports students in creating sustainable ways of living, becoming leaders in their own communities, moving away from dependence on foreign aid and resisting the pattern of rural migration to the urban fringes of Managua or other cities in Central America and the United States. SAT and the people who are teaching and training within the SAT model represent a resource for our work together, a model of content area teaching and learning that is already embedded in the communities where Puente al Conocimiento is present. However, as we noted earlier, SAT was not originally designed with English language teaching as part of the curriculum.

Globalization Rhetoric, Local Policy Implementation and Inequality

In this section, we raise our first critical question: Why is it that a language policy, when local leaders faithfully attempt to implement it, can in fact result in the disempowerment of local teachers and local students? Part of our answer has to do with the rhetoric of globalization and the way it naturalizes certain assumptions about the value of English.

Hay más apertura ahora (there is more opening now)

The rhetoric of globalization is heard everywhere in Nicaragua, and the role of English is always intertwined. In the following snapshot, we hear how Roberto, a young business graduate, views the role of English in Nicaragua:

Roberto works at a bank in Estelí, a small city in the north of Nicaragua. When asked about the role of English in Nicaragua (especially in the rural north), he says, 'In the past few years there is more commerce with the United States. Now the companies in Nicaragua are requiring English on the job applications ... *hay más apertura ahora* (there is more of an opening now)'.

In the regular MINED secondary schools, Roberto says students attend classes for 5 hours a day. They have English 3 times a week, about an hour each session. But the English teaching *'es deficiente'* (is deficient). The teachers don't know English well enough to teach it. Even with English classes 3x a week for 5 years, students get their *secundaria* diploma and still can't really use English effectively. In the rural areas, Roberto says it is even worse. Most rural areas don't even have secondary schools. Puente al Conocimiento is making a big effort by providing secondary education in the rural areas.

Students don't hear English on TV in the rural areas. If they have power, and if they have television, the TV only gets one channel and it is usually a local station with only Spanish. They can't watch TV in English.

But agricultural equipment and supplies (from tractors to seed packets to fertilizers) are often imported from the Unites States, so those items would have directions and packaging information in English. Also, any kind of technology will have information in English.

This snapshot of how Roberto sees the role of English in Nicaragua speaks volumes about corporate interests in Nicaragua and the use of English as a tool for international business, development of tourism, and so on. But Roberto also echoes the sorry picture already noted of Nicaraguan English teaching and of the teachers' deficiencies, particularly in the rural areas. This observation is further documented by Chávez's study of English teaching in Nicaragua (2006). Chávez notes, 'With so little degree of students' involvement and participation in the development of the language learning processes, it is not surprising that they do not get adequate levels of language proficiency at the end of their secondary school studies' (2006: 37). The 'natural' implication is that if Nicaraguans want to move forward in this globalizing world, access to English has to be improved and the training of English language teachers must be further professionalized.

However, Roberto's remarks seem to describe mainly the needs of urban areas in Nicaragua. We wondered, do rural communities need to 'move forward' in a similar fashion? To what extent is this marketing of English as a communication tool based in authentic local uses for English?

Local implementation of English teaching in the rural SAT program

The second part of our answer examines what the SAT *Inglés* classes are actually using to teach English, and seeks to pinpoint whether and to what degree rural communities actually 'need' English in the same way urban ones do (or might). The implementation of English language teaching in rural areas is fraught with contradictions, since the tutors charged with actually teaching English do not speak English themselves and have little in the way of support to acquire English and learn how to teach it. This is a major gap with major consequences. At the very least, given the expectations of the equivalent MINED program, it places the SAT tutors in a profoundly disempowering position that almost guarantees a sense of failure, both for them and for their rural students.

Currently, SAT tutors use a set of three leveled textbooks that were created by Bayán, the organization which is licensed by FUNDAEC to implement SAT in Honduras. These are 8 1/2 by 11 inch photocopied texts which try to follow the philosophy of the other SAT areas. They have no color and few illustrations. The level 1 book, for example, is called *Citizens of the World*.

It contains eight lessons. The first one, 'Making new friends', provides students with language used in meeting people from various countries, such as asking, 'What's your name?' 'Where are you from?' It also models how to talk about people in the third person, e.g. 'Maria is from _____'. Instructions to the teacher and students are provided in Spanish as well as English. Each lesson includes in some spots a symbol of a CD, indicating that the teacher should play a segment of a CD so that students can hear the language and repeat. However, the Nicaraguan SAT program does not have any CDs to accompany the curriculum. Furthermore, in most cases, only the tutor has a copy of the book. The students do not actually have their own copies nor is there a set of books for each classroom.

When the MA TESOL students in the Independent Study group analyzed the Level 1 book to see what was covered and where there might be gaps, they found a number of significant gaps. For example, in Lesson 1, there is no explanation of how to form information questions (sometimes known as WH questions) and the subject and verb word order switch that has to take place (e.g. 'He is from Spain' becomes 'Where is he from?'). They also found that in most lessons, activities to practice the new language in engaging ways are not provided apart from fill-in-the-blank exercises.

The main advantages of the SAT *Inglés* books are that they are cheap to reproduce, they are somewhat in alignment philosophically with the SAT content curriculum, and they have Spanish translations of all the instructions. Furthermore, the tutors who have been working with them are now somewhat familiar with them.

When we met with two classes of SAT students (2nd year and 3rd year) in 2009 at one of the rural SAT schools, we asked them what they feel they need English for. (Since we know that often interviewees will give what they believe are 'socially desirable responses' in an interview situation, we first explained that even though we are visiting from the United States, we do not necessarily think that everyone needs to learn English). The students responded, first, that English is a requirement for graduation from *secundaria*. This is an instrumental motivation that is simply a fact of life, from their perspectives. Several students also mentioned that they would like to be able to communicate with people and communities outside of Nicaragua. Thirdly, some thought that they will need English to be able to access agricultural and scientific information either printed or on the internet in English. Some are interested in music and would like to be able to understand and sing songs in English as well as other languages. And finally, some have goals of pursuing higher education degrees to become nurses, doctors, or attorneys to help their communities, and they know that English will be needed to pursue a higher degree. Many students said they hope to be 'agents of change' in their community, and that to effect change, they must become educated.

Daniel, the coordinator and trainer for Puente al Conocimiento's SAT program, confirms this information: Students see English as a necessary part of getting their secundaria diploma. *'Más de la mitad de los estudiantes ven el Inglés como un requisito…'* (more than half see it as a requirement). Students' motivations, according to him, are linked to the strength of the tutors. When tutors barely know more English than students, their ability to inspire and motivate students to learn more English is limited. Yet, Daniel continues, students do enjoy learning English when it is directly connected to the local region: *'Una de las actividades que más les gusta es traducir, y aprender vocabulario que describa su micro región, contextualizar el libro a la región de ellos'.* (One of the activities they like the best is translating and learning vocabulary that describes their local region, contextualizing the textbook to their own region.)

What do the students want to get out of learning English (in terms of future goals)?

'Algunos de los estudiantes quieren aprender Inglés porque han visto la influencia que ha tenido Puente al Conocimiento en las comuidades con las visitas de US y el querer compartir con ellos les motiva además de algunos que desean ir a la Universidad y estudiar Licenciatura en habla Inglés'. (Some of the students want to learn English because they have seen the influence Puente al Conocimiento has had in some communities with visits from residents of the Unites States; they want to be able to share and communicate with them. Some also want to go to the university and get a degree in English teaching.) This suggests that Puente al Conocimiento is creating its own micro-context for English usage. Even if there was little prior usage of English in the rural communities, Puente al Conocimiento's guided visits with interested donors and volunteers from the Unites States and other countries have shown students that English is actually useful.

Local implementation of English teaching clearly suffers from large gaps between policy and practice on the ground. MINED began promoting a new program based in communicative competence and constructivism in 2004. The plan was for this program to be used in all national schools by 2007. However, changes in national educational authorities resulted in policy changes as well, and Chávez (2006: 30) stated that 'little is known of the new policies for English as a Foreign Language (EFL) language instruction'. Furthermore, there is currently no standard assessment of English proficiency at the end of the five years of required study. According to the SAT coordinator Daniel, the only assessment would come if students wished to enter a higher education program that required English.

Puente al Conocimiento and SAT leaders want the best for rural students. They particularly want to make secondary education accessible to those who traditionally have been denied access. The goal of full participatory citizenship is unfortunately compromised by the practical realities of the English program, and of Nicaragua's changing political environment as well, which creates an uncertainty about whether any changes will actually stick. Our stance as partners has been to remain supportive of the Puente al Conocimiento staff and tutors, but also skeptical of the assumed need for English. Ever since the original needs assessment in 2008, we have continued to ask the question, 'Do rural students in Nicaragua really need English, and if so, what for?' This skepticism has helped to keep the conversation with our Nicaraguan colleagues open and has guarded us from working in ways that would legitimize the assumed superiority of English heard in the globalization rhetoric. As we have seen above, each stakeholder (MINED, the SAT students, Daniel the SAT coordinator, Puente al Conocimiento and the SJSU team) holds beliefs about the role and value of English for rural Nicaraguan secondary students. The question we turn to next is, whose understandings carry the most weight and should that weight be allocated differently?

Relationships of unequal power

The work with our Nicaraguan colleagues is saturated at every level with the sedimented legacy of colonial and modern era inequality. In addition to the macro social inequalities described at the beginning of this chapter, the partnership also shows us more localized demarcations that, when taken together with the more macro inequalities, result in the disempowerment of rural teachers and students. One of these local demarcations is the line between *'maestros'* (teachers who have a license to teach) and *'tutores'* (who are working on their *licenciatura* (teaching credential) and at the same time teach in rural areas where Puente al Conocimiento uses the SAT program). *Tutores* are expected to shoulder many or most of the responsibilities of a teacher, but without the status of a teacher. Another line of unequal power is inscribed between Puente al Conocimiento's central office leadership team in Managua and the rural northern programs. The central leadership team, though well intentioned, simply does not have the staff or resources to maintain consistently good communication with all its programs in different parts of the country. Thus, support for rural programs often slips and slides, creating a sense among the rural staff that the central office doesn't care or is too busy to see what the rural programs need in order to serve students effectively. This may be especially true in the case of the SAT English program because Puente al Conocimiento is already stretched thin by sustaining the many other elements of the SAT curricular program, as well as the food, school uniforms and school supplies it provides to all the SAT students. The English program has until recently been given lower priority than some of these more pressing needs within the SAT Program, which is understandable.

When SJSU and Puente al Conocimiento are contrasted, the subject of power relations comes into play in virtually every domain of interaction. Its manifestation stems mostly from the existing inequity in the relationship between the counterparts. This inequity is deeply rooted in the economic, educational and social advantages and disadvantages from both sides, particularly from the lack of basic resources and the inadequate living, learning and working conditions in Nicaragua.

Overall, inequality in power relations contributes to distortion in the roles of participants, institutions, and English itself. US partners' suggestions and recommendations may be taken less critically than they should, and the prestige that many US higher education institutions have abroad may also blind Nicaraguan counterparts to mistakes or recommendations that are not culturally responsive. Since English is not only the target language, but also the language spoken on the side of more privilege, it may take a connotation that obfuscates its real roles in a Nicaraguan rural context: locals may attribute to the role of English a value higher than its real one. While as foreign partners, we cannot and should not intervene to change local power dynamics, what we can do is to consistently ask questions that relate back to the authentic local needs and interests of the rural students for whom the program is designed. The students and their tutors should, we believe, acquire the inquiry skills that will enable them to study English in the ways and to the extent they see as relevant to their own needs. We can also, because of our outsider status, sometimes see possibilities and alternatives that may be 'outside of the box'. In the next section, we turn to a discussion of some of these alternatives

What are the Alternatives?

In the previous sections, we have shown how the 'natural' sounding rhetoric of English as part of globalization doesn't fit the rural communities' realities, and may contribute to their further marginalization or 'dis-citizenship', given their lack of access to basic resources, technology and trained English language teachers. So in this section, we ask, does the assumed model of Standard English language learning and teaching with a fluent, trained teacher necessarily have to be maintained? And if not, what else might be possible?

Examining the roles of English and English language education

Spanish in Central America is hardly an endangered language in the sense in which this term is typically used (Rajagopalan, 2005). However, as global markets encroach more and more into regions which previously had little contact with global trade, English may soon begin to coexist with Spanish as the bilingual norm of certain domains, such as business and tourism.

But for the rural regions, a different picture might emerge, one where limited uses of English are embraced for specific purposes (such as understanding agricultural information, using the internet, talking about cell phones, communicating with visitors, etc). Models of English as a second language (ESL) curriculum presume that immigrants to an English dominant society need to communicate with their neighbors and peers, master the language of local bureaucracies, prepare themselves for local jobs and participate in English medium cultural activities to entertain or educate themselves (Lagerspetz, 1998). Nevertheless, we should not treat ESL as the unmarked default situation for language learning, and we should avoid transferring this urgency to regions where English is not the dominant or main language used. Students in rural Nicaraguan communities do not need to learn how to communicate in a US bank, for example, or at a US doctor's office, as the staples of ESL curriculum would have them do. On the other hand, a traditional EFL or World English curriculum assumes that students want to travel to English-speaking countries as foreign students or business professionals, or interact with English-speaking tourists in their own country. The assumption of such curricula is that they will learn standard British or American English, and not a nativized variety such as Indian English or Singaporean English.

While activities such as travelling to English-speaking countries might be important for rural students now or later in their lives, they hardly sum up the present reality of rural students' needs and priorities. If any urgent issues need to be brought up, they should be the ones already embedded in the SAT curriculum: access to food, water, basic services and the right to gender equality that these rural areas may lack. Or perhaps, in the educational domain, the human right to research as described by Appadurai (2006: 176): 'the capacity to systematically increase the horizons of one's current knowledge, in relation to some task, goal or aspiration'.

As for English, we ask whether rural Nicaraguan students might benefit from having access to learning opportunities in a local variety of English or even a simplified English such as Vittachi (2010) described in his article about 'Globalese'. Nicaragua is in fact home to several communities that use a variety of English. About 30,000 people in the eastern coastal communities speak an English based creole, called Miskito Coast Creole or Nicaraguan Creole English (Spolsky, 2006; Wikipedia). Because the speakers of this creole are largely poor, and their African and Amerindian ancestry is also a target for racism, their language skills are not usually considered as a potential resource for a government that wants to promote the learning of English. However, if language attitudes were not an issue, a partnership between MINED and Creole speaking communities could be formed to create a career ladder program for future English teachers from these communities. If standard English is not necessarily the immediate goal for rural students, then why not open up opportunities for them to acquire a Nicaraguan variety of English, or even a variety like 'Globalese'? Students who continue their education would certainly need to later acquire a more standard variety as well, but acquiring a local variety or some form of 'Globalese' while in *secundaria* does not preclude further learning.

Examining the roles of *tutores*

The reason for letting go of a standard variety of English is also related to the need of the *tutores* to develop a greater sense of confidence. The philosophy behind the SAT curriculum is that *tutores* are guides who learn alongside and a little bit ahead of the students. This model closely parallels apprenticeship in informal settings, where a more experienced person guides and demonstrates a craft or a process, and a novice acquires increasing mastery by watching and participating and learning (Lave & Wenger, 1991; Rogoff, 1981). In the SAT philosophy, the *tutor* is not expected to be an expert on the curricular content. Rather, the *tutor* reads the content ahead of the students and participates in preparatory training every two weeks with other *tutores* and a leader. The *tutor* then returns to his or her school community and supports the students in acquiring and applying the new content. When guiding students in the thematic units of SAT content areas, *tutores* are well supported by the SAT trainers; *tutores* have told us that they feel a sense of ownership and self-empowerment that comes with authentic education that is relevant to their communities, and they know that they can communicate everything through Spanish. We pointed out earlier that the *tutores* are disempowered by the imposition of an additional role as English tutors. This role differs from their roles as *tutores* for the other content areas because they are asked to teach a language in which they have no proficiency, using only a Xeroxed book. To further hamper their efforts, usually the *tutor* is the only person in the class with the book.

What if the English to be learned were not so rigidly defined? What if the expectation that students learn a standard variety were eased, and instead the expectation would be to develop sufficient vocabulary and structure to use English in ways the students and community see as relevant – e.g. reading and understanding agricultural product instructions in English; having a simple conversation with a visitor who speaks English; acquiring the vocabulary of computer and cell phone use in English; learning to sing songs in English?[4] What if the *tutores* were prepared not to 'teach' a language they are not even marginally proficient in, but rather, to guide the students in explorations of English, explorations that the *tutores* would undertake as well? What if the curriculum and materials used for this exploration were mainly self-access materials, which students and *tutores* could access and use whenever they wished to?

This model, instead of being viewed as an English teaching program, could be defined as a program of apprenticeship and inquiry in languages, with English as one of its foci, but certainly not the only one. The use of such a model would require a shift in the way the *tutores* are prepared. Instead of the current training, which seeks to prepare them to teach a language they don't know, the alternative would emphasize inquiry skills, such as how to learn a song in English, how to increase vocabulary, how to talk about the region where they live with people from other countries, how to engage English-speaking visitors in language learning activities; when the internet is available, such inquiry could extend further, to searching for songs and lyrics in English, using websites relevant to students' interests, using a translation program such as Google Translate to understand agricultural information written in English, and so on.

The alternative model would also include a unit of study in which students and *tutores* investigate the roles of English and other languages in Nicaragua (Appadurai, 2006; Davis, 2011b, personal communication). This unit would be carried out primarily through Spanish and would engage SAT students and *tutores* in investigating the uses of different languages in their own regions and communities. This inquiry unit would contextualize their study of English, develop an awareness of the politics of language and help them discover their own stance with regard to the learning of English. Such a unit would contribute to and serve as a bridge between the SAT content curriculum (the theme on communication) and the English curriculum. One of the questions that students could investigate initially is 'What languages are native to Nicaragua?' By exploring language maps of their own country, they would find out that in addition to Spanish, Nicaragua's eastern coast is a place where an English creole is spoken. The eastern portion of the country also includes small populations who speak indigenous languages, namely Sumo, Miskito and Rama. Students could be asked to investigate the current uses of English in their own region, in Managua and on the Eastern coast. Through this series of inquiry topics, the goal would be to develop critical understandings of the relationships among different varieties of language in their country and region and to make a distinction between the rhetoric of English as global language and their own authentic needs and uses for English. In short, it would encourage them to discover their own uses for English as well as other languages, rather than allowing globalization rhetoric to 'use' them.

Rethinking access to technology

In considering alternative models for language inquiry in rural Nicaragua, we often encounter the issue of limited technology. The SAT curriculum was designed with very few resources in mind: books, writing tools and participants. It has been said many times that SAT is designed to be taught 'under a mango tree'. On the other hand, in the United States, our experience and practice with teaching is each day more and more dependent on access to devices such as computers, audio players and a fast network. Our experience with technology has made it challenging to create curriculum that mirrors the same independence that the rest of the SAT curriculum has over high tech devices. SAT *tutores* have reported that they feel insecure to provide models for speaking and pronunciation. Audio technology, in this case, would be a way to fill the gap, but many communities where English is taught lack the basic infrastructure to play audio devices. Most of the communities where SAT is being used in Nicaragua do not have electricity. Only one or two communities have access to the internet via solar powered devices. And while solar powered technologies may become more and more available, we cannot count on their availability on a broader scale yet.

The MA TESOL students in the independent study group gave careful attention to the audio technology issue and made the following observations: Cell phones are almost everywhere now, and we ascertained that most of the cell phones in use in Nicaragua have audio playback functionality. This means that we can in theory record small audio files to fit with English lessons, send them to Daniel or another SAT trainer and the files can then be distributed to anyone with a cell phone that has audio file capability. We have recorded a few initial segments that mesh with existing SAT Ingles lessons and are currently awaiting feedback about their usefulness. This example emphasizes the use of existing local resources and practices (cell phone use) as a pathway to innovation.

Reflections

Language practices can be likened to a natural landscape in which we experience flows, linguistic landscapes, and sedimented pathways (Appadurai, 1990; Kramsch, 2006; Pennycook, 2010). Sedimented language practices are the accumulated result of frequently used forms. 'We tend to follow them', as we do pathways. We may at times have to choose between paths, but when we ask how the paths got there, we have only to look at iterative human activity: we do them in the doing' (Pennycook, 2010: 138). In other words, it is our own practices as human societies that build up the pathways we use in language. We suggest that this notion of sedimented pathways can be applied not only to language forms and usages, but also to language policies and pedagogical practices. Recent ethnographic scholarship on language policy and planning supports the notion that we need to look at language policy not as frozen texts that determine language practices, but rather as the shaping and molding and resistance that take place as humans engage in language practices at many interacting levels (communities, classrooms, workplaces, curriculum design, national educational policy making, etc). In the words of McCarty *et al.* (2011), the New Language Policy Studies advance a view of 'language policy not as disembodied text but as situated sociocultural process' (2011: 335). Policy, says McCarty, is best understood as a verb; it never just 'is' but rather 'does' (2011: 338).

With this active view of language policy in mind, what have we learned from this partnership experience? Below, we summarize our key points:

- *Language policies that fail to take the rural context into account can lead to disempowering experiences for teachers and students.*
- *It is necessary to critically examine the role of English through local realities, rather than only through the rhetoric of globalization.*
- *Rather than assuming that standard British or American English is the target language, curriculum planners in rural areas should be encouraged to think 'against the grain', considering other varieties as possible targets for learning.*
- *The assumption that English can only be learned from qualified English teachers may contribute to the disempowerment of rural teachers. Instead, in situations where English language teachers are scarce, we would do better to embrace a model of apprenticeship and inquiry into language.*
- *Recognizing the strengths and innovations within the local context can help language planners and partners to build on local resources rather than introducing an entirely foreign set of resources.*
- *Reliance on technology can be a limitation as much as lack of technology can be.*

- As *partners, it is important to look inward at our own resources in order to make change, rather than only relying on an influx of outside funding to support our work.*

Despite the rhetoric of globalization and the institutional and national push toward English as a global language, which in a way was the reason our partnership with Puente al Conocimiento was formed, we find that the reality on the ground is quite different from what is touted in the global business world. Recognizing this local reality or 'linguascape', we have tried to identify a more local and regional path in which the use of English can be contextualized and situated, especially in rural communities which are struggling to achieve their full rights and participation as citizens.

Cornell West urged us to go 'against the grain, against the evidence'. The evidence tells us that Nicaragua's English education policy will not work without massive infusions of capital and outside experts to provide training. But our experience with our Nicaraguan colleagues suggests a more radical pathway, one that that already has some footprints: We might, in some contexts, be moving toward English learning without English teachers, as well as English learning without standard English. Both propositions fly in the face of the TESOL industry, but they might also be the only way to prevent the rhetoric of 'English as a tool of globalization' from driving an even deeper wedge between urban middle-class students and poor, rural students in places like Nicaragua.

Notes

(1) An earlier version of this paper was presented at the American Anthropological Association meeting in Montreal, November 17, 2011. We wish to thank Vaidehi Ramanathan and our colleagues who generously responded to our requests for comments. The opinions expressed in this chapter are those of the authors and do not necessarily reflect the views of any of the organizations discussed in the chapter.
(2) The name of the organization as well as personal names have been changed in order to preserve confidentiality.
(3) The use of the term *tutores* in Spanish is interesting because while it overlaps in most ways with the English cognate, it also covers more conceptual ground than it does in English. In Spanish it can mean a child's guardian as well as an instructor and a private tutor (Real Academia Española, 2012). We are grateful to Mayra S. Cerda for bringing our attention to the nuances of this term.
(4) Of course, if MINED eventually imposes a more rigid set of expectations and standards for English teaching, such flexibility may not be possible.

References

Appadurai, A. (1990) Disjuncture and difference in the global cultural economy. *Public Culture* 2 (2), 1–24.

Appadurai, A. (2006) The right to research. *Globalisation, Societies and Education* 4 (2), 167–177.
Booth, J.A. and Walker, T.W. (1999) *Understanding Central America* (3rd edn). Boulder, CO: Westview Press.
Cerezál, F. (2000) Formación de profesores de inglés en Nicaragua. *Aula* 12, 23–34.
Chávez, E. (2006) In-service teachers' beliefs, perceptions and knowledge in the Nicaraguan EFL context. *Encuentro* 16, 27–39.
CIA World Factbook. (2011) Accessed 19 February 2011. https://www.cia.gov/library/publications/the-world-factbook/geos/nu.html
Crystal, D. (2003) *English as a Global Language* (2nd edn). NY: Cambridge University Press.
Davis, K. (2009) Agentive youth research: Towards individual, collective, and policy transformations. In T.G. Wiley, J.S. Lee and R. Rumberger (eds) *The Education of Language Minority Immigrants in the USA*. Bristol: Multilingual Matters.
Davis, K. (2011a) Preface: Toward critical qualitative research in second language studies. In K.A. Davis (ed.) *Critical Qualitative Research in Second Language Studies: Agency and Advocacy*. Charlotte, NC: Information Age Publishing.
Davis, K. (2011b) Personal communication.
Devlin, R. and Pothier, D. (2006) Toward a critical theory of dis-citizenship. In R. Devlin and D. Pothier (eds) *Critical Disability Theory: Essays in Philosophy, Politics, and Law*. Vancouver: University of British Columbia Press.
Edge, J. (2006) Background and overview. In J. Edge (ed.) *(Re)locating TESOL in an Age of Empire* (pp. xii–xix). Hampshire and New York: Palgrave MacMillan.
Friere, P. (1973) *Pedagogy of the Oppressed*. NY: Seabury.
FUNDAEC (2008) http://www.fundaec.org/en/programs/sat/index.htm
González, N., Moll, L. and Amanti, C. (eds) (2005) *Funds of Knowledge: Theorizing Practices in Households, Communities and Classrooms*. NJ: Lawrence Erlbaum Associates.
IPADE. (2010) *Experiencias relevantes de educacion rural: Aportes pedagógicos y metodológicos de organizaciones de la sociedad civil Nicaragüense*. Instituto para el desarollo y la democracia (IPADE). Managua: Nicaragua.
Jaque, M. (2006) Vine para un año de voluntariado con 21, y sigo aqui con 38. May 26, *ALBA*.
Kachru, B. (1986) *The Alchemy of English: The Spread, Functions, and Models of Non-native Englishes*. NY: Pergamon Press.
Kramsch, C. (2006) From communicative competence to symbolic competence. *The Modern Language Journal* 90, 249–252.
Kumaravadivelu, B. (2008) *Cultural Globalization and Language Education*. Princeton, NJ: Yale University Press.
Kumaravadivelu, B. (2012) *Language Teacher Education for a Global Society*. New York and London: Routledge.
Lagerspetz, E. (1998) On language rights. *Ethical Theory and Moral Practice* 1 (2), 181–199.
Lave, J. and Wenger, E. (1991) *Situated Learning: Legitimate Peripheral Participation*. Cambridge, England: Cambridge University Press.
McCarty, T.L., Collins, J. and Hopson, R. (2011) Dell Hymes and the new language policy studies: Updates from an underdeveloped country. *Anthropology and Education Quarterly* 42 (4), 335–363.
MINED (2012) Accessed 5 February 2012. http://www.mined.gob.ni/index.php

Murphy-Graham, E. (2010) And when she comes home? Education and women's empowerment in intimate relationships. *International Journal of Educational Development* 30, 320–331.
Pennycook, A. (2010) *Language as a Local Practice*. NY: Taylor and Francis.
Rajagopalan, K. (2005) Language politics in Latin America. *AILA Review* 18, Special Issue on Applied Linguistics in Latin America.
Ramanathan, V. (2005) *The English-Vernacular Divide: Postcolonial Language Politics and Practice*. Clevedon: Multilingual Matters.
Ramanthan, V. (2006) The vernacularization of English: Crossing global currents to re-dress West-based TESOL. *Critical Inquiry in Language Studies* 3 (2/3), 131–146.
Ramanathan, V. and Morgan, B. (2007) TESOL and policy enactments: Perspectives from practice. *TESOL Quarterly* 41 (3), 447–463.
Real Academia Española (2012) Accessed 14 March 2012. http://buscon.rae.es/draeI/
Red MEIRCA. (2011) El proyecto de MEIRCA de formación de profesores de Inglés en CentroAmerica. *Encuentro* 20, 68–79.
Rogoff, B. (1981) Adults and peers as agents of socialization: A highland Guatemalan profile. *Ethos* 9, 18–36.
Schumann, J. (1978) The acculturation model for second language acquisition. In R.C. Gingras (ed.) *Second Language Acquisition and Foreign Language Teaching*. Washington, DC: Center for Applied Linguistics.
Spolsky, B. (2006) Accessed 29 January 2012. https://groups.google.com/group/lpren/browse_thread/thread/eed32f41a055aea0?pli=1
Thomas, W. and Collier, V. (2002) *A National Study of the School Effectiveness for Language Minority Students' Long Term Academic Achievement*. Washington, DC: Center for Applied Linguistics.
Tupas, T.R. (2008) Postcolonial English language politics today: Reading Ramanathan's The English-Vernacular divide. *Kritika Kultura* 11, 5–21.
Villegas, A.M. and Lucas, T. (2002) *Educating Culturally Responsive Teachers*. Albany, NY: SUNY Press.
Vittachi, N. (2010) A short course in Globalese. In D. Nunan and J. Choi (eds) *Language and Culture: Reflective Narratives and the Emergence of Identity* (pp. 215–222). NY and London: Routledge.
West, C. (1993) Commencement address at Wesleyan University Middletown, Connecticut, May 30, 1993.

Afterword

Vaidehi Ramanathan

My reflections in this short piece attempt to speak to concerns that are latent in the volume. I wish to address key elements of the term 'citizenship' in order to speak more directly of its implications. The orientation to this term adopted in this volume is dictated partly by my conviction that themes such as 'citizenship', 'fuller participation', 'citizenship tests', or 'refugee resettlement opportunities' cannot be the object of purely juridical treatment (at legislative or regulatory levels), nor the enactments that proceed from pre-existing definitions of 'citizens' and 'citizenship'. These themes require deliberation and reflection on the stakes involved in their articulations and their tensions, issues that can be best understood only through grounded explorations. Certainly, the various essays in this volume prompt us to do exactly this. Such an approach does not deny the importance of the legal aspects of the problem of citizenship (indeed, as I discuss in the Introduction, and as several pieces in the volume address, the juridical elements are what we need to address headlong, among other things), but refuses to frame the inquiry solely in pre-given terms. Moving our gaze to situated contexts where (dis)citizenship occurs and gets negotiated alerts us to the importance of refraining from prescribing or in some way performing the question in terms of the existing concept of 'citizenship.' As I point out in my Introduction, this term was complicit with a certain period and particular modernist and colonial agenda.

Towards skirting these murky waters but still striving to move our debates forward, I decided to shift the terms of our cognitions around 'citizenship' (where it is often viewed as a goal to be attained) to what it enables one to do: namely participate fully. Because so much around 'citizenship' is about not having rights or access, and about blocks and borders that inhibit full participation, it seemed fitting to have people who have historically known what it is like to not be able to participate – namely women – be the dominant voices of this volume. While gender is not a key issue in the essays here (indeed, only Busi Makoni's piece is the only one that truly fronts gender), concerns around being or feeling 'dis-citizened' or having a strong historical sense of the same resonate strongly for all women on our planet. It also seemed fitting to bring in Devlin and Pothier's (2006) term '(dis) citizenship' in our debates. While not all of the authors in this volume draw on this term per se, their focus on what in our local environs inhibit fuller participation underscores the 'dis-citizening' that is ever present. Shifting the terms of the debates away from passports, citizenship tests, and visas to 'being able to participate fully' opens us up to the possibility of very different, localized scenes around the term.

'(Dis)citizening', then, flows thickly as a subtext through each piece, casting long shadows that push us to articulate a variety of political and historical concerns, a task that is most demanding and difficult. Among other things, it throws up larger political questions around modernizing, late modernity and postcolonial concerns. While recently colonized countries such as India, Nigeria, Sri Lanka, Pakistan and Bangladesh are waking up to a fuller sense of themselves (many of these countries gained independence from the British Empire only between the 40s and 60s and are only just seriously grappling with the nuances of 'citizenship' for their citizens), the rapid rhetoric of globalization is pulling them in other ways, threatening fragile postcolonial borders. This is important to note because the collective identities and histories of these places are at stake, and as I mentioned in the Introduction, these are issues that we need to make more room for in our debates about globalization and citizenship. We also need to be actively addressing tensions and contradictions around globalizing surges: In what contexts are the structural inequalities around globalization apparent? Where in history – indeed, particular tellings of history – can these inequities be traced to? Where do languages and the hierarchies they get placed into and against, fit? The various pieces in this volume call our attention to these questions in different ways. They make us see that citizenship and democracies, historically built up through structural inequities and colonizing agendas, are not abstract categories but ones constituted by particular historical processes encased in regimes of power. If such a thing as a 'global citizenship' has to emerge, then our meanings around the term 'citizenship' will need to alter profoundly, and this volume moves us a step closer to this.

History, then, is crucial in this and all endeavors on citizenship and globalization. To insist on the historical in our citizenship debates is to affirm the travels of postcolonial migrations, to recognize our subjectivities emerging in translations, and to see the utter reducibility of our heterogeneous existences. It interrupts any and all claims to authorize narration, and opens us all up to the in-between spaces of translations, where when we each recognize the other's alien-ness we acknowledge our own. It is in doing so that we confront the newer grammars of our being. Language, needless to say, is at the heart of this.

A Personal Note

My forays into Applied Sociolinguistics began with Prof James Gee in 1989 at the University of Southern California. He was my dissertation mentor and his work on language ideologies and marginalizing discourses heavily influenced my thinking. I am including in the Appendix my first real paper in applied sociolinguistics written during this time and I wish to remember it for what it did for me at the time – flag off one end of a long journey. I acknowledge with profound gratitude those early impulses that have brought me to my present cognitions.

Vaidehi Ramanathan
Davis, CA
10 March 2013

Appendix: An Examination of the Relationship between Social Practices and the Comprehension of Narratives*

Vaidehi Ramanathan-Abbott

Abstract

This paper argues, with the help of an experiment, that the comprehension of narratives is as influenced by the social practices of a culture, as the production *of narratives is. I argue that the social practices of the white American middle-class culture not only influences the way 'mainstream' people tell stories, but also the way they comprehend them. I also argue that someone practiced at producing texts in a certain way, and not familiar with a given alternative way, will have a harder time comprehending the structures in text produced in the alternative way.*

Keywords: discourse analysis; narratives; literacy; cultural differences.

Introduction

In his article 'Two styles of narrative construction and their linguistic and educational implications,' James Paul Gee (1989) examines two stories, one told by a white child (called 'Sandy') and the other told by a black child (called 'Leona'). He argues, along with Scollon and Scollon (1979, 1981) that 'narrative style is associated with one's cultural identity and presentation of self' (Gee, 1989: 299). As Gee and others (Labov, 1972; Tannen, 1989)

---

* 0165–4888/93/0013–0000 $2.00 © Walter de Gruyter
Text 13 (1) (1993), pp. 117–141

have characterized storytelling in 'vernacular black culture', narratives are performances wherein the speaker uses a rich set of devices (sound effects, dialogue, the historical present) to give a theatrically involving rendition of the narrative. Narratives are not mere linear reports of 'facts', they are stories with rich plots and richly elaborated images and themes (Briggs, 1984; Hymes, 1975; Bauman, 1975). Narrators use 'poetic' devices, like repetition, parallelism, and sound play (Lord, 1960), and they expect the active participation of the audience in their storytelling. Some of these features are due to the continuing ties black culture has to historical traditions of 'oral' story telling, which go back to the founding of the U.S. and further back into African oral traditions.

On the other hand, it has been argued that narratives associated with mainstream, school-based culture in the U.S. (and much of the Anglo world as a whole), even when they have the plots and points of high interest typical of stories, tend to stress the chronological, linear flow of events, and their causal connections (Gee, 1989; Michaels, 1981; Heath, 1982). Such narratives use less 'poetic' language and tend to emphasize the 'explicitness' of the narrator as against the participation of the hearer through rich inferences left open by the text. Such narratives, even when they are stories, are in some ways still like 'reports', stressing the giving of information over the performance of the narrative and its interactional setting.

Of course, these are partly matters of degree. Since all stories have plots and require that their tellers make clear why they are worth telling (using what Labov calls 'evaluation' to signal the aspects of the story that are of 'high interest'), they all must go beyond a mere and pure recital of 'just the facts' in straight order. Mainstream story telling is influenced by the norms and values of Western-style schooling, with the high value it places on explicitness and on decontextualizing the teller and tale (or the writer and the text) from the context of telling and from the 'private' knowledge of those to whom it is directed, leaving the text 'decodable' in other contexts and by other people who may share little with the teller save the sorts of 'public' knowledge that everyone in a literate society is 'expected' to have (Scollon and Scollon, 1981; Heath, 1983; Gee, 1989).

This study wishes to move from the realm of culturally significant stylistic differences in the production of narratives to ways of comprehending narratives from different cultures. I will argue that cultural identity, and the influences of school-based literacy, shape not only the telling of stories, but their comprehension as well. This is a less studied aspect of narrative than is production, and so in many ways this study is opening up new ground in a fashion that is meant to be more suggestive than definitive.[1]

While we do know that (mainstream) people from Western culture tend to listen for certain patterns and structures in stories, and will impose these on stories from other (non-Western) cultures, stories that do not in fact 'fit' these patterns, we know much less about how 'mainstream' people, deeply influenced by school-based literacy, listen to the sorts of culturally diverse stories told by people within the wider U.S. culture we all share. This is an important matter, since most teachers in the U.S. come from 'mainstream' culture and all of them, when in the classroom, tend to act within the norms of school-based literacy values and ways of thinking, acting, talking, and reading. It has been argued that such teachers cannot properly hear the narratives told by children, such as lower socioeconomic children, from non-mainstream cultures – for example, narratives at sharing time ('show and tell', Michaels, 1981).

Gee has delineated much about the structure of narratives from different social groups, in terms of their 'lines and stanzas' and larger units (1989). I am interested in ways of getting at the structures that people hear or read in a text, not the ones that are there by virtue of how the text was produced. Of course, these two are related: the structures in a text by virtue of its production (e.g., its prosody and syntax and discourse organization) must influence how a text is perceived, but it cannot completely determine it. Further, speakers from different social groups use different sorts of prosodic signals, and use syntax and discourse organization differently – that is part of the point of the production literature. This immediately raises the question of how someone practiced at producing texts in a certain way, and not familiar with a given alternative way, will hear or read a text produced in this alternative way.

In order to investigate these questions, this paper describes an experiment in which the two narratives Gee (1989) studied, representing two different cultural traditions (one with rich ties to oral traditions, one embedded in school-based literacy traditions), were given to 'mainstream' subjects with typical substantive mainstream school-based literate backgrounds (all graduate students, in fact, with little or no experience with black story telling). The hypothesis was that these subjects would process (in hearing or in reading) the narrative from the mainstream cultural background (Sandy's) in a systematically different way than they would process the narrative from black culture. In order to determine whether or not this were the case, some quantitative measures of how people were processing the texts at a discourse level were needed. Of course, one can not ask subjects with no linguistic training to gauge the 'cohesiveness' of a text or to give us an explicit discourse analysis of the text. It was decided that the subjects' approach to comprehension could be gauged if the subjects were asked to identify what we might call 'folk semantic units' within the narratives, that is, units that allowed subjects to determine for themselves what constituted 'ideas' in the texts. Accordingly, two sorts of semantic units – 'ideas' and 'idea groups' (the definitions of these will be discussed below) – were used as tools to inspect what listeners made of these texts. Of course, the proof of the usefulness of these units lies in whether or not they display a systematic, pervasive, and interesting difference in how the listeners approach these two texts, and a difference that makes linguistic sense.

Review of Literature

In the last decade, ethnographers and discourse analysts have increasingly focused attention on narrative as a genre (Petersen and McCabe, 1991; Hudson and Shapiro, 1991; Gee, 1989; 1991; Hicks, 1991; Michaels, 1981). Despite their differences, most researchers believe that the structure of a narrative is determined in part by the social practices of a culture. Furthermore, recent research (Gee, 1990b) has studied narratives in relationship to literacy, where literacy is an inherently multiple notion ('literacies'). Literacies are social practices defined by how different social groups use writing or reading in different contexts, for different purposes, and integrate them in different ways with their other language and nonlinguistic social practices. Further, many researchers now see literacy practices as an integral part of the overall discourse practices of a social group, and, in turn, see these discourse practices as tied intimately to the group's 'world view' and sense of identity. For example, Scollon and Scollon (1981) have argued that many school-based 'essayist' literacy practices can constitute an 'identity crisis' for Athabaskans, since the values about human beings, interaction, knowledge, and presentation of self that underlie 'essayist' literacy conflict at various points with the values of Athabaskan culture. To use another example, Heath (1983) has argued that in some social groups reading privately is seen as asocial and odd; among these groups reading is often a group and participatory activity. Gee (1990b) has argued that any literacy practice is also part of what he calls a Discourse (with a capital D), where Discourses are integrated ways of being, acting, thinking, speaking, valuing, believing, and, in some cases, reading and writing, ways connected to different roles people play on different occasions or different identities they take on within the many social groups of which they are members.

Thus, narrative and literacy practices are part of a larger sociocultural whole. The issue is not one between orality and literacy per se, but between different uses, with their concomitant values, of speaking, writing, reading, hearing, and interacting. Much of the literature on orality and literacy can better be interpreted as talking about culturally different uses of language within culturally different assumptions about the nature of narratives, discourse, and social interaction generally. Thus, when Ong (1982), for instance, claims that thought and language in an oral culture is elaborate and formulaic, and that much of spoken discourse is held together by formulaic expressions like cliches, proverbs and paralinguistic features, I would prefer to see this as characterizing one family of approaches to language, based on certain needs and values, and then only in certain contexts of use.

Such practices flourish when a group wants (or needs) to pass down its central values and beliefs through stories, or has encoded a significant part of its own distinctive identity in these stories. This can happen even in the midst of a 'modern' urban culture where various non-mainstream groups, however literate they may be, may have a decided interest in retaining and passing down their values and beliefs outside the 'standard' channels of the wider society, whose 'stories' may depict them as outsiders and whose institutions (like schools) may conflict seriously with their own interests. Within black culture, the formulaic, the poetic, the allusive may be part of social practices, some of which encode their distinctive identity, some of which pass down their values, world view, and beliefs, and some of which serve to resist the oppression of the wider society (Cook-Gumperz, 1986). The performative and dramatic may serve to enact identities, socially bond people together, and offer alternatives to mainstream ways of being in the world. Such practices are not historical 'hold overs', though they have long and rich roots; they are not the mere 'absence' of school-based practices, a 'deficit' left over from failing to master something else. They are positive accomplishments integrated with socio-cultural distinctive ways of being in the world.

Rather than thinking in terms of a single dichotomy, whether orality and literacy, or any other for that matter, it is better to think in terms of a variety of different continua. While some kinds of continua have already been suggested (Tannen, 1982; Chafe, 1982), there are at least the following five continua that are relevant to any use of language, oral or written. Firstly, an *involvement continuum,* with at one end, heavily 'involved' language in which the speaker or writer is deeply involved with her audience, and, at the other end, highly 'distanced' language, wherein the speaker or writer is primarily interested in the text and not the audience. Second, an *integration continuum,* with at one end, language which is loosely integrated, and, at the other end, language that is tightly integrated through the full use of the syntactic resources of the language. Third, an *explicitness continuum,* with at one end, fairly inexplicit language that leaves much to the inferencing capacity of hearers or readers, and, at the other end, highly explicit language which leaves much less to the participation of hearers or readers through their rich inferences about meaning and connections in the text. Fourth, a *topic continuum,* which has at one end language which the speaker or writer organizes in a clear fashion around a single topic and at the other end language which is less topic centered, but more concerned with elaborating themes and images which may be tied only loosely to a single topic. Fifth, a *prosaic continuum,* with at one end language that is highly 'poetic' (using repetition, parallelism, sound play, formulas, and heavy patterning) and at the other end language that does not much use these devices.

There are undoubtedly a number of other relevant continua. These continua, and others that would be relevant, are different from an orality–literacy continuum, since each end of all these continua cover both written and oral texts (e.g., sermons, which are often oral, and 'high literature', which is written, can both be highly integrated, explicit, and topic centered, but involved and poetic at the same time – and nearly all other combinations are possible). What is relevant in discussing any use of language is placing it within such continua and also within the larger social practice of which it is a part, not identifying it as simply oral or written. It is also the case, that while all speakers in the society range across a certain portion of each of these continua, usually in the middle reaches of each, members of some groups tend to 'specialize' in certain polar regions of the continua, or favor certain points more than others across a variety of their speech genres.

A claim that is made often in the discourse and literacy literature is that many school-based practices – ranging from sharing time to essay writing – value highly language, whether written or oral, that is towards the distanced, explicit, integrated, topic centered, prosaic end of these continua (Heath, 1983; Gee, 1989; Michaels, 1981; Olson, 1977). This is held to be so, in part at least, because of the high value the school places on the essay as the 'prototype' of 'high literacy'. It has also been argued that this is so also because of the emphasis in modern, 'post-industrial', Western cultures on information, communication between relative strangers, and the dislocation ('decontextualization') of information from specific times and places. Furthermore, these values can be seen to 'filter into' and affect other written and speech genres of mainstream people, given their deep allegiance to the values of school-based literacy, influencing genres, like storytelling, which are fairly removed from the school as a primary locus. And, indeed, there can be little doubt that many genres of speech, and especially narrative, are influenced by dominant forms of literacy in a society.

Certainly the two texts that Gee studied fit within this framework. The story by Sandy (a white upper-middle class twelve year old from a 'good' suburban school) appears to reflect a different set of language practices and values from the story told by Leona (a black working class twelve year old from a 'poor' inner city school). Sandy's story achieves coherence through the use of syntactic devices one would associate with the sort of integrated, topic centered practices associated with 'essayist' literacy and its values, despite the fact that it is most certainly a story. Her language stresses the linear progress of temporally ordered events, and the structure of information, in terms of backgrounding and foregrounding information and in terms of breaking actions and events down into their 'analytic' bits. Gee (1989) found that Sandy used many more 'temporal and logical links' than Leona, and that her lines were more 'informative' than Leona's in the sense of giving 'new' information about events and characters, however small or trivial (or predictable) that information might have been. Leona's language, on the other hand, was more 'expressive' and 'performative', and she frequently interrupted a temporal or logical sequence to give expressive, dramatic, or affective 'information', rather than information about the temporally ordered events that make up the main line of the story. Her language is poetic, dramatic, performative; she develops themes and images, rather than centering around one place and one topic. Instead of syntactic devices like 'temporal and logical links', Leona makes her story cohere because of 'patterns' that she is able to create 'through the use of such devices as sound play, repetition ... syntactic and semantic parallelism, changes of rate, loudness, ... and pitch ...' (Gee, 1989: 291).

All in all, the two stories represent different 'traditions', one tied to the schools much more clearly than the other; the other tied to oral traditions and poetic storytelling much more clearly than the first. The above-mentioned features of 'rate, loudness, and pitch' are a particularly important feature as far as the current study is concerned. These are aspects of prosody (i.e. pausing, pitch, stress, duration of syllables, rate). Gee and Grosjean (1983, 1984) demonstrate how people processing a spoken text must be influenced to some degree by the prosody of the text, that is, that prosody constitutes 'clues' to interpretation (along with syntax and discourse organization). At the same time, speakers from different social groups, including Sandy and Leona, use prosody quite differently. For instance, it has been argued that black speakers like Leona tend, at least in stories, to use falling intonation at the ends of 'episodes' (Gee, 1989: 79), while mainstream speakers like Sandy tend to use it at the end of what would be 'sentences' in a written text. In addition, Leona uses a much broader range of pitch patterns and much more dramatic switches in rate than Sandy. Sandy's text sounds 'flatter' and sounds as if it has less 'affect' than Leona's. In the study to follow, I will look at the difference listening to these texts makes in comparison to just reading their transcripts. This should help delineate the role of prosody both in general and in regard to the cultural difference between Leona and Sandy.

Experiment

This study establishes that listeners and readers can identify at least two kinds of semantic units in the structure of narratives: ideas and idea groups. The first unit is based on Butterworth's notion that an idea 'is not a technical word and is reasonably free from obvious structural implications' (1975: 79). In other words, I view the idea as a natural, objective entity and not as an analytical construct. Drawing on Goldman-Eisler's conclusion that pauses 'serve the function of communication', (1972: 105) this study assumed (and we will find below) that listeners identify idea units in part by pauses. However, my primary interest will be in the nature of the size and content of these idea units as they are found by listeners and readers in the two texts, not in the specific functioning of pausing (which has been much studied elsewhere). The second kind of semantic unit used in this study is the 'idea-group'. An 'idea-group' can be defined as a set of ideas that appear to the listener or reader to 'go together'. It was felt that an identification of idea units and idea-groups would provide a measurable indication of how the listeners and readers responded to the structure of the narratives.

Subjects

There were 40 subjects, all white, middle class, literate Americans. They were of both sexes and their ages ranged from 25 to 45. They were all graduate students from universities in the Los Angeles area. None of them had any extensive experience with black storytelling (or storytelling from any other than mainstream Western culture) by their own report. The subjects were randomly divided into two groups of 20 each and asked to identify idea and idea groups in Sandy's and Leona's narratives. One group, hereafter referred to as listeners, was asked to identify the idea and idea-groups on a written transcript while listening to the spoken version of the narratives. The second group, hereafter referred to as readers, had to identify idea and idea-groups on the written transcript, without access to the spoken version of the narratives.

Methods, materials, procedures

The transcripts of the stories were not punctuated, and lines broke randomly at the right margin when they ran out of space. As Kreckel (1981: 121) says, eliminating punctuation 'helps to avoid the pitfalls of following the pattern set by punctuation and favors the adherence to the instruction in terms of message related unitization'.

The narratives used for this study were the same narratives on which Gee (1989) based his conclusions about stylistic differences in production. Both narrators are Americans. Sandy comes from a white, middle class home, Leona from a black family of a lower economic status. Sandy attended a suburban, middle class school, with an excellent reputation; Leona attended an urban school with a much poorer reputation for quality education. Sandy had had a great deal of success in school; Leona had done poorly in literacy, both in terms of reading and writing, though she was viewed by teachers as a 'good citizen' in her school. Both girls were 12 years old when their stories were recorded. Sandy told her story to an older female acquaintance with whom she was comfortable; Leona told her story to a group of her peers. In fact, these contextual differences are probably related to the sorts of socio-cultural differences discussed above. The researchers who had collected the original texts had found it difficult to get upper middle class children to meet with peers and share stories, though they had no trouble getting them to tell stories to adults. On the other hand, not only did they have no trouble getting lower socioeconomic black children to get together with peers of their own choosing and tell stories, they often had to wait some time to get their tape recorder back after they had collected the stories they wanted – the children wanted to continue to trade stories.

The narratives on which this study is based were collected as part of a project at Harvard University, School of Education, directed by Courtney Cazden and Sarah Michaels. The story by the young black girl discussed both in Gee's paper (1989) as well as in this one was collected by Charles Haynes from Harvard University at part of the project. The story by the young white girl was collected by Denise Wolf also at Harvard University.

No specific definition of what constitutes an idea was provided for either group of subjects. The subjects were to follow their own intuitions of what constituted an idea, marking what they understood to be the end of each idea with a vertical slash. The following example may serve as an illustration. Each unit that the subject felt constituted an 'idea' is placed between slashes:

(1) Well see / we have this park near our house / and it really stinks /

Once both stories were marked in this way, each subject then had to identify idea-groups. The subjects were asked to do so by marking square brackets around those ideas that they thought could be grouped together. The following example may serve as an illustration.

(2) [then my mo / him and my mother went over there / sh / and she went up to where he was sittin and I told her / and I was telling my mother that he was up to that tree / and I told him that my mother was comin' and my mother came up and she goes what's your name / and he goes I'm not gonna tell you / you're not my mother / and my mother started calling / startin' / calling names and stuff like that /]

As mentioned earlier, the listeners had to identify idea units on the written transcript while listening to the stories. They were to identify idea-groups after having identified the idea units. The following instructions were given:

You are going to listen to two stories told by two young girls. Here is a transcript of the two stories. You have to identify idea units in the stories while you are listening to them. Mark the end of each idea with a vertical slash. You have to follow your intuition as to what constitutes an idea. Once you have finished identifying ideas, put square brackets around those ideas you think go together.

No subject had any difficulty with the instructions. When subjects were unable to keep up with the ongoing narrative, they were allowed to turn the player off until they caught up with the speaker. They were also allowed to replay the stories if they felt they had failed to mark an idea. The subjects were allowed as much time as they required to finish their task. When they finished marking the idea units, they were to identify idea-groups. They were however, not allowed to relisten to the narratives when marking idea-groups.

The second group of twenty (the readers) were given almost identical instructions except that they were asked to identify the semantic units without access to the spoken version. Like the listeners, they too had to demarcate ideas with vertical slashes and idea-groups with square brackets.

Hypotheses

The main hypothesis this study wished to investigate was whether these mainstream subjects, deeply influenced by school-based literacy practices, would process Sandy's and Leona's stories in a systematically and consistently different way. These subjects certainly share much more in the way of culture and literacy background with Sandy than they do with Leona. Would this affect how they heard the two girls? A secondary question was whether listening as against reading would cause a difference in how subjects processed either or both of the two stories.

In order to investigate these questions, the data was quantitatively investigated in three areas. First, I wanted to know whether the number of idea units any particular reader or listener found in Sandy's story would correlate with the number that listener or reader found in Leona's. If there was such a significant correlation this would indicate that the subjects' were behaving consistently, that is, if one subject, for example, tended to mark more ideas than other subjects in the case of Sandy, he or she tended to do the same for Leona. This would also indicate that subjects were using the same notion of what an idea was (for them) in the case of both texts. Secondly, the number of ideas and idea-groups identified by both listeners and readers for both stories was compared. This gives some indication of how the readers and listeners 'parsed' the stories. At the level of idea-groups, it gives us some indication as to whether the subjects thought that ideas 'hung together' differently in the two stories and how they thought they 'hung together' in each case. And, third, the number of idea units agreed upon by listeners and by readers were compared. Here, I was interested in knowing if subjects agreed with each more in regard to one text than the other, since, if they did, this may well indicate that text was somehow 'easier' for them, or fit better with their discourse-level expectations.

After these quantitative measures were carried out, a more qualitative investigation of the ideas and idea-groups found in each text was carried out to begin to formulate hypotheses as to what may have caused the differences found and what the linguistic nature of these differences was (i.e., did they make any sense within a theory of discourse differences).

Results

As was expected, it makes a difference whether one reads or listens to these texts. This can be seen clearly by comparing the number of idea units identified by readers for both stories with those identified by listeners. Since the stories are of unequal length (Sandy's story had 803 words and Leona's had 669), the responses to the stories, by both listeners and readers, for ideas and idea-groups, were totalled and adjusted to a text of 1000 words. Table 1 below shows the average number of idea units identified by listeners and readers. Figure 1 gives the same information in graph form.

Table 1 and Figure 1 Average number of idea units identified by listeners and readers in the two stories

Sandy's story		Leona's story	
Listeners	Readers	Listeners	Readers
87	56.4	67.05	39.8

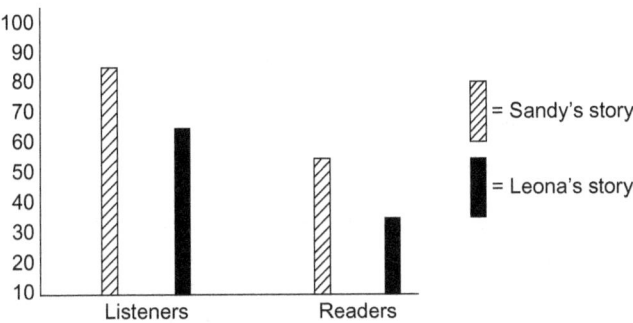

Figure 1

As Table 1 and Figure 1 show, the listeners identified more idea units than did the readers, and this held true of both stories. The mean number of idea units identified by listeners to Sandy's story was 87, while the mean number identified by the readers was 56.4, a difference of 30.6%. The mean number of idea units identified by listeners to Leona's story was 67.05, while the mean number identified by the readers was 39.8, a difference of 27.25%. Thus, readers found fewer (and, thus, longer) idea units in the two stories.

In all likelihood this is due to the lack of prosodic cues (pausing, syllable duration, pitch, stress, and rate changes) in the case of the readers. This conclusion is supported by Chafe's (1980a) claim that idea units are 'typically bounded by pauses' and that they are reconginzable by a 'coherent intonation contour', as well as the pervasive literature showing that prosodic properties are deeply implicated in planning texts and in how they are heard. It should be remembered that the listeners were looking at a written transcript while they were listening, so the difference was not due to the fact that the readers could take in more information at once; though, of course, it may be due to readers being in a 'reading mode' as against the listeners being in a 'listening mode'. As Chafe (1980a) has also pointed out,

Table 2 Correlation test

	Value of r for 18 df using of 0.05	Computed value of / for both stories
Listeners	0.444	0.729
Readers	0.444	0.561

written texts tend to have longer idea units than spoken ones, and readers may be 'primed' to look for longer idea units. Whatever the reason, hearing the stories makes a consistent difference, and that difference is to encourage the subjects to find more idea units.

However, the reading-listening difference cannot obscure the fact that both readers and listeners process Sandy's and Leona's texts differently. Table 1 and Figure 1 also show that on average both listeners and the readers identify more idea units in Sandy's narrative than in Leona's.

The listeners identified a mean of 87 idea units in Sandy's narrative and a mean of only 67.05 in Leona's, a difference of 19.95%. The readers of Sandy's narrative identified a mean of 56.4 idea units as opposed to a mean of 39.8 identified in Leona's, a difference of 16.6%.

The possibility that the above conclusion is based on mere chance or sampling error can be ruled out by the results of the following correlation test, shown in Table 2.

The results of the correlation test shown in Table 2 indicate that the computed value of r for both listeners and readers was greater that the tabled value. That is, the subjects, whether they were readers or listeners, demonstrated a significant consistency in the number of idea units they identified for Sandy and the number they identified for Leona. When correlation tests were conducted using a probability of .05 and 18 degrees of freedom, significant results were obtained. For listeners, a coefficient figure of 0.729 was obtained; for readers, a coefficient figure of 0.561 was obtained. Since in both cases the coefficient figure was significantly higher than the tables value of 0.444, one can conclude that there is a strong positive correlation between the two sets of data in both cases. Thus, there is reason to believe that, whatever the subjects are doing, they are doing the 'same' thing for Sandy and Leona; however a particular subject goes about looking for idea units, that subject appears to go about looking for idea units in the same way in both texts, and tends to find much fewer idea units in Leona's text than in Sandy's.

These results would seem to demonstrate that different structures of the stories affect the ways readers and listeners process them. Subjects, regardless of whether they are listening or reading, process Sandy's story into more frequent and shorter idea units. What is particularly interesting here is the fact that this difference cannot be due solely to the significant prosodie differences between Sandy and Leona, since even readers respond to the two texts in different ways, and, in fact, respond to Leona's text with fewer idea units, just as the listeners did.

Now, one might ask, 'Is this difference due to the fact that Leona has fewer idea units, in an objective sense, in her text than Sandy; perhaps, Leona has longer idea units than Sandy does?' First, idea units in an 'objective sense' are tone groups, that is, a string of words with a uniform intonational envelope containing one major pitch glide. Tone groups tend to be about the same size, i.e., relatively small, for all speakers, though, of course, there is some variation. Leona has a total of 143 tone groups in her text, while Sandy has a total of 151. Remember that Leona's text is, in fact, shorter (at 669 words) than Sandy's (803 words). Thus, Leona has 4.68 words per tone unit, while Sandy has slightly longer tone units than Leona, with 5.32 words per idea unit. Therefore, if readers and listeners were to reflect the 'objective' properties of the text they would find more idea units (on average) in Leona's text than in Sandy's. But, of course, they do just the reverse. Even if we remove all speech dysfluencies from each text and count only clauses, Leona has 90 and Sandy 95, which amounts to 7.47 words per unit for Leona versus 8.45 words per unit for Sandy. Once again, Leona in fact has more such units per number of words than Sandy does (though, in fact, the two are very close). Readers and listeners are not finding fewer idea units in Leona's text because there are 'objectively' fewer tone units there; there aren't, there are more.

Now I turn to an examination of the idea-groups in the two stories. As mentioned earlier, an idea-group was defined as a set of related ideas held together by a single topic. For this experiment, the subjects were told to put square brackets around those ideas they thought went together. The data is given in numerical form in Table 3 and in graph form in Figure 3.

Both readers and listeners identified more idea units in Sandy's story than they did in Leona's. Listeners to Sandy's narrative identified an average of 10.5 idea-groups from an average of 87 idea units, while listeners to

Table 3 and Figure 3 Average number of idea groups identified by both groups for the two stories

	Listeners		Readers	
	Sandy's story	Leona's story	Sandy's story	Leona's story
Idea units	87	67.5	65.4	39.8
Idea groups	10.5	17.3	8.6	14.05

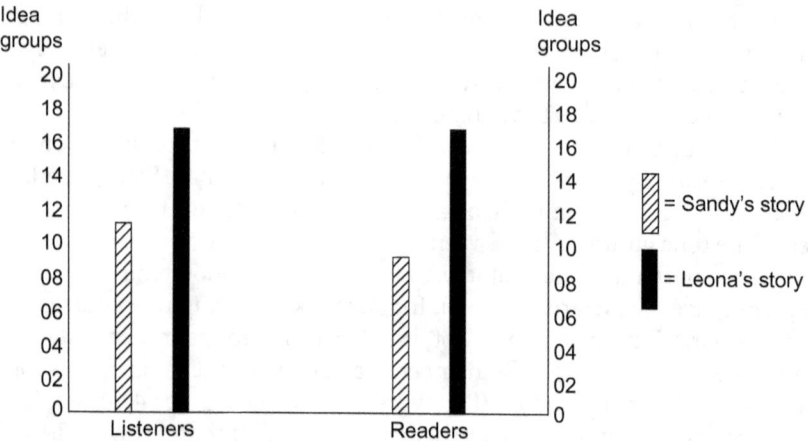

Figure 3

Leona's story identified an average of 17.3 idea-groups from an average of 67.05 idea units. Showing the same trend, readers of Sandy's story identified an average of 8.6 idea-groups from an average of 56.4 idea units, while readers of Leona's story identified an average of 14.05 idea-groups from an average of 39.8 idea units.

This fits with what was found for idea units, and, again, probably reflects the operation of prosody for the listeners and its absence for the readers. But, once again, this prosodic difference is not the whole story, because both listeners and readers identified more idea-groups in Leona's story than they did in Sandy's (the reverse of what we found in the case of idea units). Of course, we do not know what "idea-group" meant to the subject (though we will discuss this below).

Finally, we can look at the amount of agreement that existed between subjects. Not only did both groups of subjects (readers and listeners) identify more idea units and fewer idea-groups in Sandy's story, both groups also agreed on a greater number of identical idea and idea-groups in the case of Sandy's story as compared to Leona's. The data is shown in Table 4.

The figures in Table 4 indicate that for Sandy's text there was 19.9% of agreement about idea unit boundaries, by 10 and more listeners and readers, and only 2.98% of agreement for Leona's text by the same number of listeners and readers. Similarly, there was 14.9% of agreement about idea groups in Sandy's text, but only 2.98% in Leona's. This indicates that there were many more points in Sandy's story that both sets of subjects regarded as salient.

Table 4 The amount of agreement between the subjects

	Ideas	Idea groups
Sandy	19.9%	14.9%
Leona	2.98%	2.98%

Qualitative Study

These results raise interesting implications for the comprehension processes involved in the 'decomposition' (Sanford and Garrod 1981) of a text. Specifically, it raises the question of whether (and perhaps even to what degree) the structure of a text facilitates decoding processes. Theorists like Kintsch (1974) advocate that while decoding the reader parses a text into propositional units and then attempts to make connections between the propositions. Rumelhart (1975) and Thorndyke (1975), on the other hand, explain text comprehension in terms of looking for general patterns in the overall organization of a text, and use a set of general rules to segment stories. These rules also help account for the gist and recall pattern. A similar approach was put forth by Kintsch and van Dijk (1978), although their central aim was to unravel complex stories with several episodes.

Whichever decoding process the subjects used – segmenting the text into propositions or general organizational rules – the results indicate that they were using them consistently. That is, whatever it is they were looking for in Sandy's story, they seemed to be looking for the same in Leona's. Closely examining what constituted 'ideas' and 'idea-groups' for the subjects throws light on the kinds of patterns that the subjects were looking for in their parsing process. It turns out that when listeners reach agreement on an idea unit boundary for Sandy's text, this very often matches a boundary that Gee (1989) independently identified from his linguistic analysis as a 'line' and 'stanza' boundary. This is not so in the case of Leona's text. Gee's notion of 'lines' is similar to the notion of 'idea units', inasmuch as it too is characterized by intonation. A line, however, is an intonation unit that is 'cleaned up' of all speech disfluencies and errors that are typical of spontaneous speech. Specifically he defines a line as a structure made up of a 'simple clause, a verb of saying and what is said, or a 'heavy' pre or post clausal modifier' (1989: 98). Likewise, he defines a stanza as 'a group of lines about a certain topic' with each stanza capturing a single 'vignette' (1990a: 14).[2] Out of 22 places in Sandy's story where 10 or more subjects agreed on an idea unit boundary, 18 of these were line boundaries and 12 were stanza boundaries in Gee's terms.

Leona's text, on the other hand, presents quite a different picture. Out of the 12 places where 10 or more listeners agreed on an idea unit boundary, while 9 of these were line boundaries in Gee's terms, only 2 were stanza boundaries. Since stanzas are a uniting group of clauses all of which reflect a single topic, perspective, or episode, we would certainly expect listeners to notice an idea unit boundary after a stanza (since there is a significant, decisive break between stanzas). While this is true for Sandy's text, it was not for Leona's. The appendix indicates idea unit boundaries identified by 10 and more listeners for both stories.

The fact that the subjects agreed on many more idea-groups in Sandy's story than they did in Leona's also indicates that the structure of Sandy's story came further closer to meeting their discourse expectations that did Leona's. It would appear that Sandy's text comes closer to fitting the patterns that white, middle-class subjects had internalized, or at least the patterns that Gee's linguistic analysis demonstrates, than did Leona's text.

There are at least a couple of plausible explanations to account for the difference in the parsing. The first has to do with the structure of Leona's narrative; Leona narrative is built around cohering principles appropriate to her black culture. As Gee (1989) has already established, her narrative coheres because of elements she uses to 'perform' her narrative, namely graphic details, and patterns of repetition, parallelism, and sound effects. These were elements that the subjects of this study were unfamiliar with, and it is possible that these elements came in the way of their parsing process.

Another explanation has to do with the way in which Leona presents her 'given' and 'new' information (Chafe, 1970; Halliday, 1967). It is possible that the 'expressive' elements in her narrative blurs the distinction between given and new information by interrupting the temporally ordered events of her story. According to Clark and Haviland (1977) much of comprehension depends on the pattern of the given and new in speech, which is 'inherent in its syntax and associated stress pattern' (1977: 3). To ensure reasonably efficient communication the speaker tries to make the structure of his utterances match the listener's mental world; 'he agrees to convey information he thinks the listener already knows as given information and to convey information he thinks the listener doesn't yet know as new information' (1977: 4). Haviland and Clark conceive of the given-new strategy as being made up of three steps: step 1, isolating the given from the new information in the utterance; step 2, searching in one's memory for a structure that matches the given information and step 3, integrating the new information with the information found in step 2 (Clark and Haviland, 1974, 1977; Haviland and Clark, 1974). When the speaker does not present information in a way that allows the listener to effectively distinguish between the given and new, incoherence or miscommunication can result. Given the variation in the way in which the subjects responded to the two stories, it seems likely that Leona's narrative strategy does not meet with the given-new expectations of the subjects; in all likelihood, her syntax and stress patterns (discussed in Gee, 1989) thwart their expectations, thus disabling them from parsing her story along the same lines as they parsed Sandy's.

Conclusion

I have not been precise here in specifying what I mean by 'idea unit' or 'idea group'. This was done mainly because the study aimed at arriving at what the *subjects* perceived as an 'ideas' or 'idea groups'. Given the fact the study was interested in getting at the structures (of texts) that people hear or read, it seemed appropriate to allow the subjects to intuit for themselves how they recognized 'ideas' and 'idea-groups'. Furthermore, related notions of 'lines', 'intonation contours', and 'stanzas' have been researched elsewhere (Gee, 1989, 1990; Chafe, 1980a, 1980b).

The conclusions in this study are tentative, but it has provoked some interesting questions for future research: if this experiment were duplicated for black subjects – subjects whose socio-cultural background matched Leona's – would those subjects parse her story in a systematically different way from the story told by the white child, Sandy? Or would they, as products of a dominantly white ideology, parse the story the way the white subjects did? It is admittedly difficult to hypothesize about these questions; nevertheless it is important that future research address them. In doing so, we will gain a better understanding of how humans from different backgrounds perceive and comprehend texts. It will, if anything, give us a glimpse into an alternative mode of comprehension.

Appendix

Ideas identified by 10 and more listeners in Sandy's story:

Well see we have this park near our house/

and it really stinks/

but me and my friend Sarah were over there/

and we were playin on the swings//

and this other kid we call tin head cans or whatever because he goes around through garbage and stuff and picks up cans/

and go brings them to the store to get money//

and ah so they start and were playin and he starts callin us names/

and so we call him names back/

and then he starts talkin about our mothers so I take a rock and I throw it at him/

it missed him I made sure it missed him it just banged on the slide//

and then he started throwing rocks at us and now he was throwing rocks and he was spittin and everything else/

he wouldn't dare have hit us with it though and um and my mother was going down the street okay/

and she saw him spittin at 'im and un spittin at us so sh my mother went over to was trying to go over to his house but she couldn't find him//

and instead she went to Jeremy and Erica's house/

they're brats/

they ah they do everything he does except they get buckets of paint and they dump 'em on people and stuff like that//

and so then my mo him and my mother went over there sh and she went up to where he was sittin and I told her and I was telling my mother that he was up to that three/

and I told him that my mother was coming//

and my mother came up and she goes what's your name and he goes i'm not gonna tell you you're not my mother//

and my mother my mother started calling'him startin' calling names and stuff like that/

and then it turns out that he has this problem like cause he's got some disease or somethin and he doesn't quite know how to make friends or anything like that//

and one day we went over there another day and he stars whippin he starts throwin swingin chains around okay/

and he whips Sarah with a chain and whipped me with a padolock that was on the chain//

and I didn't do anything but I grabbed him okay/

and I go you hit me again and you're gonna be in so much trouble you're not gonna believe it//

so instead he just starts swinging a swing he just wasn't on it he just started swingin it he swung it into me//

I go up to him and I kicked him so hard he was like ahhhhhh (crying) and he fell after I kicked him in both his shins so it really hurt and he'd get big bruises on his shins//

and and the mark I had from the padolock was about a lump it was like that (traces out a small square on her forearm) and the mark went oohhhh/

and it was all black and blue and you could see the shape of the padolock//

and then let's see then un Sarah's father goes over and fin and talk and Sarah's mother starts talking to him not to Jay

and started to we finally find out his name was Jay/

and started talkin to his mother and the mother said I'll be glad to pay any hospital bills and anything like that//

and the kid said and Sarah goes all I want im to do is apologize and he goes like this I did apologize and urn and Sarah yeah like oh you wanna be my friend after you whipped me with a chain//

he whipped her in the he whipped her in her leg//

and once in her arm and once on her stomach/

and then she goes then I go like this after he yells at her like I'm sorry and um I go like this after he yells at her like I'm sorry and um I go like this oh yeah that's a great way to make friends whip people with chains and say hi I wanna be your friend that's dumb//

and so then the next day we went over there he was up in the tree and he has a bunch of rocks and a bucket of sand up there okay and he started throwin sand at us//

and Debbie Moraine and got sand in thrown at her she goes up to the tree she took the bucket of sand and dumped it over his head//

and he went home screamin and cryin and told his mother/ and everybody ran cause they didn't want to get in trouble anymore cept when people start with him//

[big pause] he's dumb

he's he's you threaten his life and he laughs he's got some problem

Ideas identified by 10 and more listeners in Leonas story:

I'll tell you about my ear ache, o.k./

all right this is what happened//

I was I was just up there I was up my grandmother's house especially for like two weeks or three well not two weeks two days or three or more like that a couple of days ah shoot I should say//

alright
I got this thing my ear's all buggin me an everything/

my ear was all buggin me and I was cryin I was doin all oooh oooh (laughter) oooh oooh I was doin all that and un and my mother put alcohol on though//(laughter)

an then what happened was and then what happened I was just let alone/

n I bought myself an ice cream I thought that would make me feel better I was all shuup shuup shuup shuup you know//

and then and then you know just all of a sudden I just got this terrible feelin after I stopped eatin ice cream and what not like on shoot oh go::d (laughter) my ear was killing me an I was sayin ma:: ma:://

an un we got on the train to go home an my mother said let's go to the hospital/

we had to walk down this long dark street about five miles or somethin like that (laughter) ??? we had to walk down this long street an then the hospital was there//

and this is the funny part alright you wait in there I'm sitting there oooh oooh oooh//

my mother's sittin there talkin to this lady and all (laughter) an you know excuse me madam can I help you at all oooh oooh oooh an uh then we went in the emergency because we didn't make an appointment or nothin my mother's in there for about ten minutes or what not I'm still cryin she's talkin to this lady//

and they said well we can't help you here cuz we're busy here at regular hospital we're blaa blaa and they kept goin on and on//

my mother got real mad start steamin at the lady she was all cussin her out yellin naa naa naa naa//

and then she goes what happened if my daughter was dyin an all that stuff/

she was all well urn excuse me miss if you want to pay the bill we can see you right away my way//

an then she called my hospital doctor up on the phone

I was like oooooooooh still me cryin and my mother was cussin that lady out

an she goes why don't you take a cab/

my mother say I ain't got no money now//

an then they sent a cab down for cuz she have no money she didn't pay the cab driver she just walked out she just slammed the door she said come on Rona//

an un an then an then we had they gave me this consummation or something like that for the bill this lady urn wrote it up an spit it in my mother's face??? those guys off pssst (kissing sound) thank you like that boy I was upset//

and then we had to wait for a good fifteen minutes just to get help now ah isn't that come on what if I was goin deaf or something you what I mean//

that's when I had that bad earache/

I was like oh god am I gonna die I says no what if I die ooooooooh I was just cryin there like that//

this lady was all cleanin an stuff like that she said you have an ear in FEC-TION an an everything is going well but there's something in your ear you know and I was like yea I know//

an that's about all we went home I: grubbed out on some food wait you see//

put that medicine in my ear an I was grubbin out on that food I was grubbin out shuuk mmm mmm an I was grubbin out on the food an everything//

mmm alright ADJ it's your turn

Out of 12 places where 10 or more subjects agreed on an idea unit, 9 were 'line' boundaries, 2 were 'stanza' boundaries.

Notes

*I am greatly indebted to James Gee for thinking through several of the ideas in this paper with me. The feedback I received from the editor and the anonymous reviewers was also invaluable.

(1) There has been some previous research that has investigated issues related to this study. Kintsch and Greene (1978), for instance, argue that story schémas are culture specific and that story schemata aid in both comprehending and reconstructing stories. The authors also argue that subjects, when reconstructing stories with unfamiliar story scheme, experience difficulty in recalling the gist of the story. A detailed discussion of how story conventions influence the reader's comprehension and reproduction of text can be found in Kintsch and van Dijk (1975) as well.
(2) For a detailed analysis of how lines and stanzas operate in Sandy and Leona's stories, see Gee (1989).

References

Bauman, R. (1975). Verbal art as performance. *American Anthropologist 11:* 290–311.
Briggs, C. (1984). On the fuzzy fringes of performance. Paper presented at American Anthropological Society meetings, Denver.
Butterworth, Brian (1975) Hesitation and semantic planning in speech. *Journal of Psycholinguistic Research* 4(1): 75–87.
Chafe, Wallace (1970). *Meaning and the Structure of Language.* Chicago, IL: University of Chicago Press.
(1980a). The deployment of consciousness in the production of a narrative. In Wallace Chafe (ed.), 1980b: 9–50.
—(ed.) (1980b). *The Pear Stories: Cognitive, Cultural and Linguistic Aspects of Narrative Production.* Norwood, NJ: Ablex.
—(1982). Integration and involvement in speaking, writing and oral literature. In *Spoken and Written Language: Exploring Orality and Literacy,* Deborah Tannen (ed.), 35–53. Norwood, NJ: Ablex.
Clark, Herbert and Haviland Susan (1974). Psychological processes of linguistic explanation. In *Explaining Linguistic Phenomena,* D. Cohen (ed.), 25–60. Washington, DC: Winston.
—(1977). Comprehension and the given-new contract. In *Discourse production and Comprehension,* Roy O. Freedle (ed.), 1–40. Norwood, NJ: Ablex.
Cook-Gumperz, Jenny (1986). *The Social Construction of Literacy.* Cambridge: Cambridge University Press.
Gee, James Paul (1989). Two styles of narrative construction and their linguistic and educational implications. *Discourse Processes* 12: 287–307.
—(1990a). A linguistic approach to narrative. *Journal of narrative and life history* 1(1): 15–39.
—(1990b). *Social Linguistics and Literacies: Ideology in Discourses.* London: Falmer Press.
—(1991). Memory and myth: A perspective on narrative. In *Developing Narrative Structure,* Allyssa McCabe and Carole Peterson (eds.), 1–25. Hillsdale, NJ: Lawrence Erlbaum.
Gee, James Paul and Grosjean, F. (1983). Performance structures: A linguistic and psycho-linguistic appraisal. *Cognitive Psychology* 15: 411–458.

—(1984). Empirical evidence for narrative structure. *Cognitive Science* 8: 59–85.
Goldman-Eisler, Frieda (1972). Pauses, clauses, sentences. *Language and Speech* 15: 103–113.
Halliday, M. A. K. (1967) Notes on transitivity and theme in English 2. *Journal of Linguistics* 3: 199–224.
Haviland, Susan and Clark, Herbert (1974). What's new? Acquiring new information as a process in comprehension. *Journal of Verbal Learning and Verbal Behaviour* 13: 512–521.
Heath, Shirley (1982). What no bedtime story means: narrative skills at home and school. *Language in Society* 11: 49–76.
—(1983). *Ways with Words: Language, Life and Work in the Communities and Classrooms.* Cambridge: Cambridge University Press.
Hicks, Deborah (1991). Kinds of narrative: Genre skills among first graders from two communities. In *Developing Narrative Structure,* Allyssa McCabe and Carole Petersen (eds.), 55–87. New Jersey: Lawrence Erlbaum.
Hudson, J. and Shapiro, L. (1991). From knowing to telling: The development of children's scripts, stories and personal narratives. In *Developing Narrative Structure,* Allyssa McCabe and Carole Petersen (eds.), 89–136. New Jersey: Lawrence Erlbaum.
Hymes, D. (1975). Breakthrough into performance. In *Folklore: Performance and Communication,* David Ben-Amos and Kenneth Goldstein (eds.), 11–74. Berlin The Hague: Mouton.
Kintsch, Walter (1974). *The Representation of Meaning in Memory.* Potomac, MD: Erlbaum.
Kintsch, Walter and Greene, Edith (1978). The role of culture specific schemata in the comprehension and recall of stories. *Discourse Processes* 1: 1–13.
Kintsch, Walter and van Dijk, Teun A. (1975). Comment on se rappelle et résume des histoires. *Languages* 40: 98–116.
—(1978). Toward a model of text comprehension and production. *Psychological Review* 85: 363–394.
Kreckel, Marga (1981). Tone units as message blocks in natural discourse: Segmentation of face to face interaction by naive, native speakers. *Journal of Pragmatics* 5: 459–476.
Labov, William (1972). *Language in the Inner City: Studies in the Black English Vernacular.* Philadelphia: University of Pennsylvania Press.
Lord, A. (1960). *The Singer of Tales.* Cambridge: Cambridge University Press.
Michaels, Sarah (1981). "Sharing time": Children's narrative style and differential access to literacy. *Language in Society* 10: 423–442.
Olson, David (1977). From utterance to text: The bias of language in speech and writing. *Harvard Educational Review* 47(3): 257–281.
Ong, Walter J. (1982). *Orality and Literacy: The Technologizing of the Word.* London: Methuen.
Petersen, C. and McCabe, A. (1991). Linking children's connective use and narrative macro-structure. In *Developing Narrative Structure,* Allyssa McCabe and Carole Petersen (eds.), 29–53. New Jersey: Lawrence Erlbaum.
Rumelhart, D. E. (1975). Notes on a schema for stories. In *Representing and Understanding: Studies in Cognitive Science* D. G. Bobrow and A. Collins (eds.), XX–XX. New York: Academic Press.
Sanford, A. J. and Garrod, S. C. (1981). *Understanding Written Language: Explorations of Comprehension Beyond the Sentence.* Chichester: John Wiley and Sons.
Scollon, R. and Scollon, S. B. K. (1979). *Linguistic Convergence: An Ethnography of Speaking at Fort Chipewyan, Alberta.* New York: Academic Press.

—(1981). *Narrative, Literacy and Face in Interethnic Communication.* Norwood, NJ: Ablex.
Tannen, Deborah (1982). The oral/literate continuum in discourse. In *Spoken and Written Language: Exploring Orality and Literacy,* Deborah Tannen (ed.), 1–16. New Jersey: Ablex.
—(1989). *Talking Voices: Repetition, Dialogue and Imagery in Conversational Discourse.* Cambridge: Cambridge University Press.
Thorndyke, P. W. (1975). Cognitive structures in human story comprehension and memory. Unpublished Ph.D. dissertation, Stanford University. California.

Vaidehi Ramanathan-Abbott is a doctoral student in the Linguistics program at the University of Southern California. She holds an M.A. in Literature from the University of Baroda, India, and an M.A. in Linguistics from California State University, Northridge. Her current research involves examining the discourse of patients afflicted with Alzheimer's disease. She has published the following: Frames and Coherence in Sam Shepard's *Fool for Love, Issues in Applied Linguistics* 2(1): 49–76 (1991); Review of *Language, Society and the Elderly: Discourse Identity and Ageing,* by Nikolas Coupland, Justine Coupland, and Howard Giles, *Linguistics* 30(6): 1129–1131 (1992).

Contributors

Fabio Coelho has an MA degree in linguistics and a multiple-subject bilingual teaching credential, both from San José State University. He is primarily interested in issues of language and education as they affect bilingual and multilingual language users and/or communities in the United States and Latin America. He has worked as a writing specialist at the SJSU Writing Center and has also taught English as a Foreign Language for five years in Brazil. Since 2008, he has been volunteering, along with a team from San José State University, to help a Nicaraguan organization design culturally responsive practices to meet the foreign language requirements of their rural high school curriculum. He is currently a fifth-grade bilingual teacher in the San Jose Unified School District.

Chatwara Suwannamai Duran is an assistant professor of Applied Linguistics at the University of Houston, where she teaches courses in linguistics and sociolinguistics. Originally from Bangkok, Thailand, but as one who has studied in both Europe and the United States, she has learned to appreciate and explore multilingualism in both local and global contexts. Her current research focuses on transnational families' lived experiences, multilingual repertoires and literacies that are complicated by migration, globalization and contested language ideologies in sending and receiving nations.

Emily Feuerherm began teaching English in Switzerland in 2004 after getting her Bachelor's in anthropology from the University of Arkansas. She received her MATESOL from the University of California in Davis in 2008 and is currently a PhD candidate in linguistics at the same university. She has been teaching English as a Second Language since Switzerland. She founded and currently directs the Refugee Health and Employment

Attainment Program (RHEAP) at the Sacramento Immigrant Resource Center. Her research interests include the socio-politics of language and language instruction, TESL pedagogy, immigrant studies, discourse analysis and linguistic rights.

Rosemary Henze is a professor of Linguistics and Language Development at San José State University, where she teaches courses on intercultural communication and language teaching pedagogy in the MA TESOL program. Her interests center on the role language plays in promoting (as well as hindering) social justice, positive interethnic relations and effective leadership. She is currently completing a documentary film about Muslim women's experiences in the Bay Area and collaborating with a Nicaraguan NGO to support them in meeting the foreign language requirements of their rural high school curriculum. Prior to joining SJSU in 2001, she spent 13 years with ARC Associates as a researcher and consultant focusing on bilingual education and race relations in collaboration with K-12 public schools. Her publications include *The Power of Talk* (Corwin Press, 2009); *How Real is Race?* (Rowman and Littlefield Education, 2007); *Leading for Diversity: How School Leaders Promote Positive Interethnic Relations* (Corwin Press, 2002); and 'Metaphors of diversity, equity, and intergroup relations in the discourse of school leaders' (*Journal of Language, Identity, and Education*, 2005). She received her doctorate in Education with a minor in Anthropology from Stanford University.

Ariel Loring has a PhD in Linguistics from the University of California, Davis. Her research includes interpretations and consequent implications of citizenship in different societal venues, employing ethnography, discourse analysis, lingusitic landscape and social semiotics approaches. She is interested in applied sociolinguistic issues of language policy and practice, immigration and language ideologies.

Kendall A. King is a professor of Second Languages and Cultures at the University of Minnesota, where she teaches and conducts research on language policy, sociolinguistics and child bilingualism and second language learning. She previously has served as faculty at the Center for Research on Bilingualism at Stockholm University, in the Department of Linguistics at Georgetown University and in the Department of Teaching and Learning at New York University. Her recent projects have examined transmigration, parenting practices and Spanish-Quichua-English language learning and use in Washington D.C., Minneapolis and Saraguro, Ecuador, and the relationship across (im)migration status, second language learning and school engagement for US Latino youth. She is currently researching the role of technology in supporting urban Ojibwe language revitalization. Her most recent research appears in academic journals such as *Discourse Studies, Applied Linguistics* and the *International Journal of Bilingual Education and Bilingualism*. She is also editor of the journal *Language Policy*.

Busi Makoni holds a PhD in applied linguistics from the University of Edinburgh in Scotland. She is currently working as a lecturer of the African Studies Program at Pennsylvania State University. Her research interests are in second language acquisition, language and gender, language and security of the state, feminist critical discourse analysis, language policy and planning and language rights. Some of her research has been published in the *Journal of Second Language Research, International Journal of Applied Linguistics, Discourse & Communication, Per Linguam, Current Issues in language Planning, Journal of Language, Identity and Education* and the *International Multilingual Research Journal*.

Aya Matsuda is an associate professor of English at Arizona State University, where she teaches undergraduate and graduate courses in applied linguistics. Her research focuses on the global spread of English, its use as an international language and its implications for pedagogy, and her work on these topics has appeared in several leading journals as well as a number of edited collections. She has recently edited *Principles and Practices of Teaching English as an International Language* (Multilingual Matters, 2012) and co-edited, with Patricia Friedrich, the 'World Englishes' and 'Language Ideology' sections of *The Encyclopedia for Applied Linguistics* (Blackwell, 2012). She currently serves on the editorial board of *World Englishes*.

Teresa L. McCarty is the George F. Kneller Chair in Education and Anthropology at the University of California, Los Angeles and the Alice Wiley Snell Professor Emerita of Education Policy Studies at Arizona State University. A sociocultural anthropologist and applied linguist, she has worked with Indigenous education programs in the United States, Canada, Mexico, New Zealand, Australia and Russia, and has published widely on indigenous/bilingual education, educational language policy, critical literacy and ethnographic studies of schooling. Her books include *A Place To Be Navajo – Rough Rock and the Struggle for Self-determination in Indigenous Schooling* (Erlbaum, 2002), *Language, Literacy, and Power in Schooling* (Erlbaum, 2005), '*To Remain an Indian*' – *Lessons in Democracy from a Century of Native American Educa-*

tion (with K.T. Lomawaima, Teachers College Press, 2006), *Ethnography and Language Policy* (Routledge, 2011) and *Language Planning and Policy in Native America – History, Theory, Praxis* (Multilingual Matters, 2013).

Julia Menard-Warwick received her MATESL degree from the University of Washington in 1987. She taught English as a foreign language (EFL) in Nicaragua for one year, and then English as a second language (ESL) at a small community college in Washington State for 10 years. She received her PhD degree from University of California Berkeley in 2004; her dissertation study was published by *Multilingual Matters* in 2009 as *Gendered Identities and Immigrant Language Learning*. Since 2004, she has been a professor of Applied Linguistics at University of California Davis. Her research on English language teaching (ELT) at Chilean University was conducted in 2005 and 2006, and funded by the Binational US-Chile Fulbright Foundation. Since then, she has continued to teach intensive courses for the Masters in English Teaching program at the Chilean University as a visiting scholar. Her research interests include second language learning and teaching, narrative analysis and language ideologies. She is currently working on a book about ELT in Chile and California.

Kate Menken is an associate professor of Linguistics at Queens College of the City University of New York (CUNY), and a Research Fellow at the Research Institute for the Study of Language in Urban Society at the CUNY Graduate Center. Previously, she was a researcher at the National Clearinghouse for Bilingual Education and an English as a second-language teacher. She holds an EdD from Teachers College, Columbia University. Her research interests include language education policy, bilingual education and emergent bilinguals in secondary schools. Recent books are *English Learners Left Behind: Standardized Testing as Language Policy* (Multilingual Matters, 2008) and *Negotiating Language Policies in Schools: Educators as Policymakers* (co-edited with Ofelia García, Routledge, 2010). She is also associate editor and review editor for the journal *Language Policy*, and Co-Principal Investigator of the CUNY-New York State Initiative for Emergent Bilinguals (NYSIEB) project.

Gemma Punti holds a PhD in second languages and cultures education from the University of Minnesota. She is currently a language lecturer at the Center for Learning Innovation at the University of Minnesota, Rochester. Her research interests include race, language, immigration status and first and second-generation youth education and has appeared in the *Journal of Linguistics and Education*. In particular, she is interested in the life experiences of undocumented Latino young adults. She is originally from Catalonia, Spain, and a native speaker of Catalan. This background has also largely influenced her interest in language policy, and language revitalization and maintenance.

Vaidehi Ramanathan is a Professor of Applied Sociolinguistics in the Linguistics Department at the University of California, Davis. Her research interests span all domains of literacy, including teacher education, minority languages, language policies and unequal power relations between English and the vernaculars in postcolonial contexts. She is also interested in aging, health and disability studies as well language learning and literacy studies. Her publications include: *Language, Body and Health* (co-edited, Mouton de Gruyter, 2011), *Bodies and Language: Health, Ailments, Disabilities* (Multilingual Matters, 2010), *The English-Vernacular Divide: Postcolonial Language Politics and Practice* (Multilingual Matters, 2005), *The Politics of TESOL Education: Writing, Knowledge, Critical Pedagogy* (Routledge, 2001) and *Alzheimer's Discourse: Some Sociolinguistic Dimensions* (Lawrence Erlbaum, 1997). She has also edited a special issue of *Language Policy*, with a focus on health and co-edited a special issue of *TESOL Quarterly* with a focus on language policies.

Gopinder Kaur Sagoo is a doctoral researcher based at the MOSAIC Centre for Research on Multilingualism, School of Education, College of Social Sciences, University of Birmingham. Funded by the Economic and Social Research Council, her study examines a Sikh-inspired early childhood project in the UK and considers its contributions to understandings of participatory citizenship and children's holistic development. Herself a British-born Sikh with a family background in East Africa, she holds a Joint Honors degree in French and Russian (Cambridge) and a Masters in South Asian Area Studies (London, School of Oriental and African Studies). This reflects an abiding interest in language, culture, discourse and society and the exploration of perspectives and practices from a transnational, Sikh-faith heritage positioning.

Jacqueline Widin has extensive experience in teaching English as an additional/international language and in teaching and research of tertiary led pre- and in-service teacher training programs in and outside of Australia. She has a particular interest in the relationship between language learning and human rights and the sociopolitical dynamics of the English language teaching field. She is currently a senior lecturer at the University of Technology Sydney and manages the TESOL and Applied Linguistics Education programs. She is the author of *Illegitimate Practices: Global English Language Education*.

Keiko Yasukawa is a lecturer in adult education at the University of Technology, Sydney. She coordinates courses and teaches in the areas of adult literacy and numeracy. Her research interests include the critical examination of the nexus between policy and practice in adult literacy and numeracy, and adult literacy and numeracy teacher development. She is one of the editors of *Literacy and Numeracy Studies*: An international journal in the education and training of Adults.

Index

ABE (adult basic education) classes, 178–80
Abrego, L.J., 93, 94
academic language, and emergent bilinguals in US, 222
accountability, pressures of, 214–19
achievement, ideologies of, 94
activity theory, 173
adult education
  in Australia, 167–85
  and lifelong learning policies, 170
  and US citizenship, 190–206
advancement, discourses of, 92, 99–113
Africa, 19–32
Allen, G., 148
'allied others', 117
American Indians, 116–36
Amway see also multi-level marketing (MLM) discourses, 95, 97, 98–9, 101, 103–7, 111
Appadurai, A., 245
Appiah, K.A., 178
Arviso, M., 130
Asian American Community Center (AACC), 191–2
assimilation, as citizenship construct, 9, 171–3, 219–21, 234
assumed knowledge, 202–3
Australia, 167–85, 190
authoritative discourses, 83–4, 88

Baker, C., 44, 212
Bakhtin, M., 75, 84

banking model of education, 197
Banks, J.A., 189, 204
Bashir (Iraqi refugee), 57, 58–9, 64–5
beliefs about citizenship: teacher-student enactments, 193–6
Benally, A., 121
Benjamin, W., 4
Bhai Sahib, 146, 151–2, 153, 154, 159
Biesta, G., 150
bilingual education, 40, 128, 210–28
bilingualism see also multilingualism
  'emergent bilinguals' as a term, 37
  referring to learners as bilinguals, 36–7, 47
  US Americans as emergent bilinguals, 209–28
Birch, B., 169, 170
Blommaert, J., 76, 202
Blum Martinez, R., 136
body language, 24, 26–7
borders, 1–4, 8, 22–3, 43, 150
bottom-up policies see also top-down policies, 9, 124–5, 189
Bourdieu, P., 194
Brayboy, B.M.J., 120, 121, 131
Briggs, C., 97
Bronfenbrenner, U., 148
bullying, 62
business language
  English as see also global language, English as, 78–9
  Spanish as, 75, 245

call-center workers, 75
cell phones as tool for teaching, 248
censorship, in Chile, 88–9
Chávez, E., 240, 242
Chile, language ideologies of English teachers, 73–89
China, English in, 75
Chinese used by politicians in US, 41
Choi, P.K., 75
citizenship see also discitizenship; full participation; global citizenship
  assimilation as citizenship construct, 9, 171–3, 219–21, 234
  benefits of, 195–6
  'citizenship minus', 30, 211, 227
  citizenship-as-practice, 150, 167–8, 189
  classroom as space of citizenship, 173–5
  deficit, assimilation and integration constructs, 171–3
  definitions, 22–4, 43, 88, 147, 152, 160, 167–8, 170, 188, 189–90, 209–10
  dynamic, two-way models of, 185
  faith-inspired/spiritual citizenship, 151–9, 238
  'flexible' citizenship, 60, 196
  full participation see full participation
  and globalization, 3–4
  history of, 189–90
  integration, as citizenship construct, 171–3
  in the media, 188
  multiple, overlapping citizenship, 120
  and Native Americans, 119–20
  OECD definitions, 170
  partial citizenship, 20, 31
  as a process, 1, 4, 9, 253–5
  productivity, 1, 4, 9, 168, 171, 173–5, 185
  Ramanathan's reflections on, 253–5
  rights and responsibilities, 160
  and Sikh faith-derived concepts, 146
  surface and peripheral meanings, 197–201
  transformative citizenship, 4, 9, 76, 84, 147, 189, 204
  and undocumented people, 2–3
citizenship programmes, 172, 188, 189, 190–206
citizenship tests, 3, 168–9, 172, 189–205
classroom as space of citizenship, 173–5, 188–206
classroom literacy, 202
Cleghorn, A., 149
code switching, 157–8
Coelho, F.O., 231–50
cognitive aspects of multilingualism, 37
Cohn, D., 93, 94
colonialism, 3, 65, 120–1, 149, 171, 233–4, 243
communities
  building communities in classrooms, 167–85, 200–1
  and MLM schemes, 106–10
  Sikh visions of, 152, 154
composition studies, 37–8
constant comparative method, 192
consumerism (vs citizenship) in Chile, 87–9
Cook, V.J., 37
Cornwall, A., 160
'cosmopolitanism', 178
country as keyword in refugee accounts, 63–9
courtrooms, 19–32
covert vs overt language policies, 19, 20, 31, 127, 134, 234–5
Crawford, J., 40
creoles, 246, 247
critical citizenship education, 204, 205
critical interpretive approaches, 53, 55, 69
critical pedagogy, 233
Crystal, D., 42, 43, 235
cultural context
  and bilingual education, 224–5
  and citizenship programmes, 172
  and the comprehension of narratives, 256–78

cultural advantages of multilingualism, 44
cultural value in language varieties, 75
and education, 150
English as key to global culture, 78–9, 84, 234, 241
ignoring in rape trials, 28
intercultural communication, 22
language acquisition and cultural assimilation, 234
'multicultural' meaning 'minority', 38
and multi-level marketing companies, 95–6, 100
music (popular) as motivation to learn English, 82, 84, 86, 89
in Navajo schools, 129–35
popular culture more of a reason to learn English than financial, 84, 86–7
for refugees, 63, 65, 67–8
the safety zone theory, 121–36
in Sikh nursery project, 154
taking account of personal histories and cultures of learners, 4–8, 180–4, 200–1
translation across cultures, 4–8
Cummins, J., 212
customary law, 23

Dahlberg, G., 149, 160
David, T., 149
de facto vs *de jure* language policies, 19, 20, 31, 127, 134, 234–5
deficit constructs
of citizenship, 171–3
of language learners, 35–8, 45–7, 172, 176, 217–18, 225
DeJaeghere, J.G., 190, 204
denizenship, 24, 31, 211
Devlin, R., ix, 1, 20, 23, 30, 32, 167, 180, 185, 210–11, 233, 254
dharam, 151–2, 159
disabilities, people with, 167–8, 173, 210–11

discitizenship
bridging, 180–5
definitions, 22–4, 167–8, 210–11
Devlin and Pothier quote, ix
and language rights, 30
and Native Americans, 119
and poverty, 231–50
Ramanathan's reflections on, 253–5
underexplored in research, 2
and US language education policies, 209–28
discrimination
multilingualism as a 'surrogate means' to, 41
against refugees, 61–2
dispositions, 153–4, 158–9
'diverse' meaning 'minority', 38
Drew, P., 29
Duran, C.S., 35–49

Eades, D., 24, 28
early childhood education, 153–4
economic advantages of multilingualism, 44, 77–8, 79, 87
Edge, J., 234
education *see also* teachers
adult education, 167–85, 190–206
bilingual education, 40, 128, 210–28
deficit view of language learners, 35–8, 45–7, 172, 176, 217–18, 225
early childhood education, 145–61
immersion education, 131, 132, 135
MLM schemes providing, 104–6, 112
of Native American people, 117, 121, 123–35
roles in building citizenship in Australia, 167–85
of rural poor in Nicaragua, 231–50
of undocumented Latino youth in US, 93–4
and US language education policies, 209–28
Elahi, B., 70 n.1

ELLs (English Language Learners) see also
　　ESL (English as a Second Language)
　'ELL' vs 'multilingual users', 35, 37, 46–7
　LTELLs (long-term English language
　　learners), 210, 212, 214, 221–4
emergent bilinguals
　'emergent bilinguals' as a term, 37
　US Americans as emergent bilinguals,
　　209–28
EM-NALPA (Esther Martinez Native
　　American Languages Preservation
　　Act), 129–35
endangered languages, 128–35, 149
Engestrom's expansive learning model,
　　173
English
　the case for *not* learning, 245
　code switching with Punjabi in Sikh
　　nursery, 157–8
　English proficiency as toughest part of
　　citizenship test, 194
　English-only movements, 40, 210, 211,
　　214–21, 225
　global language, 43, 66, 78–80, 235
　'imperialist' language, 82, 87
　and Iraqi refugees, 65–7, 68–9
　as key to global citizenship, 66, 73, 80,
　　234, 239–44, 250
　language ideologies of teachers in Chile,
　　73–89
　learning alongside vocational education,
　　176–8
　learning without teachers in Nicaragua,
　　231–50
　and Navajo communities, 127, 128,
　　130–1, 134
　NCLB as de facto English policy, 127, 134
　teacher-English, 194–5
　US Americans as monolinguals, 35–49
　in Zimbabwe, 22
English as a Second Language (ESL)
　in Australia, 172
　should not be default situation, 245

　vs bilingual education in New York,
　　210, 214–21
　vs 'multilingual users', 35, 36–8, 45,
　　46–7
English Language Learners (ELLs) see also
　　ESL (English as a Second Language)
　'ELL' vs 'multilingual users', 35, 37, 46–7
　LTELLs (long-term English language
　　learners), 210, 212, 214, 221–4
English Regents test, 216
English-only movements, 194
entextualization, 97–8, 101
Erickson, F., 150, 152
Erikson, F., 122
ESL (English as a Second Language)
　in Australia, 172
　should not be default situation, 245
　vs bilingual education in New York,
　　210, 214–21
　vs 'multilingual users', 35, 36–8,
　　45, 46–7
ethnicity
　Iraqi refugees in US, 63–8
　and use of non-dominant language, 75
ethnographic research, 151, 188–206
euphemism
　rape trials and *isihlonipho sabafazi,* 26–7
　using 'multilingual' to avoid
　　stigmatization, 45
Every Child Matters (UK DES 2004), 148
'everyday' language, learning, 176–8
eye contact, 24

Fairclough, N., 53
feminine vs masculine language, 19–32
Feuerherm, E., 52–70
'figured worlds', 151, 155–9, 161
Fillerup, M., 132, 133, 134
Fitzsimmons, S., 212–13
'flexible' citizenship, 60, 196
Flexible Learning Centre, 179–80
Ford School for Adults, 191, 192
Fort Defiance, 130

Foucault, M., 117
frames of interpretation, 28
Freire, P., 197, 233
French
  in Corsica, 75
  used by politicians in US, 41
full participation
  and adult learners, 173
  and bilingual education, 209–13, 226–7
  as citizenship construct, 1, 8–10, 147
  and globalization, 88
  and indigenous communities, 136
  and multilingualism, 43
  in Nicaragua, 243
  Ramanathan's reflections on, 253–5
  and the role of English teachers, 167
  and women, 22–3
funding
  for FL education in US, 42
  for Navajo education, 123–7
  pressures of accountability in US schools, 214–19

García, O., 37, 47, 211
Gaventa, J., 160
Gee, J.P., 2, 100, 202, 255
gender
  of book's authors, 2
  cross-cultural teaching, 89
  and discitizenship generally, 2, 253–4
  isihlonipho sabafazi (women's language of respect), 19–32
  and refugee status, 57–62
  translation across cultures, 5–8
Gentil, G., 37
geographical domain of Iraqi refugees in US, 63–8
Giddens, A., 43
Gingrich, Newt, 41
global citizenship
  and consumerism, 88–9
  cultural rather than economic benefits of English promoted in Chile, 84

English as key to, 66, 73, 80, 234, 239–44, 250
  and individual monolingualism, 43–4
  and nationhood, 190
  in Nicaragua, 232
  and notions of 'citizenship', 254
  opportunities compromised by monolingual ideology, 42–3
  teachers' role in, 169, 170–3
global language, English as, 43, 66, 78–80, 235
Globalese, 235, 246
globalization
  as applied linguistic metanarrative, 3–4
  and local policy implementation, 239–44, 249–50
glocalization, 234–5
Godley, A.J., 75
Gonzales, R., 93, 94
governmentality, problems of, 117–18
Grimmitt, M., 154
Griswold, O., 190
Groß, C., 95, 101, 111
Gujarati, 5–8
Guo, S., 171
Gupta, A., 149, 150
Gutiérrez, K., 173, 174, 176, 177, 178

Hamilton, M., 170
Hammar, T., 24, 211
Han, C., 172
'hard work results in success' discourse, 101–4, 112
Hawaiian Native Americans, 120, 135–6
Haysom, L., 19
hegemonic language ideologies, 74–6
Heller, M., 44
Henze, R., 231–50
Herbalife see also MLM, 95, 97, 99, 101–2, 105, 107, 108, 110
hijab as keyword in refugee accounts, 57, 61–2, 68–9

Hindi, 158
Holland, D., 151
Holm, A. and W., 125–6, 130
home languages, importance of see also bilingualism; multilingualism, 121, 158, 209–12, 219–21, 222–8
Honduras, 233, 237, 238, 240
Hong Kong, 75
Hornberger, N.H., 125, 224
human rights and language rights, 20, 22
Huntsman, John, 41

identity
  Bakhtin's 'ideological becoming', 76
  based on difference, 8
  and bilingual education, 225
  'figured worlds', 151, 155–9, 161
  'identity kits' and multi-level marketing, 97, 98
  identity politics and globalization, 3–4
  Iraqi refugees in US, 57–68
illegal immigrants, 2–3, 92–113, 228 n.2
immersion education, 131, 132, 135
immigrants
  citizenship programmes, 171–3
  illegal immigrants, 2–3, 92–113, 228 n.2
  Iraqi refugees in US, 52–70
  undocumented Latino youth and multi-level marketing, 92–113
  and US language education policies, 209–28
  and the use of English in US, 39–41, 75
'imperialist' language, English as, 82, 87
implicit language ideologies, 19, 20, 31, 74, 127, 134, 234–5
'inclusion', 171
India
  Indian early childhood education, 150
  Indian immigrants to US and use of English, 75
indigenous communities
  Australian, 169, 181–4

isihlonipho sabafazi (women's language of respect), 19–32
  Native American, 116–36
instrumentalist approaches to learning support, 180
integration, as citizenship construct, 171–3
interdependence hypothesis, 212
internet
  and cultural exchange, 43
  and multi-level marketing to Latino people, 95–6
  and popular culture, 78, 84
  as premier global institution, 88
  using as research tool, 236, 237
interpretation see translation
Iraqi refugees in US, 52–70
isihlonipho sabafazi (women's language of respect), 19–32
Isin, E., 24
Islamic countries, 234

Jenson, J., 22, 31
Johnson, D., 224
Johnson, F.T., 131
Jones, S.P., 44
Julian, T., 128

Kaomea, J., 117
Kapchan, D.A., 97–8
keywords (research tool), definition of, 56
King, K.A., 92–113
Kira, I.A., 61–2
knowledge, assumed/neglected, 203–4
Koehn, D., 94, 113 n.2
Korean, 75
Krauss, M., 128
Kumaravadivelu, B., 83, 88, 174, 234

L2 education
  the 'deficit' view of, 35–8, 45–7, 172, 176, 217–18, 225
  in US, 42–3
  vs 'multilingual users', 45

labels, problems with, 45
language, literacy and numeracy (LLN) classrooms and citizenship, 168–85
language reclamation, 128–35, 149
language revitalization, 129–35, 149
language rights, 20, 22, 30, 48, 135
language-in-education projects, 117, 127, 132, 136
Latino youth, 92–113
law and language, intersection, 20
Leeman, J., 75
legal system and *isihlonipho sabafazi* (women's language of respect), 19–32
Legatz, J., 131
Leibowitz, A., 116–17, 122, 136
'LEP' (limited English proficiency) vs 'multilingual users' see also ESL (English as a Second Language), 35, 37
Levinson, B., 150
life stories as research tool, 55, 69
lifelong learning, 170–3
Linde, C., 55
lingua francas, 43, 66, 235
lingua-denizens, 31
LLN (language, literacy and numeracy) classrooms and citizenship, 168–85
Lo Bianco, J., 20
local vs national policies, 53, 214, 234, 239–44
Lomawaima, K.T., 116, 117, 118, 119, 120, 121, 128, 130, 135
López, L.E., 133
Loring, A., 188–206
LTELLs (long-term English language learners), 210, 212, 214, 221–4
Luke, A., 118, 127
Lukes, M., 40

Machuca (Chilean film), 86–7
Mackey, W., 39
Makoni, B., 19–32
Manuelito, K., 124
Marshall, T.H., 13 n.1, 20, 23, 30, 32

Martinez, G., 75
Martin-Jones, M., 150
Matsuda, A., 35–49
McCarty, T.L., 116–36, 249
MDE Latino see Amway
Mellinkoff, D., 20
Menard-Warwick, J., 73–89
Menken, K., 209–28
MLM (multi-level marketing) discourses, 94–113
mobile phones as tool for teaching, 248
modality, importance of addressing, 203–4
Moje, E.B., 173, 175
Moll, L.C., 135
monolingualism
 in Australia, 172
 in Chile, 74–5
 dominant ideology in US, 35–49, 211, 217–18, 221, 223–4, 226
Morgan, B., 52, 170, 184
Moss, P., 149, 160
Motha, S., 38
motivation to learn English
 in Chile, 82–3
 in Nicaragua, 241–2
Moulián, T., 87
multi-competence, 37
'multicultural' meaning 'minority', 38
multi-level marketing (MLM) discourses, 94–113
multilingual writers, 37
multilingualism
 in Australia, 172
 cognitive aspects of multilingualism, 37
 economic advantages of multilingualism, 44, 77–8, 79, 87
 'multilingual users' as a term, 35, 36, 45
Navajo (Diné) communities, 131–2
 in Sikh nursery project, 151, 152, 154
 US Americans as emergent bilinguals, 209–28
 US Americans as monolinguals, 35–49

Murphy-Graham, E., 233
music (popular) as motivation to learn English, 82, 84, 86, 89

Nadia (Iraqi refugee), 56–7, 61–2, 63–4, 65, 67–8
NALA (Native American Languages Act), 128–35
names, changing personal, 196
narratives see also life stories as research tool, 256–78
National Curriculum (UK), 148
national security, languages critical for, 42
nationality
    Iraqi refugees in US, 63–8
    and use of non-dominant language, 75
Native America, 116–36
native speaker teachers, 195
naturalization see citizenship programmes
Navajo (Diné) communities, 117, 120, 123–35
Ndebele speakers and *isihlonipho sabafazi*, 19–32
neglected knowledge, 203–4
New York and US language education policies, 209–28
New Zealand, 149
Ng, R., 171
Nicaragua, 231–50
Niño-Murcia, M., 75
Nishkam Nursery Project, 145–61
'NNES' (non-native English speakers) vs 'multilingual users' see also ESL (English as a Second Language), 35, 37, 45, 46–7
No Child Left Behind (NCLB), 127, 134–5, 215, 217
Noberto (MLM case study), 96, 98–9, 103–4, 105–6, 107, 109–10, 111
non-standard varieties
    Native Americans, 128
    in US, 41
    vs official status languages, 21

non-verbal communication, 24, 26–7
NSIEA (Navajo Sovereignty in Education Act), 134
nursery education, 147–50

observer's paradox, 56, 65
O'Donnell, J., 111
OECD (Organisation of Economic Co-operation and Development), 170
official status languages
    and the public/private distinction, 20–1
    in Zimbabwe, 22
Ong, A., 60
oppression, 171
overt vs covert language policies, 19, 20, 31, 127, 134, 234–5

partial citizenship, 20, 31
participation, full see full participation
particularity, practicality and possibility, 175
Passel, J.S., 93, 94
pathways, language, 249
Patricia (MLM case study), 96, 99, 101–2, 105, 107, 111
peripheral dimensions of citizenship, 199–201
personal names, changing, 196
Pfeiffer, A., 127
phonotactic assimilation, 196
pidgin, 235
Pitt, K., 170
policy transfer/policy borrowing, 170
popular music as motivation to learn English, 82, 84, 86, 89
Pothier, D. ,ix, 1, 20, 23, 30, 32, 167, 180, 185, 210–11, 233, 254
poverty and discitizenship, 233
power
    language as means of social control, 116–17, 136
    language policies as questions of, 20–1, 234
    and MLM discourses, 112

unequal power relations in Nicaraguan education, 234, 243–4
pre-school education, 147–50
private vs public language, 21, 30
Prochner, L., 149
productivity and citizenship, 168, 171, 173–5, 185
pro-social communicative competence, 170–3
Puente de Hózhǫ́ Trilingual Magnet School, 131–4
Punjabi, 151, 157
Punti, G., 92–113
pyramid schemes see multi-level marketing (MLM) discourses

Rajagopalan, K., 232, 245
Ramanathan, V., 52, 119, 170, 184, 211, 233, 234
rape trials, 25–32
reclamation, language, 128–35, 149
Refugee Employment Acquisition Program (REAP), 54–5, 70
refugees
  definitions and statistics, 53–4
  keywords in refugee accounts, 52–70
  and the use of English in US, 39–41
Reggio Emilia, 149
register
  code and style shifting, 158
  immigrants adapting language use to social situation, 75
  isihlonipho sabafazi (women's language of respect), 19–32
  private vs public language, 21, 30
religion
  and citizenship, 170
  faith-inspired/spiritual citizenship, 146, 151–4, 238
  and indigenous communities, 121
  in multi-level marketing schemes, 105–6
  symbols of religion, 61–2
  in US citizenship test, 197

research, calls for further
  on law and language intersection, 20
  on multilingual Americans, 46
researcher's/observer's paradox, 56, 65
resettlement policies for refugees in US, 52–70
revitalization, language, 129–35, 149
rights
  the human right to research, 245
  human rights and language rights, 20, 22
  of Indigenous Peoples, 118–20, 123
  language rights, 20, 30, 48, 135
  life without, 194
  as part of definition of citizenship, 189
  the 'right to participate fully', 8
  rights and responsibilities, 189–90
rituals (as discourse), 97–8, 105
Roessel, M., 135, 136
Rogers, A., 171
Rough Rock school, 124, 127, 128, 135
Ruiz, R., 135
Rushdi (Iraqi refugee), 56–7, 59–61, 63, 65–7, 68–9
Russian speakers and US citizenship, 191, 195

Sacramento Immigrant Resource Center (SIRC), 54
safety as keyword in refugee accounts, 57–62, 68–9
safety zone theory, 117, 121–36
Sagoo, G.K., 145–61
Saxena, M., 150
Schiffman, H., 31
sex, talking about (for Ndebele women), 25–31
Shan, H., 171
Shankar, S., 75
Shoffler, Pam, 107–8
Shona, 22
Short, D., 212–13
Siebens, J., 128

Sikhs, 145–61
simplification (as teaching strategy), 245–6
Singapore, 190
Singh, D., 168, 171
Singh, R., 152, 158–9
Small, Dorothy, 127
small stories, 104
social class see also *isihlonipho sabafazi* (women's language of respect)
  rural poor in Nicaragua, 231–50
  and the use of English in Chile, 80–3, 84
social control, language as means of, 116–17, 136
spaces, constructing, 3, 167–85
Spanish
  in Chile, 77, 78, 84
  language of global business, 75, 245
  and multi-level marketing companies, 95–6, 100
  and Navajo communities, 131–2
  Spanish-speaking emergent bilinguals in New York, 216, 219–21
Spolsky, B., 124, 125
standardized varieties of English, 245
Stearns, P., 147
storytelling, 256–78
substantive equality, 32, 210–11
subtractive education, 128, 211–14, 221–4, 227
Sweden, 149

teachers
  as agents of change, 170–1
  FL teachers in US, 42
  language ideologies of English teachers in Chile, 73–89
  learning without teachers in Nicaragua, 231–50
  native speaker teachers, 195
  Navajo teachers, 125

  roles in building citizenship in Australia, 167–85, 190
  roles in building citizenship in Singapore, 190
  simplification (as teaching strategy), 194–5, 245–6
  teacher-English, 194–5
  teaching strategies in Sikh nursery, 155–9
  understanding about citizenship, 193–5
  'teaching to the test', 197–201, 205
technology in rural Nicaragua, 248
temporal language in *isihlonipho sabafazi*, 26
terrorism, 54, 62, 69, 152
testing
  citizenship tests, 3, 168–9, 172, 189–205
  pressures of accountability in US schools, 214–19
texts, choice of, 5–8, 75, 85, 240–1
thematic analysis, 77
theory of linguistic transfer, 212
Thetela, P., 28
Third space, 173–85
Thonus, T., 213
Tobin, J., 149
Tollefson, J.W., 20
Toohey, K., 36–7
top-down policies, 9, 122, 124–5, 170, 227–8
transformative citizenship, 4, 9, 76, 84, 147, 189, 204
translation
  and citizenship generally, 4–8
  isihlonipho sabafazi (women's language of respect), 24
  of self, 64–5, 68–9
  translation theory, 3
transnational policies, 170
transnationality, 60
tribal sovereignty, 118–20, 135
trust responsibility, 119–21, 126, 130

Tséhootsooí Diné Bi'ólta', 129–31, 134
Turner, B., 13 n.1
tutores in Nicaragua, 243, 246–8
two-way translations, 4

undocumented people, 2–3, 92–113
United Kingdom (UK)
  adult literacy policies, 170
  assimilation vs multiculturalism, 172
  Chileans' negative associations with English-speaking countries, 81–3
  citizenship programmes, 171–3
  Nishkam Nursery Project, 145–61
United States (US)
  assimilation vs multiculturalism, 172
  Chileans' negative associations with English-speaking countries, 81–3
  cultural context and narrative comprehension, 256–78
  early childhood education, 148
  ethnographic study of classroom meanings of citizenship, 188–206
  FL education, 42–3, 47
  Native America, 116–36
  refugees in, 52–70
  Third space, 173–5
  undocumented Latino youth and multi-level marketing, 92–113
  US Americans as emergent bilinguals, 209–28
  US Americans as monolinguals, 35–49, 75
  US Constitution, 116, 119, 189
universality of English see also global language, English as, 78–80
Uricuoli, B., 97

Valenzuela, A., 211–12
varieties of languages
  and EFL, 245–7
  and language ideology, 74–5
  non-standard varieties, 21, 41, 128
  official status languages, 20–1, 22
  standardized varieties of English, 245
Viri, D., 121
Vittachi, N., 235, 245
vocational education, 176, 179–80
Vygotsky, L., 148

Walby, S., 24
Walker, J., 170, 172
Warhol, L., 128
West, Cornell, 235
Widin, J., 167–85
Wiley, T.G., 40, 41
Wilkins, D.E., 116, 119, 120, 130
Williams, R., 56
Wilson Adult School, 191, 192
Winn, P., 87
women
  book's authors, 2
  Iraqi refugees in US, 57–62
  isihlonipho sabafazi (women's language of respect), 19–32
  in Nicaragua, 232
Woolard, K.A., 74–5
writing skills, 37, 222
Wyman, L., 127

Yasukawa, K., 167–85

Zimbabwe, 19–32

For Product Safety Concerns and Information please contact our EU Authorised Representative:

Easy Access System Europe

Mustamäe tee 50

10621 Tallinn

Estonia

gpsr.requests@easproject.com

www.ingramcontent.com/pod-product-compliance
Lightning Source LLC
Chambersburg PA
CBHW071157300426
44113CB00009B/1237